AND BOOK TRAINING PACKAGE AVAILABLE

ExamSim

Experience realistic, simulated exams on your own computer with interactive ExamSim software. This computer-based test engine offers knowledge and scenario-based questions like those found on the real exam and review tools that can show you where you went wrong on the questions you missed and why. ExamSim allows you to mark unanswered questions for further review and provides a score report that shows your overall performance on the exam.

Knowledge-based questions present challenging material in a multiple-choice format. Answer treatments not only explain why the correct options are right, they also tell you why the incorrect answers are wrong.

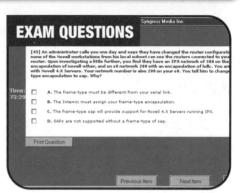

Applied **scenario-based questions** challenge your ability to analyze and address complex, real-world case studies.

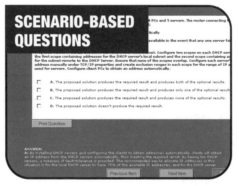

Additional CD-ROM Features

Complete hyperlinked **e-book** for easy information access and self-paced study.

DriveTime audio tracks offer concise review of key exam topics for in the car or on the go!

The **Score Report** provides an overall assessment of your exam performance as well as performance history.

System Requirements:

A PC running Microsoft® Internet Explorer version 5 or higher

CCA Citrix®
MetaFrame XP™ for
Windows Administrator
Study Guide

(Exam 220)
Second Edition

CCA Citrix® MetaFrame XP™ for Windows Administrator Study Guide

(Exam 220)
Second Edition

Syngress Media, Inc.

Osborne McGraw-Hill

New York   Chicago   San Francisco   Lisbon   London   Madrid
Mexico City   Milan   New Delhi   San Juan   Seoul   Singapore   Sydney   Toronto

Osborne/**McGraw-Hill**
2600 Tenth Street
Berkeley, California 94710
U.S.A.

To arrange bulk purchase discounts for sales promotions, premiums, or fund-raisers, please contact Osborne/**McGraw-Hill** at the above address. For information on translations or book distributors outside the U.S.A., please see the International Contact Information page immediately following the index of this book.

CCA Citrix® MetaFrame XP™ for Windows Administrator Study Guide (Exam 220), Second Edition

34567890 1FGR 1FGR 0198765432

Book p/n 0-07-219320-4 and CD p/n 0-07-219321-2
parts of
ISBN 0-07-219319-0

Publisher Brandon A. Nordin	**Project Manager** Jenn Tust	**Technical Reviewer** Raj Harie
Vice President and Associate Publisher Scott Rogers	**Acquisitions Coordinator** Jessica Wilson	**Copy Editor** Michael McGee
Editorial Director Gareth Hancock	**Editorial Management** Syngress Media, Inc.	**Production and Editorial** Apollo Publishing Service
Associate Acquisitions Editor Timothy Green	**VP, Worldwide Business Development** **Global Knowledge** Richard Kristof	**Series Design** Roberta Steele
Acquisitions Editor Nancy Maragioglio	**Technical Editor** Melissa Craft	**Cover Design** Greg Scott

This book was published with Corel VENTURA™ Publisher.

9000 Regency Parkway, Suite 500
Cary, NC 27512
1-800-COURSES
www.globalknowledge.com

From Global Knowledge

Global Knowledge supports many styles of learning. We deliver content through the written word, e-Learning, Classroom Learning, and Virtual Classroom Learning. We do this because we know our students need different training approaches to achieve success as technical professionals. This book series offers each reader a valuable tool fore Citrix MetaFrame XP 1.0 Windows Administration Exam (Exam 220).

Global Knowledge is the world's largest independent IT trainer. This uniquely positions us to offer these books. We have trained hundreds of thousands of students worldwide. Global Knowledge captured those years of expertise in this series. The quality of these books shows our commitment to your lifelong learning success.

For those of you who know Global Knowledge, or those of you who have just found us for the first time, our goal is to be your lifelong training partner. Global Knowledge commits itself daily to providing all learners with the very best training.

Thank you for choosing our training. We look forward to serving your needs again in the future.

Warmest regards,

Duncan Anderson
President and Chief Executive Officer, Global Knowledge

v

About Syngress Media

Syngress Media creates books and software for Information Technology professionals seeking skill enhancement and career advancement. Its products are designed to comply with vendor and industry standard course curricula, and are optimized for certification exam preparation. You can contact Syngress via the Web at www.syngress.com.

Contributors

Ralph Crump (CCEA, CCNP\DP, MCSE, MCNE, ASE) is a Senior Consultant for an integration and services firm in Atlanta, Georgia. He develops large-scale Networking and Security solutions for Enterprise customers, also specializing in Citrix and thin-client technologies. He is currently pursuing his Cisco CCIE certification as well as the Citrix Certified Instructor for MetaFrame XP. In addition, Ralph currently co-hosts the Atlanta Citrix Users group in the Atlanta area.

Travis Guinn (CCA, MCSE, CCSA, CCSE, A+) is currently a Senior Technical Officer with JPMorgan Chase in Dallas, TX. He has worked in the IT industry for 10 years and started one of the first Windows NT based ISPs in Charleston, South Carolina, where he gained extensive experience in TCP/IP and large scale dial-in solutions from US Robotics. Travis then worked for a large Citrix integrator for three years on projects involving MetaFrame, 3Com Total Control, Checkpoint Firewall-1, RSA SecurID, AVT RightFax, and a Windows 2000 based Managed Service Provider initiative.

Craig Luchtefeld (CCEA, MCSE, MCP+I) is a Network Engineer at STL Technology Partners, a Bloomington, IL based company that focuses on web and network solutions, custom programming, and technical training. Craig has more than eight years of computer and computer network experience and specializes in the field of Terminal Services and Citrix-based technology.

In his spare time, Craig enjoys spending time at home with his wife, Mandy, in addition to reading, skating, mountain biking, and computer gaming.

Ron Oglesby (CCEA, CCI, MCSE, CSA) is Citrix Consultant in Chicago and has worked with every Citrix product since WinFrame 1.5. Ron was named as one of the "Original CCEAs" by Citrix's Certification staff for being one of the first 50 CCEAs in the world. He has managed and been part of teams whose function was the design, implementation and troubleshooting of large corporate Citrix environments. His current projects have drawn him into the world of web development for incorporating company intranets with Citrix's application portal technology, Nfuse. Ron has trained hundreds of Administrators on the proper configuration and management of MetaFrame 1.8 and MetaFrame XP.

When not working with computers, he enjoys bodybuilding, motorcycles, and spending time with his daughter Madison, wife Dina, and their three cats.

Heather Simpson (CCEA, CCA, MCSE) currently works as a Senior Consultant for All Bases Covered in San Diego, CA. Heather has provided consulting services on a number of MetaFrame implementation projects, spanning small to enterprise-sized corporations. Outside of server-based computing, she enjoys spending her time hiking, biking, and surfing.

James Spadaro (CCEA, MCSE, CCNA, CNA) is a systems integration specialist for an outsourcing firm in Philadelphia, PA. He currently manages a large group of Citrix WinFrame and MetaFrame servers, providing fortune 500 companies with 24-hour access to custom pension and benefit management software. James has a business degree from Michigan State University and has several years of LAN/WAN experience, specializing in remote access and thin-client solutions.

Joel W. Stolk (CCA, CCNA, MCSE) has been working with Citrix and related thin client technologies for over five years. His professional background includes many years of field consulting experience in Texas and California. He currently works at Trammell Crow Company in downtown Dallas as the MetaFrame Operations Engineer.

Joel enjoys snowboarding, snow skiing, surfing, and writing electronic music in his spare time. His music can be found at http://www.mp3.com/exobyte.

Connie Wilson (CCA, MCSE, MCP+I, CNA) has worked in the IT industry for over 15 years, with her most recent positions in Consulting. She is currently the Senior Network Engineer for GE Capital in Phoenix, AZ where she built and now manages the Citrix MetaFrame server farm.

Kevin Wing (CCEA, MCSE, CCNA) is a System Engineer for Pomeroy Computer Resources. He has a BA in Communications from Western Kentucky University and has worked with computers for his entire life, beginning with Atari

400s and working his way upward. He has been in the profession for seven years, and began working on VAX/VMS and Digital Unix machines, then progressing to NT systems. He has worked with Citrix for three years.

His hobbies include computers, pipe smoking, and reading. Kevin lives in Nashville, TN with his fiancé, Cathy and three cats.

Technical Editor

Melissa Craft (CCA, CCNA, MCSE, Network+, CNE-5, CNE-3, CNE-4, CNE-GW, MCNE) designs business computing solutions using technology to automate processes, and using business process reengineering techniques.

Early on in her career, Melissa threw herself at the task of truly understanding network engineering, gaining a myriad of technology certifications and, at the same time, deploying projects for clients. Over the years, Melissa has successfully designed, implemented and integrated networks ranging in size from a few nodes to over 100,000 nodes. This consulting experience incorporated extensive project management, needs-analysis, LAN and WAN design, deployment and operational turnover.

In 1997, Melissa began writing magazine articles regarding networking and the technology industry. In 1998, Syngress Media hired Melissa to contribute to an MCSE certification guide. Since then, Melissa has continued to write about various technology and certification subjects.

Currently, Melissa works on Microsoft Solutions for CompuCom Systems, Inc. CompuCom is a systems integrator headquartered in Dallas, Texas. CompuCom provides business services, IT design, project management and support for distributed computing systems. Melissa is a key contributor to the business development of Microsoft technology-based solutions. As such, she develops enterprise-wide solutions and methodologies focused on client organizations. These technology solutions touch every part of a system's lifecycle—from network design, testing and implementation to operational management and strategic planning.

Melissa holds a bachelor's degree from the University of Michigan, and is a member of the IEEE, the Society of Women Engineers and American MENSA, Ltd. Melissa currently resides in Glendale, Arizona with her family, Dan, Justine and Taylor, and her two Great Danes (a.k.a Mobile Defense Units), Marmaduke and Apollo as well as her Golden Retriever (a.k.a. Mobile Alarm Unit) Pooka.

Technical Reviewer

Raj Harie (CCA, MCSE, MCP+I, CNE) has been working with network operating systems for the last five years. After studying for a Commerce degree in Grahamstown, South Africa, he embarked on a career in Information Technology. He completed his Novell CNE in Intranetware and his MCP+I and MCSE before moving to London, England and taking a position as a Systems Engineer at Westcon UK, a worldwide distributor headquartered in New York, USA. After achieving his CCA status in Winframe and MetaFrame, along with plenty of hands on experience, he rose to a position of Senior Systems Engineer with a team of Citrix Technical staff under his wing, before the call of the African bush lead him back to his native South Africa. He is currently employed as the Citrix Channel Manager for the South African division of Westcon in the Enterprise Business Unit, overseeing the technical and commercial needs of a fast growing channel that encompasses South Africa and the neighboring states.

ACKNOWLEDGMENTS

We would like to thank the following people:

- Richard Kristof of Global Knowledge for championing the series and providing us access to some great people and information.
- All the incredibly hard-working folks at Osborne/McGraw-Hill: Brandon Nordin, Scott Rogers, Timothy Green, Gareth Hancock, and Jessica Wilson.

CONTENTS AT A GLANCE

CONTENTS

This book's primary objective is to help you prepare for the CCA Citrix MetaFrame XP 1.0 for Windows Administration exam (Exam 220). As the Citrix program continues to evolve, it will become increasingly important that current and aspiring IT professionals have multiple resources available to assist them in increasing their knowledge and building their skills.

At the time of publication, all the exam objectives have been posted on the Citrix Web site and the beta exam process has been completed. Citrix has announced its commitment to measuring real-world skills. This book is designed with that premise in mind; its authors have practical experience in the field, using Citrix MetaFrame in hands-on situations.

Because the focus of the exams is on application and understanding, as opposed to memorization of facts, no book by itself can fully prepare you to obtain a passing score. It is essential that you work with Citrix MetaFrame XP 1.0 to enhance your proficiency. Toward that end, this book includes many practical step-by-step exercises in each chapter that are designed to give you hands-on practice as well as guide you in truly learning CCA Citrix MetaFrame XP 1.0 for Windows Administration, not just learning *about* it.

In This Book

This book is organized around the actual structure of Exam 220 administered at Sylvan Prometric and VUE Testing Centers. Citrix has let us know all the topics we need to cover for the exam. We've followed their list carefully, so you can be assured you're not missing anything. Each chapter covers a major aspect of the exam, with an emphasis on the "why" as well as the "how to" of administering Citrix MetaFrame XP 1.0 for Windows.

In Every Chapter

We've created a set of chapter components that call your attention to important items, reinforce important points, and provide helpful exam-taking hints. Take a look at what you'll find in the chapters:

- Each chapter begins with the **Certification Objectives**—what you need to know in order to pass the section on the exam dealing with the chapter topic. The Certification Objective headings identify the objectives within the chapter, so you'll always know an objective when you see it!

- **Certification Exercises** are interspersed throughout the chapters. These are step-by-step exercises. They help you master skills that are likely to be an area of focus on the exam. Don't just read through the exercises; they are hands-on procedures that you should be comfortable completing. Learning by doing is an effective way to increase your competency with the language and concepts presented.

- **From the Classroom** sidebars describe the issues that come up most often in the training classroom setting. These sidebars give you a valuable perspective into certification- and product-related topics. They point out common mistakes and address questions that have arisen from classroom discussions.

- The **CertCam** icon that appears in many of the exercises indicates that the exercise is presented in .avi format on the accompanying CD-ROM. These .avi clips walk you through various system configurations and are narrated by Kevin Wing, CCEA, MCSE, CCNA.

- **Scenario & Solution** sections lay out specific scenario questions and solutions in a quick and easy-to-read format.

SCENARIO & SOLUTION

You have three servers. All three support 50 users each. You notice though that when one server goes down performance on the other two servers suffers greatly. What is going on?	Load balancing is allowing the users that were dropped to reconnect to the remaining two servers. This is obviously overloading those servers and could possibly cause a domino effect where each server may come down in turn. To resolve this, change the load evaluator for all three servers to allow only the number of users on the server that it can support.
You have recently created a new load evaluator that will limit the number of users who can log on to your server. You then wait a day and notice that the user count has not been limited to your amount and it is actually a lot higher than what you specified. What is the problem?	By just creating an evaluator you have done nothing more than build a set of rules. You must assign that evaluator to your servers in order for your rules to take effect.
You notice that several users have just logged off one of your servers, decreasing the load significantly. You wait several minutes, but none of your existing users are being routed to that server. What is the problem?	There is no problem. Load balancing only takes place at login. New users will be routed to this server but existing connections will remain where they are currently.

- The **Certification Summary** is a succinct review of the chapter and a re-statement of salient points regarding the exam.

- The **Two-Minute Drill** at the end of every chapter is a checklist of the main points of the chapter. It can be used for last-minute review.

- The **Self Test** offers questions similar to those found on the certification exam. The answers to these questions, as well as explanations of the answers, can be found at the end of the particular chapter. By taking the Self Test after completing each chapter, you'll reinforce what you've learned from that chapter, while becoming familiar with the structure of the exam questions.

- The **Lab Question** at the end of the Self Test section offers a unique and challenging question format that requires the reader to understand multiple chapter concepts to answer correctly. These questions are more complex and more comprehensive than the other questions, as they test your ability to take all the knowledge you have gained from reading the chapter and apply it to complicated, real-world situations. These questions are aimed to be more difficult than what you will find on the exam. If you can answer these questions, you have proven that you know the subject!

Some Pointers

Once you've finished reading this book, set aside some time to do a thorough review. You might want to return to the book several times and make use of all the methods it offers for reviewing the material:

1. *Re-read all the Two-Minute Drills,* or have someone quiz you. You also can use the drills as a way to do a quick cram before the exam.

2. *Review all the Scenario & Solution sections* for quick problem solving.

3. *Re-take the Self Tests.* Taking the tests right after you've read the chapter is a good idea, because it helps reinforce what you've just learned. However, it's an even better idea to go back later and do all the questions in the book in one sitting. Pretend you're taking the exam. (For this reason, you should mark your answers on a separate piece of paper when you go through the questions the first time.)

4. *Complete the exercises.* Did you do the exercises when you read through each chapter? If not, do them! These exercises are designed to cover exam topics, and there's no better way to get to know this material than by practicing.

5. *Check out the Web site.* Global Knowledge invites you to become an active member of the Access Global Web site. This site is an online mall and an information repository that you'll find invaluable. You can access many types of products to assist you in your preparation for the exams, and you'll be able to participate in forums, on-line discussions, and threaded discussions. No other book brings you unlimited access to such a resource. You'll find more information about this site in Appendix B.

The CD-ROM Resource

This book comes with a CD-ROM that includes test preparation software and provides you with another method for studying. You will find more information on the testing software in Appendix A.

How to Take the Citrix Certified Administrator Exam for MetaFrame XP

This introduction covers the importance of the Citrix Certified Administrator (CCA) certification for MetaFrame XP and prepares you for taking the actual examination. It gives you a few pointers on methods of preparing for the exam, including how to study, register, what to expect, and what to do on exam day. The Citrix Certified Administrator certification program was created to address the needs of IT managers trying to find qualified Citrix MetaFrame professionals. Additionally, certification is extremely important to Citrix resellers. Citrix offers various levels of reseller programs including "Silver" and "Gold" Solutions Provider Programs. Because Citrix requires resellers to maintain a set number of CCAs on staff in order to achieve and maintain preferred reseller status, CCAs continue to enjoy the results of the high demand for CCA certified professionals. After all, the benefits of preferred reseller status often warrants the creation of new positions for Citrix Certified Administrators. Citrix has been on the IT scene for several years. It is now possible to distinguish Citrix professionals by their experience level in addition to certification. Experience, however, does not indicate the same solid understanding of the fundamentals of the language that the certification exams demand. In order to succeed on the Citrix Certified Administrator exam, a candidate must demonstrate a comprehensive understanding of the core server-based computing concepts. And in order to succeed on the CCA exam for MetaFrame XP, the candidate must also demonstrate knowledge of server farms, which differ from single-server computing environments.

Why Vendor Certification?

Certification helps identify you as a Citrix expert. It is a tool that IT managers can use to identify those who have a solid grasp of the core language concepts. This is not to say that there are not good Citrix professionals that aren't certified, but when taken into consideration with experience, certification can be a powerful tool to the

IT manager or consultant. Considering the Citrix-mandated requirements for CCA staffing at authorized Citrix Solutions Providers, CCA certification can be an extremely valuable addition to your hard-earned credentials.

Some people become certified as an aid to compete in the demanding IT marketplace. Some companies use the exam as the final phase of a Citrix training course. Others take it purely for the challenge. Whatever your reasons for tackling the exam, this book will help you prepare for it.

It would be nice to know some statistics about the exam such as the pass/fail ratio and the number of people certified. Citrix, however, has decided to keep this information confidential. The actual questions on the exam are also kept confidential and are even copyrighted. The questions and materials in this book are therefore based largely upon the experience of those who have previously taken and passed the exam as well as on Citrix's publicly stated course objectives.

Over the years, technology vendors have created their own certification programs because of industry demand. This demand arises when the marketplace needs skilled professionals and an easy way to identify them. Vendors benefit because it promotes people skilled in their products. Professionals benefit because it boosts their careers. Employers benefit because it helps them identify qualified people.

Technology changes too often and too quickly to rely on traditional means of certification, such as universities and trade associations. Because of the investment and effort required to keep certification programs current, vendors are the only organizations suited to keep pace with the changes. In general, such vendor certification programs are excellent, with most of them requiring a solid foundation in the essentials, as well as their particular product line.

Corporate America has come to appreciate these vendor certification programs and the value they provide. Employers recognize that certifications, like university degrees, do not guarantee a level of knowledge, experience, or performance; rather, they establish a baseline for comparison. By seeking to hire vendor-certified employees, a company can assure itself that it has also hired a person skilled in the specific products the company uses.

Technical professionals have also begun to realize the value of certification and the impact it can have on their careers. By completing a certification program, professionals gain an endorsement of their skills from a major industry source. This endorsement can boost their current position, and it makes finding the next job even easier. Often, a certification determines whether a first interview is even granted.

Today, a certification may place you ahead of the pack. Tomorrow, it may be a necessity to keep from being left in the dust.

A Brief History of Citrix

Since 1989, Citrix Systems, Inc. (NASDAQ:CTXS) has established itself as a global leader in providing application server software and services for enterprises. Citrix's application server software and services offer the ability to run any application on virtually and device with any type of connection.

Citrix application server software and services enable organizations to run applications on servers that can be accessed from a variety of client devices. Since the applications are installed and updated on servers instead of on each individual client, the complexity, time, and resources required to manage the applications are reduced. Local and remote users can easily access the latest applications over the Internet or via other connections.

These are exciting times indeed for professionals involved in selling, implementing, and maintaining Citrix-based thin-client solutions. As reported in the March 27, 2000 edition of *Business Week* magazine, Citrix had the second-best three-year return on the S&P 500, up 4,911%.

Citrix's Certification Program

Currently there are three main Citrix certifications. They are the Citrix Certified Administrator (CCA) for MetaFrame XP, the Citrix Certified Sales Professional (CCSP), and the Citrix Certified Enterprise Administrator (CCEA). Citrix maintains a Web site for its certification programs at http://www.citrix.com/. This Web site will give you current information about Citrix certifications and exams.

The Citrix Certified Administrator for MetaFrame XP Exam

The CCA for MetaFrame XP 1.0 exam (Sylvan exam number 220) is designed to test your basic knowledge and competence of MetaFrame XP administration itself. It requires detailed knowledge of such topics as performance optimization, Program Neighborhood, Load Balancing, and advanced system management. It does not test any issues related to advanced administration or configuration and primarily tests your knowledge and understanding of MetaFrame core concepts and administration utilities.

The CCSP Exam

The Citrix Certified Sales Professional (CCSP) program is a sales certification for individuals who demonstrate general knowledge of Citrix products, technologies, and services. The audience for the CCSP program is Citrix business partners who work in a sales and marketing capacity. These partners include members of the Citrix Solutions Network (CSN), Citrix Business Alliance (CBN), and Citrix Consulting Partners.

The Citrix Certified Enterprise Administrator Exams

The CCEA is an advanced certification that demonstrates an individual has an extensive knowledge of Citrix technology, as well as a wealth of experience installing and administering Citrix MetaFrame or WinFrame and knowledge of Management Services. In order to achieve this level of recognition, you must first achieve CCA certification for at least one of the Citrix platforms. Once certified as a CCA, you must then pass four of the following seven exams available through Sylvan Prometric Testing Centers:

- #910- Citrix Resource Management Services
- #911- Citrix Resource Manager
- #920- Citrix Installation Management Services
- #921- Citrix Installation Manager
- #930- SecureICA™ and Security
- #940- Load Balancing and Program Neighborhood™
- #950- Citrix NFuse Administration Exam

Computer-Based Testing

In a perfect world, you would be assessed for your true knowledge of a subject, not simply for how you respond to a series of test questions. But life isn't perfect, and it just isn't practical to evaluate everyone's knowledge on a one-to-one basis.

For all of its certifications, Citrix evaluates candidates using a computer-based testing service operated by Sylvan Prometric. This service is quite popular in the industry, and it is used for a number of vendor certification programs, including Novell's CNE and Microsoft's MCSE. Thanks to Sylvan Prometric's large number of facilities, exams can be administered worldwide, generally in the same town as a prospective candidate.

e x a m
W a t c h

For the most part, Sylvan Prometric exams work similarly from vendor to vendor. However, there is an important fact to know about Citrix's exams: They use the traditional Sylvan Prometric test format, not the newer adaptive format. However, care should be taken that items marked for review are just that, marked only for review. Once you provide an answer and progress to the next question , you are not allowed to go back to previous questions and modify previous answers. Citrix Administrator Advice: Many experienced test takers do not go back and change answers unless they have a good reason to do so. Many of the current Citrix exams do not allow you to change an answer when you feel you may have misread or misinterpreted the question the first time.

To discourage simple memorization, most Citrix exams present a different set of questions every time the test is administered. In the development of the exam, hundreds of questions are compiled and refined using beta testers. From this large collection, a random sampling is drawn for each test.

Each Citrix exam has a specific number of questions and test duration. Testing time is typically generous, and the time remaining is always displayed in the corner of the testing screen, along with the number of questions remaining. If time expires during an exam, the test terminates, and incomplete answers are counted as incorrect.

At the end of the exam, your test is immediately graded, and the results are displayed on the screen. Scores for each subject area are also provided, but the system will not indicate which specific questions were missed. A report is automatically printed at the proctor's desk for your files. Your score report will instruct you to fax your results directly to Citrix and will provide you with the appropriate fax number.

In the end, this computer-based system of evaluation is reasonably fair. You might feel that one or two questions were poorly worded; this can certainly happen, but you shouldn't worry too much. Ultimately, it's all factored into the required passing score.

e x a m
W a t c h

When I find myself stumped answering multiple-choice questions, I use my scratch paper to write down the two or three answers I consider the strongest, and then underline the answer I feel is most likely correct. Here is an example of what my scratch paper looks like when I've gone through the test once:

21. B or <u>C</u>
33. <u>A</u> or C

Test Structure

Because Citrix holds the exam questions confidentially, it may happen that you will come across a question that doesn't appear to have a correct answer. Citrix does try to quality-check the exam thoroughly, but without an outside review, some badly formulated questions may appear.

Unfortunately, there isn't much you can do about this when you are taking the exam. You can't write the question down and take it with you, so I'd recommend trying to remember the question before you leave and check it out later. If you still believe the question to be in error, contact Citrix as soon as possible and try to work out a solution. This at least helps to keep others from having the same problem in the future.

There aren't supposed to be any multiple-choice questions that don't have any correct answers. There may be some that have multiple correct answers, but they should all have at least one. If you find a question that you think has no correct answers, pick the answer that is closest to being correct, and contact Citrix about the question after the exam.

Types of Test Questions

Citrix exams pose questions in a variety of formats, most of which are discussed here. As candidates progress to the more advanced certifications, the difficulty of the exam is intensified, both through the subject matter as well as the question formats.

True/False

The classic true/false question format is not used in the Citrix exams, for the obvious reason that a simple guess has a 50% chance of being correct. Instead, true/false questions are posed in multiple-choice format, requiring the candidate to identify the true or false statement from a group of selections.

Multiple Choice

Multiple choice is the primary format for questions in Citrix exams. These questions may be posed in a variety of ways.

"SELECT THE CORRECT ANSWER" This is the classic multiple choice question, where the candidate selects a single answer from a list of about four choices. In addition to the question's wording, the answers are presented in a Windows "radio button" format.

"SELECT ALL THAT APPLY" The open-ended version is the most difficult multiple-choice format, since the candidate does not know how many answers should be selected. As with the multiple-answer version, all the correct answers must be selected to gain credit for the question. If too many answers are selected, no credit is given. This format presents choices in check box format, but the testing software does not advise the candidates whether they've selected the correct number of answers.

Fill in the Blank

Fill-in-the-blank questions are less common in Citrix exams. They may be presented in multiple-choice or freeform response format.

Tips on Taking the Exam

There are 40 questions on the exam. You will need to get at least 28 of them right in order to pass- just over 68 percent. You are given 60 minutes to complete the exam.

There are no penalties for wrong answers as opposed to incomplete answers, so it's better to at least attempt to answer than not to give one at all.

Tips on Studying for the Exam

First and foremost, give yourself plenty of time to study. MetaFrame is a unique platform, and you cannot expect to cram what you need to know into a single study session. It's a field best learned over time, by studying a subject and then applying your knowledge. Build yourself a study schedule and stick to it, but be reasonable about the pressure you put on yourself, especially if you're studying in addition to your regular duties at work.

exam
ⓦatch

One easy technique to use in studying for certification exams is the 15-minutes per day effort. Simply study for a minimum of 15 minutes every day. It is a small, but significant commitment. If you have a day where you just can't focus, then give up a 15 minutes. If you have a day where it flows completely for you, study longer. As long as you have more of the "flow days", your chances of succeeding are extremely high.

Another excellent way to study is through case studies. Case studies are articles or interactive discussions that offer real-world examples of how technology is applied to meet a need. These examples can server to cement your understanding of a technique or technology by seeing it put to use. Interactive discussions offer added value because you can also pose questions of your own. Citrix offers examples of its case studies at its Web Site (http://www.citrix.com/).

Scheduling Your Exam

The Citrix exams are scheduled by calling Sylvan Prometric directly at (800) 481-3926. For locations outside the United States, your local numbers can be found on Sylvan's Web site at http://www.2test.com. Sylvan representatives can schedule your exam, but they don't have information about the certification programs. Questions about certification should be directed to Citrix's training department.

These representatives are familiar enough with the exams to find them by name, but it is best if you have the specific exam number handy when you call. After all, you wouldn't want to be scheduled and charged for the wrong exam.

Exams can be scheduled up to a year in advance, although it's really not necessary. Generally, scheduling a week or two ahead is sufficient to reserve the day and time you prefer. Currently, same day testing is unavailable for Citrix exams. You are required to schedule your exams at least 24 hours in advance. When scheduling. operators will search for testing centers in your area. For convenience, they can also tell you what testing centers you've used before.

Sylvan accepts a variety of payment methods, with credit cards being the most convenient. (Quick scheduling can be handy, especially if you want to re-take an exam immediately). Sylvan will mail you a receipt, and confirmation of your testing date, although this often arrives after the test has been taken. If you need to cancel or reschedule an exam, remember to call at least one day before your exam, or you'll lose your test fee.

When registering for the exam, you will be asked for your ID number. This number is used to track your exam results back to Citrix. It's important that you use the same ID number each time you register, so that Citrix can follow your progress. Address information provided when you first register is also used by Citrix to ship certificates and other related material. In the United States, your Social Security Number is commonly used as your ID number. However, Sylvan can assign you a unique ID number if you prefer not to use your Social Security Number.

Arriving at the Exam

As with any test, you'll be tempted to cram the night before. Resist that temptation. You should know the material by this point, and if you're too groggy in the morning, you won't remember what you studied anyways. Instead, get a good night's sleep.

Arrive early for your exam; it gives you time to relax and review key facts. Take the opportunity to review your notes. If you get burned out on studying, you can usually start your exam a few minutes early. On the other hand, I don't recommend arriving late. Your test could be cancelled, or you may not be left with enough time to complete the exam.

When you arrive at the testing center, you'll need to sign in with the exam administrator. In order to sign in you'll need two forms of identification. Acceptable forms include government-issued Ids (for example, passport or drivers license), credit cards, and company ID badge. One form of ID must include a photograph.

Aside from a brain full of facts, you don't need to bring anything else to the exam. In fact, your brain is about all you're allowed to take into the exam! All the tests are "closed book", meaning you don't get to bring any reference materials with you. You're also not allowed to take any notes out of the exam room. The test administrator will provide you with paper and a pencil. Some testing centers may provide you with a small marker board instead.

Leave your pager and telephone in the car, or turn them off. They only add stress to the situation, since they are not allowed into the exam room, and can sometimes still be heard if they ring outside of the room. Purses, books, and other materials must be left with the administrator before entering the exam. While in the exam room, it's important that you don't disturb other candidates; talking is not allowed during the exam.

Once in the testing room, the exam administrator logs onto your exam, and you have to verify that your ID and the exam number are correct. Before the test begins you will be required to complete a brief survey to help Citrix better understand the demographics of people taking Citrix exams. Following your completion of the survey, you will be provided with facts about the exam, including the duration, the number of questions, and the score required for passing. Then the clock starts ticking, and the fun begins.

The testing software is Windows-based, but you won't have to access the main desktop or any of the accessories. The exam is presented in full screen, with a single question per screen. Navigation buttons allow you to move forward and backward between questions. In the upper-right corner of the screen, counters show the number of questions and the time remaining. Most importantly, there is a "Mark" check box in the upper-left corner of the screen- this will allow you to return to revisit tough questions that may prompt subsequent additional study.

Submitting Your Answers and Scoring

When you're confident with all of your answers, finish the exam by submitting it for grading. After what will seem like the longest ten seconds of your life, the testing software will respond with your score. This is usually displayed as a bar graph, showing the minimum passing score, your score, and a PASS/FAIL indicator.

If you're curious, you can review the statistics of your score at this time. Answers to specific questions are not presented; rather, questions are lumped into categories, and results are tallied for each category. This detail is also printed on a report that has automatically been printed at the exam administrator's desk.

As you leave the exam you'll need to leave your scratch paper behind, or leave it with the administrator (Some testing centers track the number of sheets you've been given, so be sure to return them all). In exchange, you'll receive a copy of the test report.

This report will be embossed with the testing center's seal, and you should keep it in a safe place. Your score report will instruct you to fax your results directly to Citrix and will provide the appropriate fax number.

In a few days, *weeks, or months,* Citrix will send you a package in the mail containing a nice paper certificate and lapel pin. You will be given a license to use logos available for download on your personal stationary and business cards.

Retake Policy

If you don't pass the exam, don't be discouraged. Try and have a good attitude about the experience, and get ready to try again. Consider yourself a bit more educated. You know the format of the test a little better, and the report shows which areas you need to strengthen.

If you bounce back quickly, you'll probably remember several of the questions you may have missed. This will help you focus your study efforts in the right area. Serious go-getters will re-schedule the exam for a couple of days after the previous attempt, while the study material is still fresh in their minds.

Ultimately, remember that Citrix certifications are valuable because they're hard to get. After all, if anyone could get one, what value would it have? In the end, it takes a good attitude and a lot of studying, but you can do it!

CITRIX® CERTIFIED ADMINISTRATOR

1

Introduction to MetaFrame XP

M etaFrame XP is the next generation in Citrix's long line of excellent thin client application server solutions. Citrix has done an outstanding job of listening to their customers and channel partners to bring into its new product the features needed to really maximize the potential of thin client technology. MetaFrame's scalability has dramatically improved, as well as its license management capabilities. With new features such as per session time zone support, SpeedScreen 3, and the Citrix Management Console, MetaFrame should become even more popular and successful.

MetaFrame XP is the next platform release for Citrix and is optimized for use with advanced Windows platforms, and tuned specifically for Internet use. This new architecture should allow Citrix to deploy any application, to any device, over any connection, with a highly competitive power and flexibility. With the new XP family of solutions, Citrix has integrated advanced management features into its higher end product suites to maximize a customer's return on investment (ROI). These features capitalize on Citrix's proven track record in load balancing, network monitoring, and application deployment.

Citrix's use of the XP moniker is in no way related to Microsoft's use of the same for its next version of Windows. Citrix and Microsoft followed different development paths to arrive at the same name, and did consult with each other as to the impact of the similarity, deeming it an acceptable solution for both. MetaFrame XP is compatible with Windows NT 4.0 Terminal Server Edition, Windows 2000, and the upcoming Windows XP.

CERTIFICATION OBJECTIVE 1.01

Identifying the Key Benefits of Deploying MetaFrame

Deploying MetaFrame in heterogeneous environments enables companies to provide best-of-breed and legacy applications to their entire enterprise, with little regard to the client platform. This flexibility allows IT departments to deploy the desktop best suited to their type of business, whether it be Windows, Macintosh, or Unix/Linux, while maximizing return on investment (ROI). MetaFrame also empowers companies to provide applications to a remote or mobile work force through the Internet or through low speed WAN connections.

The key benefits of MetaFrame are:

- **Reach** MetaFrame allows administrators to reach users over a wide range of mediums and hardware platforms. From LAN (local area network) to WAN (wide area network) to Wireless on Windows, Pocket PC, Mac OS, and Unix/Linux, MetaFrame delivers a rich user experience.

- **Performance** By utilizing Citrix's Independent Computing Architecture (ICA) protocol, MetaFrame provides unparalleled performance over any connection and on any platform.

- **Simplicity** MetaFrame provides a simple method of deploying complex applications to a remote or mobile workforce while minimizing the administrative burden inherent in the many-to-one relationship of users and servers. Citrix NFuse furthers this simplicity by removing the need to administer and configure the users' local ICA client. All configuration information can be provided from a simple Web site.

- **Management** MetaFrame XP now includes the new Citrix Management Console (CMC), a comprehensive interface that combines all MetaFrame administrative functions into a single application, ensuring administrators no longer need switch between several task specific applications to manage a server farm. CMC now provides better support for a scalable farm paradigm by allowing administrators to manage a server farm as a single entity, instead of having to manage each server individually. The CMC will also function at any time, from any location.

- **Security** MetaFrame has always allowed administrators to tightly control the users' environment while optimizing the users' computing accessibility and productivity. MetaFrame, combined with Windows 2000 and Group Policy Objects (GPOs), can further tailor the users' environment to take maximum advantage of the computing power and security of a controlled atmosphere.

MetaFrame XP includes a host of new features in answer to the many requests of users and administrators, such as:

■ **Enhanced scalability**   Independent Management Architecture (IMA) provides a scalable architecture that allows server farms to be installed quickly, span several subnets, and yet still be managed from a centralized perspective. It also introduces a level of fault tolerance that permits any one server to fail, without affecting the entire farm.

■ **Integrated security**   XP now integrates 128-bit encryption into the base product to help secure your data.

■ **NFuse integration**   XP ships with NFuse, which provides Program Neighborhood functionality to Web-based clients.

■ **Licensing**   IMA provides single point license installation and management as well as enterprise-wide license pooling.

■ **SNMP support**   MetaFrame now supports alerting and limited control using third-party products and SNMP (Simple Network Management Protocol) traps.

■ **Printer management**   IMA provides a single point of control for printer drivers with automatic driver replication and client printer mapping.

■ **Application migration**   All MetaFrame 1.8 published applications can be seamlessly migrated to XP, and yet retain all settings.

■ **Interoperability**   XP server farms can coexist with both MetaFrame 1.8 and MetaFrame for Unix servers.

■ **Installation**   XP supports both attended and unattended installation.

■ **Shadowing options**   Shadowing can now be configured to require user notification, or be disabled completely during installation.

■ **Display options**   XP supports higher screen resolutions and more color depth than MetaFrame 1.8.

Independent Management Architecture

A major advance in Citrix MetaFrame administration and management is Independent Management Architecture (IMA). IMA is both an architectural model and a communications protocol. This new management foundation is key to the execution and control of Citrix products.

IMA provides not only an architectural foundation, but also a server-to-server communications bridge on UDP (User Datagram Protocol) 2512 for license pooling, published applications, and load balancing information. IMA enables you to group servers into farms regardless of their location or subnet. Organizations gain several advantages with IMA:

- SNMP support. Citrix now supports the sending of SNMP traps, and offers full support of some of the top SNMP monitoring packages.

- Auditing of administrative actions.

- Centralized management of published applications and load balancing information.

- ICA client browsing of published applications without using UDP broadcasts.

- Shadowed sessions which now support logging to track which administrator shadowed whom and when.

- A central repository of license information.

Citrix Management Console

The Citrix Management Console (CMC) provides a single point of contact for the administration of all facets of a MetaFrame XP server farm (as shown in Figure 1-1). CMC is a Java-based console capable of running on any Windows NT or Windows 2000 computer, thus freeing the administrator from having to perform administrative functions on a Citrix server.

CMC is designated as an optional installation when installing MetaFrame XP. If loaded, it also installs and configures the components necessary for communication over the IMA protocol. CMC combines the duties of several MetaFrame 1.8 utilities into one tool, such as Citrix Server Administration (mfadmin.exe), Citrix Licensing (plicense.exe), Published Application Manager (appcfg.exe), and Load Balancing Administration (lbadmin.exe).

on the job *Remember that the CMC will run on any NT 4.0 or Windows 2000 workstation. This makes it easier to administer your farm without having to log in to a session just to run the tools.*

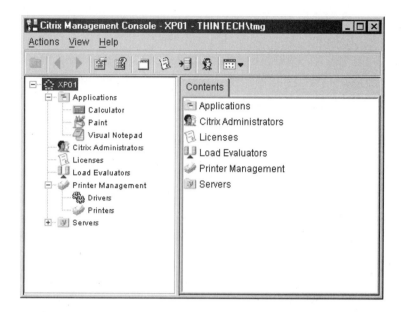

FIGURE I-I

Citrix
Management
Console

Hardware Independence

Citrix clients provide hardware independence by supporting a vast selection of hardware platforms. There are ICA clients for almost all hardware platforms in use, thus giving users of all platforms access to Windows applications. Companies can take advantage of its centralized processing power to extend the life of aging desktops. 386, 486, and Pentium class machines can easily be deployed as thin client terminals, and still run the latest software, such as Office XP, that would not perform well on slower processors. This independence allows companies to deploy the best and most cost-effective hardware platform for their processing needs, without regard to the platform's ability to run Windows applications.

Applications Deployed Regardless of Desktop OS

ICA clients are available for a multitude of desktop operation systems, and thus provide users with connectivity to Windows-based applications regardless of which operating systems they use. With Microsoft possessing such a large share of the market in desktop operating systems, they have easily attracted more developers than any other platform. This means your chances of needing to provide the functionality of a Windows-based application are very high, even if you don't use Windows as your primary platform. By using MetaFrame and the appropriate client, you can deploy mission critical Windows-based applications to users not running a Windows OS, without having to deploy a second desktop or "dual boot" a single desktop. See Table 1-1 for a list of operating systems that have ICA clients.

on the job

People running Unix workstations enjoy not having to have two computers at their desk in order to run all their Windows applications. Remember though, not all ICA client versions support all features.

| TABLE 1-1 | ICA Client Platform Support |

Platform	Version
Windows 32-bit	Windows 9x/ME, Windows NT 3.51, NT 4.0 (Workstation and Server), and Windows 2000/XP
Windows 16-bit	Windows 3.1 or later (running in enhanced mode) and Windows for Workgroups 3.11 or later; also supports client devices running OS/2 2.1, OS/2 Warp Connect 3.0, and OS/2 Warp 4.0 or 4.5
Windows CE	Windows CE 2.0 or later
EPOC	EPOC release 5
Java	Most platforms that implement Sun's Java Virtual Machine (JVM) Version 1.1 or later
Macintosh	System 7.1 or later with installation of Apple's Thread Manager, System 7.5.3, and Mac OS 8 or later
Unix	SCO UnixWare 7 Hewlett Packard HP-UX 10.x and later Sun Solaris 2.5.1 and later (SPARC); Version 2.6 and later (x86) Sun SunOS 4.1.4 Silicon Graphics IRIX 6.2 and later Digital UNIX 3.2 and later IBM AIX 4.1.4 and later
Linux	RedHat 6.1, SuSE 6.4, Slackware 7.0, Debian 2.2, and Caldera 2.4 Linux ARM Netwinder Linux 2.2.14
DOS	3.3 and later

Reduced Costs

Using MetaFrame to deploy applications and centralize management can greatly reduce your total cost of ownership (TCO) by using inexpensive and low maintenance thin clients, and by reducing the amount of administrative time integrating and upgrading applications. Deploying 30 servers to support 1500 users not only has the potential of saving millions of dollars today, but tomorrow as well. Whereas desktop workstations typically get replaced or "refreshed" every three years or so, thin client terminals have a five to six year refresh cycle, and only cost 60-75% of a full workstation.

The administrative burden to support these clients is also reduced, because the rate of failure with thin clients is miniscule compared to that involving PCs. As a result, users will have less chance of causing problems due to a restricted environment. In many situations, help desk and desktop support personnel never have to visit the users, because all application support can be done by "shadowing" them. Shadowing is a feature of WinFrame and MetaFrame that allows administrators to see the same screen as a user, and even share control of the keyboard and mouse in order to show users how to perform a task. By keeping your help desk and desktop people *at* their desks, and giving them the ability to see what the user sees, your trouble tickets should become a lot less troublesome.

exam
ⓦatch   *Be sure to learn which platforms have ICA clients available.*

Now that you have been introduced to MetaFrame XP, review the following points for the exam.

SCENARIO & SOLUTION	
What are the key benefits of MetaFrame XP?	Reach, Performance, Simplicity, Management, and Security.
What is IMA?	Independent Management Architecture. Both an architecture model and a protocol.
What is the IMA protocol?	Server-to-server communications UDP port 2512.
The CMC is what?	Citrix Management Console. A one-stop administration point.

FROM THE CLASSROOM

What Makes a Thin Client Deployment Beneficial?

A common question raised in classrooms has to do with just how a thin client deployment is better than a well-integrated fat client deployment. When thinking about this, a good thing to consider is the total picture, as well as just what issues you or your support team spend time resolving in a normal fat client rollout. Issues such as color scheme, screensavers, crashed hard drives, and unauthorized applications are a few of the top problems I have seen in traditional desktop environments. A thin client deployment is a culture change that may have to be introduced gradually, but the return on this is that users have a more stable platform. This platform will typically be more restricted than a fat client would be, but when users are limited as to the amount of time they can spend on non-work-related tasks at their workstations, the more time they will spend on work-related

tasks. This increased productivity can often be enough to entice CIOs and/or CTOs to buy into a thin client solution. Another point to consider is the time which support staff spends attending hardware failures and onsite applications. Thin client terminals typically do not have hard drives, so if a hardware failure occurs, the downtime experienced should be dramatically reduced. The hardware replacement can also be performed by a non-technical staff member if the location is remote and no onsite support personnel are at hand. The application support issue can be greatly reduced both by shadowing and by allowing your help desk or desktop support personnel to resolve issues and close tickets without leaving their desks. This also reduces the amount of time wasted traveling to a user's location, whether it be down the street or down the hall.

—Travis Guinn, MCSE, CCA, A+, CCSE, MCP+I

EXERCISE 1-1

CertCam 1-1

Requiring Auditing for Shadowing

Some companies may place restrictions on, or even completely disallow, the use of session shadowing due to privacy, classification, or financial concerns. To implement global settings for shadowing, it must be done during the installation of

MetaFrame XP, and cannot be changed once it is installed. The following exercise will show you one of the possible settings that requires all shadowing activity be logged for auditing purposes.

1. Run setup.exe from the MetaFrame XP CD.

2. Accept the License agreement.

3. Choose Next at the Welcome screen.

4. Choose Next at the Network ICA Connections screen.

5. Choose Next on the TAPI (Telephony Application Programming Interface) Modem Setup.

6. Choose Next on the ICA Session Shadowing screen, depicted in Figure 1-2.

7. Choose Allow Shadowing Of ICA Sessions On This Server.

8. Select Prohibit Shadow Connections Without Logging (as shown in Figure 1-3).

9. Continue with setup.

FIGURE 1-2

ICA Session
Shadowing
Wizard

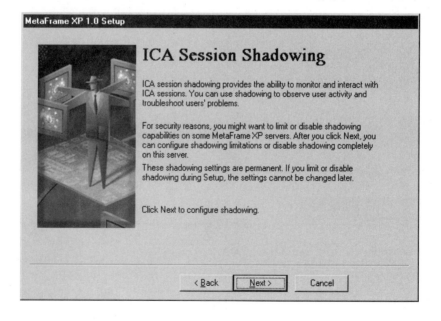

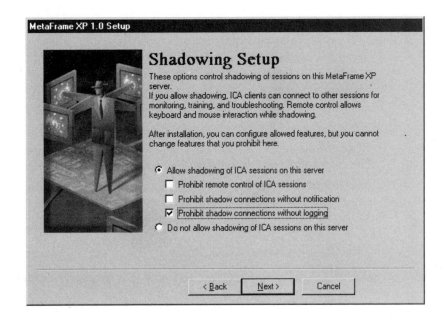

FIGURE 1-3

ICA Session
Shadowing
configuration
options

CERTIFICATION OBJECTIVE 1.02

Understanding Digital Independence

Digital Independence is the marketing term Citrix uses to describe the concept of being able to run any application, on any device, over any network connection, wireless to Web. Attaining "Digital Independence" means being freed from the traditional restrictions and intricacies of technology so everything can compute. Citrix MetaFrame helps organizations effectively compete in the digital age by allowing users to access their applications freely, without restraint to a particular platform or connection. Digital Independence enables Web browsers, PDAs (personal digital assistants), and network appliances to access applications regardless of the method of connection. Whether they use LAN, broadband Internet, wireless, or public Web browser kiosk, Digital Independence gets users connected to their data.

Browsers

Web browsers allow users to access Citrix NFuse sites where they receive the same applications that would be provided by a full Program Neighborhood client. The users can then launch their applications using either an ActiveX-, Netscape Plug-In-, or Java-based ICA client. These Web clients are installed on demand and reduce the administrative burden of distributing the client to users. Now, almost any platform that can support a Web browser can provide users with Program Neighborhood functionality. This freedom empowers users to access company data anywhere they can log on to a Web browser. So, whether they are aboard a cruise ship or shopping at the mall, clients can retrieve company information easily and securely.

Mobile Devices

Mobile devices and mobile Internet access is quickly becoming mainstream and, as it does, Citrix will be there to bring ICA clients to mobile devices. Today, with wireless service providers like Ricochet, Omnisky, and AT&T, more and more people are using the Internet without wires. Motorola has a new service called iDen that allows 64Kb connections from your laptop via your mobile phone. Ricochet, meanwhile, enables laptop and Windows CE users to utilize PC Card-based modems to access the Internet at up to 128 Kbps in most major cities. These networks are constantly being expanded to service more users and will eventually cover the entire country. New technologies like Bluetooth and 802.11b are also being brought into use with higher bandwidth or specialized applications.

Net Appliances

Net appliances are becoming more and more popular as companies begin to find the right niche and price-point. Net appliances typically come with a keyboard, mouse, and small screen, but no hard drive. The OS is usually embedded in ROM (read-only memory) or FLASH and no files are stored locally. The low power of the CPU (Central Processing Unit) prevents the appliance from running mainstream applications natively, but with the use of an ICA client, the appliance can run any application the server can provide. Most net appliances provide a parallel or USB (Universal Serial Bus) port for a printer, so documents created in an ICA session can be printed locally.

EXERCISE 1-2

Adding a Network Appliance to Your Network

Adding a network appliance to your network is extremely easy. In this exercise, we will step through the procedure to add a generic network appliance.

1. Unpack the net appliance and verify that all parts are present.
2. Set up the device by plugging in the power, keyboard, and mouse.
3. Connect the network cable and power on the device.
4. Follow the instructions in the device manual to enter the setup of the device.
5. If no DHCP server is available, assign the device an IP address.
6. In the browser configuration, enter the DNS alias for the data collector and port for the XML service.
7. Depending on the device, select a published application to connect to.
8. If the device has a local browser, the start page could be set to the NFuse server.
9. Save the configuration and reboot the device.
10. Test the configuration by connecting to the MetaFrame server.

As yet, net appliances have not seen the success of PDAs; their manufacturers are still trying to fine-tune the target market of consumers and corporate users that will benefit most from their unique capabilities. As more and more net appliances become available and their features and capabilities are enhanced and refined, more corporations may find they present an easy and inexpensive way to allow users to connect from home.

exam
ⓦatch

Digital Independence is any app, any connection, and any device.

Now that you know about Digital Independence, review these points for the exam.

SCENARIO & SOLUTION	
What is NFuse?	Browser-based access to Program Neighborhood features.
What are net appliances?	Inexpensive diskless workstations, great for running ICA clients.
What is Digital Independence?	Any application, on any device, over any connection.

CERTIFICATION OBJECTIVE 1.03

Identifying the Benefits of MetaFrame Interoperability

MetaFrame XP is fully backwards-compatible with WinFrame and MetaFrame 1.x. This allows you to upgrade your servers incrementally and still maintain full capacity. MetaFrame XP supports two modes of operation: native mode and mixed mode. Mixed mode allows you to operate your new XP server in a MetaFrame 1.8 server farm seamlessly. Table 1-2 lists the different versions of MetaFrame XP available and the features each one supports. With XP in mixed mode, you do however lose some of the advanced functionality. Table 1-3 outlines these issues. It is recommended to have at least Service Pack 2 for MetaFrame 1.8 installed on all MetaFrame 1.8 servers before adding MetaFrame XP to the farm.

When operating in mixed mode, MetaFrame is actually two separate farms. One farm is the XP servers, and the other is the 1.8 servers. Mixed mode allows up to two farms to operate together in what appears to be one unit to ICA clients. Mixed mode configures one server to be the master ICA browser to respond to broadcasts, and the pre-server option to respond to broadcast requests when the master ICA browser is disabled. To optimize your browsing, Citrix recommends that ICA clients be configured to use TCP/IP+HTTP (Transmission Control Protocol/Internet Protocol+HyperText Tranfer Protocol) for browsing and that you log multiple servers in the address list. These servers must have both the Extended Markup Language (XML) Service and Feature Release 1 installed if they are to use MetaFrame 1.8.

TABLE 1-2		XPs	XPa	XPe
MetaFrame Versions and Their Supported Features	Citrix Management Console (CMC)	X	X	X
	Active Directory Support	X	X	X
	Enterprise-class Scalability	X	X	X
	Centralized Printer Management	X	X	X
	Application Publishing	X	X	X
	Centralized License Management	X	X	X
	Advanced Load Management		X	X
	Application Packaging and Delivery			X
	System Monitoring and Analysis			X
	Monitoring and Analysis			X
	Network Management			X

The limitations of mixed mode can be seen in Table 1-3, which follows.

exam
ⓦatch *Be sure to acquaint yourself with the limitations of mixed mode.*

TABLE 1-3 Mixed Mode Limitations

ICA browser election	The MetaFrame XP server becomes the master ICA browser.
ICA license gateways	In mixed mode, license gateways do not function for license pooling. License pooling must be set up using CMC.
Program Neighborhood service	The Program Neighborhood service must be stopped and started on all pre-Service Pack 2 MetaFrame 1.8 servers if you migrate the farm to native mode before all the servers are upgraded.
Farm names	The server farm name must be exactly the same as the MetaFrame 1.8 farm name.
Subnet issues	You must have at least one MetaFrame 1.8 server in every subnet that contains MetaFrame XP servers to run in mixed mode.
Active Directory and user logons	MetaFrame 1.8 does not support Active Directory. In mixed mode, users cannot enter their username as a user principal name (UPN) (user@domain).

EXERCISE 1-3

Switching MetaFrame XP from Mixed to Native Mode

Once a farm has been fully migrated to MetaFrame XP, the XP farm can be switched to native mode. This allows you to take full advantage of all the new features in MetaFrame XP.

1. Open Citrix Management Console by going to Start | Programs | Citrix and choosing Citrix Management Console.

2. Log in to the farm that needs to be switched.

3. Select the farm at the root of the tree, as shown in Figure 1-4.

4. Switch to the Interoperability tab, as shown in Figure 1-5.

5. Uncheck the Work With MetaFrame 1.8 Servers In The Farm check box to place the farm in native mode.

6. Click OK to close the dialog box.

FIGURE 1-4

Farm Properties

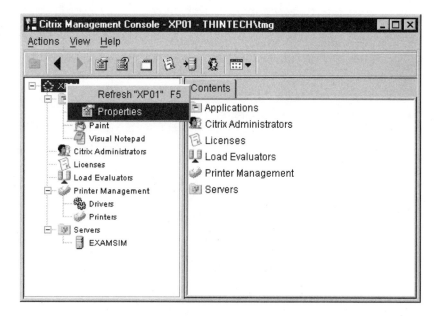

FIGURE 1-5

Setting
interoperability

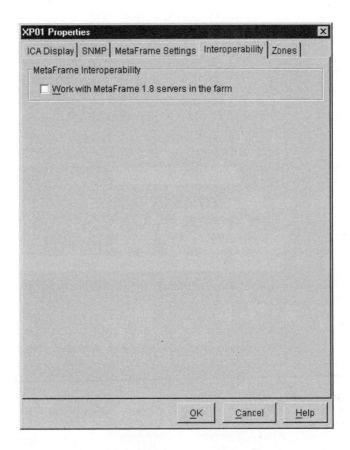

Master Browser Elections

MetaFrame follows specific criteria when selecting a master ICA browser. The following measures determine the new master browser:

1. ICA browser version

2. Manual master browser designation by an administrator

3. Domain controller

4. Longest uptime

5. Server name in alphabetical order

A new master browser is chosen when:

1. Two master browsers are detected on the same subnet

2. A Citrix Server is started

3. The master browser does not respond to another ICA browser

4. The master browser does not respond to an ICA client

You can use the **qserver** or **query server** command to determine which server is acting as the master browser. The master will have a capital M at the end of its line.

on the **Job** *Take care in implementing your first XP server, as it will try to take over as master ICA browser. If you have users accessing published applications, you may experience problems if the master ICA browser suddenly changes.*

exam **Watch** *Be familiar with the causes for ICA browser elections.*

exam **Watch** *Be sure to know what features each version provides.*

Interoperability is an important feature of XP; so here are a few points to review for the exam.

SCENARIO & SOLUTION	
What is native mode?	Native mode is a pure XP environment that gives you all the benefits of XP.
What is mixed mode?	Mixed mode allows an XP farm to operate with a 1.8 farm and presents the two farms as one to the clients.
What are some limitations of mixed mode?	ICA browser elections, license gateways, farm names, AD and subnet requirements.
What version contains all the Citrix products?	XPe

CERTIFICATION SUMMARY

MetaFrame XP is a major advance in thin client technology. Citrix has taken all the feedback from partners and customers and enhanced MetaFrame to include the most sought-after features. These features make MetaFrame XP more scalable and more stable, while still maintaining full compatibility with existing MetaFrame 1.8 installations.

MetaFrame XP adds the Independent Management Architecture and the Citrix Management Console to enhance the administrator's ability to monitor and control the operation of farms from a central location. The CMC consolidates several legacy management applications into one easy-to-use application that can run on workstations as well as MetaFrame servers.

Citrix's concept of hardware independence presents new possibilities in providing access to business applications. Eventually, users will be accessing corporate data from holographic projections of a terminal from their wrist watch. When they do, Citrix will be there to maximize the ability of that mobile processor while minimizing the amount of bandwidth required. For now, users are free to use Windows-, Unix-, Linux-, and Java-based platforms (as well as others), to access business applications.

MetaFrame XP introduces a new paradigm of licensing. We don't have to buy a license for each server with a few user licenses, and then add bump packs. Load balancing, resource management, and installation services are no longer add-on products. Licensing now supports an unlimited amount of servers, allowing us to only pay for the users' licenses. Add-on products are bundled into one of the three target solutions and factored into the per user price. XP*s* provides base functionality for small scale deployments. XP*a* is the ideal for mid-size farms that need load balancing but not installation services or network management. XP*e* includes all the Citrix products in one complete solution.

TWO-MINUTE DRILL

Identifying the Key Benefits of Deploying MetaFrame

❏ Reach allows administrators to supply applications to users where low bandwidth or hardware limitations prevented their use before.

❏ Performance provides users with LAN speed response times over low speed connections with less powerful hardware.

❏ Simplicity defines MetaFrame's ability to reduce both the deployment time of an application and worries over incompatibilities with existing applications.

❏ Management issues are reduced with the CMC, which provides a consolidated view of the farm as a whole.

❏ Security can be tightly controlled to provide users with a safe and stable platform.

Understanding Digital Independence

❏ Freedom from broadband connections and high-powered hardware allows companies to leverage older platforms and still deliver the latest applications to their users.

❏ Versatility describes Citrix's ability to provide Digital Independence with the concept of any application, on any device, over any connection, wireless to Web.

❏ "Any application" is Citrix's goal to make all applications function on a Citrix platform. Windows and Unix are both available now, with more platforms to come.

❏ Citrix is working hard to provide ICA connectivity on every type of connection, from LAN to wireless.

❏ Citrix continues to develop clients for more and more platforms in order to achieve the goal of "any device."

Identifying the Benefits of MetaFrame Interoperability

❑ MetaFrame XP is backwards-compatible with MetaFrame 1.8 and WinFrame 1.8 in order to provide simultaneous operation during migration to XP.

❑ MetaFrame XP's interoperability allows the migration to XP to be transparent to the user.

❑ MetaFrame XP's data store technology allows XP to be scalable far beyond previous versions.

❑ Mixed mode provides legacy browsing functionality while the farm is migrated to an all XP environment.

❑ Native mode eliminates UDP browsing and enables many of the new features of XP.

SELF TEST

The following questions will help you measure your understanding of the material presented in this chapter. Read all the choices carefully as there may be more than one correct answer. Choose all correct answers for each question.

Identifying the Key Benefits of Deploying MetaFrame

1. Which version of MetaFrame XP does not support load balancing?

   A. 1.8

   B. XP*s*

   C. XP*a*

   D. XP*e*

2. Which of the following are key benefits of MetaFrame? (Choose all that apply.)

   A. Reach

   B. Complexity

   C. Performance

   D. Security

3. In MetaFrame XP, Citrix Server Administrator, Load Balancing Administrator, and Published Application Manager are replaced by what?

   A. CMC

   B. DAT

   C. IMA

   D. ICA

4. Your company wants to deploy an inexpensive, simple device to its employees for home use. It should integrate monitor, keyboard, and mouse and have no hard drive, but it should be capable of running the ICA client. It should be able to access the Internet and print out documents to a local printer. What device would be best suited for this scenario?

   A. PDA

   B. Calculator

   C. Net appliance

   D. Commodore

5. You need to provide your users with easy access to a Citrix-based application without the need to deploy the ICA client manually. What Citrix technology would best meet these requirements?

A. ICA

B. IMS

C. RMS

D. NFuse

6. How does MetaFrame XP interoperate with MetaFrame 1.8?

A. Through native mode

B. Through mixed mode

C. Through heritage mode

D. Through lineage mode

7. The CMC will run on NT 4.0 and Windows 2000 platforms using what method?

A. ActiveX

B. Java

C. MMC

D. Web Portal

Understanding Digital Independence

8. IMA uses what port for communication?

A. 1494

B. 1604

C. 2512

D. 2513

9. Your help desk is very busy visiting user desktops to fix simple problems. What feature of MetaFrame can help reduce physical visits to the desktop?

A. Installation Management Services

B. Resource Management Services

C. SecureICA Services

D. Shadowing

10. What are the install options for implementing shadowing? (Choose all that apply.)

    A. Prohibit remote control of ICA sessions

    B. Prohibit shadow connections without notification

    C. Prohibit shadow connections without logging

    D. Do not allow shadowing of ICA sessions on this server

11. What is Digital Independence?

    A. Where do you want to go today?

    B. Any application, on any device, over any connection.

    C. Vendor diversity in thin client deployments.

    D. Platform freedom for ICA clients.

12. Identify the NFuse Web clients. (Choose all that apply.)

    A. C++

    B. ActiveX

    C. Java

    D. Plug-In

13. What is a major limiting factor on net appliances when running mainstream applications locally?

    A. Low power CPU

    B. Large hard drive

    C. Small screen

    D. No mouse

Identifying the Benefits of MetaFrame Interoperability

14. How many farms does XP utilize to implement interoperability?

    A. Five

    B. Four

    C. Two

    D. One

15. What modes of operation does MetaFrame support? (Choose all that apply.)

    A. Interoperability

    B. Mixed

    C. Compatibility

    D. Native

16. Which version of MetaFrame XP does not support load balancing?

    A. XP*s*

    B. XP*a*

    C. XP*e*

    D. None of the above. (They all support load balancing.)

17. You have completed your migration from MetaFrame 1.8 to MetaFrame XP and are now ready to move to native mode. How would you go about making the change?

    A. Reinstall MetaFrame on the first XP server to reinitialize the database and choose native mode operation during the installation.

    B. From CMC, choose the Properties option of the server farm and from the Interoperability tab, uncheck the Work With MetaFrame 1.8 Servers In The Farm box.

    C. On the master browser, open a command window and type **qserver /native**. Stop and start the Program Neighborhood service, as well as the ICA browser service, on all servers in the farm.

    D. From CMC, delete the server farm and create a new one with a different name.

18. What two items will cause an ICA master browser election?

    A. Two master browsers are detected on the same subnet.

    B. A domain controller is rebooted.

    C. The ICA master browser does not respond to a client.

    D. A MetaFrame server is shut down.

LAB QUESTION

You are the lead engineer for a firm with a medium-sized Citrix farm of about 50 MetaFrame 1.8 servers. After migration, you expect your farm to grow to 100+ servers which could be in different locations. Provide a brief overview of how to begin your migration to MetaFrame XP that will allow for a seamless transition to the new platform.

SELF TEST ANSWERS

1. ☑ **B.** MetaFrame XP*s* is intended as a small-scale server and does not include load balancing.
   ☒ **A, C,** and **D** are incorrect because they all support load balancing.

2. ☑ **A, C,** and **D** are correct because they are all key benefits of deploying MetaFrame.
   ☒ **B** is incorrect because a key benefit of deploying MetaFrame is its simplicity, therefore complexity would be incorrect.

3. ☑ **A.** Citrix Management Console (CMC) replaces most of the MetaFrame 1.8 management utilities.
   ☒ **B** is incorrect because DAT stands for Digital Audio Tape. This is a type of magnetic media. **C** is incorrect because IMA stands for Independent Management Architecture, which is the concept and protocol that CMC uses. **D** is incorrect because ICA stands for the Independent Computing Architecture, a performance-improving protocol.

4. ☑ **C.** A net appliance is an ideal solution, allowing home users to access the Web, e-mail, and Citrix applications, and yet keep maintenance costs down.
   ☒ **A** would be a costly solution due to the requirements necessary for PDAs to access the Internet. Therefore, it would not best fit this scenario. A calculator is not capable of running an ICA client (yet), thus **B** would not be a correct answer. Commodore is also not capable of running an ICA client, therefore **D** would be incorrect.

5. ☑ **D,** NFuse, is correct. It would allow you to simply distribute a URL to your users and allow the NFuse site to automatically install the ICA client.
   ☒ **A,** ICA, is the protocol the connection would use to make the connection, but would not directly allow you to access the URL, thus it is incorrect. **B,** IMS, is used for installing packaged applications to the servers in your farm, therefore it is incorrect. **C,** RMS, is used to monitor the system for faults and performance thresholds and therefore is incorrect.

6. ☑ **B,** Through mixed mode, is correct. MetaFrame XP uses mixed mode to interoperate with MetaFrame 1.8.
   ☒ **A,** Through native mode, is how an XP farm operates after all legacy 1.8 servers have been upgraded, therefore it is incorrect. **C,** Through heritage mode, and **D,** Through lineage mode, cite invalid modes, thus they are incorrect.

7. ☑ **B,** Java is correct. CMC uses Java, allowing it to be independent of the Citrix server.
   ☒ **A,** ActiveX, is not used in the CMC, therefore it is incorrect. **C,** MMC, is incorrect because there are no Citrix snap-ins for MMC yet. **D,** Web Portal is incorrect because at the present time there are no Web-based utilities for managing Citrix.

Understanding Digital Independence

8. ☑   C, 2512, is the UDP port IMA uses for communication.
☒   Since **C** is correct, **A**, **B**, and **D** are therefore incorrect.

9. ☑   D, Shadowing, allows administrators to view and control the user's desktop. This can eliminate many visits to the desktop.
☒   **A**, Installation Management Services, is used to install and deploy applications across server farms, therefore, it is incorrect. **B**, Resource Management Services, is used to monitor server performance, thus it is not correct. **C**, SecureICA Services, provides encryption to the ICA data stream, but does not reduce the help desk's visits to the desktop. Therefore, it is not correct.

10. ☑   A, B, C, and D are all correct. All these options are available during install.

11. ☑   B is correct. Any application, on any device, over any connection is the marketing definition for Citrix's Digital Independence concept.
☒   Since **B** is correct, **A**, **C**, and **D** are therefore incorrect.

12. ☑   B, C, and D are correct. Citrix utilizes ActiveX, Java, and Plug-In technologies to provide Web-based clients.
☒   **A**, C++, is incorrect because C++ is not used to provide Web-based clients.

13. ☑   A, Low power CPU, is correct. Net appliances typically have very low power processors that prevent mainstream applications from running successfully.
☒   **B** is incorrect because net appliances typically do not have hard drives. **C** is incorrect because, while net appliances may have smaller than normal screens, that would not prevent them from running applications. **D** is incorrect because net appliances do have pointing devices.

Identifying the Benefits of MetaFrame Interoperability

14. ☑   C is correct. XP actually places a MetaFrame 1.8 farm and a MetaFrame XP farm that co-operates with the MetaFrame 1.8 farm.
☒   Since **C** is correct, **A**, **B**, and **D** are therefore incorrect.

15. ☑   B, Mixed, and D, Native, are correct. MetaFrame XP uses two modes of operation to support legacy MetaFrame 1.8 and WinFrame 1.8 farms. Mixed mode provides a backward compatibility that should only be used while migrating the farm to XP. Native mode supports all the new features available in XP.

   ☒   **A**, Interoperability, and **C**, Compatibility, are not valid modes for MetaFrame XP, therefore they are incorrect.

16. ☑   **A**, XP*s*, does not support load balancing. It is intended as a small-scale server used for a small number of users.
   ☒   **B**, XP*a*, and **C**, XP*e*, are incorrect because they both support load balancing. **D**, None of the above, is incorrect because XP*s* does not support load balancing.

17. ☑   **B** is correct. To change to native mode, all that is required is to uncheck the box on the Interoperability tab.
   ☒   **A**, **C**, and **D** are incorrect because they will not change the farm to native mode.

18. ☑   **A** and **C** are correct. An ICA browser election occurs when either event occurs.
   ☒   **B** and **D** are incorrect because these events do not cause ICA browser elections.

LAB ANSWER

Begin with setting up a data store server. We expect to expand our Citrix offering in the future so we choose to implement a dedicated data store on a Microsoft SQL 2000 server. After the database administrator certifies the SQL server, we begin with upgrading the server we expect to become the data collector. Once the server is upgraded to Windows 2000 Server, MetaFrame XP is installed. We create a new XP farm with the same name as the 1.8 farm and set the XP farm to run in mixed mode. A second server is migrated and the applications are integrated and tested on the new platform, which is then certified to be production ready. We include the new server as a publisher of the applications and test the farm interoperability. After a successful test, we slowly begin migrating the remainder of the servers until all are on board. A procedure is developed to update the Program Neighborhood to use TCP/IP+HTTP instead of UDP for ICA service location. Everything is thoroughly tested and the migration is deemed a success.

2

MetaFrame Installation Process

I t may sound like a cliché, but planning really is the key to successful installations. Without suitable hardware and software, an installation may fail, or even worse, you could end up with an unstable system. Selecting your hardware is especially critical. Making the wrong choices can wreak all sorts of havoc. In the real world, there's little time for mistakes. Therefore, taking the time to check system requirements and carefully plan your installation is crucial.

Pre-installation Tips

Here are a few tips that, if followed, can save you time and stress during your installation.

1. Before you begin the installation, read the documentation that accompanies the software or operating system. Find out what is required and what decisions you may need to make during the installation. Remember to check the Microsoft Hardware Compatibility List (HCL); it's also a good idea to check the knowledge bases of both Microsoft and Citrix for new, platform-specific issues. It may influence which hardware you decide to use. The HCL can be found at http://www.microsoft .com/hcl/ and at Citrix's Web site, http://www.Citrix.com.

2. Analyze your existing systems and collect your data. See what you have to work with and what you may need to do before beginning the installation. Check the hardware manufacturer's and software vendor's Web sites, downloading any BIOS updates, service packs, or upgrades that might be needed—even for your new hardware.

3. Make sure you have all the required drivers for the various hardware components such as Basic Input/Output System (BIOS), Network Interface Cards (NICs), Redundant Arrays of Inexpensive Disks (RAID) controllers, and video before you begin.

4. Prepare and test your hardware. If installing new servers, check each one to make sure that cards are seated well, shipping protection has been removed, and all components are as they should be. Before installing the software, turn on the power and run any diagnostics provided by the vendor. By taking a step-by-step approach, you'll find you have fewer problems and a far more stable system.

To keep things simple, consider purchasing all your equipment from the same vendor and have it configured identically. Make sure the components that make up your servers are identical as well. If you are implementing multiple servers, you will appreciate the time saved on configuration issues. With the right equipment and proper planning, you can eliminate many of the obstacles faced when implementing or upgrading your systems.

on the job

Don't forget that user education is an extremely important aspect in moving from a traditional networked environment to a server-based one. When planning your deployment, make sure that user-training sessions are taken into account. This, more than anything else, will reduce the number of administration and support problems after deployment.

Sizing your server is an equally important issue, especially in a server-based computing scenario. Since the server, not the workstation, does all the processing, it is essential to have adequate resources and applications for the number of users you will support. An underpowered server will not advance the idea of a server-based, thin client environment.

The following sections outline the hardware and software specifications required for a successful installation of MetaFrame XP. Keep in mind that these are the bare minimums for the installation. Later, in the section on planning and sizing, we will discuss real-world implementations and what resources are needed for optimal performance.

CERTIFICATION OBJECTIVE 2.01

Identifying Software and Hardware for MetaFrame XP

MetaFrame XP is an add-on product and requires an existing Microsoft operating system running Terminal Services. It is compatible with the hardware listed on the Microsoft Windows Hardware Compatibility List (HCL), so if you have carefully selected your equipment for the operating system, MetaFrame will be supported as well. In the sections that follow, you will find the hardware and software requirements for both the server and the clients. Which operating system you choose will depend on the size of your user base and the load of applications that will be run. Use the Microsoft recommendations for selecting the operating system.

Server Software Requirements

As an add-on product, MetaFrame XP must be installed onto an existing Microsoft operating system. The following lists the operating system requirements:

Operating Systems

MetaFrame XP can be installed on these Microsoft operating systems:

- Microsoft Windows NT 4.0, Terminal Server Edition with Service Pack 5 or later
- Windows 2000 Server with Service Pack 1 or later
- Windows 2000 Advanced Server with Service Pack 1 or later
- Windows 2000 Datacenter Server with Service Pack 1 or later

If using the Windows 2000 family of servers, the Terminal Services component must be installed prior to installing MetaFrame XP. It is not installed by default. If the component was not installed initially, it can be installed later by using Add/Remove Programs in the Control Panel or from Configure Your Server in Administrative Tools, as shown in Figure 2-1. From the Configure Your Server screen, select Application Server.

If installing MetaFrame XP on a Windows 2000 family server, make sure you do not use one that will act as a Domain Controller. Unless users are given the Log On Locally right, they will not be able to log on to a Terminal Services session on a domain controller. Whether you are using NT 4.0 Terminal Server or Windows 2000, it is not advisable to run Terminal Services and MetaFrame from a domain controller. The caveat is that Terminal Services can be installed on Windows 2000 Server in remote administration mode, as shown in Figure 2-2. In that case, Terminal Services would be used to remotely administer the server, and the Administrators Group would require Log On Locally rights, but separate licenses would not be necessary.

exam
ⓦatch

Make sure you understand the operating system requirements for installing MetaFrame XP. It is a common misconception that MetaFrame XP cannot be run on Windows NT 4.0 Terminal Server Edition.

FIGURE 2-1

The Windows
2000 Configure
Your Server
screen

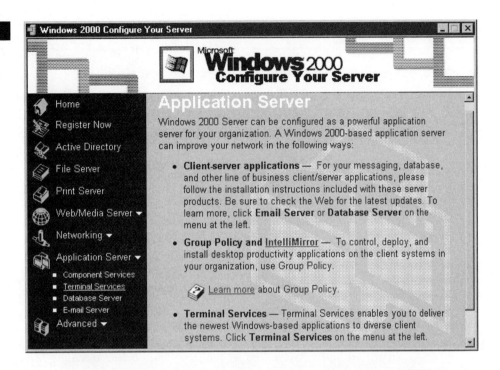

FIGURE 2-2

Selecting the
Windows 2000
Server Terminal
Services modes

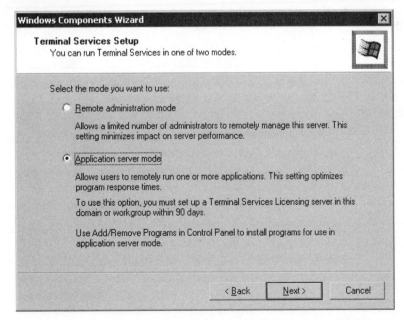

EXERCISE 2-1

How to Determine if Terminal Services Are Installed

How can you tell if Terminal Services have already been installed on a Windows 2000 Server? A quick way to check is to look in the Administrative Tools folder. If you have a Windows 2000 family server currently installed, use the following exercise.

1. Log into the server.

2. Double-click My Computer.

3. Double-click the Control Panel.

4. Double-click Administrative Tools.

When Terminal Services have been installed, the Administrative Tools folder will contain the four Terminal Server shortcuts, Terminal Services Manager, Terminal Services configuration, Terminal Services Client Creator, and Terminal Services Licensing, as shown in Figure 2-3. If already installed, be sure to double-check your hardware and software settings for compliance before installing MetaFrame XP.

FIGURE 2-3

Windows 2000 Server Administrative Tools with Terminal Services installed

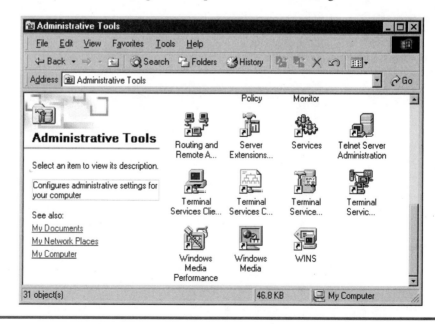

exam
ⓦatch

Terminal Services are not installed by default under the Windows 2000 Server family operating systems, and must be installed prior to installing MetaFrame XP. Terminal Services may be selected during the installation or added later via Add/Remove Programs or Configure Your Server.

Other Software Requirements

Depending on your environment and how you intend to configure your server, you may also need to install additional software to support various components:

- Microsoft Internet Information Server (IIS) version 4.0 or later and Microsoft Java Virtual Machine (JVM) must be installed prior to installing MetaFrame XP if Citrix NFuse will be used to publish applications.

- In mixed environments, where Novell Netware will be used in conjunction with Windows NT 4.0 Terminal Server Edition and MetaFrame XP, the Netware client must be installed prior to installing MetaFrame XP.

- You may also choose to install Adobe Acrobat Reader if you plan to read or print the documentation found on the installation CD. Adobe Acrobat reader can be downloaded free of charge from: http://www.adobe.com/products/acrobat/readstep.html.

Hardware Requirements

The hardware requirements for MetaFrame XP are based upon the requirements for the operating system it is run on. Thus, the hardware requirements will vary by operating system. Table 2-1 lists the bare minimums required to install just the Windows operating systems, and does not take into account other factors that may affect server performance and user experience. In the next section, we will go over server sizing and recommendation issues.

MetaFrame XP Operating Requirements

In addition to the hardware required for the operating system, MetaFrame XP requires additional resources. Again, these figures do not take into account factors that affect server sizing and performance. The next section will cover server sizing and recommendations.

TABLE 2-1 Minimum Hardware Requirements for the Operating System

OS	CPU	RAM	Disk Space	Free Disk Space
NT 4.0 Terminal Server Edition	Pentium or better	32MB	1GB	At least 128MB free
Windows 2000 Server/Advanced Server	P133 or faster Pentium or compatible	256MB	2GB	At least 1GB free
Windows 2000 Datacenter Server	Eight-way or better array of PIII Xeon	256MB	2GB	At least 1GB free

Minimum Requirements for MetaFrame XP

The following are the hardware and software minimums that must be adhered to when installing MetaFrame XP. Remember, these are in addition to those required by the operating system.

- 75MB of disk space for a standard MetaFrame XP installation.

- 25MB minimum disk space for the Citrix Management Console. (Note: Citrix Management Console, which you will learn about in a later chapter, can be installed on any Windows NT or 2000 computer providing it meets or exceeds the minimum hardware and software requirements. Those requirements will be discussed later in this section.)

- 64MB of random access memory (RAM) for MetaFrame XP services and Independent Management Architecture Services (IMA).

- 64MB additional RAM for the Citrix Management Console.

- 1.7MB of RAM for each Idle Session awaiting a connection.

- Super Video Graphics Array (SVGA) Display supporting at least 800×600×256.

- Multiple processors are recommended.

Optional Components

During the installation, you will be prompted to install optional components such as the Independent Computing Architecture (ICA) Clients and NFuse if you have MetaFrame XP*a* or XP*e*, however, you will need additional disk space.

- 200MB of disk space for installing all ICA Client software.

- 20MB of disk space if installing NFuse.

- 6MB for the Resource Manager plug-in and an additional .075MB of space per metric hour for Management Reporting.

- 315KB of disk space for the Installation Manager plug-in.

- 2569KB of disk space for Installer Service.

- 8151KB of disk space for Citrix Packager.

- 1-5MB of disk space for Microsoft Software Installation (MSI) Service. (Note: This component is native to Windows 2000 but must be installed on Windows NT 4.0 Terminal Server Edition.)

- 10MB of disk space for MetaFrame Simple Network Management Protocol (SNMP) agent for Hewlett Packard (HP) Open View or Tivoli Netware.

Remember that these are the minimum hardware requirements. In the real world, more is better, especially where processors and memory are concerned. Server-based computing places the workload on the server, thus clients can get by with fewer resources. Put your money into your servers, making sure you have plenty of resources and room for expansion. The prices involved may seem exorbitant, but you can lower your total cost of ownership (TCO) by spending less on client machines and upgrading them less frequently.

Citrix Management Console Requirements

The Citrix Management Console is a Java Application that allows for the management of all MetaFrame XP servers within a server farm from one central location, such as an NT 4.0 or Windows 2000 Pro computer. It is installed by default with MetaFrame XP on the server but can be installed on another computer as a standalone console, provided it meets the minimum hardware and software requirements. MetaFrame XP is not required on the workstation to run the Citrix Management Console. In order for a computer to be used as a console, it will need to meet the minimum hardware requirements for the operating system, as well as specific requirements for Citrix Management Console. Those requirements are shown in Table 2-2.

TABLE 2-2	Minimum Requirements for Citrix Management Console
Software	Sun Java Runtime Environment (JRE) version 1.3 is installed by default with JRE.
CPU	A Pentium or better.
RAM	An additional 64MB above what is needed for the operating system.
Disk Space	An additional 25MB is needed for the Citrix Management Console and JRE installation.

Now that you know some of the basic server requirements, here is a quick reference for possible scenario questions relating to hardware and software requirements.

SCENARIO & SOLUTION

Your client wants you to install MetaFrame XP on an existing Windows 2000 Server. What should you do first?	Analyze the system and find out if it meets or exceeds software and hardware requirements.
You have installed MetaFrame XP on a server running Windows 2000 Server. You attempt to log in to a client session but are unable to do so. What could be the problem?	You have installed MetaFrame XP on a Windows 2000 Server that is acting as a domain controller. By default, users do not have the right to log on locally.
You plan to use Citrix NFuse to publish your applications. What other software do you need to install on your server?	Internet Information Server (IIS) 4.0 or later and Microsoft Java Virtual Machine (JVM).
Jim has a P100 machine with 64MB RAM and a 500MB hard disk. Every time he tries to install Windows 2000 Server with Terminal Services, the installation fails. What could be the problem?	The machine does not meet the minimum hardware requirements to install Windows 2000 Server. He will need at least a P133 with 256MB RAM and a 2GB hard disk.
Your client has an existing server farm comprised of Windows NT 4.0 Terminal Servers. She'd like to implement MetaFrame XP but has been told she must upgrade to Windows 2000 Server. Is this correct? If not, what, if any, requirements must be met?	No, MetaFrame XP can be run on Windows NT 4.0 Terminal Server Edition without having to upgrade to Windows 2000 Server. The servers must meet the standard hardware and software requirements for the operating system and MetaFrame XP.

Citrix Independent Computing Architecture

Citrix's Independent Computing Architecture (ICA) is a Distributed Presentation Services protocol that allows clients to establish sessions with the MetaFrame XP server and to run server-based applications as if they were installed locally. Though the client device does not require a hard drive, it can still run the most up-to-date programs. Being platform independent, ICA can run on practically any client platform. As a Universal Application Client, it supports all Windows 16- and 32-bit applications, yet requires very few resources on the client side.

All this is possible because ICA separates the program logic from the user's keystrokes and mouse clicks. One hundred percent of application processing occurs on the server side. Only keystrokes, mouse clicks, and screen updates are carried between the client and server. Since no data moves between the client and server, it only requires, on average, 10-20KB of network bandwidth per session and is optimized for connections as low as 14.4 Kbps. In fact, the technology is so efficient that client devices with very few resources can run the latest 32-bit applications.

on the job

Given enough resources, several ICA sessions can be run at the same time on a single client. This can prove helpful to administrators who must log in as another user to configure or test applications, while remaining logged in as Administrator. A single client device having only a P133 processor and 32MB of RAM can run four sessions without any noticeable degradation in performance.

The ICA client uses the ICA presentation layer protocol to transmit user keystrokes and mouse clicks from the client device to the MetaFrame XP server. Various transport and connection protocols can be used with the ICA client. They include:

- Transmission Control Protocol/Internet Protocol (TCP/IP)
- Internetwork Packet Exchange/Sequenced Packet Exchange (IPX/SPX)
- Network Basic Input/Output System (NetBIOS)
- NetBIOS Extended User Interface (NetBEUI)
- Virtual Private Network (VPN)
- Wireless connections
- Internet and intranet connections

- Direct asynchronous connections (dialup)
- WAN links such as T1, T3, 56K, and X.25

exam
ⓦatch

Remember that the ICA protocol resides at the presentation layer and runs on top of a network protocol such as TCP/IP, IPX, SPX, or NetBEUI.

ICA Client Software Requirements

As stated earlier, the ICA client enables almost any client device to connect to a MetaFrame server. It can be run on practically any platform allowing diverse clients to access the applications installed on the server. The following are current platforms that ICA supports:

- 386, 486, Pentium, and higher. Computers that would normally not be able to run today's operating systems or software can be used as thin client devices that require very few resources.
- Unix
- PowerPCs
- X-based devices
- Networked computers
- Windows-based terminals
- ICA-based information appliances
- RISC

on the
ⓞob

Because ICA requires so few resources, older computers with as little as a 386 processor and 16MB of RAM can be used as thin client devices. Only the operating system, appropriate drivers, and the ICA client need be installed locally. A full load of current, 32-bit applications can be accessed from the MetaFrame XP server as well as all networked printers without installing anything else on the client computer.

Industry vendors such as Compaq, HP, IBM, Sun Microsystems, Wyse, Sharp, NEC, and others have begun including Citrix ICA in their new hardware and software products. The list of devices and operating systems ICA can be run on is growing rapidly.

Supported Client Operating Systems

ICA currently supports the client operating systems shown in Table 2-3.

Remember that the ICA client can run on virtually any operating system, including Win16, Win32, WinCE, DOS, Unix, MAC, and OS/2.

Requirements for Win32 ICA Client   The Win32 ICA client is used for newer operating systems and provides the Citrix Program Neighborhood that allows users to browse published applications within the server farm. The minimum requirements necessary for the Win32 ICA client are:

- The 32-bit version of the Windows ICA Client can be installed on Windows 9x, Windows NT 3.51 or 4.0 (server or workstation), Windows 2000, and Windows ME.

- The processor must be at least an 80386 for Windows 95, but later operating systems will require a faster processor. Use Microsoft's recommendations for newer operating systems.

- Windows 9x requires at least 8MB of RAM, while Windows NT 3.51 and 4.0 require 16MB of RAM. Again, for the newer operating systems, stick with Microsoft's recommendations. (Note that, the figures given here are bare minimums.)

- Available hard disk space.

TABLE 2-3   Client Operating Systems Supported by ICA

Windows and Windows-based Terminals	Win32, Win16, WinCE
Handheld devices	WinCE, PocketPC, EPOC
DOS clients	DOS16, DOS32
Web clients	ActiveX Control, Netscape Plug-in, Java
Unix clients	Linux, Sun Workstation, HP-UX, IBM-AIX, Compaq Tru64, SCO, SGI IRIX, X-11
Macintosh client	Motorola and PowerPC
OS2 client	OS2 Warp

- VGA or SVGA display adapter and a color monitor.

- A Windows-compatible mouse or other pointing device.

- A floppy drive for high-density 3.5-inch diskettes.

- A network interface card for connections to the MetaFrame XP server.

- An approved network transport protocol, such as TCP/IP, IPX, SPX, and NetBIOS.

- An optional Windows-compatible sound card for audio support.

- An optional Windows-compatible modem for dial-up support.

- If using the Win32 ICA Client with NFuse, the client device will also need a standard Web browser such as Internet Explorer 4.0 or greater, or Netscape Navigator or Communicator 4.0 or greater.

Win16 ICA Client   The Win16 ICA client is for use on older operating systems and does not support Program Neighborhood. Win16 clients use Remote Application Manager and must configure specific access to published applications. The minimum requirements for running the Win16 client are as follows:

- Windows 3.1 or greater running in enhanced mode.

- Windows for Workgroups, 3.11 or greater.

- Ability to support TCP/IP, NetBIOS, IPX, SPX, and asynchronous connections.

- Can use TPC/IP 32 or other Winsock-compliant stack (for Windows for Workgroups 3.11 or later).

- Available hard disk space.

- VGA display adapter and a color monitor.

- A Windows-compatible mouse or other pointing device.

- A floppy drive for high-density 3.5-inch diskettes.

- A network interface card for connections to the MetaFrame XP server.

WinCE ICA Client   The Windows CE client is required for many handheld and Windows Terminal devices. Before installing the client, make sure you have the correct client for the device you will run it on. Requirements for the Windows CE client are as follows:

- A Windows CE device, usually a handheld or Windows Terminal.
- Should be able to work with Windows CE 2.0 or later.
- A display that supports at least 16 colors or gray scales.
- A network adapter for connections to a local area network using TCP/IP, or a modem for dialup using SLIP or PPP.
- The appropriate WinCE ICA client. Clients are available for SH3, SH4, X86, MIPS, PowerPC, and ARM.

Note: Windows CE ICA clients are available through Citrix OEM partners.

on the

ob

A handheld or pocket PC with ICA installed can be used to perform administrative tasks remotely. Together with wireless networking, an administrator can finally get away from his or her desk.

Web ICA Clients   Web ICA clients are necessary to run published applications via the Internet. The following describes Web ICA clients and the requirements for their use:

- The ICA Web client is an add-in to Microsoft Internet Explorer and Netscape Navigator or Communicator. The Internet Explorer version uses ActiveX Control and the Navigator version uses the Netscape plug-in.
- Should support Windows 3.1 in enhanced mode, as well as Windows 3.11, Windows 9x, Windows NT 3.51, and 4.0 (server or workstation), Windows 2000, and Windows ME.
- Only TCP/IP connections can be made using the Web browser client.

Non-Windows ICA Clients

Other operating systems can also act as clients and connect to the MetaFrame XP server. This allows MetaFrame XP to coexist in various computing environments, thus earning the name "Independent Computing Architecture." The current list of operating systems is shown next.

ICA Clients DOS   There aren't many PCs around that still run DOS exclusively, but I have seen environments where certain legacy applications still operate using DOS. With the correct ICA client, even older machines running legacy applications can connect to a MetaFrame server and run the latest 32-bit applications. The requirements for the ICA DOS clients are as follows:

- The ICA 16-bit DOS client supports DOS 3.3 or later as well as DOS full-screen mode, and can use NetBIOS, IPX, SPX, TCP/IP, or asynchronous connections.

- The ICA 32-bit DOS client supports DOS 4.0 or later as well as DOS full-screen mode and can use NetBIOS, IPX, SPX, TPC/IP, or asynchronous connections.

ICA Client for Unix   The Unix ICA client connections must use TCP/IP and support the following platforms:

- DEC 3.2 or greater
- HP-UX 10.x or greater
- IBM AIX 4.1.4 or greater
- Linux Red Hat 5.1 or greater; other versions may work
- SCO and UnixWare 7 (UnixWare 2.1 and OpenServer 5 require respective binary compatibility modules from SCO)
- SGI IRIX 6.2 or greater
- Solaris 2.5.1 or greater
- SunOS 4.1.4 or greater

ICA Client for Macintosh   Supports Macintosh 7.5.3 or greater. Version 7.1 is also supported, but requires Thread Manager System from Apple. Only TCP/IP can be used for connections.

ICA Client for Java   Supports with an installed Java Virtual Machine using JDK 1.0 and JDK 1.1. Only TCP/IP can be used for connections.

ICA Client for X-11   Supports devices using X-ll through the Unix Integration Services (UIS) option package.

Here are a few more possible scenario questions you may encounter.

SCENARIO & SOLUTION

The Systems Administrator has a handheld computer that runs Windows CE. She'd like to be able to use the device to connect to a MetaFrame XP session for administrative purposes. Is this possible?	Yes. If her WinCE device uses SH3, SH4, X86, MIPS, PowerPC, or ARM there is a Citrix ICA client that will allow her to run a MetaFrame session.
The IT manager is attempting to save the company money, but new operating systems and software constantly require upgraded equipment. Everyone needs either new PCs or more RAM and disk space. Is there anything else he can do?	Yes. Use the existing PCs capable of running the current software, install the appropriate ICA client and connect to a Citrix MetaFrame XP server installed with the most current operating system and software.
You are starting up a new business and need all new hardware and software for your office employees. How can you lower your total cost of ownership (TCO)?	Purchase servers that are server-based-computing ready. Purchase thin client machines and/or use existing computers, but install with ICA client.

FROM THE CLASSROOM

Dumb Terminal Versus Thin Client

You should now have a good idea of what the hardware, operating system, and software requirements are to run Citrix MetaFrame XP in a server-based environment. If you're a fan of nostalgia or were around when the primary way of accessing data on a computer was via a "dumb" terminal, you might see some resemblance. It's true, the "thin client" device and the "dumb terminal" have some similarities. However, the mainframe/dumb terminal scenario served up specific, usually proprietary applications. It did not empower the user with mainstream applications and the freedom to move about virtually as if one were on a standalone computer. With Citrix MetaFrame XP and ICA, there are far more possibilities. Not only can thin client devices be deployed at less than half the cost of PCs, and used for a longer period without upgrading, but older PCs that would be discarded as obsolete can continue to be used as thin clients without upgrading and with no degradation in performance.

—*Connie Wilson, MCSE, MCP+I, CCA, CNA*

CERTIFICATION OBJECTIVE 2.02

Server Planning and Sizing

The previous portion of this chapter covered the minimum hardware and software requirements for MetaFrame XP. Remember, the minimum requirements do not take into account the number of users on a system, the type of applications deployed, or other factors that affect server performance and user experience. As a matter of fact, sometimes the minimum requirements will barely support a single user! For this reason and because the MetaFrame XP server does 100 percent of the application processing, it is extremely important that the environment and user base be analyzed closely before implementing MetaFrame XP.

This next section will cover the planning and sizing issues related to MetaFrame XP. Just as with hardware requirements, server-sizing issues begin with those appropriate for the Windows NT 4.0 Terminal Server Edition or Windows 2000 Server family/Terminal Services operating environments. The minimum hardware requirements just don't work when you begin adding users and applications. In a server-based environment, it is highly advisable to load up your server's processors and RAM. Remember, more is better in a multiuser environment.

Sizing Factors

What factors affect the sizing of a MetaFrame XP server? Are these factors different than those of a "normal" NT/Windows 2000 Server? To answer these questions, use the sizing model of the underlying operating system (NT 4.0 TSE or Windows 2000 family with Terminal Services). Estimate how many users will be connecting to this/these server(s), and determine what types of applications will be used. You will also need to take into account where the users are when they connect.

Three items that interact and affect performance of MetaFrame XP and the user experience are:

- User load
- Application load
- Network bandwidth

Whether you are using Windows NT 4.0 Terminal Server Edition or Windows 2000 Server family as your operating system, a multiuser system will require more resources than that of a single-user system. In order to determine your server's particular hardware requirements, it is recommended you do a pilot setup of MetaFrame XP. Use performance tools and monitor the percentage of total processor time, memory pages per second, percentage of network utilization, and hard disk I/O rates. If you will be running MetaFrame XP in mixed mode with MetaFrame 1.8 servers, do not include the MetaFrame XP servers in the sizing calculations as they do not require the same resources.

User Load

The user load on a system can drastically affect its hardware requirements. The more users, the more resources are needed. It is not only the number of users that can affect system performance, but the way they use the system. Generally speaking, users can be divided into two groups: Power Users and Typical Users. Power Users will utilize more resources than Typical Users. Power Users are depicted as being more computer savvy, running more applications at one time, cutting and pasting between remote and local applications, and generally stressing the system more. Typical Users, on the other hand, are depicted as having one or two applications open at a time, and tend to be less sophisticated in their approach. One Power User is equivalent to two Typical Users in terms of processor utilization and RAM consumption. The exact processor, RAM, and network bandwidth requirements cannot be accurately determined until a baseline using at least five users, has been established.

on the job

This, of course, is a generalization, but in my experience, the Typical User can stress the system just as much or more than the Power User, albeit unknowingly. For instance, a Typical User browsing with Netscape may leave for lunch with the browser hung. As a result, processor usage can skyrocket, impacting all users connected to that server.

Application Load

An accurate measure of work load cannot be taken without considering the type of applications that will be deployed on the server. Certain applications will consume more memory than others, as well as processing time and disk space. Microsoft Office 2000 applications will eat up at least 10MB of RAM each, while Office XP consumes 12MB, and Outlook another 2MB! Applications that may interact with other backend servers, especially through a WAN link, can consume far more. Even hardware drivers consume resources. If your server runs additional drivers for tape drives or other hardware, you will need to consider the amount of RAM as well as the processor used.

Older DOS or Windows 3.x, 16-bit applications will consume more resources than native 32-bit applications. On Windows NT and Windows 2000 platforms, 16-bit applications are run in a process referred to as WOW or Win16 on Win32. WOW translates 16-bit applications in enhanced mode, which causes additional overhead, consuming more resources. This reduces the number of users per processor by 20-40 percent and increases the amount of RAM needed by 25-50 percent. If your environment uses a mixture of 16- and 32-bit applications, you may want to consider placing them on separate servers so the number of users impacted are kept to a minimum. If you cannot separate the two, you will need to adjust your resources to accommodate the 16-bit applications.

Other applications that can affect system performance are applications that run in the background, such as Microsoft Word spell and grammar checking. Streaming video and audio programs can also consume a great deal of resources. It is often recommended these be turned off by default.

Network Bandwidth

Network bandwidth also plays an important role in system performance and user experience. Since all the processing occurs on the server and clients are in constant communication, server-based computing requires more, not less, available network bandwidth. A number of steps can be taken to optimize the network for MetaFrame XP:

- Manually set the link speed on network cards.
- Add an additional network card (dual-homed) and route heavier traffic separately from typical user traffic.

- Keep other server resources on the same subnet.
- Use a high-speed, preferably switched, Ethernet network.
- You may also want to analyze the traffic on your network using Perfmon or a third-party utility to help determine your requirements and locate bottlenecks.

Recommended Hardware Configurations

Now that you have seen some of the factors that can affect server performance and the user experience, let's take a look at the "recommended" configurations for MetaFrame XP servers.

Storage

Although it is important to make sure you have adequate drive space on your MetaFrame XP server, the size should stay relatively static. It is highly recommended you maintain all user data on separate servers. MetaFrame XP is meant to be an application server and as such, no data should be stored on it. It is more important to make sure the drives and controllers you select provide for the fastest throughput you can achieve.

Drives and Controllers Typically, a RAID setup is recommended in a multiprocessor environment. Hardware RAID is highly advised as it consumes fewer resources than software RAID on both Windows 2000 and Windows NT 4.0 Terminal Services Edition. If RAID is not an option, stick to fast SCSI drives. Because system throughput is so important on a server, IDE and EIDE drives are not recommended. Citrix recommends installing at least two controllers for quad and eight-way servers: One controller for the operating system disk usage, and one for the applications and temporary files, keeping the two separated and the access load evenly divided between the two.

Configuration First, always use NTFS, particularly on the system partition. NTFS allows for better security, performance, and fault tolerance, and saves disk space due to its smaller cluster size. Second, place your system files on a separate partition from your applications. For instance, create a 4GB partition for the system and use the rest of the disk space for the applications. Third, if you have the resources, place the swapfiles on a separate hard disk from your system files as this can increase system performance. Be aware however, that if the swapfile is not on C:, a dump file will not be created after a server crash. If you need to create a dump file, create a temporary swapfile on C:, then remove it afterwards. Keep in mind that a server with a large amount of RAM can create a huge dump file if configured to do a complete dump. Windows NT 4.0 Terminal Server does not have the option to do a small or kernel dump as Windows 2000 does. A complete dump file could take hours and the server would be unavailable until finished.

Disk Space   The amount of disk space needed for a MetaFrame XP server will vary, and reflect the space required by:

- The operating system
- MetaFrame XP and the related components installed
- Swapfiles, temp files, and user profiles
- The number and type of applications installed
- The various drivers, protocols, and add-on utilities installed
- The registry size

It would be difficult for anyone to recommend an exact amount of disk space needed for a MetaFrame XP server; there are too many variables. The best you can do is add together the space needed for each piece: the operating system, MetaFrame and its components, the expected number of connections, applications, swapfiles, and registry. Again, don't skimp. You do not want to run out of disk space.

Keep in mind that the registry will be larger than that of a typical server. Not only are entries made for most applications, but the user hives will be much larger. Citrix recommends at least 40MB for servers with single processors, and at least 100MB for quad and eight-way servers. Swapfiles will tend to be larger as well. The standard recommendation for swapfiles is 2.5 times the amount of installed RAM. If a server has 2GB of RAM, that's a big swapfile! The technical staff planning the server implementation should investigate and do the math, then come up with a reasonable amount of disk space that will accommodate the current load, with enough additional space for drivers, updates, upgrades, and programs that may be added in the future. Remember to install only the drivers, protocols, and application components relevant to your environment.

Determining the amount of disk space needed per connected user is also difficult to gauge. Programs such as Internet Explorer, Netscape Navigator, and Microsoft Office can cause user profiles to grow to huge proportions. A standard rule of thumb is 100MB per connected user, but if profiles are not handled efficiently, the space required for user profiles could run into gigabytes!

on the Job *To reduce the amount of space on your server consumed by user profiles, move as many user profiles as you can to the user's home directory. (Typically, home directories are stored on a server other than the MetaFrame server.) Move temporary Internet files, Outlook.pst files, Favorites, Recently Used, and user-specific configurations used for Office and other programs to their home directories. It's also a good idea to limit the amount of space used for temporary Internet files and/or have them dump each time the program is closed. Smaller profiles will not only keep the disk space more static, they will shorten the time it takes a user to log in.*

Processors and Buses   Processor and bus architecture make a big impact in the load a MetaFrame XP server can handle. Stick with higher-performance buses such as Extended Industry Standard Architecture (EISA) or Peripheral Component Interconnect (PCI) buses, because they support the higher sustained data rates needed. As for processors, a good rule of thumb is 15 connections per Pentium or higher processor. A dual-processor system is highly recommended. Also, be sure your server has the space to expand when more processing power is needed.

As an administrator, you can take several steps to lessen the impact on the server's processors:

- Disable or minimize use of screensavers, animation, and sound.
- Disable background grammar-checking in Microsoft Word.

■ Dedicate one server to be the master ICA browser.

■ Stop/disable unneeded services and processes.

Memory   The amount of RAM needed increases linearly with the number of users connected to the server. As mentioned before, users typically belong to one of two groups, Power Users or Typical Users. Citrix recommends an additional 8MB for each Power User and 4MB of RAM for each Typical User. To do the math for a Windows 2000 Server with MetaFrame XP having eight Power Users and seven Typical Users, the equation would look something like this: 256MB + 128MB + (8 × 8) + (7 × 4) = 476MB. That's 256MB required for Windows 2000, 128MB required for MetaFrame XP and Citrix Management Console, 64MB recommended for the eight Power Users, and 28MB recommended for the seven Typical Users.

exam
ⓦatch

Remember that Citrix recommends an additional 8MB of RAM for each Power User and an additional 4MB of RAM for each Typical User.

EXERCISE 2-2

CertCam 2-2

Resource Requirements for Software Applications

To get closer to a real requirement for RAM, take a look at the applications you will deploy. Each application will consume a portion of RAM. Find that number for each application and multiply it by the number of users who will run the application(s), then add it to the total.

Here's an easy way to find out just how much RAM an application uses. This exercise can be performed on any available Windows NT or Windows 2000 workstation or server.

1. Log in to the server.

2. Open an application such as Microsoft Word.

3. Right-click the task bar.

4. Select Task Manager.

5. Click the Processes tab once.

6. Click Mem once to sort by Memory consumed.

This same process can be repeated for each application you plan to run. Experiment by running several applications at once. Figure 2-4 shows the resources used while running Outlook, Internet Explorer, and Word.

FIGURE 2-4

Windows Task Manager

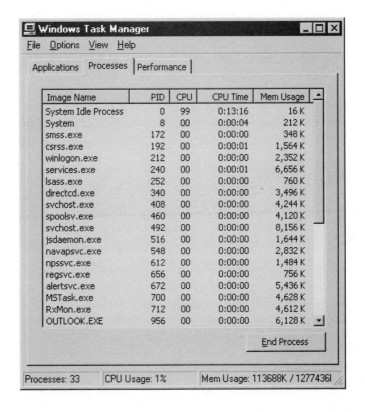

Image Name	PID	CPU	CPU Time	Mem Usage
System Idle Process	0	99	0:13:16	16 K
System	8	00	0:00:04	212 K
smss.exe	172	00	0:00:00	348 K
csrss.exe	192	00	0:00:01	1,564 K
winlogon.exe	212	00	0:00:00	2,352 K
services.exe	240	00	0:00:01	6,656 K
lsass.exe	252	00	0:00:00	760 K
directcd.exe	340	00	0:00:00	3,496 K
svchost.exe	408	00	0:00:00	4,244 K
spoolsv.exe	460	00	0:00:00	4,120 K
svchost.exe	492	00	0:00:00	8,156 K
jsdaemon.exe	516	00	0:00:00	1,644 K
navapsvc.exe	548	00	0:00:00	2,832 K
npssvc.exe	612	00	0:00:00	1,484 K
regsvc.exe	656	00	0:00:00	756 K
alertsvc.exe	672	00	0:00:00	5,436 K
MSTask.exe	700	00	0:00:00	4,628 K
RxMon.exe	712	00	0:00:00	4,612 K
OUTLOOK.EXE	956	00	0:00:00	6,128 K

Processes: 33   CPU Usage: 1%   Mem Usage: 113688K / 1277436l

FROM THE CLASSROOM

Promoting Server-based Computing and Creating a Good User Experience

Planning and sizing go hand-in-hand with user experience. Before moving forward and converting to a server-based/thin client environment, plan your deployment carefully. If you work for a large company, find out what plans are being made in the areas of collaboration, digitization, and telecommuting. Many businesses today have these and other goals in mind and are cutting back on travel and office space to save money. Make absolutely sure you've configured your servers with resources enough that you can provide all of them to your users. Don't skimp on the processors or RAM. If you are serious about becoming a server-based environment, make sure the user experience doesn't suffer. Users who have become accustomed to having PCs on their desks, with disk drives, CD-ROM drives, speakers, and whatever else they can add, will balk at being put on thin client machines. To overcome this, first make sure

you properly train your users to work in the new environment efficiently. Training is a huge issue that should not be overlooked. By properly training not only your IT staff but also your users, you will save yourself many late nights and many headaches. Secondly, make sure the servers have been tested sufficiently. If the servers are constantly crashing or the applications are buggy, it will provide ammunition to the opponents of server-based computing. Third, make sure that the users have all the tools they will need to do their job. If this means setting up a server for the applications that are resource hogs or problematic, do it. If all the complaints are about things that aren't really necessary to doing their job, they won't last. If, however, the overall user experience is not good, you can kiss the dream of server-based computing good-bye.

—*Connie Wilson, MCSE, MCP+I, CCA, CNA*

Network Adapters   Use high-speed network interface cards (NICs) in each server. Consider separating network access so that users connect to the server through one adapter, and the server connects to other servers on the network through another.

Having read the preceding section on sizing of server components, you should now be able to answer the scenario questions that follow.

SCENARIO & SOLUTION

You have been tasked with setting up a Windows 2000 Server/MetaFrame XP test server. You've been told to choose one of the existing test servers and generate a purchase request for any additional hardware or software you require. The most likely choice for a test server has one PIII 400MHz processor, 128MB of RAM, and a 9GB hard disk. Five Power Users will run standard Office applications in order to create baselines. What, if any, additional resources should you request and what is your estimate of how many connections this server can support?	This server appears to be acceptable in all but the amount of RAM installed. To estimate the RAM needed, add the base requirements for Windows 2000 Server, the MetaFrame XP minimum requirements for MetaFrame services and the Management Console, as well as the minimum RAM needed for the five Power Users. This works out to be 424MB. You can also assume that the Office applications will use about 10MB each, and every Power User will have at least two applications open. That comes to 524MB of RAM. Create a purchase order for the additional 396MB of RAM. The single 400 MHz processor and 9GB hard disk are sufficient.
Your environment consists of two MetaFrame XP servers with the same hardware configuration. Microsoft Office and several 16-bit accounting programs have been installed on both servers. There are 20 users in the office who primarily use Office 2000 and they are load balanced between two servers. Scott and Michelle in Accounting generate reports using the 16-bit applications every afternoon. Everything runs smoothly during the mornings, but in the afternoon response time on both servers slows to a crawl. Why is this happening? What can be done to correct the situation?	In the afternoons, Scott and Michelle from Accounting generate reports using 16-bit applications. 16-bit applications can consume 25-50 percent more resources than 32-bit applications, leaving fewer for the other applications and connections. The situation could be remedied in three different ways: (1) Add more resources to the existing servers; (2) Add a third server and place the 16-bit applications on it exclusively. Do not use this server in load balancing; (3) If the additional hardware is not in the budget, you can confine the two accounting users to one server and only run the 16-bit applications there. Remove the load balancing. All applications will be installed on both servers in case of a server crash.

Planning and Sizing for the MetaFrame XP Data Store

When planning your MetaFrame XP installation, you will need to make some decisions regarding the database that will be used for the server farm's data store. These are:

- What database will be used. The type of database used will be influenced by how many servers are in your server farm, the number and type of applications deployed, and the number of concurrent connections to the server and the server's hardware configuration.

■ How the MetaFrame XP servers will access the data store. MetaFrame XP servers have the option of accessing the data store directly (by local connection) or indirectly (through another MetaFrame XP server). If using a direct connection to the data store, Open Database Connectivity (ODBC) drivers are required. If using indirect access, a MetaFrame XP server will connect to another MetaFrame XP server that connects to the data store directly. Although this method, when used with an SQL database does not require ODBC to be installed on every MetaFrame XP server, it is not recommended for use with mission-critical server farms because the connecting server creates a single point of failure.

As previously stated, Microsoft Access, Microsoft SQL, and Oracle can be used for the data store; however, MetaFrame XP should not be installed on an SQL or Oracle server. It must run on either Windows NT 4.0 Terminal Server Edition or the Windows 2000 Server family.

If using Microsoft Access, you will not need to install drivers or perform configuration since the database engine and ODBC drivers are default components of Windows NT 4.0 Terminal Server Edition and the Windows 2000 Server family. Access will support small to medium environments. See Table 2-4 for details.

MetaFrame XP required Microsoft SQL Server 7 with Service Pack 2 or SQL Server 2000. If the MetaFrame server will directly access the database, it will also need Microsoft SQL ODBC, driver version 3.70.08.20 or later, installed. Windows 2000 family servers have the necessary drivers pre-installed. Windows NT 4.0 Terminal Server Edition requires Microsoft Data Access Components (MDAC) version 2.6. Microsoft SQL Server and Oracle are scalable and will work in any environment but are recommended for large to enterprise-sized environments. See Table 2-4 for details.

TABLE 2-4   Sizing for the MetaFrame XP Data Store Database

	Small	Medium	Large	Enterprise
Servers	1-50	25-100	50-100	100 or more
Named Users	Less than 50	Less than 3000	Less than 5000	More than 3000
Applications	Less than 100	Less than 100	Less than 500	Less than 2000

Supported Oracle versions are:

- Oracle 8i, version 8.1.6
- Oracle 7, version 7.3.4
- Oracle 8, version 8.0.6

If using an Oracle database, the Oracle Net 8, version 8.01.06.00, client and ODBC drivers must be installed on servers directly accessing the database.

e x a m
ⓦ a t c h *Be prepared to answer questions regarding the choice, requirements, and sizing of the database for the MetaFrame XP data store.*

Planning for Availability

Making sure that the servers on your network are up and available is extremely important, even more so within a server-based computing environment. Consider for a moment what would happen if a server catastrophe occurred in a server-based computing environment. The applications are all on the server, the clients may not even have hard disks on their machines. If the server goes down, productivity comes to a complete halt. The users may as well go home if their jobs revolve around a computer. The downtime can also be financially disastrous to the company. Fortunately, there are steps you can take to decrease the likelihood of a catastrophe. High availability is achieved through redundancy of server components and redundant systems.

Redundant Server Components

While planning your server implementation, along with the configuration decisions that will affect the installation, you should plan your strategy for high availability. Examine your hardware components and look for points of failure. Which components are most likely to fail? How can you reduce the likelihood of downtime if a component does fail? The answer is to duplicate those components, removing the single point of failure. Let's look at some of the common hardware components likely to fail and disable your server:

- Hard disks
- Controllers

- Power supplies
- Network interface cards
- RAM
- Corrupt operating system

Hard Disks   The impact of hard disk crashes can be reduced by implementing RAID (Redundant Array of Independent Disks). RAID is a disk subsystem made up of several drives of the same size that appear as a single drive thereby improving reliability, response time, and/or storage capacity. Selecting the correct RAID level is a complex process, and each has its own strengths and drawbacks. For example, RAID1 offers the best performance and is best suited to data that is accessed often, while RAID5 is cheaper and appropriate for data that is archived and only accessed infrequently.

RAID can be implemented as either hardware or software. Hardware RAID uses a RAID controller that includes RAID management software, a CPU, and memory. The management software uses its own processor and memory, minimizing impact on the performance of the host. Software-based RAID does not have its own CPU and memory, instead using that of the server. This leads to a degradation of server performance. Software-based RAID5 is not recommended for use with MetaFrame XP.

For high availability purposes, it is recommended that you mirror your hard drives. A RAID1 configuration is acceptable but there are third-party products on the market that can increase the likelihood of availability in the event of a server catastrophe. Some products, such as DuoCor's XactCopy, creates a backup on a separate drive that can be booted to in the event of a disk failure or system corruption.

Memory   Use error-correcting code memory (ECC RAM) in your server to reduce the number of page faults that result in server crashes. Bad memory is a major cause of mysterious system problems. ECC memory includes special circuitry that tests for the accuracy of data as it passes through memory and corrects any errors it finds.

Controllers, Power Supplies, and NICs   Most server vendors will configure servers with redundant components such as controllers, power supplies, and NICs.

The management software that accompanies the server can be configured to fail-over to the online spare if the primary fails.

Hot-swappable Components   Employing hot-swappable components can further enhance the benefits of using redundant components. In the past, if a component failed and had to be replaced, the server would have to be shut down to do so. This scenario could be called a cold swap. Today, hot-swappable server components are available that can be changed out while the server is online, without interrupting service. Others can detect a failure and automatically swap over to a redundant component (automatic-swap). Components that are typically hot-swappable include hard disks, power supplies, and NICs.

Other Considerations   In general, it is best to protect your MetaFrame XP servers the same as you would any other server by:

- Keeping the servers separated in an environmentally-controlled room. This will prevent them from overheating or collecting moisture.
- Placing all servers on uninterruptible power supplies (UPSs) in case of a power outage.
- Securing the room the servers are kept in to prevent unauthorized access and potential accidents.
- Monitoring the servers regularly. Look for any potential problems and nip them in the bud, if possible.
- Creating regular backups that include the registry.

Load Balancing Across Multiple Servers

Load Manager is an option that installs with MetaFrame XP but requires a separate license to activate. Its function is to balance the workload across servers in a MetaFrame XP server farm.

Load balancing works by distributing the clients that connect across the servers in the server farm. Applications or entire desktops can be published and load balanced providing that all servers have the application or desktop in common. When a user launches a published application or desktop, Load Manager determines which server in the farm has the lightest load and places the user on that server.

Load Manager is not a fault-tolerant solution like clustering, but a high-availability feature. If a server in the server farm crashes, the users connected to that server will be knocked off and will lose any data not saved beforehand. They are not automatically connected to another server to continue their sessions. Load Manager does ensure that no one server has too heavy a load. This reduces latency and response time.

exam
Ⓦatch

Load balancing is not a fault-tolerant solution. It provides for high availability because there are redundant servers in the server farm.

CERTIFICATION SUMMARY

At this point, you should have a clear idea of the installation, planning, and sizing issues faced prior to implementing a MetaFrame XP server farm. For the exam, be sure to read over and remember the minimum and recommended resources needed for the server, the Citrix Management Console, the ICA client, and each user connection. There are sure to be at least a few questions covering these. Bandwidth consumed and factors affecting performance are likely targets as well. Any topic that covers "minimum," "recommended," or "required" will show up in some form.

What follows are a few points you should read over, understand, and remember. After you have read through the drill, continue to the Self Test area and see how well you do. Keep testing yourself until you can answer each question correctly. You will then be prepared for any question or scenario the exam may throw at you. Good luck!

TWO-MINUTE DRILL

Identifying Software and Hardware Requirements for MetaFrame XP

❑ MetaFrame is an add-on product and requires Windows NT 4.0 Terminal Server Edition or Windows 2000 Server, Advanced Server, or Datacenter Server as the operating system.

❑ When installing Windows 2000 Server, Terminal Services is not installed by default.

❑ Do not install MetaFrame XP on a domain controller. If installed on the Windows 2000 Server family, users will not be able to log in without Log On Locally permissions.

❑ The minimum requirements for MetaFrame XP are 75MB of hard disk space, 64MB of RAM for MetaFrame XP services and IMA, and a Pentium or higher processor.

❑ 200MB of disk space is required to store all the ICA clients.

❑ The Citrix Management Console is a Java applet and can be installed on a workstation as a standalone console. It does not require that MetaFrame XP be installed, but does require 25MB of disk space and 64MB of RAM.

❑ ICA consumes 10-20KB of network bandwidth.

❑ ICA runs at the Open Systems Interconnect (OSI) Presentation Layer.

❑ ICA can run on Windows and Windows-based terminals, handheld devices, DOS clients, Web clients, Unix clients, Mac clients, and OS/2 clients.

Performing Server Planning and Sizing Issues

❑ The MetaFrame XP server performs 100 percent of the application processing.

❑ User load, application load, network bandwidth, and location of the user all affect system performance.

❑ A Typical User requires at least 4MB of RAM and a Power User requires at least 8MB of RAM. One Power User is equivalent to two Typical Users.

❑ Disk space needed for MetaFrame XP will reflect the operating system, MetaFrame and its components, swapfiles, temp files and user profiles, applications installed, drivers, protocols, utilities, and registry size.

❑ EISA and PCI buses are recommended because they support higher sustained data rates.

❑ Databases that can be used for the MetaFrame XP data store are Microsoft Access, Microsoft SQL, and Oracle.

❑ Microsoft Access is recommended for small to medium server farms only, while Microsoft SQL and Oracle are appropriate for any environment.

❑ Redundant server components, such as hard disks, controllers, and NICs, are recommended to provide fault tolerance.

❑ Load balancing is not a fault-tolerant solution but a high-availability feature.

SELF TEST

The following questions will help you measure your understanding of the material presented in this chapter. Read all the choices carefully as there may be more than one correct answer. Choose all correct answers for each question.

Identifying Software and Hardware Requirements for MetaFrame XP

1. What operating systems can MetaFrame XP be run on? (Select all that apply.)

   A. Mac

   B. Linux

   C. Windows NT 4.0 Terminal Server Edition

   D. The Windows 2000 Server family

2. Joe will be installing a MetaFrame XP server to provide Microsoft Windows 2000 for a small department of ten clerical users. He is given a server that had been used in another department prior to an upgrade. The server is a 200MHz PIII with 128MB of RAM and 1GB of disk space. All the clients will be PCs running Windows NT and using TCP/IP. His boss would like him to use the Windows 2000 operating system. What must he do prior to installing MetaFrame XP?

   A. Install Windows 2000 Server and TCP/IP, then install MetaFrame XP and configure.

   B. Install Windows 2000 Server, TCP/IP, and Terminal Services prior to installing MetaFrame XP. Install the Citrix 32-bit client on the users' PCs.

   C. Upgrade the RAM to 512MB, add an additional hard disk with at least 1GB of space, and install Windows 2000 Server, TCP/IP, and Terminal Services. Install MetaFrame XP and the Citrix ICA clients on the users' PCs.

   D. Add an additional hard disk with at least 1GB of disk space, install Windows 2000 Server, TCP/IP, and Terminal Services then install MetaFrame XP. Install the ICA clients on the user's PCs.

3. You plan to install Citrix NFuse to publish applications. What additional software components must you install first? (Select all that apply.)

   A. ActiveX

   B. Java Virtual Machine

   C. Internet Information Server

   D. Anti-virus software

4. Jackson has installed Windows 2000 Server on a PIII 400MHz machine with 1GB of RAM and a 10GB hard disk. He runs DCPROMO and configures DNS, WINS, and DHCP. Later, he decides he will make this a MetaFrame XP server, so he installs Terminal Services and MetaFrame XP. He logs in to the server as administrator and, since all appears okay, he decides to test the server as a user from a client machine. He installs the Citrix ICA client on a PC running Windows 2000 Pro. He then connects to the server and attempts to log in, but is unable to. What could be the problem?

   A. The server doesn't have the minimum requirements to support MetaFrame XP.

   B. His account has been locked out.

   C. He has installed MetaFrame on a domain controller and does not have Log On Locally permissions.

   D. He has configured his ICA connection incorrectly.

5. What component must be installed prior to installing MetaFrame XP if Novell Netware is be used in the same environment?

   A. IPX/SPX

   B. The Netware client

   C. Java Virtual Machine

   D. TCP/IP

6. How much RAM is required for MetaFrame XP and IMA?

   A. 80MB

   B. 64MB

   C. 280MB

   D. 512MB

7. The ICA protocol runs at what layer of the OSI model?

   A. Network Layer

   B. Presentation Layer

   C. Data Link Layer

   D. Application Layer

8. What percentage of application processing is done on the server?

   A. 10 percent

   B. 25 percent

   C. 80 percent

   D. 100 percent

9. How much bandwidth does the ICA protocol use on average?

   A. 5 Kbps

   B. 30-40 Kbps

   C. 8 Kbps

   D. 10-20 Kbps

10. What is the recommended amount of RAM required for each Power User connecting to a MetaFrame XP server?

    A. 10MB

    B. 15MB

    C. 8MB

    D. 12MB

11. Scott oversees six MetaFrame XP servers and would like to find a way to monitor the servers without going into the data center and logging in to each one. What can Scott do to ease his administration tasks?

    A. Use Event Viewer to monitor all servers.

    B. Install Citrix Management Console on a Windows 2000 Pro PC and monitor all servers from there.

    C. Purchase a third-party add-on to monitor all servers.

    D. Install Citrix Management Console on the servers.

Server Planning and Sizing

12. The MetaFrame XP server you installed for the clerical department has done so well that the engineering department has decided they too wish to lower their total cost of ownership by installing a MetaFrame XP server. They have chosen to spend their budget on a new server (with the proper resources to support their group) rather than upgrade or buy new PCs. Their

specialized engineering software is updated frequently and always needs more resources than the last update. It is your job to make sure they spend their money wisely and purchase a server that will support the group and run their programs in the same manner they are accustomed to on a PC. What must you do to ensure this?

A. Purchase a server that covers the minimum resources needed to run Windows 2000 Server and MetaFrame XP. Make sure their PCs have enough resources to run the Citrix ICA client software, and train the users on how to work efficiently in their new environment.

B. Purchase a server with 256MB of RAM, a 5GB hard disk drive, and install TCP/IP as your network protocol.

C. Plan out your installation beforehand, adding together the resources required by the operating system, MetaFrame XP, and the applications that will be run off the server.

D. Begin by planning your installation. Find out what resources the operating system and MetaFrame XP require. Talk to the users in the engineering department and find out how they are accustomed to working. If they are Typical Users, using only one application at a time and not doing anything too tricky, add at least an additional 4MB of RAM for each. If they are Power Users who have several applications running at once and a good grasp of Windows concepts, add an additional 8MB of RAM for each. Add at least an additional 100MB of disk space for each user. Evaluate the amount of resources required by the applications that will be run. The applications are currently installed on the users' PCs so you could run them and check Task Manager for the amount of RAM needed. The documentation that came with the software should tell you the amount of disk space and RAM required for each, as well as the processing speed. Check to find out if the users will all be accessing the server from the LAN, or if there are any remote users accessing from a WAN, dial-up connection, or RAS. When you have gathered all the information, do the math and find what your minimum requirements will be to support the users and application load placed on the server. To these figures, add additional resources to ensure the users' experience is comparable to their experience on a PC.

13. What databases are supported for a MetaFrame XP data store? (Choose all that apply.)

A. Oracle

B. Microsoft Access

C. Microsoft SQL

D. Paradox

14. What type of memory is recommended for the server?

    A. EDO RAM

    B. ECC RAM

    C. VRAM

    D. Flash RAM

15. Diane has been called in as a consultant at a company that has just implemented a server-based computing environment using Windows 2000 Advanced Server and MetaFrame XP. An employee who has since left the company did the installation and no one can figure out why their servers seem to be running so slow. Users say that the performance is okay part of the day, but later slows to a crawl, especially in the afternoons. What could be the possible cause(s) and what can be done to correct the situation? (Select all that apply.)

    A. The users' PCs need more RAM. Upgrade PCs to 128MB of RAM.

    B. Older DOS programs are running on the server during afternoon hours. Place DOS programs on a separate server or find updated 32-bit software.

    C. Users are checking the stock market with streaming video tickers. Create policy to restrict streaming video.

    D. The server's anti-virus software is set to scan in the afternoons. If a complete scan is necessary, set the time for later at night when users are not logged in.

16. Evelyn is in the planning stages of implementing a MetaFrame XP server farm. She has gathered information on the users, applications, and hardware, and feels she has identified the resources necessary to equip her servers for MetaFrame XP so they will perform optimally. What else must she size and decide upon before she is finished with the planning stage?

    A. Clients

    B. Upgrading user PCs

    C. Which database she will use for the data store and where it will be placed

    D. What applications to run

17. Randy has been asked to assist in planning a new MetaFrame XP server farm for the credit department. It is essential that the servers be available 24/7, thus they are looking to Randy to suggest ways to improve availability and reduce chances of downtime. What are some of the options Randy can suggest? (Select all that apply.)

    A. Use Citrix load balancing

    B. Use redundant parts such as controllers, power supplies, and NICs

C. Use RAID with hot-swappable drives

D. Keep an online, hot spare server

18. Maurice has been hired as a consultant for XYZ Company. They have decided to move to a server-based environment and want Maurice to spec out the systems they will need to order for the new servers, then assist with the installation and testing. Maurice is not familiar with the users, applications, or environment. What should Maurice do to judge the amount of RAM and disk space necessary, in addition to that required for the operating system and MetaFrame XP?

A. Ask for a list of users and a list of the applications to be installed on the servers, then add together total users and applications and multiply by 16.

B. Add up the users and multiply by 8.

C. Ask for a list of the users slated for the servers, as well as a list of the applications that will be installed. Visit with as many users as possible to discover what they do and how they will use the server. Categorize each user as a Power User or a Typical User. Add up the Power Users and multiply by 8 to get the amount of RAM needed for each Power User. Add up the Typical Users and multiply by 4 to get the amount of RAM necessary for each Typical User. Add 100MB of disk space for each user as well. Research each application to discover the resources needed to run them. When all the data has been collected, add these figures to the amount of RAM and disk space needed by the operating system and MetaFrame XP to get the minimum requirements.

D. Add 128MB of RAM for each application and 64MB of RAM for each user.

19. Ken has decided to start his own small business and has obtained a loan that will cover most of the equipment he needs to begin. He has purchased two servers with enough resources to support the applications he will run, as well as the number of users he will employ. Next, Ken will need client machines for the employees, but he's running short on funds and can't afford the new PCs he planned on. He does have several older PCs around, but they don't have enough resources to run the software they will be using. What can Ken do to get his business up and running without having to acquire more funds? (Select all that apply.)

A. Purchase as many PCs as he can with the money he has left, and create local accounts on each machine so the users can share PCs.

B. Have the employees work in shifts so there are enough PCs for each user on each shift.

C. Load the older PCs with the appropriate Citrix ICA client and configure.

D. Instead of purchasing PCs for each user, purchase thin client devices.

20. The Management at Acme Widget Corporation has decided to merge two of their divisions into one business unit. They also are looking to lower their TCO and are thinking of changing from a traditional client/server environment to a server-based environment, using MetaFrame XP. One of their concerns is that the two divisions have not standardized their clients. Several different platforms such as Windows, Linux, Mac, and WinCE are currently in use and to replace them would not be cost-effective. How can they overcome this problem?

    A. Install and configure the appropriate Citrix client for each platform and operating system.

    B. Trade in the machines that do no conform to a standard.

    C. Purchase new machines for only the most productive employees and give the older machines to the least productive.

    D. Borrow from another area's budget to purchase new machines.

LAB QUESTION

In this exercise, you will be challenged to use your knowledge and creativity to provide a solution that would work in a real-world scenario. You will be the planner and architect of a new server-based computing environment using Windows 2000 Advanced Server and MetaFrame XP. Your job is to evaluate the following information and build a system that will support the environment.

XYZ Company is made up of three divisions, Sales, Production, and Shipping. All three divisions are physically located in the same building, but each division's departments are in separate offices. There is an existing Ethernet LAN, Windows 2000 Advanced Server domain controller, two backup servers, and a RAS server.

The Sales division has two departments: Sales and Support. The Sales staff carry laptops and use a database of the company's products. Users in the Support area will typically have several applications open at once, including Outlook, Access, and NetMeeting.

Production has three departments: Clerical, Engineering, and Accounting. The clerical employees use Microsoft Office and Outlook, but seldom have more than two applications open at one time. The Engineering staff, meanwhile, use complex programs that tax system resources in addition to using Outlook and MS Office. Accounting employees have several proprietary programs, some of which are older, 16-bit DOS programs and may have several applications open at once, including Outlook and NetMeeting.

The Shipping division has two departments: Clerical and Docking. The clerical employees use the same programs as the clerical employees in the Engineering department, while the dock workers use a specialized program that employs touch-screens. Table 2-5 shows the divisions, departments, and number of users.

TABLE 2-5   Divisions, Departments, Users, and Applications

Division	Department	Number of Users	Applications
Sales	Traveling Sales Staff	25	Database, Outlook, MS Word
	Support Staff	10	Outlook, Collaboration tools
Production	Clerical	10	MS Office, Outlook
	Engineering	15	Complex engineering programs, Office, Outlook
	Accounting	12	Proprietary DOS apps, MS Office, Outlook
Shipping	Clerical	5	MS Office, Outlook
	Docking	15	Specialized shipping applications

Using the preceding information, design an environment that will allow for optimal performance and availability.

SELF TEST ANSWERS

Identifying Software and Hardware Requirements for MetaFrame XP

1. ☑ C and D. MetaFrame XP can be run on Microsoft Windows NT 4.0 Terminal Server Edition, Service Pack 4 or later and Microsoft Windows 2000 Server, Advanced Server, or Datacenter Server, Service Pack 2 or greater.
   ☒ A and B can run on the Citrix ICA client only.

2. ☑ C. The server Joe was given did not have the minimum amount of RAM necessary to install Windows 2000 Server, nor did it have the minimum disk space needed, so he had to upgrade the hardware on his server before installing Windows 2000 Server.
   ☒ In answer A, the installation would have failed because there were not enough resources and Terminal Services would need to be installed. Answer B has Terminal Services installed but still needs additional RAM and disk space. In D, Joe is still lacking the necessary RAM to install Windows 2000 so his installation would not be successful.

3. ☑ B and C. Both Microsoft Java Virtual Machine (JVM) and Microsoft Internet Information Server, version 4.0 or later must be installed.
   ☒ Neither answers A nor D are needed for NFuse.

4. ☑ C. After Jackson installed Windows 2000 Server, he ran DCPROMO, promoting his server to domain controller status. By default, users cannot log in to the domain controller unless they have Log On Locally permissions.
   ☒ A is incorrect because his server does have enough resources to run Windows 2000 Server and MetaFrame. Answer B is also incorrect because he would have received a message telling him his account had been locked out. Answer D is incorrect because he was able to connect to the server. If he hadn't configured the connection correctly, he would never have gotten to the login screen.

5. ☑ B. The Novell Netware Client must be installed prior to installing MetaFrame XP.
   ☒ A, C, and D can be installed afterwards, though it is a good idea to plan ahead and install all necessary protocols in advance.

6. ☑ B. 64MB of RAM is required to run MetaFrame XP and IMA.
   ☒ A, C, and D are all greater than the amount required, thus they are incorrect.

7. ☑   **B.** The ICA protocol runs at the Presentation Layer of the OSI model.
   ☒   **A, C,** and **D** are incorrect because Citrix ICA protocol uses other protocols to manage transport and connection.

8. ☑   **D.** 100 percent of the processing is performed on the MetaFrame XP server. Only the mouse clicks, keystrokes, and screen updates travel between the server and the client.
   ☒   **A, B,** and **C** are all incorrect, as they would put a portion of the processing on the client.

9. ☑   **D.** Citrix ICA uses an average of 10 to 20 Kbps and is optimized for connections as low as 14.4.
   ☒   **A** and **C** are incorrect as they are less than the actual amount consumed, while answer **B** is far more than the amount consumed.

10. ☑   **C.** Each Power User connecting to the MetaFrame XP server will require at least 8MB of RAM, while each Typical User will require at least 4MB of RAM.
   ☒   **A, B,** and **D** are all incorrect, as they exceed the recommended amount of RAM that each Power and Typical User would require. Exceeding the recommended amount is not a bad thing, because more is definitely better, but it is not the correct answer in this case.

11. ☑   **B.** Scott can install the Citrix Management Console on any Windows NT or Windows 2000 Pro PC and monitor all the MetaFrame XP servers from there.
   ☒   **A** is incorrect because the Event Viewer will only allow you to view event logs on all the servers in a domain, but not monitor performance. **C** is not necessary as Citrix Management Console is part of MetaFrame XP. **D** is incorrect because installing the Management Console on each server is unnecessary.

Server Planning and Sizing

12. ☑   **D** is by far the best answer. In this scenario, you will have made sure you exceeded the minimum requirements for the operating system and MetaFrame XP, and that you have collected the proper information about the users and applications.
   ☒   **A** covers only the minimum requirements necessary to install the operating system and MetaFrame XP. After the applications have been installed and the users connected, the system would be overtaxed and the users' unhappy with their experience. **B** was also incorrect, as 256MB of RAM is the minimum requirement for Windows 2000 Server. As a result, the user experience would still be underpowered. Answer **C** only addresses half the issue. The application load and user load must be figured into the sum of the installed resources.

13. ☑ **A, B,** and **C.** Microsoft Access can be used in small environments, while Microsoft SQL and Oracle can be used in all environments.

☒ **D** is incorrect, because Paradox is not supported.

14. ☑ **B.** ECC RAM or error-correcting code RAM, because it helps cut down on page faults that result in server crashes.

☒ **A,** EDO RAM or Extended Data Output Dynamic RAM is fast but does not include the special circuitry that tests for the accuracy of data as it passes in and out of memory. **C,** VRAM or Video RAM, is a type of RAM used by video adapters to enhance graphic performance. **D,** Flash RAM is non-volatile memory similar to EPROM. It holds semi-permanent data that can be rewritten.

15. ☑ **B, C,** and **D.** In **B,** older DOS programs can consume 25-50 percent more resources than 32-bit programs. If the programs were essential, it would be wise to move them to a second server where the performance would affect the least users. **C** could also be the problem. Streaming video and real-time stock tickers can consume significant resources. **D** is also correct. If your environment requires full anti-virus scans, run them at a time when most, or all, users are off the servers.

☒ **A** is incorrect because the client machines require very few resources and if the performance was good in the morning, RAM would not cause it to slow.

16. ☑ **C.** Evelyn will also need to select a database, either Access, MS SQL, or Oracle, and decide where to place the data store. She can use Access if there will be 50 or fewer users. If not, she will need to decide upon MS SQL or Oracle.

☒ **A** and **B** are incorrect as the Citrix client requires few resources. Answer **D** is also incorrect because deciding what applications to run would have been included in her information gathering process.

17. ☑ **A, B, C,** and **D.** Load balancing increases availability and keeps the servers in a farm from being overburdened. Hot-swappable and redundant parts such as controllers, power supplies, and NICs are important as well. In the event of a failed component, the redundant item will take over. An online spare server is also a good idea. If a server fails, simply move users to the spare.

18. ☑ **C.** To find the minimum amount of resources needed to support a number of users, first find out if they are Power or Typical Users. Each Power User requires 8MB of RAM, while each Typical User requires 4MB of RAM. Then look at the applications that will be installed and make sure you have sufficient resources for those as well. Check the manufacturer's system requirements and, if possible, run Task Manager while an application is running on a PC to see

how much memory each consumes. Add the totals together with the operating system and MetaFrame XP requirements and you should have a good base to start with.

  ☒ **A** is incorrect although you would probably end up with enough RAM. **B** does not address the applications at all, and **D** will give you plenty of RAM, but doesn't address disk space.

19. ☑ **C** and **D**. Using the existing PCs with the Citrix client installed can save money. Since all the processing will take place on the server, the clients don't require as many resources. Thin client devices are also much less expensive than PCs because they have no hard drives and don't require as much RAM.

  ☒ **A** could create more problems and restrict productivity, and **B** might create more expenses and less employee satisfaction.

20. ☑ **A**. The Citrix ICA client is platform-independent and can run on all the mentioned platforms, enabling all clients to connect to the MetaFrame XP server.

  ☒ **B, C,** and **D** are not cost-effective and may lend to user dissatisfaction.

LAB ANSWER

Looking at the information just shown, you'll notice there are seven departments and 92 employees. All three divisions are physically located in the same building and the Windows 2000 Advanced Server domain controller, two backup domain controllers, and RAS server are already up and running on an Ethernet LAN. With this in place, our focus is primarily on the MetaFrame XP servers and the clients.

First, let's look at the users and the programs they typically run and define them as either Typical or Power Users. Table 2-6 shows the users divided into Typical and Power User categories.

TABLE 2-6	Department(s)	Number of Users	Classification
Typical and Power Users	Clerical	15	Typical Users
	Engineering	15	Power Users
	Docking	15	Typical Users
	Sales	25	Power Users
	Support	10	Power Users
	Accounting	12	Power Users

That gives us a total of 30 Typical Users and 62 Power Users. In addition to the minimum server resources required by the operating system and MetaFrame XP, we will add in 4MB of RAM for each Typical User and 8MB of RAM for each Power User. We'll also figure in 100MB of disk space for each user. Table 2-7 shows what will be needed at this point.

Without knowing what resources and disk space the applications will require, we'll have to use an educated guess. I'd recommend at least another 1GB of RAM and at least four 9GB drives on a RAID controller. This should be sufficient for the applications and swapfile. As for the processor, we need at least a PIII, 133MHz for Windows 2000 Advanced Server, but we should check the software to find out what its minimum requirements are. Most will require at least a 200MHz processor. My recommendation would be for a 500MHz, dual-processor machine. A server with 2GB RAM, 36GB of disk space, and dual 500MHz processors should be able to support XYZ's environment. However, since we want to build in high availability, we'll add three more servers and configure them in a server farm, then load balance the users between the four. For the Accounting users, I'd add a fifth server to run the older DOS programs, so they will not impact all users. And for redundancy, a sixth server to act as a hot spare with all the applications installed. Each server, in addition to its processor, RAM, and hard disks, will have redundant, hot-swappable power supplies, controllers, and NICs.

TABLE 2-7	Resources Consumed	
Component	**RAM**	**Disk Space**
Windows 2000 Adv. Server	256MB	2GB/1GB free
MetaFrame XP with IMA and Management Console	128MB	100MB
Power Users	496MB	6.2GB
Typical Users	120MB	3GB
Total	1GB	11.3GB

CCA
CITRIX® CERTIFIED ADMINISTRATOR

3

Installing MetaFrame and Various Setup Options

CERTIFICATION OBJECTIVES

A s an integral part of using any platform, the installation of Citrix MetaFrame XP must be completed correctly and with a proper server farm design to be successful. Understanding the features available with Citrix MetaFrame XP, and how they are affected during the installation is critical to the implementation of any Citrix MetaFrame XP environment.

The first step to deploying Citrix MetaFrame XP starts with a single server. The first server must be implemented correctly as it sets the base for all future installations within a MetaFrame XP server farm. Once this is completed, servers can be added to the farm as necessary to support the requirements of the organization. Options available to automate the installation of additional Citrix MetaFrame XP servers include support for automated installation scripts and server cloning.

Another issue affecting the deployment of Citrix MetaFrame XP is proper server farm design. Items such as data store location and database type, zone layout and locations, and single versus multiple farms must be carefully considered prior to implementing MetaFrame XP. In addition, understanding how MetaFrame XP interacts with previous versions of MetaFrame can be an enormous factor in moving forward with this solution. Connecting clients is yet another factor that must be considered.

Each of these items is discussed in-depth throughout this chapter providing tips and techniques for correctly implementing each aspect. Knowledge of how each of these items are implemented and coexist together will ensure that every Citrix MetaFrame implementation is a success.

CERTIFICATION OBJECTIVE 3.01

Installing a Single XP Server

Once the hardware and software to support Citrix MetaFrame XP have been set up and configured, the next step is to complete the installation. Although Citrix provides a very simplistic installation routine, it is important to select the correct options during installation. Failure to do so could cause undesirable results or require a new installation altogether.

To start the installation process for Citrix MetaFrame XP, place the CD into the CD-ROM drive and allow the Autorun to start. Figure 3-1 displays the splash screen provided for the installation. If the Citrix splash screen does not appear automatically, or Autorun is disabled on your computer, you may manually execute the installation program using the following program: *<cddrive>*:\autoroot.exe.

FIGURE 3-1

This splash screen is used to start the server installation process

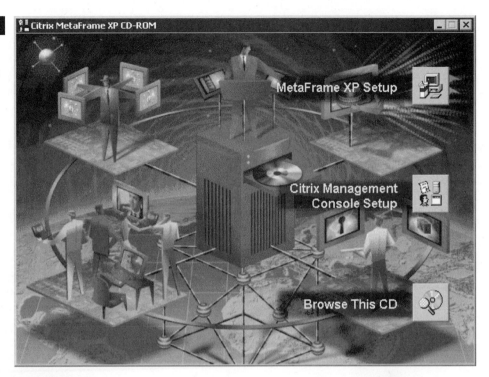

EXERCISE 3-1

CertCam 3-1

Installing Citrix MetaFrame XP

This exercise will teach you how to properly install Citrix MetaFrame XP. Various options will be discussed throughout the course of this chapter. However, an installation using the default options will be used for this exercise. Options that are selectable during installation include:

- Data store
- Citrix farm name \ zone name
- Interoperability with earlier versions
- Administrative options
- NFuse and client software setup

1. Select the MetaFrame XP Setup option from the Citrix splash screen. (See Figure 3-1.)

2. Select the button labeled I Agree to accept the End User License Agreement.

3. Select Next to continue onto the Welcome screen, as shown in Figure 3-2.

4. Press Next to allow Citrix to configure the data store.

5. Choose to create a new Citrix farm or add this server to an existing farm. (See Figure 3-3.) Only add Citrix MetaFrame XP servers to an existing XP server farm. (Interoperability with earlier releases of MetaFrame is discussed later in this chapter.)

6. Select the type of Citrix data store that will be used by this server. Advanced data store configuration options must be completed prior to this installation. This includes options such as installing and configuring SQL or Oracle for use as a data store. (See Figure 3-4.)

7. Select the zone in which this server will operate. (See Figure 3-5.) By default, the zone name is the TCP\IP network address. For example, a server with an address of 192.168.1.5 with a network mask of 255.255.255.0 would have a zone name of 192.168.1.0.

FIGURE 3-2

The Citrix
Welcome screen

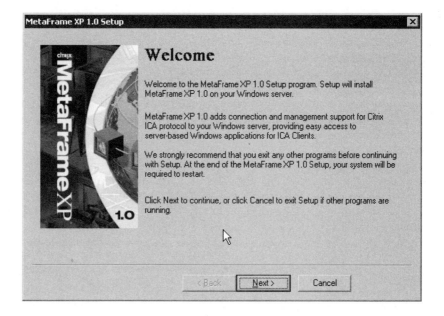

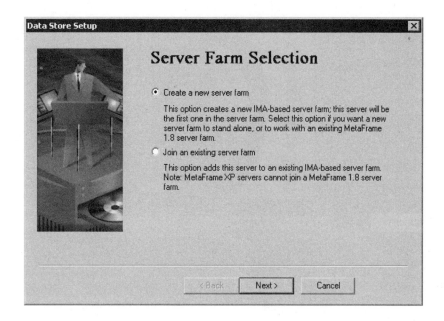

8. Select the name of the Citrix server farm. (See Figure 3-6.) If the option
   to add a server to an existing farm were selected in step 5, this option

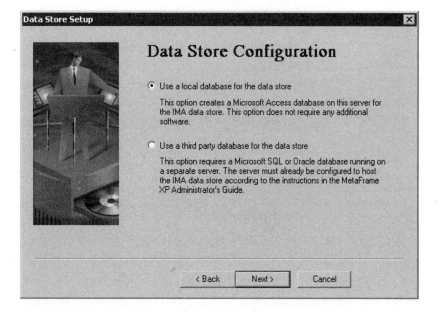

FIGURE 3-5

Installation option to specify zone name

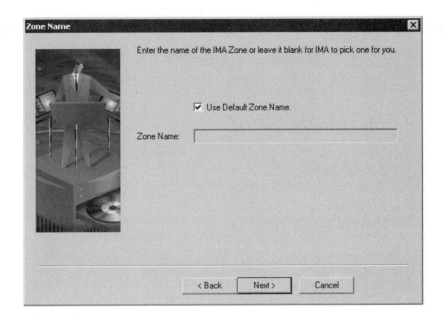

would require you to specify an existing farm that is reachable on the network.

FIGURE 3-6

Selecting the name of the Citrix server farm

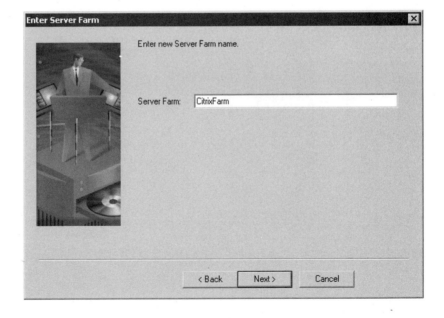

9. Press Next to confirm the name of the Citrix farm.

10. Select the interoperability mode allowing for either native mode (only MetaFrame XP servers) or mixed mode (XP and MetaFrame 1.8 servers). (See Figure 3-7.) This option can be changed after installation is completed.

11. Select the User ID that will be granted administrative privileges within the Citrix MetaFrame farm. (See Figure 3-8.) This must be a user ID that is already created.

12. Select Next to accept network options. Additional protocols such as Internetwork Packet Exchange, or IPX, can only be selected if they are installed on this server. (See Figure 3-9.)

13. To add modems within Citrix MetaFrame, checkmark the Add Modems button and follow the prompts. (See Figure 3-10.) Once completed, select Next to continue.

14. Select Next to continue configuring ICA Session Shadowing.

15. Configure shadowing options to be used with the Citrix farm. (See Figure 3-11.)

FIGURE 3-7

Option to support interoperability with Citrix MetaFrame 1.8

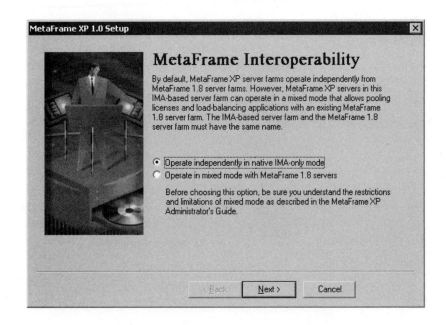

FIGURE 3-8

Citrix farm
administrative
user ID

FIGURE 3-9

Configuring
network options

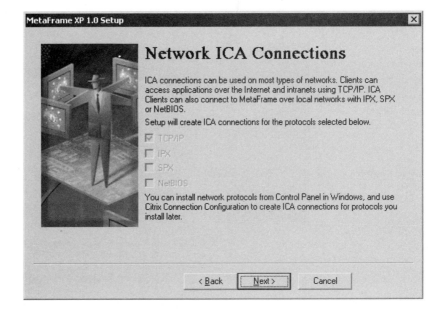

FIGURE 3-10

Configuring
MetaFrame to
use existing
modems

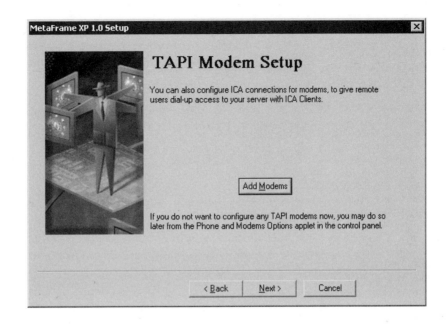

FIGURE 3-11

Shadowing
options

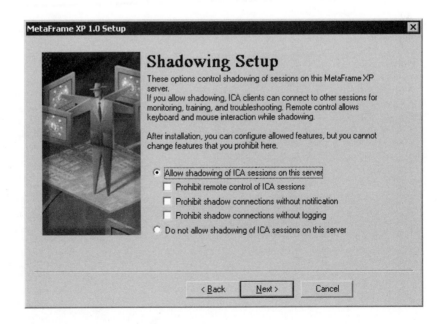

Due to the requirements of customers such as financial institutions, shadowing options selected here are permanent. Once they are chosen, reinstalling Citrix MetaFrame is the only method by which these options can be altered.

16. Select Next to continue. This dialog box discusses remapping drives within Citrix MetaFrame XP. (See Figure 3-12.)

17. Select the drive letters to use when reassigning server drives. (See Figure 3-13.) By default, no drive remapping is done.

When reassigning drive mappings with Citrix MetaFrame, any application that will be installed on this server should be completed AFTER the Citrix installation. Applications such as Microsoft Office use drive letters in registry entries as well as configuration files, resulting in application issues if implemented prior to the drives being reassigned.

18. Select the port to be used with the Extensible Markup Language, or XML services. (See Figure 3-14.) This option is used in cooperation with NFuse technologies (as discussed in Chapter 11). Select Next.

FIGURE 3-12

Drive mapping options

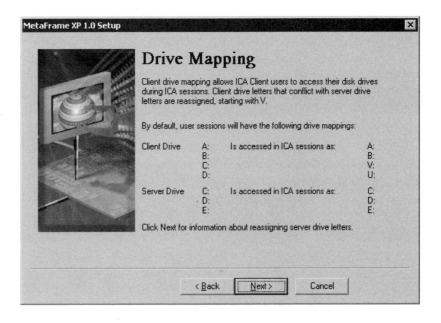

FIGURE 3-13

Selecting new
drive letters

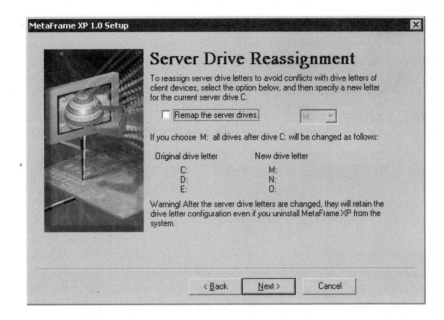

19. By default, NFuse is selected for installation with MetaFrame XP.
    (See Figure 3-15.) Press Next to continue. (NFuse is discussed in depth
    later in Chapter 11.)

FIGURE 3-14

XML Service
configuration

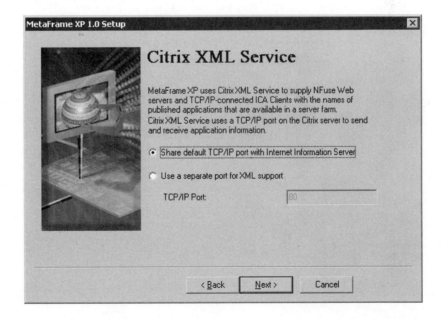

FIGURE 3-15

NFuse installation
options

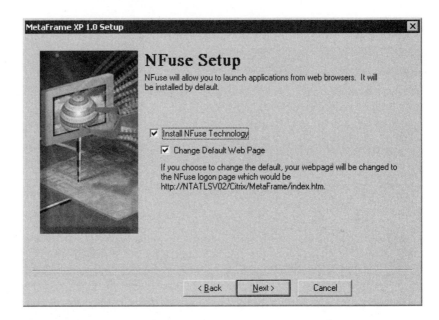

20. Now that all installation options have been elected, press Next to process these selections. Once Next is pressed, the Citrix MetaFrame software will be installed, the server farm created, and each of the options chosen will be implemented. (See Figure 3-16.)

FIGURE 3-16

Installation
confirmation

21. When prompted, select Next to begin configuring Independent Computing Architecture, or ICA client distribution.

22. Choose the location from which to copy client files. (See Figure 3-17.) These files are stored on the server to assist with the deployment and update of Citrix clients.

23. Press Next using the default options to continue. Choosing Custom allows the selection of particular clients to be installed on the server for distribution. (See Figure 3-18.)

24. Input licenses for use with Citrix MetaFrame XP and add-on products. (See Figure 3-19.) Licenses can be activated once the MetaFrame installation is completed and the server has restarted.

25. Select the product code to be used with Citrix MetaFrame XP. (See Figure 3-20.) Press Next to continue.

on the **Job**

The product code is a new license feature in MetaFrame XP. It is critical that the product codes are used correctly. For example, to add a Citrix MetaFrame XP server to an existing farm does not require a server license as in older versions. Instead, only the product code must be entered and then existing user connection licenses will be pooled between servers, by default, within the same farm.

FIGURE 3-17

Client distribution setup options

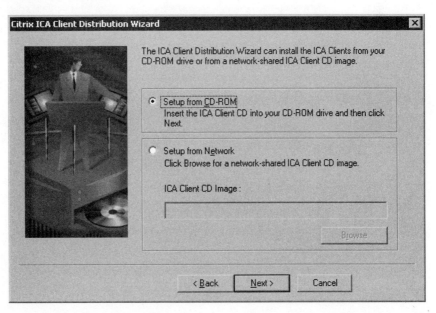

Citrix ICA Client Distribution Wizard

The ICA Client Distribution Wizard can install the ICA Clients from your CD-ROM drive or from a network-shared ICA Client CD image.

○ Setup from CD-ROM
Insert the ICA Client CD into your CD-ROM drive and then click Next.

○ Setup from Network
Click Browse for a network-shared ICA Client CD image.

ICA Client CD Image :

Browse

< Back   Next >   Cancel

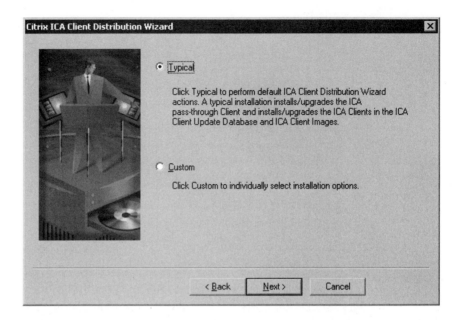

26. Once all items are completed, press Restart to complete the installation. (See Figure 3-21.) When the server has rebooted, Citrix MetaFrame XP will be installed and available for use.

FIGURE 3-20

Selecting the
Citrix product
code

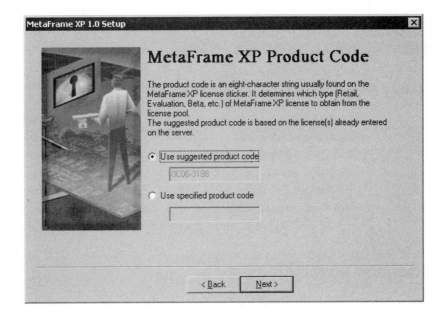

FIGURE 3-21

Restarting the
server after
installation

CERTIFICATION OBJECTIVE 3.02

Deploying Multiple, Identical XP Servers

As with any medium to large server environment, the ability to proficiently install and configure new server installations can save large amounts of time and energy. Citrix MetaFrame XP proves to be no exception to this rule. To facilitate the installation of multiple servers quickly and efficiently, Citrix has provided several methods to automate the installations. Table 3-1 provides a brief description of the various methods available for Citrix MetaFrame XP server deployment. Each method is discussed in detail along with any caveats that must be accounted for.

Unattended Installations

The first option for deploying multiple, identical XP servers available to administrators is the capability to complete an unattended installation. Unattended installations use an answer file to input automated responses during installation of MetaFrame XP. This allows an administrator to install Citrix with minimal involvement while maintaining consistency.

Similar to the Microsoft Windows unattended installation, a sample answer file is provided on the MetaFrame XP CD. The unattend.txt file is located in the \W2K\MF and \TSE\MF directories for Windows 2000 and Terminal Server Edition, respectively. Each question that appears during installation can be

| TABLE 3-1 | Citrix MetaFrame XP deployment methods comparison |

	Standard Installation	Unattended Scripts	Server Cloning
Installation of the first server in a farm	Yes	No	No
Hands-free installation	No	Yes	No
Requires third-party software	No	No	Yes
Requires basic scripting knowledge	No	Yes	No
Requires manual registry modifications	No	No	Yes

automated from within this file. To use the answer file during the set up of MetaFrame XP for Windows 2000, the following command must be used:

```
E:\W2K\MF\setup.exe /u:answerfile
```

E represents the drive letter of the CD-ROM, or the network share where the MetaFrame XP file has been copied, while *answerfile* is the modified unattend.txt file. A full path to the unattend.txt file must be specified if it is not located in the same directory as the setup executable.

Figure 3-22 displays an example of the unattended answer file.

Each section is carefully explained along with options available and warning messages on using these options. Once the answer file is configured, it is critical that proper testing be performed to ensure the installation is successfully completed. Many of these options require a reinstallation to properly reconfigure a server if they are implemented incorrectly.

FIGURE 3-22

Unattended installation answer file

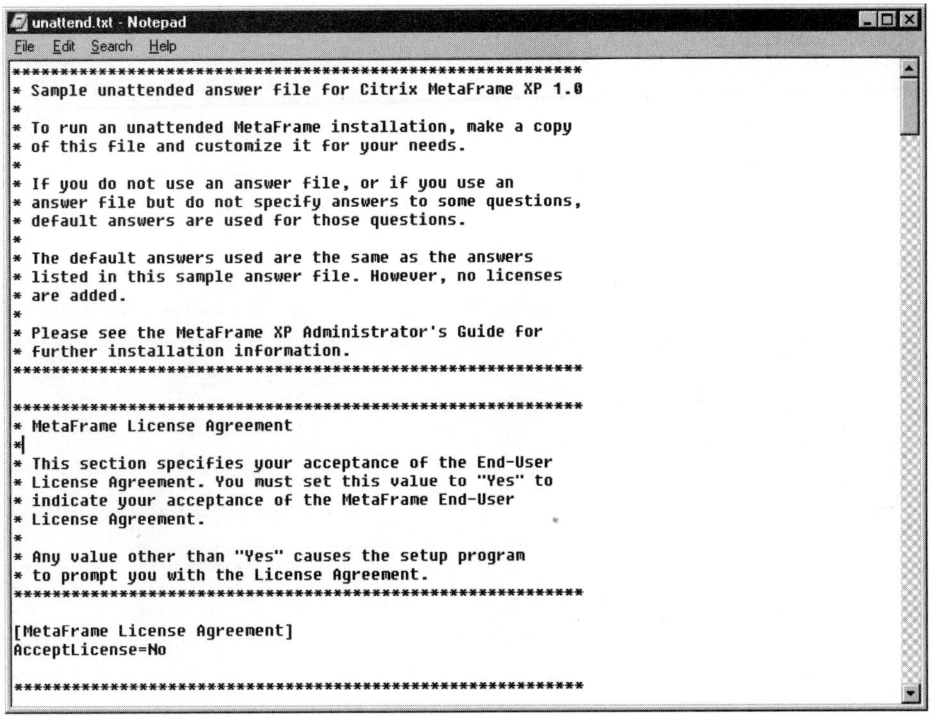

```
*********************************************************************
* Sample unattended answer file for Citrix MetaFrame XP 1.0
*
* To run an unattended MetaFrame installation, make a copy
* of this file and customize it for your needs.
*
* If you do not use an answer file, or if you use an
* answer file but do not specify answers to some questions,
* default answers are used for those questions.
*
* The default answers used are the same as the answers
* listed in this sample answer file. However, no licenses
* are added.
*
* Please see the MetaFrame XP Administrator's Guide for
* further installation information.
*********************************************************************


*********************************************************************
* MetaFrame License Agreement
*
* This section specifies your acceptance of the End-User
* License Agreement. You must set this value to "Yes" to
* indicate your acceptance of the MetaFrame End-User
* License Agreement.
*
* Any value other than "Yes" causes the setup program
* to prompt you with the License Agreement.
*********************************************************************

[MetaFrame License Agreement]
AcceptLicense=No

*********************************************************************
```

EXERCISE 3-2

Creating an Unattended Installation for Citrix MetaFrame XP

This exercise will provide instructions on creating an unattended installation for Citrix MetaFrame XP. This can only be completed for servers added to an existing farm. The first server in a Citrix MetaFrame farm must be installed and configured prior to using this procedure.

1. Ensure that the server farm you are adding servers to is reachable and functioning properly.

2. Copy the installation CD files of the version you are installing to a network share. For example, Citrix MetaFrame XP for Windows 2000 only requires the \W2K directory for installation.

3. If a direct connection to a Microsoft SQL or Oracle database is required for the data store, the following steps must be completed. Otherwise, continue with Step 4.

   A. The MF20.dsn file must be copied from the first server in the Citrix farm to a network share. By default, this file is located in the "\Program Files\Citrix\Independent Management Architecture" directory.

   B. Modify the MF20.dsn file to remove the entry "WSID=MF_Server." An example of the MF20.dsn file is shown in Figure 3-23.

   C. Save the MF20.dsn file to the network share.

4. Modify the unattend.txt file to include the Citrix settings you require. Be sure to insert the location of the MF20.dsn file, if applicable. Once completed, save the unattend.txt file to the network share. The following sections should not be modified:

   A. [Farm Settings] – This is only used for the first server in a farm.

   B. [Indirect Connect Settings] – Not used if direct connections are required.

   C. [Direct Connect Settings] – Not used if indirect connections are required.

5. Connect to the network share containing your installation files and run setup.exe with the /u:*answerfile* option as discussed earlier in this chapter.

FIGURE 3-23

Example of the
MF20.dsn file

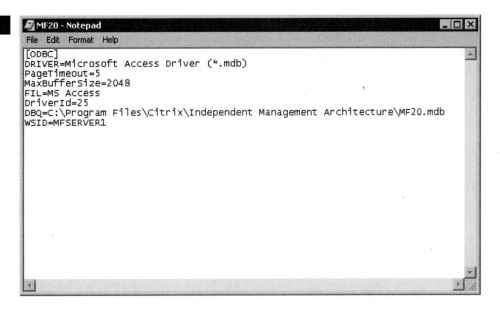

FIGURE 3-23

Example of the
MF20.dsn file

 Be cautious when modifying the MF20.dsn file. Any errors within this file will cause the Citrix MetaFrame XP installation to fail. Also, any items that are missing from the unattend.txt file will cause the installation to stop and prompt the administrator for a response before continuing.

Simultaneous Installations

An issue facing administrators when completing multiple installations of Citrix MetaFrame XP is the ability to perform simultaneous installations. Although this can be done successfully, there are a few guidelines that must be followed to minimize issues that may arise. As servers are installed, they must all communicate with the data store to properly complete the implementation process. When multiple servers try to access the same data locations within the data store, timeouts can occur. Proper planning for these types of issues can immediately resolve most problems before they occur.

Citrix recommends that no more than TEN installations occur simultaneously. When a server attempts to access an index within the data store in use by another Citrix installation, a "deadlock" occurs. The server will then attempt to retry after a short interval to access the index again. If it continues to be unsuccessful, the server installation will fail. By only allowing ten simultaneous installations, this reduces the likelihood of a failed implementation due to this behavior.

Be sure to set the preference for the designated data collector in each zone to Most Preferred in the Citrix Management Console. This ensures that the server chosen remains the data collector throughout the installations. By default, the first server installed into a farm has its preference set to Most Preferred.

Server Cloning

Another common method of deploying multiple, identical servers is through the technique of cloning. This has become an extremely popular alternative to manual installations for servers and workstation operating systems. Several major vendors provide operating system cloning applications. Microsoft has even added additional cloning capabilities into its latest operating system to facilitate easy installation and deployment.

To properly support these environments, Citrix has added support for cloning Citrix MetaFrame XP servers. This does not include the cloning application, only the requirements and capability to use Citrix within this environment. The following sections describe the items needed to support cloning a MetaFrame XP server.

Preparing a Citrix MetaFrame XP Server

The following items describe steps to be taken prior to creating an image of MetaFrame XP. Once these steps have been completed, the server cloning application can be utilized to create an image to be deployed.

- A server installed as the first in a farm with an Access database cannot be cloned.
- Do not use a server with an SSL certificate installed.
- Select the default zone name during installation.
- Delete the wfcname.ini file located on the root of the drive where Citrix MetaFrame XP was installed.
- Stop the Independent Management Architecture service and set it to manual startup.
- Delete the following registry keys:

```
HKEY_LOCAL_MACHINE\Software\Citrix\IMA\Runtime\HostId
HKEY_LOCAL_MACHINE\Software\Citrix\IMA\Runtime\ImaPort
HKEY_LOCAL_MACHINE\Software\Citrix\IMA\Runtime\MasterRanking
HKEY_LOCAL_MACHINE\Software\Citrix\IMA\Runtime\PSRequired
HKEY_LOCAL_MACHINE\Software\Citrix\IMA\Runtime\RassPort
HKEY_LOCAL_MACHINE\Software\Citrix\IMA\Runtime\ZoneName
```

Configuring an Imaged Citrix MetaFrame XP Server

The following outlines the steps necessary to image a MetaFrame XP server using cloning applications. Once these steps are completed, the server is ready to be utilized by users.

- The server name and Security Identifier, or SID, must be changed correctly to support operating system functions and Citrix MetaFrame XP. The SID is used within Microsoft Operating Systems to uniquely identify each device. These changes are traditionally done by the cloning application.

- Add the following registry key and set the value to the name of the MetaFrame XP server

  `HKEY_LOCAL_MACHINE\Software\Citrix\IMA\ServerHost`

- Edit the wfcname.ini file located on the root of the drive where Citrix MetaFrame XP is installed and replace the server name with the new machine name.

- Set the Independent Management Architecture service to start automatically.

- Reboot the server to apply the changes and start MetaFrame XP.

Now that server deployment techniques have been discussed, here are a few questions to test your knowledge.

SCENARIO & SOLUTION	
What is the name of the template file provided by Citrix for installation scripting?	Unattend.txt
What is the name of the service used to stop and start Citrix MetaFrame XP?	Independent Management Architecture
What is the maximum recommended number of simultaneous installations?	Ten
When performing an unattended installation, what file must be modified if SQL or Oracle is used as the data store?	MF20.dsn

CERTIFICATION OBJECTIVE 3.03

Designing a Server Farm

When preparing to implement Citrix MetaFrame XP, a complete server farm design can mean the difference between a failed implementation and a complete success. Critical issues such as how many farms will be used, network connectivity, how zones will be used, and the data store must be meticulously planned to properly prepare for an installation. Once the business requirements and project analysis are complete, a design can be compiled taking into account each of these items. Within this section, the most critical components will be discussed, including single versus multiple farms, zone designs, and data store issues.

Single Farm

The most common implementation of Citrix MetaFrame XP is using a single server farm. Single farms can be used in both small businesses and large enterprises, due to the increased scalability and reliability. Factors such as database performance, hardware platforms, and network connectivity all play a role in deciding upon using a single farm.

Benefits of using a single farm include:

- Centralized administration
- Minimized administrative overhead
- Pooled licensing

Multiple Farms

Based upon the business requirements of organizations, some implementations require the use of multiple farms. Although this adds an additional level of complexity to an environment, it also comes with its own set of benefits. These benefits include:

- Decentralized administration
- Minimized network traffic

- Minimized security risks associated with network traffic and traversal of firewalls for intra-farm communication
- Data store replication is not required
- Segmented licensing – the ability to license farms separately versus one large pool

Zone Design

A critical component of a MetaFrame XP farm, zones are responsible for collecting data from other servers within the farm and distributing it effectively. Each zone elects a data collector whose role replaces the need for the ICA master browser in earlier versions of MetaFrame. Placement and configuration of zones within a MetaFrame XP farm can greatly affect performance and efficiency of the Citrix farm. As shown in Figure 3-24, zones can be modified via the Citrix Management Console under the Properties dialog box for the Citrix farm.

FIGURE 3-24

Configuring zones with the Citrix Management Console

CitrixFarm Properties

ICA Display | SNMP | MetaFrame Settings | Interoperability | Zones

This tab displays the zones in the server farm. You can select one or more servers in the tree to move them or select a single server to set its data collection preference.

- 192.168.1.0 [NTATLSV02]
  - ✓ NTATLSV02

New Zone ...

Remove Zone ...

Rename Zone ...

Move Servers ...

Set Preference ...

OK | Cancel | Help

Citrix recommends that no more than 100 servers operate under a single data collector. Approximately 70 resolutions per second are supported under a single data collector allowing for optimum performance. Several factors play a role in the performance of the data collector, including:

■ Number of users connected

■ Number of simultaneous logons

■ Number of published applications being load-balanced

To properly test a zone design, careful monitoring must occur to determine any bottlenecks caused by an overworked data collector. Although Citrix recommends maintaining as few zones as possible within a farm, multiple zones will be required if a single data collector cannot handle the load. When requiring multiple zones, try separating zones by subnet to help minimize network traffic. In addition, consider dedicating a data collector for the MetaFrame farm if needed to support the environment. It is recommended to maintain a dedicated data collector for each zone that contains 50 or more servers.

Data Store

As the new method by which MetaFrame XP stores information, the data store is another critical component that must be properly planned. Available in several different flavors, the data store allows administrators to customize their environment to meet the business needs. Based upon ODBC-compliant database engines, MetaFrame XP currently supports three database formats and two connection methodologies.

As discussed in Chapter 2, MetaFrame XP supports Microsoft Access, Microsoft SQL, and Oracle as the data store. Determining which application to use for the data store is based upon several criteria. Table 3-2 illustrates the various usage guidelines.

TABLE 3-2   Data Store Platform Guidelines

	Small	Medium	Large	Enterprise
Servers	1-50	25-100	50-100	100 +
Users	<100	<3000	<5000	>3000
Applications	<100	<100	<500	<2000
Recommended Data Store	Access, MS SQL, or Oracle	MS SQL or Oracle	MS SQL or Oracle	MS SQL or Oracle

Another factor in the data store is the mode of access. Citrix supports two modes of access: direct mode and indirect mode. Direct mode allows servers to communicate directly with the data store database to maximize performance. This, however, requires more sophisticated database engines, such as MS SQL or Oracle. Indirect mode was designed to work around the limitations of Access as a database application. By utilizing indirect mode, each server must communicate directly with the IMA services on the host server. The single host server is then the only service directly communicating with Access preventing database corruption. It is recommended that you understand how each of these modes of operation functions and when to utilize the proper mode.

exam

ⓦatch

For scalability purposes, MS SQL or Oracle is always recommended for medium to large farms. Access should only be used in small environments.

In addition to the platform guidelines and modes of operation, there are also some base considerations used for specific scenarios. These items are dependent upon the environment in which they are used. Considerations include:

- Database replication is not supported with Access
- IMA start time is directly impacted by database performance
- Access only supports indirect mode to maintain the integrity of the database
- Large server farms should only use MS SQL or Oracle to maintain acceptable performance levels
- Access is best used in centralized farms
- Use MS SQL or Oracle with farms employing a large number of printer drivers

Now that you are familiar with issues related to designing server farms, here are several scenario questions.

SCENARIO & SOLUTION

What is the recommended limit for servers in a single zone?	100
What database platform(s) is recommended as a data store for enterprise environments?	MS SQL or Oracle
What database platform, used for a data store, only supports indirect mode?	Access

CERTIFICATION OBJECTIVE 3.04

Migrating MetaFrame 1.8 Server Farms to XP

Many users of Citrix MetaFrame XP currently maintain Citrix farms based upon older versions. The need to provide backwards compatibility is a key component of any upgrade strategy. Citrix provides the capability for Citrix MetaFrame XP to operate in a "mixed" environment consisting of MetaFrame 1.8 servers and MetaFrame XP servers. Although there is little configuration required by an administrator to activate these functions, the underlying architecture can be far more complex.

Citrix provides two modes of operation related to interoperability. First, native mode provides support for farms consisting of only MetaFrame XP servers. This method of operation does not support older servers in the farm and is the recommended mode, unless 1.8 servers exist within the server farm. By operating in native mode, MetaFrame XP takes full advantage of many of the new features while operating without much of the overhead existing in MetaFrame 1.8 implementations.

The second mode of operation, or mixed mode, provides the backwards compatibility that MetaFrame 1.8 requires to operate in a MetaFrame XP environment. Although the MetaFrame XP server still functions under the new IMA architecture, it also enables the older ICA Browser and Program Neighborhood services to support communications with MetaFrame 1.8. Each mode is discussed to provide more detail on how each option is used in MetaFrame XP.

exam
ⓦatch

Mixed mode operation is only recommended for migrating Citrix MetaFrame 1.8 servers to MetaFrame XP. It was not designed to operate as a permanent solution.

XP Native Mode

As mentioned earlier, MetaFrame XP supports two modes of operation. Native mode provides compatibility within a server farm consisting of Citrix MetaFrame XP 1.0 servers only. A farm containing only MetaFrame XP servers takes full advantage of the new feature set provided in the product, along with several network enhancements. Since the Citrix MetaFrame XP architecture and features are discussed in depth throughout this book, a limited discussion of how these apply to interoperability is provided here.

Advantages for using native mode include:

- ICA Browser service is disabled on all servers within the farm limiting the broadcast traffic required on your network. IMA traffic used in its place is not based on broadcast traffic.

- Program Neighborhood services are disabled on all servers within the farm.

- Data collectors are used instead of the ICA browser service. This is a more stable solution.

- Data is not shared with Citrix MetaFrame 1.8 servers located within the same farm.

XP Mixed Mode

To properly support backwards compatibility in a MetaFrame 1.8 server farm environment, mixed mode operation can be enabled. Though recommended only as a migration or temporary option, it does offer additional services and capabilities to administrators. With these features, however, come several stipulations that must be accounted for. Within this section, the features and caveats will be discussed to properly prepare you for using this capability.

Features provided by mixed mode operation include:

- ICA Browser compatibility with MetaFrame 1.8 is enabled on every MetaFrame XP server in the farm.

- Program Neighborhood compatibility with MetaFrame 1.8 is enabled on every MetaFrame XP server in the farm.

- MetaFrame 1.8 and MetaFrame XP servers with the same farm name are displayed as a single farm to clients.

- MetaFrame XP servers can respond to legacy UDP client requests.

- Published applications can be load-balanced across MetaFrame XP and MetaFrame 1.8 servers with the same farm name.

- License pooling is available between MetaFrame XP and MetaFrame 1.8 servers on the same subnet.

- The MetaFrame XP Citrix Management Console provides intelligence for interoperability with MetaFrame 1.8.

- MetaFrame XP servers will win ICA browser elections, providing more stable data storage.

Interoperability Considerations

Due to the nature of the operation of interoperability mode, several factors must be taken into consideration when using it. Each of these items can impose a significant affect on the use of Citrix services if not carefully accounted for. Each item is discussed and recommendations for usage are provided.

Citrix Farm Name

To properly support both Citrix MetaFrame 1.8 and MetaFrame XP in the same farm, the name of the server farm must be identical across both server platforms. When installing MetaFrame XP into an existing MetaFrame 1.8 server farm, you must create a new farm during the installation of the first server with an identical farm name. This allows the data store to be created with the appropriate information, and communication between the two farms will automatically take place. Although they are two separate farms, to the users, applications, and management utilities, they are operating as a single entity.

Application Migration

Based upon the nature of Citrix MetaFrame providing access to applications, migration of these applications cleanly is critical to the success of any implementation. Within interoperability mode, MetaFrame XP provides the ability to operate in cooperation with MetaFrame 1.8 to continue providing application services to users. In addition, there are methods for migrating published applications and their associated settings into a MetaFrame XP farm.

It is recommended not to publish applications while operating in a mixed mode environment. Although this capability exists, it must be performed correctly to accomplish this task. Additionally, when published applications are migrated to MetaFrame XP, a log is maintained in the Winnt\System32 directory. This log can assist in troubleshooting issues that may arise.

There are several rules that must be followed when dealing with published applications in this type of environment:

- Applications installed prior to MetaFrame XP being added to the farm will upgrade successfully.

- The back up of published application settings is recommended to help resolve any issues that may arise.

- Newly published applications must first be published via Published Application Manager from the MetaFrame XP server. Once completed, it must then be published via the Citrix Management Console. This order must be observed for application publishing to succeed.

- Applications viewed via the MetaFrame 1.8 version of Published Applications Manager can disappear under certain circumstances. Using the MetaFrame XP version of this utility resolves this issue.

- Do not use Published Application Manager to remove MetaFrame XP servers from the list providing this application.

- Application modified by the MetaFrame XP version of Published Applications Manager cannot be later modified by the version provided with MetaFrame 1.8.

License Pooling

One of the most important features of using mixed mode operation is the capability to share licenses between MetaFrame 1.8 and MetaFrame XP servers. MetaFrame 1.8 servers with connection licenses installed can share these with all servers located within the mixed mode server farm. In addition, MetaFrame XP servers can pool connection licenses it maintains to any MetaFrame 1.8 server within the farm located on the same subnet. Although this can really help in migrating to MetaFrame XP, there are several caveats that must be accounted for.

First, MetaFrame XP servers automatically win ICA browser elections. When acting as the master browser, MetaFrame XP converts ICA license gateways to ICA gateways. In addition, if ICA gateways exist prior to the installation of MetaFrame XP into the server farm, licensing updates can take up to 48 hours due to backup ICA browsers. This can affect how licensing operates within your farm. Also, MetaFrame XP servers handle connection licenses differently in mixed mode as compared to native mode. By default, connection licenses are available to all servers within a farm, in all subnets in native mode. Within mixed mode, these licenses are statically assigned to servers within a particular subnet for a farm. To manually assign licenses to specific servers, administrative intervention is required to ensure they are delineated to the appropriate devices.

Load Balancing

A new feature available with Citrix MetaFrame includes advanced load-balancing criteria from which to choose. Unfortunately, this capability is not available in a mixed mode server farm. When load-balancing applications across a mixture of MetaFrame versions, only the basic load-balancing parameters in MetaFrame 1.8 are available. In addition, a few rules are necessary for this to function properly.

These rules include:

- A MetaFrame XP server must be the master ICA browser.
- Only the default load balance should be configured for all MetaFrame servers.
- Application publishing rules, as described earlier, must be considered since they also apply to load-balancing support.
- The Qserver utility must be used to determine load values across a mixed mode farm.

Load evaluation occurs differently in a mixed mode farm. Although unusual compared to native environments, it is required to support client requests. The evaluation process includes the following:

1. ICA client connects to the master ICA browser to determine application availability.
2. MetaFrame XP servers are queried to determine lightest load based upon user connections.
3. MetaFrame 1.8 servers are queried to determine lightest load based upon user connections.
4. The master browser then chooses between the MetaFrame XP server and the MetaFrame 1.8 server with the least number of connected users. If both servers contain equal values, the MetaFrame XP server will then be chosen.

ICA Browser Elections

Once MetaFrame XP is operating in mixed mode, the ICA browser service is enabled on all servers in the farm. The master browsers generally maintain and provide information to clients on license usage and application availability. This was a service required in earlier releases of Citrix MetaFrame. MetaFrame XP servers can now participate in "browser elections" with MetaFrame 1.8 servers on the same subnet. Used to determine the server maintaining the master information base about the server farm, it is a critical component when operating MetaFrame 1.8 server farms.

Master browser elections are based upon specific criteria. When one of these items occurs, a master browser election is forced to determine who should maintain this role. If any of the following take place, it will trigger a browser election:

■ Citrix MetaFrame server is started

■ Current master browser does not respond to a request

■ Two master browsers are detected on the same subnet

Once a browser election is triggered, the server is chosen based upon several items. Listed is the hierarchy of the election process in order starting with the first rule:

1. ICA Browser version (higher takes precedence)

2. Configured as master browser (w/ Server admin tool or registry)

3. Citrix server is Windows 2000 domain controller

4. Length of time ICA browser has been running

5. Computer name

exam
Watch

Citrix MetaFrame XP servers always win master browser elections over MetaFrame 1.8 due to the first rule. The version number of MetaFrame XP is 2.0, which is greater than MetaFrame 1.8.

ICA Gateways

Based upon the network architecture of previous versions of MetaFrame, broadcast traffic was used to communicate between servers and server farms. To allow servers to communicate across networks, ICA gateways were required. ICA gateways provided virtual links between servers and farms to tunnel all traffic in order to allow

MetaFrame to scale outside a single network. Although MetaFrame XP does not require ICA gateways to perform this function, they are still used for backwards compatibility with MetaFrame 1.8.

ICA gateways are currently supported in mixed mode operation to allow master ICA browsers to communicate across subnets. To identify ICA gateways on MetaFrame XP servers, the Qserver utility must be used. These must be taken into consideration as plans for the upgrade of existing MetaFrame 1.8 servers using ICA gateways are migrated to MetaFrame XP.

License Migration

As part of migrating from an older release of MetaFrame to MetaFrame XP, licensing issues must be taken into account. Citrix provides a service known as Subscription Advantage, where clients meeting defined criteria receive free upgrade licenses to MetaFrame XP. Additional information related to these licenses can be found at the Citrix Web site.

There is one important technical note worth mentioning when migrating a license. When upgrading from MetaFrame 1.8, an existing base license and connection license must be installed. When adding a MetaFrame XP upgrade license, it will not function properly without finding these original licenses in place.

Citrix Farm and Server Management

To assist with interoperability issues, MetaFrame XP provides updated versions of the Citrix administration utilities used to manage MetaFrame 1.8 servers. It is recommended that you use the updated version of these utilities as they address many of the issues related to interoperability not fixed in the earlier releases. In addition, specific rules apply to using these utilities so as not to inject problems into this environment.

As mentioned earlier, it is recommended you use the MetaFrame XP version of Published Application Manager to handle applications across a mixed mode farm. In addition, the Citrix Administration utility can be used to manage some settings across both MetaFrame 1.8 and MetaFrame XP servers simultaneously. The use of the MetaFrame XP Citrix Management Console, or CMC, is generally the preferred administration tool.

EXERCISE 3-3

Configuring an Existing Citrix MetaFrame XP Farm to Operate in Mixed Mode

This exercise will allow an administrator to configure a Citrix MetaFrame XP server farm to operate in compatibility mode, or "mixed mode," and permit interoperability with previous versions of MetaFrame. It assumes that the Citrix farm was not installed, or is not currently operating in "mixed mode."

1. Open the Citrix Management Console by selecting Start | Programs | Citrix | Citrix Management Console.

2. Enter the information required to log on to the Citrix farm including farm name, server name, User ID, and password. (See Figure 3-25.)

3. Select the farm object at the top of the tree. Right-click the object and select Properties (Figure 3-26).

4. Select the Interoperability tab on the Properties dialog box. Check the box labeled Work With MetaFrame 1.8 Server In The Farm to enable mixed mode operation. Select OK on the prompt shown in Figure 3-27.

5. Once completed, the MetaFrame XP servers in the farm will now be able to communicate with MetaFrame 1.8 servers. Subnet license allocation options will also now be available for configuration.(See Figure 3-28.)

FIGURE 3-25

Citrix
Management
Console logon

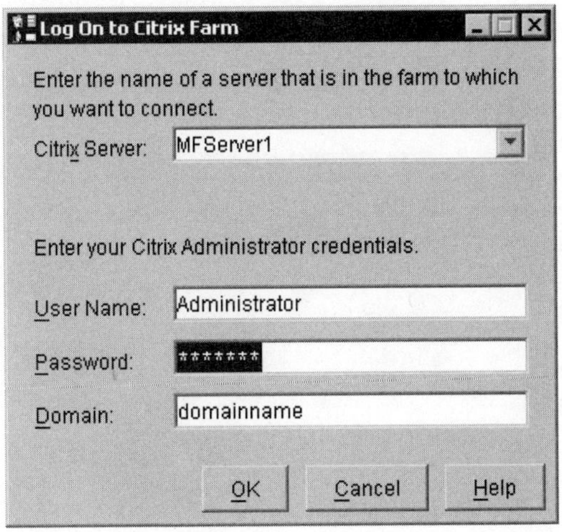

Log On to Citrix Farm

Enter the name of a server that is in the farm to which you want to connect.

Citrix Server: MFServer1

Enter your Citrix Administrator credentials.

User Name: Administrator

Password: *******

Domain: domainname

OK   Cancel   Help

FIGURE 3-26

Citrix
Management
Console

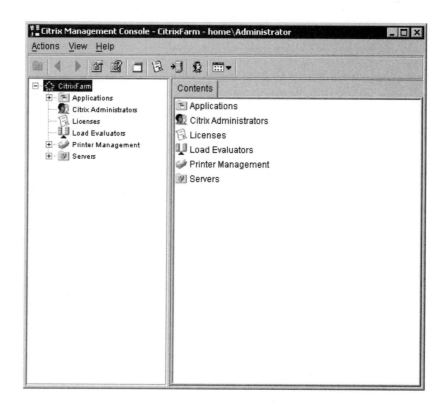

6. After interoperability mode has been activated, an additional tab is now available on the Properties dialog box of each server object located in the Citrix Management Console. As shown in Figure 3-29, these options allow an administrator to customize several of the options discussed throughout this chapter related to mixed mode operation.

FIGURE 3-27

Accepting the
activation of
interoperability
mode

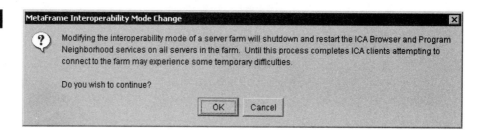

FIGURE 3-28

Configuring
MetaFrame
interoperability
options

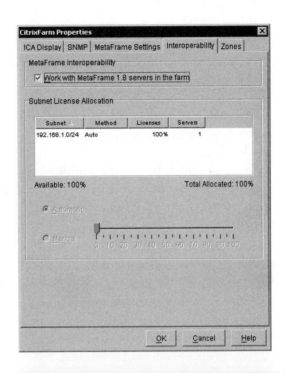

FIGURE 3-29

Server options
available for
configuring
interoperability
with MetaFrame
1.8

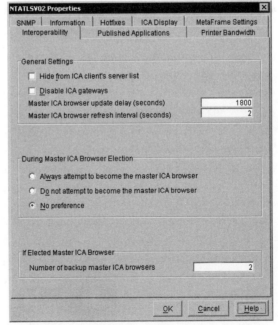

Network Traffic Increases

Because of the new architecture in MetaFrame provided by IMA services, network traffic is handled differently as compared to older versions. In older versions of MetaFrame, traffic was primarily broadcast-based causing network performance and security issues. Now, MetaFrame XP provides a much more scalable, stable, and secure network infrastructure to support communications from client-to-server and server-to-server.

In order to support backwards compatibility, mixed mode operation requires that MetaFrame XP not only maintain its own internal network infrastructure, but emulate the MetaFrame 1.8 networking components as well. If not planned for properly, there could be a potentially large network impact.

Server-to-server Communication

Within MetaFrame XP, server-to-server communication is accomplished by utilizing Transmission Control Protocol, or TCP port 2512. Each server uses a direct channel to other servers as required via this single port. As compared to MetaFrame 1.8 using User Datagram Protocol, or UDP port 1604, this new architecture provides a much more reliable and scalable solution.

Once interoperability mode is activated, Citrix MetaFrame XP must now support both methods of communication. Therefore, MetaFrame XP servers will continue to use TCP port 2512 to communicate with each other, but will use UDP port 1604 to work with MetaFrame 1.8 servers. Traffic thereby increases a great deal as the number of servers located within the Citrix farms increases. Although this functionality works, it is something that, again, must be planned carefully to minimize any network impact.

Client-to-server Communication

As discussed earlier in this chapter, MetaFrame 1.8 networking is primarily broadcast-based. Client communications requirements related to interoperability mode are similar to server requirements, as clients also use UDP port 1604 to locate Citrix services. In addition, because MetaFrame 1.8 relies on the master browser to provide these services to clients, additional network overhead can quickly increase. As with server-to-server communication, care must be taken to provide services to clients without impacting the existing environment.

Now that you are familiar with issues related to interoperability, here are several scenario questions and their solutions.

SCENARIO & SOLUTION

What port do MetaFrame XP servers use to communicate with each other?	TCP port 2512
What is the first item that determines the master browser during an election?	ICA browser version
What port do MetaFrame 1.8 servers use to communicate with each other?	UDP port 1604
What Citrix utility is used to determine load-balancing values in a mixed mode farm?	Qserver

FROM THE CLASSROOM

Real-world Usage of Interoperability Mode

One of the most confusing issues when dealing with MetaFrame XP is interoperability mode and how it should be utilized. Due to its complex nature and interaction problems with MetaFrame 1.8, it is really only recommended as a temporary solution. In most cases, I do not suggest using it.

As you probably noticed throughout this section, there are a lot of caveats to using mixed mode, and this lists only the most common issues. Older versions of MetaFrame had concerns associated with many of the items that had been removed in XP, such as the ICA browser server and Program Neighborhood. By turning on interoperability mode, you enable these services on all XP servers to communicate with MetaFrame 1.8 servers. Many of the utilities don't work properly, or you have to use advanced command-line functions to find out valid information.

Due to the complexity involved in using this feature, try to avoid it if possible. Nevertheless, you should be familiar with the subject for the test.

—Ralph (JJ) Crump – CCNP\DP, CCEA, MCSE, MCNE

CERTIFICATION OBJECTIVE 3.05

Connecting Clients to MetaFrame XP

Once the Citrix MetaFrame XP server has been installed and configured, the next step involves deploying client software to each workstation. An integral part of using Citrix MetaFrame, these components are required to allow clients to connect to Citrix services.

Citrix provides support for many of the major operating systems, including Windows 32-bit operating systems, Linux, Unix, Macintosh, DOS, Windows CE, and Web browsers including Netscape and Internet Explorer. Citrix also provides the ability to simplify the installation of clients as well as automatically distribute updates. Understanding the options available as an administrator can ease the burden of rolling out clients throughout an organization. Installation of the Citrix ICA client is discussed in detail in Chapter 9.

Client Distribution

The first step to distributing clients is determining the method by which they will be installed. Several methods of installation are available, including: installing from diskettes, installing from a network share, and installing from a central Web site. Each step has its own advantages and pitfalls. However, all of the options together provide a great overall solution to distributing clients to each workstation.

Client Diskette Creation Utility

The first method of installing clients is by using 3.5" diskettes. The old style of software installation, this method works well in small environments or especially when used for remote access over modem lines. The diskettes can be given to users with instructions for installation with minimal involvement.

To help in using this methodology, Citrix provides a utility that will automatically create the appropriate diskettes based upon the client platform. As shown in Figure 3-30, the client diskette creation utility is accessible by selecting Start | Programs | Citrix | MetaFrame XP | ICA Client Creator.

FIGURE 3-30

ICA Client
Creator utility

The ICA Client Update Utility

During the installation of Citrix MetaFrame XP, client files are installed and configured within a database for distribution. This database can be configured with the appropriate client files and updated as new clients are released. As clients connect to the Citrix server, they can be configured to automatically update themselves to prevent the need to reinstall the new clients throughout the organization. Citrix provides a utility to manage this database known as the ICA client update utility.

This utility is available by selecting Start | Programs | Citrix | MetaFrame XP | ICA Client Update Configuration. As shown in Figure 3-31, this utility allows you to specify update options based upon the client platform as well as make global specifications for all clients.

Options available with this utility include:

- Addition or deletion of ICA clients from the update database
- Creating a new client update database
- Configuring options for client updates
- Configuring options for the client update database (as shown in Figure 3-32)

Shadowing

Another feature available for administrators and users within Citrix MetaFrame XP is the ability to control a user session by remote. Known as "shadowing," this capability allows administrators to manage and troubleshoot user sessions, thereby providing further functionality to this multiuser environment. This service allows administrators to interact directly with user sessions, including providing keyboard and mouse input into the MetaFrame XP session simultaneously with the user. Used

FIGURE 3-31

ICA Client
Update
Configuration

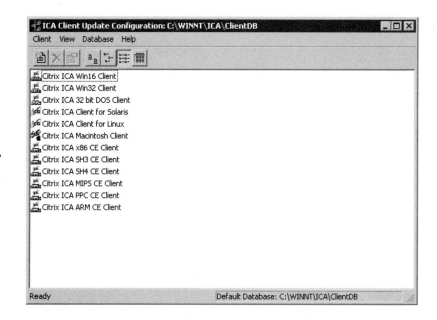

commonly for training exercises, user monitoring, and troubleshooting, this adds to the administrator's arsenal of tools when using Citrix MetaFrame XP.

FIGURE 3-32

ICA Client
update database
options

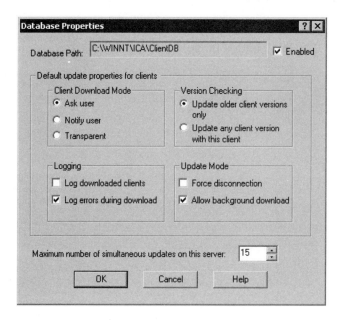

Enabling Shadowing

In order to utilize the shadowing capabilities of MetaFrame XP, it must first be activated. As shown earlier in this chapter, shadowing first must be allowed during the initial installation process. Once the installation is completed (as shown earlier in this chapter), the default options are set up.

EXERCISE 3-4

CertCam 3-4

Configuring Shadowing Options for MetaFrame XP

This exercise will allow an administrator to access and configure shadowing options on a single MetaFrame XP server. The options available within this exercise are directly related to the shadowing selections chosen during installation.

1. Select Start | Programs | Citrix | MetaFrame XP | Citrix Connection Configuration.

2. Right-click the ICA_TCP protocol, and select Edit.

3. In the Edit Connection dialog box, select the Advanced button to configure connection settings (as shown in Figure 3-33).

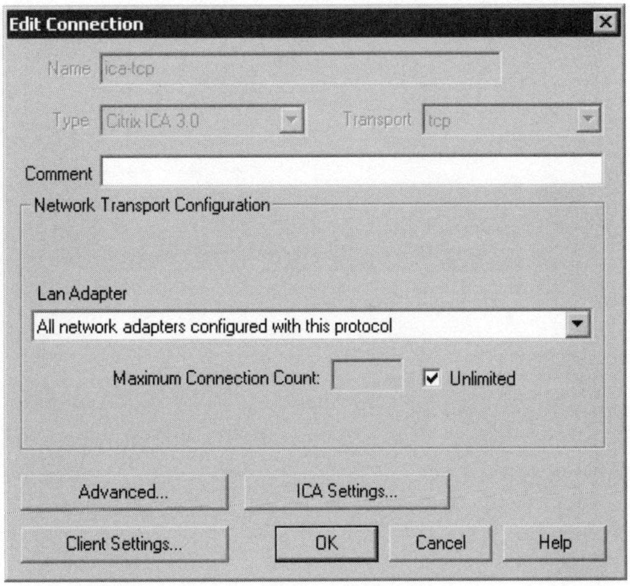

FIGURE 3-33

Configuring the ICA protocol connection settings

Edit Connection	✕
Name: ica-tcp	
Type: Citrix ICA 3.0 Transport: tcp	
Comment:	
Network Transport Configuration	
Lan Adapter	
All network adapters configured with this protocol	
Maximum Connection Count: ___ ☑ Unlimited	
Advanced... ICA Settings...	
Client Settings... OK Cancel Help	

4. Select the Shadowing drop-down box and choose the appropriate option for your environment. Once completed, press the OK button to continue (Figure 3-34).

5. Select OK to continue. Defined shadowing options will now take effect for all new client sessions.

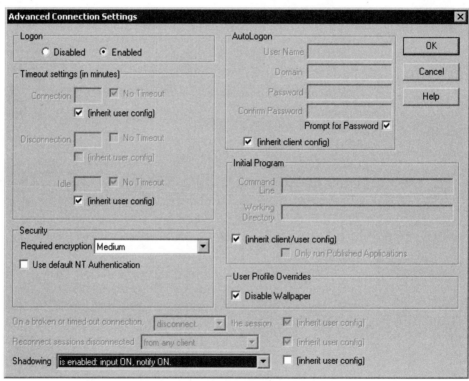

FIGURE 3-34

Configuring
shadowing
options

CERTIFICATION SUMMARY

An integral factor in the stability of MetaFrame XP has a great deal to do with the initial installation. Proper installation sets the pace for the performance and stability of every server, and must be performed correctly. During the course of installing a single server, a variety of options must be configured, including the data store, farm name, zone information, administrative options, interoperability with MetaFrame 1.8, NFuse, and licensing. Proper selection of how these items will be used must be performed during this step. For example, once shadowing options are selected during installation, they cannot be altered without reinstalling MetaFrame XP.

For larger environments where multiple servers require deployment, Citrix has provided support for automating the installation process. Support for unattended installation scripts and server cloning assist administrators in deploying multiple MetaFrame XP servers with minimal involvement, and with consistency. Both options require planning to test and implement each technology. This includes understanding the caveats involved.

A key component of implementing MetaFrame XP is designing the server farm. It is necessary that this be done prior to any installation work. The design should be based upon the existing computing environment, and take into consideration any business requirements that may affect it. Accounting for items such as single versus multiple farms, the data store database and how it is accessed, and zone layout is necessary to properly prepare for MetaFrame XP.

To allow environments a migration path from older versions of MetaFrame, Citrix has provided the capability for MetaFrame XP to coexist in the same farm as MetaFrame 1.8. Although a temporary solution, this allows a seamless migration path for users and administrators, if planned properly. Understanding this feature is critical to preventing any negative impact on the existing environment.

Once MetaFrame XP has been installed, client software must be made available for deployment. Similar to MetaFrame 1.8, MetaFrame XP provides the capability to maintain a database of client files and information for deployment. Utilities are available to assist in managing this environment, as well as automate the client installation and update process.

TWO-MINUTE DRILL

Installing a Single XP Server

❑ The default zone name installed is the network address for the server.

❑ Once shadowing options have been selected, only a reinstallation of MetaFrame XP can alter those chosen.

❑ The Citrix product code is a new feature used with licensing services.

Deploying Multiple, Identical XP Servers

❑ Unattend.txt, located with the setup executable, can be used to automate the installation of MetaFrame XP.

❑ No more than ten simultaneous installations are recommended.

❑ Server cloning is supported by MetaFrame XP, but requires manual changes after the server is installed.

Designing a Server Farm

❑ The database used for the data store is determined by factors such as user connections, number of applications, and scalability.

❑ No more than 100 servers should exist within a single zone.

❑ A dedicated data collector is recommended in larger MetaFrame XP environments.

Migrating MetaFrame 1.8 Server Farms to XP

❑ Interoperability mode, or mixed mode, can be activated either during installation or via the Citrix Management Console.

❑ Mixed mode operation causes the ICA Browser and Program Neighborhood services to run on all MetaFrame XP servers

❑ Various caveats exist that must be considered when using mixed mode operation, including farm naming, license pooling, application migration, ICA browser elections, and ICA gateway usage.

Connecting Clients to MetaFrame XP

❑ MetaFrame XP maintains a database of client files and information used in automating and updating the client installation.

❑ The ICA Client Update Configuration utility is used to manage the client database.

❑ Options such as shadowing are determined in the Citrix Connection Configuration utility.

SELF TEST

The following questions will help you measure your understanding of the material presented in this chapter. Read all the choices carefully as there may be more than one correct answer. Choose all correct answers for each question.

Installing a Single XP Server

1. What is the default zone name used by MetaFrame XP during the installation of a single server?

   A. Citrix server name

   B. Farm name

   C. IP subnet

   D. Administrator ID

2. Which of the following options are NOT configured during the installation of MetaFrame XP?

   A. Citrix farm name

   B. Interoperability mode

   C. Shadowing options

   D. Load balancing

3. Based upon company standards, the ability to shadow connections causes some concern in regards to sensitive data that could be seen on management's computers. In order to implement MetaFrame XP, users must be aware that they are being monitored, and all shadowing activity must be recorded. Which shadowing options during installation support these objectives? (Select all that apply.)

   A. Prohibit Remote Control of ICA Sessions

   B. Prohibit Shadow Connections Without Notification

   C. Do Not Allow Shadowing of ICA Sessions on this Server

   D. Prohibit Shadow Connections Without Logging

4. What service is configured during installation of MetaFrame XP to support the use of published applications via NFuse?

   A. Shadowing

   B. XML

   C. TAPI modem setup

   D. Drive remapping

Deploying Multiple, Identical XP Servers

5. What file is used as a template for a scripted installation of MetaFrame XP 1.0 for Windows 2000?

   A. \W2K\MF\unattend.txt

   B. \MF\Setup\install.exe

   C. \TSE\MF\unattend.txt

   D. \W2K\MF\install.exe

6. Your company maintains an existing server farm and decides to add 15 new servers to support continued growth. You want to minimize the time required for installation and the configuration that must occur, while maintaining consistency throughout the server farm. What option best suits these requirements?

   A. Use a third-party application to clone a MetaFrame XP server and image all new server installations.

   B. Create an unattended installation using unattend.txt as a template. Specify the unattend.txt during setup to automate the installation process.

   C. Automated installations are not recommended for this scenario. Use the manual installation process.

   D. None of the above.

7. What is the maximum number of simultaneous installations of MetaFrame XP that should occur within a single farm?

   A. 100

   B. 50

   C. 10

   D. 5

8. As part of a MetaFrame XP server deployment, server cloning will be used to automate the installation process. After installing a server to base the image from, several modifications must be made to ensure correct functionality once the servers are deployed. Which of the following items must be completed prior to imaging this server for deployment?

   A. Select the default zone name during installation.

   B. Delete the wfcname.ini file located on the root of the drive where Citrix MetaFrame XP was installed.

   C. Set the Independent Management Architecture service to Automatic in the services applet.

   D. All of the above.

Designing a Server Farm

9. When designing a MetaFrame XP server farm, the database used for the data store is dependent upon issues such as number of servers, number of users, and so on. Which database technologies are recommended for large enterprise environments with more than 100 servers? (Choose all that apply.)

    A. MS SQL

    B. Access

    C. Oracle

    D. Pervasive SQL

10. When designing a zone configuration for a MetaFrame XP server farm, several factors determine this configuration. What is the maximum number of servers allowed, per zone, within a farm?

    A. 10

    B. 25

    C. 50

    D. 100

11. Which data store database application does not support direct mode for MetaFrame XP server farms?

    A. MS SQL

    B. Oracle

    C. Pervasive SQL

    D. None of the above

12. When designing server farms, there are several considerations that must be taken into account. Each one can drastically affect the outcome if not properly planned. Which of the following does not represent a farm design consideration?

    A. Database replication is not supported with Access

    B. License pooling

    C. Access is best used in centralized farms

    D. None of the above

Migrating MetaFrame 1.8 Server Farms to XP

13. What port is enabled on all MetaFrame XP servers for server-to-server communication for MetaFrame 1.8 communication within the same farm?

    A. TCP 2512

    B. TCP 2513

    C. UDP 2512

    D. UDP 1604

14. While operating in interoperability mode, MetaFrame XP must support and participate in ICA master browser elections. Based upon the following items, what is the proper sequence by which browser elections are decided?

    1. Citrix server is the Windows 2000 domain controller

    2. ICA Browser version (higher takes precedence)

    3. Configured as master browser (w/server admin tool or registry)

    4. Computer name

    5. Length of time ICA Browser has been running

       A. 1, 4, 3, 5, 2

       B. 2, 3, 1, 5, 4

       C. 3, 2, 5, 1, 4

       D. 2, 1, 3, 4, 5

15. While operating in mixed mode environments, application publishing and migration must be performed carefully to prevent inaccurate results. What process must be completed to ensure applications are published correctly within a mixed mode server farm? (Choose all that apply.)

    A. New applications must be published to MetaFrame 1.8 servers using Published Application Manager on the MetaFrame 1.8 server.

    B. New applications must be published to MetaFrame 1.8 servers using Published Application Manager on the MetaFrame XP server.

    C. Applications modified with the MetaFrame XP Published Application Manager cannot later be administered from a MetaFrame 1.8 server.

    D. Applications modified with the MetaFrame XP Published Application Manager can later be administered from a MetaFrame 1.8 server.

6. Published application load evaluation occurs differently in a mixed mode farm than with a MetaFrame XP server farm operating in native mode. What is the order by which the load is evaluated for client requests?

1. MetaFrame XP servers are queried to determine lightest load based upon user connections.

2. MetaFrame 1.8 servers are queried to determine lightest load based upon user connections.

3. The ICA client connects to the master ICA browser to determine application availability.

4. The master browser then chooses between the MetaFrame XP server and the MetaFrame 1.8 server with the least number of connected uses. If both servers contain equal values, the MetaFrame XP server will then be chosen.

    A. 2, 3, 1, 4

    B. 1, 2, 3, 4

    C. 3, 1, 2, 4

    D. 4, 2, 1, 3

Connecting Clients to MetaFrame XP

17. What utility is used to manage the client database stored on the MetaFrame XP server?

    A. The ICA Client Update Configuration utility

    B. The Client Connection Configuration utility

    C. The ICA Client Creation utility

    D. The Citrix Management Console

18. As new client updates are released, the MetaFrame XP server allows administrators to automatically update clients as they initiate sessions. An administrator wants these upgrades to occur automatically without notifying the user while monitoring all downloads to determine who has been upgraded. Within the ICA Client Update Configuration utility, what options not set by default must be selected to support these requirements?

    A. Log downloaded clients

    B. Log errors during download

    C. Transparent client download mode

    D. Update older client versions only

19. Which of the following are valid uses of the shadowing capabilities for client sessions within MetaFrame XP?

    A. Troubleshooting

    B. Training

    C. Monitoring

    D. None of the above

20. What utility is used to configure shadowing options for MetaFrame XP?

    A. The ICA Client Update Configuration utility

    B. The Client Connection Configuration utility

    C. The ICA Client Creation utility

    D. The Citrix Management Console

LAB QUESTION

You are an administrator who must design and install MetaFrame XP within your environment. You plan to upgrade your existing MetaFrame 1.8 farm consisting of three servers to MetaFrame XP while adding two more servers to the farm. In addition, you must ensure that all applicable farm settings and applications are upgraded without any user impact on the existing client base. Lastly, each client must automatically be upgraded to the latest client to support this change without any notification. Lastly, you must be able to monitor client installation usage to determine what clients have not been upgraded yet. Determine the steps required to upgrade your existing MetaFrame 1.8 farm to MetaFrame XP while meeting all of the previous requirements.

SELF TEST ANSWERS

Installing a Single XP Server

1. ☑ C is correct. The default name used for a zone during installation is the IP subnet, or TCP\IP network number of the server. It is recommended to change this option from the default of multiple farms existing within the same subnet.
   ☒ A, B, and D are incorrect as they are not used for the zone name.

2. ☑ D is the correct answer. Load balancing is not configurable during installation. However, it can be administered once the MetaFrame XP farm is operational.
   ☒ A, B, and C are incorrect as they are all options available for configuration during installation.

3. ☑ Answers B and D are correct. The options to Prohibit Shadow Connections Without Notification and Prohibit Shadow Connection Without Logging meet the business requirements described.
   ☒ A is incorrect because remote control of sessions is required. C is incorrect because this option would disable shadowing altogether.

4. ☑ B is the correct answer. In order for NFuse to function properly with published applications, XML services are used to facilitate communication between these components.
   ☒ A is incorrect because shadowing is used for controlling user sessions by remote. C is incorrect as TAPI modem setup is used for asynchronous connections. D is incorrect because drive remapping is used to support environments where the default drive selections are not permissible.

Deploying Multiple, Identical XP Servers

5. ☑ A is the correct answer. Unattend.txt located in the \W2K\MF directory is the template used for scripted installations.
   ☒ B and D are incorrect as these are not valid utilities. C is incorrect as the unattend.txt file located within the \TSE\MF directory is used for Windows NT 4.0 Terminal Server Edition installations.

6. ☑ B is the correct answer. Using unattended installation scripts provides an automated method of installation while minimizing the configuration required after the installation is complete.

☒ **A** is incorrect as cloning requires several manual modifications, once completed, to properly configure MetaFrame XP. **C** is incorrect because automated methods will work correctly in this scenario. **D** is incorrect because an answer is provided.

7. ☑ **C** is the correct answer. The maximum number of recommended simultaneous installations within a server farm is 10. This prevents servers from timing out and causing installations to fail.

   ☒ **A**, **B**, and **D** are incorrect as they are not valid recommendations.

8. ☑ **A** and **B** are correct. To support server cloning, the default zone name must be used, and the wfcname.ini file must be deleted from the root of the drive where MetaFrame XP is installed.

   ☒ **C** is incorrect because the Independent Management Architecture service must be set to manual in the services applet to prevent it from starting. **D** is incorrect because answer **C** does not provide a correct response.

Designing a Server Farm

9. ☑ **A** and **C** are the correct answers. In large environments with a large number of servers, MS SQL and Oracle are designed to provide the scalability necessary to support this configuration.

   ☒ **B** is incorrect as Access should only be used in small environments. Answer **D** is incorrect because Pervasive SQL is not supported by MetaFrame XP.

10. ☑ **D** is the correct answer. Up to 70 resolutions can occur per second, resulting in a maximum number of 100 servers, per zone, within a farm.

    ☒ **A**, **B**, and **C** do not apply to designing zone configurations.

11. ☑ **D** is the correct answer. Based upon the architecture of Access, indirect mode allows MetaFrame to maintain the database while storing data from multiple sources.

    ☒ **A** and **B** are incorrect as both are recommended for use with direct mode as a data store within MetaFrame XP. **C** is incorrect as Pervasive SQL is not supported by MetaFrame XP.

12. ☑ **D** is the correct answer. When designing server farms, all of the items listed directly impact the outcome. Database replication with Access directly impacts scalability in larger environments while license pooling affects farm layout. Access usage in centralized farms also deals directly with scalability issues with MetaFrame XP.

    ☒ **A**, **B**, and **C** are incorrect answers as they are all farm design considerations.

Migrating MetaFrame 1.8 Server Farms to XP

13. ☑ D is the correct answer. UDP port 1604 is used by the legacy version of MetaFrame to communicate via server-to-server communications. This port is activated to support communication between MetaFrame XP servers and MetaFrame 1.8 servers.

    ☒ A is incorrect because it is only used in server-to-server communications between MetaFrame XP servers. B is incorrect because it is used to support communication from the Citrix Management Console to the server. C is incorrect because it is not used by MetaFrame for any function.

14. ☑ The correct answer is B. When an election occurs to determine the ICA master browser, the ICA Browser version always takes precedence. Next, any server configured as master browser followed by Windows 2000 domain controllers win out. If not elected yet, the next criterion is the length of time the ICA Browser has been operational, and lastly, the computer decides if no other criteria was matched.

15. ☑ B and C are correct answers. New applications must be published to MetaFrame 1.8 servers using Published Application Manager on the MetaFrame XP server. Once administered in this manner, they cannot later be modified from the older version of the utilities.

    ☒ A and D are incorrect because they directly contradict the answers provided in B and C.

16. ☑ C is the correct answer. Load-balancing services and how they are evaluated maintain different standards in mixed mode to support backwards compatibility. Once the farm is migrated into native mode, advanced evaluators can be used to further define application load balancing.

    ☒ A, B, and D are incorrect as they are not placed in the proper sequence to determine server load values.

Connecting Clients to MetaFrame XP

17. ☑ A is the correct answer. The ICA Client Update Configuration utility is used to manage the database storing client files and update parameters.

    ☒ B is incorrect because it is used to manage ICA sessions from the client to the server. C is incorrect because it is utilized to create installation media for client implementation. D is incorrect because the Citrix Management Console is used to manage server and farm properties.

18. ☑ **A** and **C** are correct. To support these requirements, the options to log downloaded clients and transparent client download mode must be selected.

    ☒ **B** and **D** are incorrect as they are already selected by default.

19. ☑ **A, B,** and **C** are correct answers. Common uses of shadowing include troubleshooting user sessions, training users, and monitoring usage.

    ☒ **D** is incorrect because correct answers are provided.

20. ☑ **B** is the correct answer. The Client Connection Configuration utility is used to manage shadowing options. Settings specified during installation of MetaFrame always override any options located within this utility.

    ☒ **A** is incorrect as it is used to manage the ICA database located on the MetaFrame XP server. **C** is incorrect because it is utilized to create installation media for client implementation. **D** is incorrect as the Citrix Management Console is used to manage server and farm properties.

LAB ANSWER

The following steps are required to install MetaFrame XP into the existing MetaFrame 1.8 environment. The additional steps needed to meet each of the requirements are placed throughout this list where required.

1. Select a data store design to meet the farm requirements. Based upon the criteria, any of the database options could fit into this environment.

2. Create a zone design that fits this environment. Because this is a single small farm without mention of remote sites, the single default zone should be sufficient.

3. Back up all servers and application settings in case problems arise.

4. Install MetaFrame XP on the server acting as the ICA master browser. Configure required components during installation, including name of existing MetaFrame 1.8 farm, data store design, and activation of interoperability mode.

5. Configure published applications to work with MetaFrame XP server and ensure all functionality exists.

6. Upgrade the two remaining MetaFrame 1.8 servers to MetaFrame XP and ensure complete functionality exists.

7. Once completed, remove interoperability mode from the server farm.

8. Add and configure two new MetaFrame XP servers into the existing server farm.

9. Upgrade client update database if not completed during installation of each server. Configure database options to upgrade without intervention and to log all software client downloads.

4

Using Citrix Technologies

M etaFrame XP improves upon several existing features and introduces a few new
ones. Citrix has improved the ICA protocol to allow for a more robust user
experience and support of new features. One of the improvements is the
Independent Management Architecture (IMA), which is the new management structure and
server-to-server protocol used to administer the majority of XP server components by
consolidating several MetaFrame 1.8 management applets into one Citrix Management Console
(CMC). Citrix has also updated the SpeedScreen 3 technology to include predictive text entry
and instant mouse click feedback.

CERTIFICATION OBJECTIVE 4.01

Identifying the Components of the ICA Packet

ICA is a general purpose presentation protocol developed by Citrix to provide the
Windows community with functionality similar to that of X Windows on Unix.
The ICA protocol, however, is much more efficient and robust, allowing more
features and better performance over lower bandwidth connections. ICA is the
physical line protocol used for communication between the client and the Citrix
MetaFrame application server. The name of the data protocol that exports the
application's graphical screen image is called thinwire. Thinwire is a logical data
stream that flows encapsulated in an ICA packet. ICA must guarantee the delivery of
the thinwire data stream with no errors and no missing or out-of-sequence data. The
output of the thinwire protocol driver is a logical data stream that is sent through a
virtual channel API, which takes the data stream and encapsulates it into an ICA
packet. Once the ICA packet is formed, it optionally passes through a series of
protocol drivers to add functionality like encryption, compression, and framing. It is
then put on the transport layer and sent to the client. Once at the ICA client, the
data packet passes through the same layers in opposite order, resulting in the
graphical display of the remote application user interface on the client.

ICA packets consist of a required one-byte command, followed by optional data.
This packet can be prefixed by optional components, negotiated at connection time,
to manage the transmission of the packet. The nature of the transmission medium
and user-defined options (e.g., encryption) influence the total packet definition.
ICA packets consist of the format depicted in Figure 4-1.

FIGURE 4-I	ICA packet format

Frame head	Reliable	Encryption	Compression	Command	Command Data	Frame Trail

Only the command component will always be present in an ICA packet. All other components are optional.

- **Frame Head**   Optional framing protocol header. Prefix for framing stream-oriented transport data.

- **Reliable**   Optional reliable transmission protocol header. Prefix for error detection and recovery.

- **Encryption**   Optional encryption protocol header. Prefix for managing encrypted data.

- **Compression**   Optional compression protocol header.

- **Command**   Beginning of base ICA protocol packet.

- **Command Data**   Optional data bytes associated with the specified command.

- **Frame Trail**   Optional framing protocol trailer. Suffix for framing asynchronous transport data.

The ICA protocol stack is dynamically configured to meet the needs of each transport protocol. For example, IPX is not reliable, so a reliable protocol driver is added above the IPX transport driver. However, since IPX is a frame-based protocol, a frame driver is not included. TCP is a stream protocol so a frame driver is included, and TCP is reliable, so a reliable driver is not added to the stack.

There are several different categories of ICA commands. These categories are discussed in the listing that follows:

1. **Control Commands**   Control commands are a category of ICA command packets that manage the connection to the application server and the relationship to the local client user interface. Control commands include the following:

   - Server browsing
   - Connection initialization and negotiation

- Screen control between the application server and the local client user interface
- Keyboard and mouse input to the application server
- Control of the keyboard indicator lights

2. **Full-Screen Text**   A set of ICA command packets that permit the Citrix server to control the local client display in a full-screen text mode. These commands are normally not needed for Windows applications, however, they are important for supporting older, DOS-based clients. These commands involve less data transfer; therefore they typically have high display performance. Command packets are used to perform the following functions:

- Set the text modes
- Write characters
- Adjust character attributes
- Scroll
- Control the cursor

3. **Keyboard**   An ICA command packet containing one or more PC scan codes transmits keyboard data from the client to the server.

4. **Mouse**   ICA command set used to track mouse coordinates and button states.

5. **Virtual Channel Commands**   The ICA protocol supplies simultaneous control of multiple *virtual channels*. A virtual channel is used by application layer objects on a session-based connection to provide additional functions to the client in parallel to the ICA protocol. Some of the virtual channels are shown in Table 4-1.

exam
ⓦatch

The only component of the ICA packet that will always be present is the command section.

ICA data packets use optional protocol drivers to provide functionality across various network architectures. These drivers are not necessary for the operation of ICA itself and their use is negotiated during the ICA handshake that occurs at the

TABLE 4-1 Virtual Channels

Thinwire Virtual Channel	An ICA virtual channel protocol used to transmit presentation commands from applications running on the server to the ICA client. The thinwire protocol has been optimized for transmission of Windows display objects across low-bandwidth links.
	Command and object-specific intelligent compression with state persistence (e.g. run-length encoding for bitmaps)
	Outboard complex clipping and complex curve drawing
	Intelligent caching of Windows objects, such as bitmaps, brushes, glyphs, and pointers
	Remote SaveScreenBitmaps
	Cross-session persistent caching
Printer Spooling Virtual Channel	A dedicated virtual channel used to transmit printer spooler data from the server to the client
Drive Mapping Virtual Channel	A virtual channel used to provide client drive mapping and file system functions
Parallel Port Mapping Virtual Channel	Provides access to the client's parallel port
Serial Port Mapping Virtual Channel	Provides two-way full-duplex access to client serial ports
Clipboard Virtual Channel	Provides a virtual mapping that allows users to copy and paste from the local clipboard to the server clipboard, and vice versa

beginning of a session. Protocol drivers for the most ubiquitous transport protocols such as TCP/IP (Transmission Control Protocol/Internet Protocol), NetBIOS (Network Basic Input/Output System), IPX/SPX (Internet Packet Exchange/Sequenced Packet Exchange), and PPP/SLIP (Point-to-Point Protocol/Serial Line Internet Protocol) are available but can be removed and/or replaced due to their position under the ICA protocol. This architecture provides ICA with a protocol independence that allows it to continue regardless of new networking technologies that may be developed.

Using ICA Over the Internet

A great way to provide access to applications to remote and home users is to allow connections to your MetaFrame servers over the Internet. This can come in many forms such as directly connecting to a server or published application, using NFuse to deliver a Web-based solution, or a VPN to provide access to Citrix servers residing on a private network.

on the *Job* *Using ICA over the Internet is a great way to provide connectivity to users, but it is susceptible to latency and other network conditions. For mission–critical access, provide a backup access method such as a modem bank for dial-in.*

ICA uses TCP port 1494 to establish sessions over TCP/IP and requires that this port be open on any firewalls between the client and server. Previous versions of WinFrame and MetaFrame used UDP port 1604 for ICA browsing traffic. Many companies had security concerns about allowing UDP traffic across their firewalls due to its connectionless nature. Citrix has addressed this concern in XP by using an XML (Extensible Markup Language) service on HTTP (Hypertext Transport Protocol) port 80 (or any other unused port you designate) for obtaining server and farm information.

on the *Job* *Migrating your clients to use HTTP instead of UDP traffic is much easier to get approved by security. It is also more reliable since it is no longer connectionless.*

EXERCISE 4-1

CertCam 4-1

Configuring the ICA Client to Use TCP/IP+HTTP

To start migrating your clients to an XP environment, begin by changing your client settings to use TCP/IP+HTTP if you have FR-1 running on your existing MetaFrame 1.8 servers. To do this:

1. Make sure that FR-1 and the XML service is installed on your ICA master browser.

2. Start Program Neighborhood and select the properties of your farm or connection, as shown in Figure 4-2.

FIGURE 4-2   Farm properties

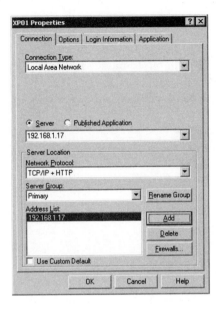

3. Change the network protocol to TCP/IP+HTTP.

4. Click the Add button to add an entry for your MetaFrame server and XML port.

5. Enter the new server location address and port as shown in Figure 4-3.

6. Click OK on the property page.

7. Your connection will now use XML over port 80 (or whichever port you entered as your XML port) to obtain server and application lists.

FIGURE 4-3

Server and XML
port definition

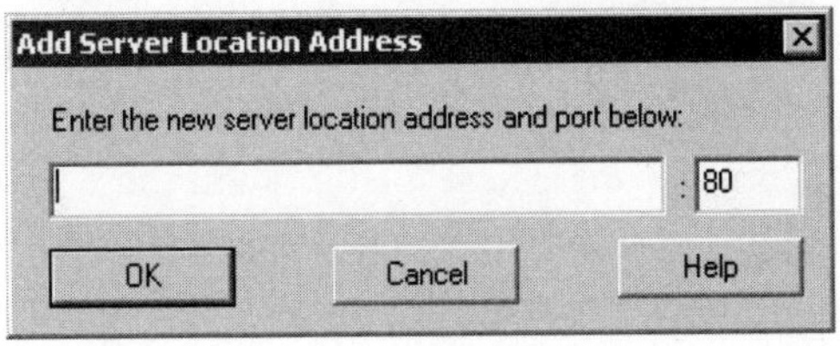

MetaFrame XP farms running in native mode will not respond to UDP broadcasts by default. There are two methods that allow an XP server to respond to UDP broadcasts.

1. Run the farm in mixed mode to provide compatibility to older clients while you complete your migration.

2. Set the individual server or farm to respond to client broadcasts.

Since UDP broadcasts do not cross subnets, you will need to enter one or more IP addresses or DNS (Domain Name System) names of the master ICA browser (data collector in XP) to allow the client to find the server and published applications. This also is true after you migrate to TCP/IP+HTTP as the client will still need to find the data collector server to obtain information on servers and published applications.

Using ICA Over Wireless LANs

Wireless LANs are becoming more prevalent now with the 802.11b standard equipment being available to home users as well as corporations. Many companies are installing wireless access points throughout their offices to provide easy access to corporate data as employees move about the building conferring with other staff on various projects. Conference rooms are a common place to find wireless connectivity because it provides LAN access to everyone in the room without the hassle of wires.

ICA is ideal for access to applications across wireless links as the bandwidth degrades with distance. 802.11b provides 1MB connectivity at the outer range, but this isn't always enough to run corporate applications. By using ICA to establish a session with a MetaFrame server, the lower bandwidth is more than enough to provide wireless users with LAN–like speeds.

As wireless technology proliferates further into the mainstream, places like airports and coffee shops are providing wireless access to the Internet while you wait for a connection or have a latte. Soon there will be 802.11b access points hanging from light posts where you can check your stocks, make restaurant reservations, or log in to the corporate VPN and MetaFrame to check your e-mail while waiting for the bus.

Now that you have a better idea of the structure of the ICA packet, here are some possible scenario questions and their answers.

SCENARIO & SOLUTION

What section of the packet is always present?	The command section
What are two common protocol headers?	Compression and encryption
What is used to provide additional functionality to the ICA protocol?	Virtual channels

CERTIFICATION OBJECTIVE 4.02

Listing the Benefits of SpeedScreen Technology

Starting with Feature Release 1 for MetaFrame 1.8, Citrix introduced SpeedScreen 3 technology. SpeedScreen 3 enhances the feel of responsiveness of an application and further reduces bandwidth usage. SpeedScreen 3 shows significant measurable improvement over previous versions.

Low bandwidth connections, such as modems, or high latency connections, like satellite WAN connections, can cause frustrations for users when entering data into an application. Previously, when a user typed a character into a MetaFrame-delivered application, the key press had to travel to the server and a signal from the server had to then return to the client before the character was displayed on the screen. For fast typists, this delay was very disconcerting as whole sentences were typed in but did not appear on the screen for several seconds. To solve this problem, SpeedScreen 3 provides predictive text entry allowing users to immediately see the text as it is typed, without waiting for the data to return from the server.

exam
ⓦatch

This technology only works with applications that use the standard Windows API for handling text entry.

The second major feature of SpeedScreen 3 is allowing the mouse to provide immediate feedback as well. In previous versions, a user could click on an icon in a published desktop and the mouse would appear as if nothing had happened, prompting the user to click on the icon several more times thus launching multiple instances of applications. SpeedScreen 3 provides the user with an immediate change in the cursor to inform the user the action is pending.

High-latency networks can create an elevated sense of frustration for users due to the delays of sending data to and from the servers. SpeedScreen 3 enables users to receive almost instantaneous responses to mouse movements and keystrokes. SpeedScreen can also be customized by using the Latency Reduction Manager from the Citrix | MetaFrame XP program group depicted in Figures 4-4 and 4-5. Figure 4-6, meanwhile, shows the latency reduction settings on the ICA client.

Delays between entry and echo of mouse movements and keyboard input are one of the primary frustrations client users experience with a high-latency network connection. SpeedScreen features in MetaFrame XP and the ICA client software enable almost instantaneous echoing of mouse movements and keystrokes at the ICA client. Use the SpeedScreen Latency Reduction Manager to customize SpeedScreen settings for a MetaFrame XP server, individual published applications, and input controls within applications. You can save a SpeedScreen configuration file and then deploy the file across your server farm.

To launch SpeedScreen Latency Reduction Manager, from the Start menu, choose Programs | Citrix | MetaFrame XP | SpeedScreen Latency Reduction Manager.

FIGURE 4-4

The SpeedScreen Latency Reduction Manager

FIGURE 4-5

Server Properties
in the Latency
Reduction
Manager

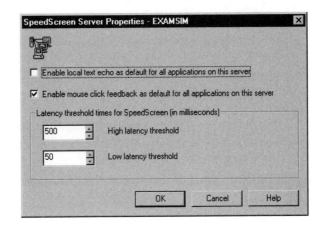

By default, instant mouse click feedback is enabled and local text echo is disabled for all applications. You can enable local text echo on an application-by-application basis only. If you use this feature, the programs to which you apply it must use only standard Windows APIs for displaying text, or the settings will not work correctly. Test all aspects of an application with local text echo in a non-production environment before enabling text echo for your users.

FIGURE 4-6

Client
SpeedScreen
settings

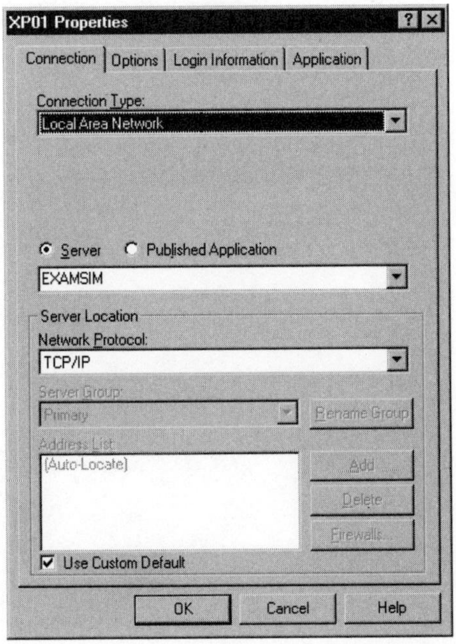

With SpeedScreen Latency Reduction Manager, you can also configure local text echo settings for individual input fields within an application. See the application help for the SpeedScreen Latency Reduction Manager utility for more configuration information.

on the !
job *Make sure to test all your applications on a non-productive server and have real users test them when making changes to SpeedScreen settings. Some applications may not perform perfectly with local text echo.*

EXERCISE 4-2

CertCam 4-2

Setting SpeedScreen Settings on the ICA Client

The client also has some SpeedScreen settings to manipulate. In this exercise, we will enable the predictive text entry setting on our client.

1. Open Program Neighborhood, then open the properties page to your farm.

2. Select the Default Options tab and choose the drop-down list in the SpeedScreen Latency Reduction section. Set it to "On" as shown in Figure 4-7.

FIGURE 4-7

Client-side SpeedScreen settings

XP01 Properties	? X

Connection | **Options** | Login Information | Application |

☑ Use data compression
☐ Use disk cache for bitmaps
☐ Queue mouse movements and keystrokes

☐ Enable Sound   ☑ Use Custom Default
Medium sound quality

Encryption Level: ☑ Use Custom Default
Basic

┌ SpeedScreen Latency Reduction ──────────
│ On ▼   ☑ Mouse Click Feedback
│   ☑ Local Text Echo

┌ Windows Properties ──────────
Window Colors: ☐ Use Custom Default
High Color (16 bit) ▼

Window Size: ☐ Use Custom Default
800 X 600 ▼

OK | Cancel | Help

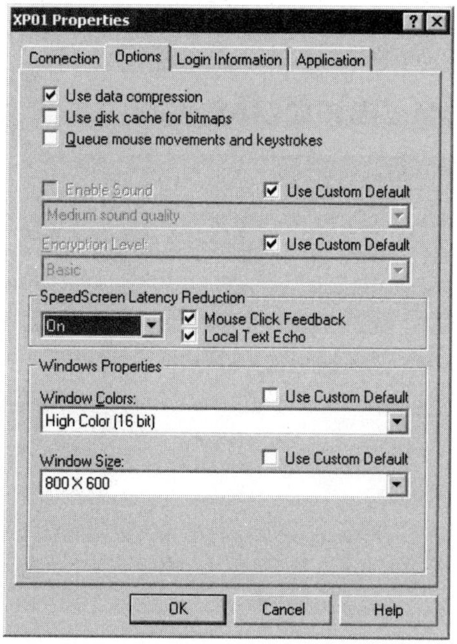

3. Check the box for local text echo and close the properties page.

For general information about SpeedScreen options, see the online help in the SpeedScreen Latency Reduction Manager. You can deploy SpeedScreen settings for each application or server you configure by copying the entire contents of the %systemroot%\system32\ss3config directory to each server in the farm.

on the **job**

Be aware that applications developed using MFC (Microsoft Foundation Classes) generate application window names dynamically and may receive settings even when the application name is in the exception list. This is because the Latency Reduction Manager uses window names to identify items listed in the exception record.

CERTIFICATION OBJECTIVE 4.03

Discussing the Features of Independent Management Architecture

The Independent Management Architecture is an advanced server-to-server communications protocol as well as a management design that is the foundation of Citrix's ability to scale MetaFrame XP beyond previous versions and enhance its management capabilities. IMA provides a single integrated platform to manage, maintain, and support your entire company's installation and security efforts on all your application servers. IMA also allows administrators to group servers into farms logically, rather than geographically, to provide the best in performance, fault tolerance, and manageability.

exam **Watch**

All IMA traffic is on TCP port 2512 and can be changed if necessary.

IMA and MetaFrame XP provide a lot of new features and capabilities. Some of the benefits of IMA are listed in the following.

- Administrative actions are now auditable.

- Session shadowing can now be logged and audited.

- MetaFrame XP now supports SNMP (Simple Network Management Protocol) to provide alerts and administrative action.

- All Citrix configuration information is now stored in a central location.

- The CMC provides a centralized management tool to administer Citrix servers and license data.

- ICA clients no longer need UDP broadcasts to locate servers and published applications.

While IMA and CMC have replaced the older architecture that Citrix was built on, it is still fully backwards-compatible with all previous ICA client software. Citrix has also provided all the older management utilities to assist in making your transition as smooth as possible. This design extends Citrix's Digital Independence slogan to include the ability to manage from anywhere, anytime as well.

Zones

Zones are a new concept with MetaFrame XP. They can be used to group MetaFrame servers together in logical collections. By using zones, server farms can span multiple geographic locations. Each zone has its own data collector, which acts much like a master browser in MetaFrame 1.8. By default, a zone consists of all the XP servers on a single subnet. You can create and configure additional zones from the Zones tab on the Farm Properties dialog box. See Figure 4-8 for an illustration of the zone properties page.

exam
ⓦatch
There is only one data collector per zone and no backups. All MetaFrame servers contain the information necessary to become the data collector.

Single farms with member servers in different geographic locations benefit from using multiple zones to localize the data collection services and reduce WAN traffic. Making servers members of different zones is very easy. Simply select the server from the list of zones in the Zones tab and move it to another zone.

FIGURE 4-8

Zones
configuration
page

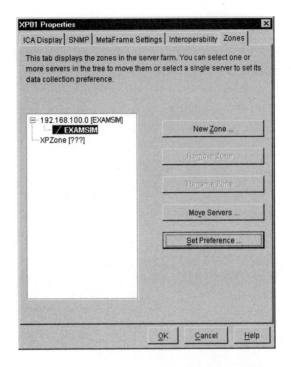

There is a preset limit of 256 open connections to the data collector. Refer to the documentation to increase this number if you have more than 256 servers in a zone.

Data Store

MetaFrame XP introduces a new method of storing server configuration data, as well as licensing data and farm administrators. The data store is created when you install the first MetaFrame XP server, and can use Microsoft Access, Microsoft SQL Server, or Oracle as the database engine. Microsoft Access is suitable for farms of up to 50 servers, while SQL Server and Oracle are suitable for farms of any size. See Table 4-2 for the supported versions of each product. This centralized database of information is the core to XP's scalability and stability.

Connections to the data store can be of two types: direct and indirect. Direct connections require that the XP server have the correct ODBC driver installed

TABLE 4-2   Database Versions Compatible with MetaFrame XP

Database	Supported Versions
Microsoft Access	Terminal Server and Windows 2000 include compatible drivers
Microsoft SQL	Microsoft SQL Server 7 Service Pack 2 and SQL 2000 Version 3.70.08.20 SQL ODBC driver 2000 includes this driver, Terminal Server requires MDAC 2.6
Oracle	Oracle8i, Version 8.1.6 Oracle 7, Version 7.3.4 Oracle 8, Version 8.0.6

and configured so the server can communicate directly with the database server. Indirect connections use a central XP server to connect via direct mode to the database server, while other XP servers connect indirectly through that server. Indirect connections eliminate the need to install ODBC (Open Database Connectivity) drivers on every server, but the intermediary server becomes a single point of failure.

exam
ⓦatch   *Be sure to know the databases that the data store supports.*

Data Collectors

Data collectors in MetaFrame XP are analogous to an ICA master browser. Each zone contains one MetaFrame XP server that is configured as the data collector. The data collector receives information from each of the other XP servers in the zone. Like the master browser in previous versions, the data collector maintains a list of all servers and the applications they serve, along with the TCP/IP addresses of each server. XP servers use TCP connections for server-to-server communications unlike previous versions that used UDP.

Data collectors are chosen via elections much like NT domain controllers and MetaFrame 1.*x* ICA master browsers. If a new server joins the farm or the data collector becomes unavailable, the farm holds an election for a new data collector. There are four levels of preference in selecting a new data collector. The levels are shown in Figure 4-9.

By default, all servers are set to the default preference except for the first server in the farm, which is set to most preferred and is the farm's first data collector. You can change these levels via the Zones tab on the farm properties page in the CMC. When an election occurs, the farm attempts to select a server from the highest

FIGURE 4-9

Data collector
preference levels

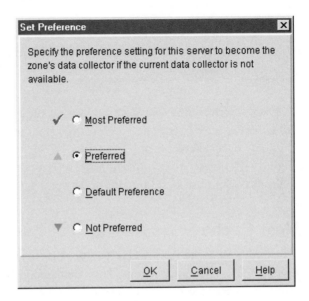

preference level: most preferred. If no servers from the level are available, it continues down the list until, as a last resort, it attempts to select one from the not preferred list.

EXERCISE 4-3

CertCam 4-3

Setting the Data Collector Preference Level

In this exercise, we will set the preference level to lowest on a server that is to be used for data collection only as a last resort.

1. Open the CMC and log in to your farm.

2. Select the farm name in the left pane and choose Properties from the Actions menu.

3. Choose the Zone tab from the properties page, as shown in Figure 4-8.

4. Expand the zone by clicking the plus sign (+) next to the zone name.

5. Select the server to change, then click the Set Preference button.

6. Set the preference to Not Preferred in the dialog box shown in Figure 4-9.

7. Click OK and then OK again to close out the dialog boxes.

Data collectors also act as communication gateways between the zones of a farm. All servers in a zone send their unique information only to the local data collector, thus only data collectors send data across WAN links to other data collectors. Figure 4-10 depicts an example of how zones are used in conjunction with data collectors to minimize the amount of data sent across the WAN.

The Local Host Cache

The local host cache is an Access database that is stored locally on each server in the farm to cache farm information. This database increases performance because it is not necessary to contact the data store every time a client queries the server. The database contains the following types of information:

■ Basic information on all servers in the farm

FIGURE 4-10   Data collector and zone architecture

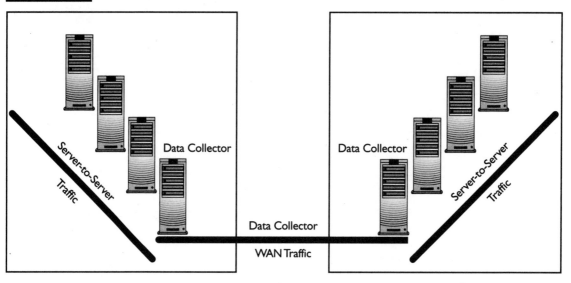

- All Windows domain trust relationships in the farm
- Names and properties of all applications published within the farm
- Information specific to itself

The local host cache also maintains enough information to allow the server to operate for up to 48 hours in the absence of the data store. During this period, the server will continue to attempt to contact the data store on a regular basis. If the data store is not contacted within 48 hours, the server will invalidate its licensing information and discontinue taking new connections.

If the local host cache gets out of sync with the data store, it can manually be refreshed by issuing the command: **dsmaint refreshlhc**. The cache will only get out of sync if the IMA service (which is responsible for maintaining the cache) misses a sync or change event. If the cache database becomes corrupt, it can be re-created from the ODBC object in the Control Panel. Refer to your documentation for the specific procedure.

Now that you have a better idea of IMA, here are some possible scenario questions and their answers:

SCENARIO & SOLUTION

What port does IMA use for communication?	TCP 2512
What enhancements does IMA bring to shadowing?	Logging / auditing
How many farms can be in one zone?	No farm can be in a zone. Zones are a part of farms.

Bandwidth Requirements for a Server Farm

MetaFrame XP uses a central data store and data collectors to manage all the configuration and event data for a farm. This task generates network traffic each time a farm event occurs. Bandwidth considerations must be made when designing a server farm to control the amount of bandwidth used for IMA traffic. A single server retrieves approximately 275KB of data from the data store each time it starts up. In larger farms, the data read is a function of the amount of servers in the farm, the number of published applications, and the number of printers in the farm. The total data read can be estimated by using the formula 275 + (0.5 × #Applications) + (5 × #Servers in Farm) + (92 × #Print Drivers in the Farm) = Total KB read. This is an approximate formula from a test lab, so your mileage may vary.

In a farm with multiple sites, it is recommended that the data store be replicated to reduce the amount of WAN traffic. If a replicated data store is not an option, the use of third-party bandwidth management devices may help control IMA traffic across the WAN. As the farm grows and the amount of data to transmit increases, the data the server tries to read may take longer to transfer across the connection than the service normally allows. In some cases, the servers may display error messages indicating the IMA service did not start. This error is normal and can be disregarded, as the service will start normally after all data is received.

Data Collector Traffic

Each zone will contain one data collector to maintain farm information for that zone. Each data collector updates all other data collectors each time an event occurs in its zone. These events cause WAN traffic and must be taken into consideration when calculating WAN usage. Table 4-3 lists some of the events and the associated WAN traffic.

TABLE 4-3	Event	Approximate Data Transmitted
Data Collector Event Traffic	Session connection established	3KB
	Session disconnect	2.3KB
	Session reconnect	3KB
	User logoff	1.5KB
	CMC server inquiry	2.2KB
	Publishing a new application	9.0KB + 1KB × #Servers in Farm
	Starting a new data collector	20KB

FROM THE CLASSROOM

How Can I Reduce My IMA Bandwidth Consumption?

If not properly designed and managed, data collector traffic can consume a large amount of bandwidth very quickly. Consider all the options when designing your zone and farm strategy. A zone is typically only one subnet, but that is not a limitation. A zone can span multiple subnets and even sites. If you have a farm that spans four sites, you could configure it as one zone. A central data collector would reside at the main location and all data would be sent to it. As each event occurs, the data only traverses the WAN one time from the client to the central data collector. Otherwise, the data would travel over the WAN three times, once from the data collector for the zone to each of the data collectors for the other zones.

—*Travis Guinn, MCSE, CCA, A+, CCSE, MCP+I*

The use of zones must be carefully considered when designing farms. For each zone, there is one data collector. Each time an event occurs in one zone, the data collector must update every other data collector. For a farm with six zones, the event data must be transmitted from the originating zone five times to be replicated to the other zones.

CERTIFICATION OBJECTIVE 4.04

Recognizing Listener Ports, Idle Sessions, ICA Sessions, and Client Device Licensing

ICA sessions begin when the client initiates a connection to the server. The server has listener ports available for each type of connection to accept these requests and begin the connection process. There is typically one listener for each protocol or connection listed in the Connection Configuration utility. When a listener port receives a connection, it dynamically uses one of the available idle sessions (or Winstations) for the client to connect to. By default, there are two idle sessions. If many users are logging in at once, the default two sessions may not recycle quickly enough and users will see their connections time out. To prevent this, the number of idle sessions may be increased by editing the registry value of `HKEY_LOCAL_MACHINE\SYSTEM\CurrentControlSet\Control\` `Terminal Server\IdleWinstationPoolCount` to a higher value in increments of two. Beware that each idle session consumes resources. Figures 4-11 and 4-12 show the CMC as well as the idle sessions and listener ports.

Another item you will see in the CMC's Sessions tab is the list of ICA sessions, which are the actual user connections after they are connected and logged on. The Sessions tab will provide you with the state of the connection, for instance: Active, Listen, Idle, Disconnected, or Down. You will also see what protocol the client is using, such as RDP or ICA, and by double-clicking on the connection session, specific data will be displayed.

FIGURE 4-11

Listener ports

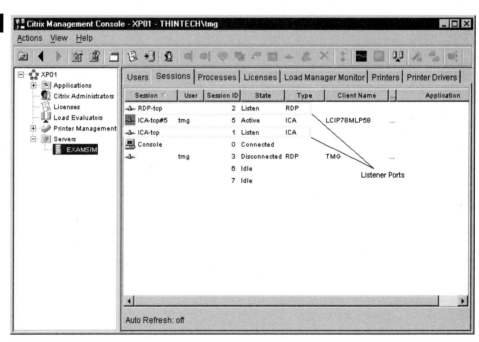

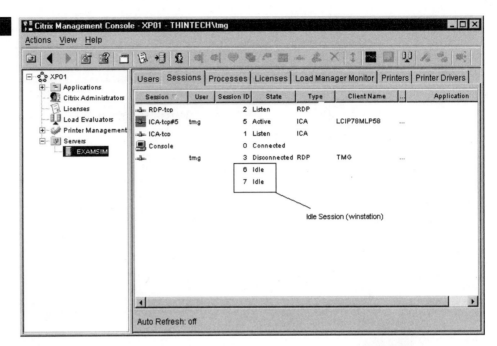

FIGURE 4-12

Idle sessions

CertCam 4-4

EXERCISE 4-4

Creating Additional Idle Sessions

In this exercise, we create two additional idle sessions to accommodate the large number of users we are seeing log on first thing in the morning.

1. Open the Registry Editor by going to Start | Run and typing: **regedit**.

2. Navigate down to the key
   HKEY_LOCAL_MACHINE\SYSTEM\CurrentControlSet\Control\
   Terminal Server.

3. In the right-hand pane, locate the IdleWinstationPoolCount value, as shown in Figure 4-13.

4. Double-click the value and change the number to 4.

5. Close Registry Editor and reboot the server.

FIGURE 4-13

Idle session
(Winstation)
configuration

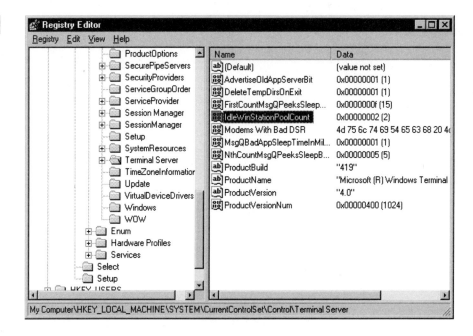

Client Device Licensing

When using MetaFrame in a farm environment, users may not always receive every application from the same server. To prevent multiple client licenses from being consumed, Citrix has provided client device licensing. This allows the user to start sessions on multiple servers from the same client and only consume one license. The servers are required, however, to pool licenses to enable the license sharing.

Now that you have a better idea of port listeners and idle sessions, here are some possible scenario questions and their answers.

SCENARIO & SOLUTION

What is the default number of idle sessions?	There are two idle sessions by default.
How many licenses does a client device use when running two apps from one server and one app from another?	One, if the licenses are pooled.
Can you increase the number of idle sessions?	Yes, via a registry modification.

CERTIFICATION SUMMARY

The ICA protocol is a general-purpose presentation protocol that Citrix developed to provide extensible functionality over a wide range of connections. With its protocol independence, extensibility, and bandwidth management capabilities, ICA provides an excellent foundation for thin client solutions. Now building on the new Independent Management Architecture, Citrix has introduced a new server-to-server protocol that can also be extended to provide for new features. IMA and CMC provide a unified management paradigm to ease the administrative burden by consolidating management functions into one application.

Taking user suggestions is key to Citrix's ongoing developmental success. In the past, the most requested features from users involved better response time while speed typing over slow links, and immediate feedback of mouse clicks to inform the user that the action was being performed. SpeedScreen 3 has fulfilled these requests with predictive text entry and instant mouse feedback.

MetaFrame XP uses the same type of connection scheme as MetaFrame 1.8 with listener ports and idle sessions. For large farms that have many users logging in at the same time, the number of idle sessions may need to be increased to prevent users from getting timeouts while the existing idle sessions recycle. Once the MetaFrame user connects and logs on, they constitute an ICA session. ICA sessions can be monitored from the CMC's Sessions tab and specific information can be obtained from each session by drilling down to its properties. Client device licensing allows users to start multiple sessions from one client to one or many MetaFrame servers and only consume one pooled license.

TWO-MINUTE DRILL

Identifying the Components of the ICA Packet

❑ ICA is a general purpose presentation protocol that provides X Windows–like functionality to the Windows community.

❑ ICA is the physical line protocol used for communication between client and server.

❑ Only the command portion of the packet is always present.

❑ ICA uses virtual channels to add functionality to the protocol.

Listing the Benefits of SpeedScreen Technology

❑ SpeedScreen 3 provides predictive text entry to provide instant visual feedback on high-latency lines.

❑ SpeedScreen 3 provides instant visual feedback for mouse actions by changing the cursor to indicate that the command has been executed.

❑ SpeedScreen 3 can be configured per application on the server.

❑ SpeedScreen 3 can be enabled or disabled manually from the client.

Discussing the Features of Independent Management Architecture

❑ IMA is both an architecture and a protocol.

❑ IMA traffic uses TCP port 2512.

❑ IMA provides that all configuration information is stored in a central location.

❑ Administrative actions such as shadowing can now be logged and audited.

❑ Farms are made up of zones. Where a farm's spans multiple subnets and locations, a zone is typically one subnet.

❑ The data store is the central database that contains all the farms configuration information.

❑ The data collector is the zone traffic cop that gathers all zone data and forwards it to all other data collectors.

❏ The local host cache is a subset of the data store and speeds performance by caching farm information on the local server. This also allows the server to run for up to 48 hours without being able to contact the data store.

Recognizing Listener Ports, Idle Sessions, ICA Sessions, and Client Device Licensing

❏ Listener ports accept the connections for the specific protocols and direct them to an idle session.

❏ Idle sessions are the connection point for new users. Once an idle session is used to connect a user, it recycles itself to another idle session.

❏ By default there are two idle sessions.

❏ Client device licensing allows multiple sessions from the same device to consume only one license.

SELF TEST

The following questions will help you measure your understanding of the material presented in this chapter. Read all the choices carefully as there may be more than one correct answer. Choose all correct answers for each question.

Identifying the Components of the ICA Packet

1. What is the data protocol that exports the screen image?

   A. ICA

   B. Thinwire

   C. TCP

   D. FTP

2. While analyzing a sniffer trace of ICA traffic, you begin examining the contents of the ICA packets. On an IPX network, using SecureICA and a dial-up connection, what packet components would you expect to find? (Choose all that apply.)

   A. Command

   B. Encryption

   C. Compression

   D. Reliable

3. Which ICA clients support full-screen test mode?

   A. Windows 32

   B. Windows 16

   C. Java

   D. DOS

4. You need to provide UDP broadcast compatibility to your farm as you migrate from MetaFrame 1.8 to MetaFrame XP. What must you do to the XP farm to enable it to interoperate with MetaFrame 1.8?

   A. Run the XP farm in compatibility mode with a different farm name.

   B. Configure the XP farm with the same farm name as the 1.8 farm and run the XP farm in mixed mode.

   C. From Published Application Manager on the 1.8 master browser, choose farm scope and select the Interoperability Mode check box.

   D. Nothing. XP and MetaFrame 1.8 are fully compatible and do not need any special settings to work together.

5. What transport protocols does ICA currently support?

   A. IPX

   B. SPX

   C. DLC

   D. NetBEUI

Listing the Benefits of SpeedScreen Technology

6. When was SpeedScreen 3 first available?

   A. WinFrame 1.5

   B. MetaFrame 1.0

   C. Feature Release 1

   D. MetaFrame XP

7. Your Citrix implementation is primarily for medical transcriptionists who work from home. Their primary application is a word processor and they are complaining that the text they type does not show up until several seconds after they type it. What feature of SpeedScreen would help alleviate this problem?

   A. Instant mouse feedback

   B. Predictive text entry

   C. Client side caching

   D. Repainting only changed areas of the screen

8. How are SpeedScreen 3 settings configured?

   A. Per server

   B. Farmwide

   C. Per client

   D. Per application

9. What application is used to configure SpeedScreen settings?

   A. Latency Reduction Manager

   B. Citrix Management Console

   C. Published Application Manager

   D. Citrix Server Administration

10. You need to deploy the settings for SpeedScreen to all 80 servers in your farm. What directory needs to be copied to all the servers?

    A. %systemroot%\system32\ss3config

    B. %systemroot%\system32\ss3

    C. %systemroot%\system32\SpeedScreen

    D. %systemroot%\system32\ThinWire

Discuss the Features of Independent Management Architecture

11. IMA operates on which port?

    A. TCP 1494

    B. UDP 1604

    C. TCP 80

    D. TCP 2512

12. You are trying to present to management the reasons to upgrade to MetaFrame XP. While covering IMA, what are some of the points you would discuss?

    A. Session shadowing can now be logged.

    B. Administrative actions can be audited.

    C. Licensing information is distributed across all servers.

    D. All configuration data is stored in a central database.

13. You are creating a large farm with servers in five geographical locations. You create a single farm and set up each location as a zone. By default, how many data collectors will there be?

    A. One

    B. Five

    C. Two

    D. Four collectors and one data store

14. What three databases can support data store services?

    A. IBM DB2

    B. Microsoft SQL Server

    C. Oracle

    D. Microsoft Access

15. When setting up connections to the data store, a server can be configured one of two ways: direct connections and indirect connections. When setting up indirect connections, what is the biggest drawback?

    A. Slow performance

    B. Single point of failure

    C. Increased WAN utilization

    D. Requires multiple data stores

Recognizing Listener Ports, Idle Sessions, ICA Sessions, and Client Device Licensing

16. You are manning the help desk one morning and receive calls from users who have tried numerous times to get a connection to your MetaFrame XP farm. You have a large farm with 2000+ users and have plenty of capacity. It is about 9 A.M. so there are many users connecting to the farm at one time. You see that this behavior has become more and more common. What is the best immediate solution?

    A. Install additional servers

    B. Disable logons to the busiest servers

    C. Configure additional idle sessions

    D. Reboot all the servers in the farm

17. What is the requirement to enable client device licensing?

    A. Use MetaFrame XP*e*

    B. Enable license pooling

    C. Run the farm in native mode

    D. Use a MetaFrame 1.8 server as the master browser

18. To increase the count of idle sessions, what value in the registry must be incremented?

    A. IdleSessionCount

    B. IdleWinstationPoolCount

    C. NumIdlePortListeners

    D. IdleSessionTime

19. Identify some of the possible states an ICA session can be in. (Choose all that apply.)

    A. Neutral

    B. Active

    C. Listen

    D. Down

20. What are the two types of connections that you may see a user being connected with?

    A. ICA

    B. HTTP

    C. RDP

    D. XML

LAB QUESTION

Your manager tasks you to draw up a design to handle your upcoming MetaFrame XP deployment. You currently plan on creating a single farm with four zones to cover your four data centers that contain 50 servers each. You plan on having your Microsoft SQL Server data store at the main data center. Using the example in Figure 4-14, decide how you would use the various techniques to provide IMA connectivity to your farms. Remember to consider direct and indirect connections, zoning possibilities, and replicated data stores. The WAN connections are used for other mission-critical data as well as ICA and IMA traffic and over-usage should be minimized. Each zone will provide redundancy for every other zone and the loss of one zone would not cause a loss of service to users.

FIGURE 4-14   Lab Example

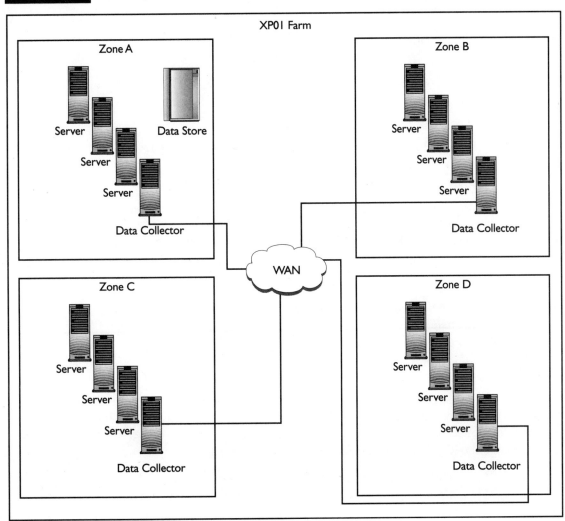

SELF TEST ANSWERS

Identifying the Components of the ICA Packet

1. ☑ **B.** Thinwire is correct because it is the portion of ICA that handles the graphical screen image.
   ☒ **A**, ICA, is incorrect because it contains thinwire. **C**, TCP, is incorrect because TCP is the lower level protocol that ICA and thinwire can ride on. In addition **D**, FTP, is incorrect because FTP is for transferring files.

2. ☑ **A, B, C,** and **D** are all correct. A command is always included in every ICA packet. SecureICA is an encryption service so the encryption header would be included. Dial-up should always use compression and IPX is not a reliable protocol so a reliable header is added.

3. ☑ **D**, DOS, is correct. Only the DOS client (both 16- and 32-bit versions) support running a text mode application in full-screen text mode on the client.
   ☒ Since **D** is correct, **A, B,** and **C** are therefore incorrect.

4. ☑ **B,** Configure the XP farm with the same farm name as the 1.8 farm and run the XP farm in mixed mode, is correct. MetaFrame XP provides mixed mode to interoperate with legacy MetaFrame 1.8 farms during a migration. A requirement in mixed mode is that both farms have the same name.
   ☒ **A**, Run the XP farm in compatibility mode with a different farm name, is incorrect because XP does not have a compatibility mode, it has mixed mode, and again the farm names must match. **C**, From Published Application Manager on the 1.8 master browser, choose farm scope and select the Interoperability Mode check box, is incorrect because MetaFrame 1.8 has no facility to interoperate with XP. **D**, Nothing. XP and MetaFrame 1.8 are fully compatible and do not need any special settings to work together, is also incorrect because you do have to configure the XP farm to be compatible with MetaFrame 1.8.

5. ☑ **A, B,** and **D**, IPX, SPX, and NetBEUI are all supported by the ICA client.
   ☒ **C**, DLC, is a mainframe protocol and is not currently supported by ICA, therefore it is incorrect.

Listing the Benefits of SpeedScreen Technology

6. ☑ **C,** Feature Release 1, is correct. Citrix first included SpeedScreen 3 technology in Feature Release 1 for MetaFrame 1.8.
   ☒ **A**, WinFrame 1.5, did not have a SpeedScreen feature set, thus it is incorrect. **B**, MetaFrame 1.0, included SpeedScreen 2, thus it is incorrect. **D**, MetaFrame XP, includes SpeedScreen 3 but it was not the first, thus it is incorrect.

7. ☑ **B.** Predictive text entry is correct because it provides instant local text echo to allow users to see text as it is typed instead of waiting for the screen update from the server (even over high-latency connections).

☒ **A,** Instant mouse feedback would not satisfy the typists' need to see the text any faster, thus it is incorrect. **C,** Client side caching, only helps after an image has been displayed on the client screen. The character would still have to be sent to the server and return to be displayed. **D,** Repainting only changed areas of the screen, still would not help as this is a standard feature of ICA, thus it is also incorrect.

8. ☑ **D,** Per application, is correct. All SpeedScreen 3 settings are configured on a per application basis.

☒ Since **D** is correct, **A, B,** and **C** are therefore incorrect.

9. ☑ **A,** Latency Reduction Manager, is correct. All server-side SpeedScreen settings are controlled from the Latency Reduction Manager.

☒ Since **A** is correct, **B, C,** and **D** are therefore incorrect.

10. ☑ **A,** %systemroot%\system32\ss3config, is correct. All Speed-Screen settings are saved in the %systemroot%\system32\ss3config directory and can be copied to all servers in the farm to deploy identical settings throughout.

☒ **B, C,** and **D** are not valid directories, therefore they are incorrect.

Discuss the Features of Independent Management Architecture

11. ☑ **D.** 2512 is correct. IMA uses TCP port 2512 for all traffic.

☒ **A,** TCP 1494 is the port on which ICA session traffic operates, so it is incorrect. **B,** UDP 1604, is used for legacy ICA browsing, thus it is incorrect. **C,** TCP 80, is used for Web traffic, therefore it is incorrect.

12. ☑ **A,** Session shadowing can now be logged, **B,** Administrative actions can be audited, and **D,** All configuration data is stored in a central database, are all correct.

☒ **C,** Licensing information is distributed across all servers, is incorrect because, like the configuration data, all licensing information is also stored in a central database.

13. ☑ **B,** Five, is the correct answer. By default, each zone will contain one data collector.

☒ Since **B** is the correct answer, **A** and **C** are incorrect. **D,** Four collectors and one data store, is also incorrect because there will be actually be five data collectors and one data store. A data store does not function as a data collector.

14. ☑ **B, C,** and **D** are correct. The default data store is the Microsoft Access database, but for larger installations, a more robust and powerful database such as Oracle or Microsoft SQL Server is recommended.

    ☒ **A,** IBM DB2, is incorrect. There is currently no support for DB2.

15. ☑ **B,** Single point of failure, is correct. When using indirect connections, you must set up one server with a direct connection and point all other servers to it. This introduces a single point of failure if the single server fails.

    ☒ **A,** Slow performance, is not correct because the performance will not be affected. **C,** Increased WAN utilization, is incorrect because in most cases it will reduce WAN utilization by only one server if transmitting across the WANB to the data store. **D,** Requires multiple data stores, is incorrect because while it is possible to have multiple replicated data stores, using indirect connections would not require it.

Recognizing Listener Ports, Idle Sessions, ICA Sessions, and Client Device Licensing

16. ☑ **C,** Configure additional idle sessions, is the best solution. Users are connecting faster than the idle sessions are recycling. Adding more idle sessions will allow users to connect at a faster rate and not get timeouts.

    ☒ **B,** Disable logons to the busiest servers, would not solve the problem because load balancing will be pushing users to the other servers already, thus it is incorrect. **A,** Install additional servers, would help the problem but it would not necessarily solve it, and you already have adequate capacity to service your users. This would be an unnecessary expense that would not be a complete fix, thus it is not the best solution and is incorrect. **D,** Reboot all the servers in the farm, would not only cause all users to lose the connections they have, it would probably increase the rate of timed-out connections as all the users that have trickled in over the last hour will suddenly be attempting to reconnect all at once. Not to mention, you may lose your job. This is not the best solution and therefore incorrect.

17. ☑ **B,** Enable license pooling, is correct. Client device licensing prevents a single client from consuming multiple licenses if connecting to multiple servers to run applications. To enable it, you must have licenses pooled and the license the client acquires must be a pooled license.

    ☒ **A,** Use MetaFrame XP*e*, is incorrect because license pooling is also available in other versions of MetaFrame. **C,** Run the farm in native mode, is incorrect because client device licensing also works in mixed mode. **D** is incorrect because the use of a MetaFrame 1.8 server as the master browser is not allowed in a mixed or native mode MetaFrame XP deployment.

18. ☑ **B,** IdleWinstationPoolCount is correct. This value, located in the key `HKEY_LOCAL_MACHINE\SYSTEM\CurrentControlSet\Control\Terminal Server`, controls the number of idle sessions (or Winstations) the server maintains. Keep this number as low as possible because each idle session requires system resources.
    ☒ **A, C,** and **D** are not valid values and therefore are incorrect.

19. ☑ **B, C,** and **D** are correct. ICA sessions can be in one of five states: Active, Listen, Idle, Disconnected, and Down.
    ☒ **A,** Neutral, is not a valid state for ICA connections, thus it is incorrect.

20. ☑ **A,** ICA, and **C,** RDP are correct. The two types of connections currently supported by Terminal Services and MetaFrame are ICA and RDP.
    ☒ **B,** HTTP is used for Web browsing not ICA connections, thus it is incorrect.
    D, XML, is for ICA service location, not connection, thus it is also incorrect.

LAB ANSWER

To minimize use of the WAN connection and to avoid loading ODBC drivers on 200 servers, they can be configured to use indirect connections to the dedicated data collector and configure the data collector as the only direct connection. Since the loss of connectivity to the data store will not cause an outage to the users for 48 hours, it is determined that the single point of failure that the usage of indirect connections introduces is outweighed by the bandwidth savings and administrative time saved by not loading and maintaining ODBC drivers. (See Figure 4-15.)

FIGURE 4-15 Lab answer

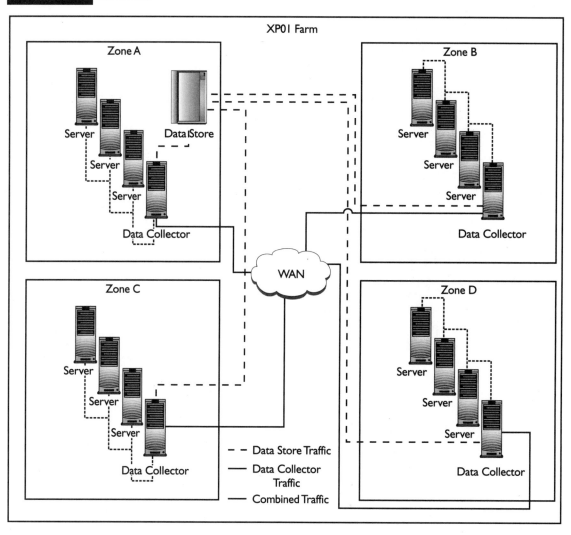

5

MetaFrame XP
Administration

T he majority of the monitoring and management tasks of Citrix MetaFrame XP servers are accomplished using the Citrix Management Console or CMC. The CMC is a Java-based extensible program used solely for administration of IMA, Independent Management Architecture, based (XP) MetaFrame servers. Allowing the administrator a single seat of administration, the CMC reduces the administrative overhead for an organization. The CMC administrative tool is to MetaFrame XP servers what the MMC, Microsoft Management Console, is to Windows 2000 servers. Similar to the way administrators add snap-in administrative tools to their MMC consoles, add-on management tools, such as Load Manager, Resource Manager, and Installation Manager for MetaFrame servers, automatically snap into the CMC when installed.

CERTIFICATION OBJECTIVE 5.01

Understanding the Citrix Management Console

The Citrix Management Console is a useful tool, which displays data for IMA-based MetaFrame XP servers. In Figure 5-1, you will see a screen shot of the CMC, in which items are arranged in a *tree view* in the left pane. The server farm, GLOBAL in this case, displays at the top of the left pane with all management tools or *node items* displayed beneath it. Each node item with a (+) next to it will reveal nested specific items and features of the server farm beneath them when clicked. Node items are containers that house objects representing resources or items that can be managed in the server farm, such as Applications and Citrix Administrators. An example of an object is W2KSERVER, which lies beneath the Servers node item. In Figure 5-1, W2KSERVER is the name of a MetaFrame XP server on the network being managed, whereas GLOBAL is the IMA-based server farm name.

In the right pane of the CMC, a *tab view* is displayed. The tab view allows administrators to configure a number of parameters for each item simply by clicking its associated tab. For example, you can manage the users or sessions (or processes, licenses, and so on) associated with W2KSERVER, shown in Figure 5-1, simply by clicking the Users tab or Sessions tab while the W2KSERVER is selected. If you wish to manage users or sessions associated with a different server, you can select the other server and switch to the appropriate tab.

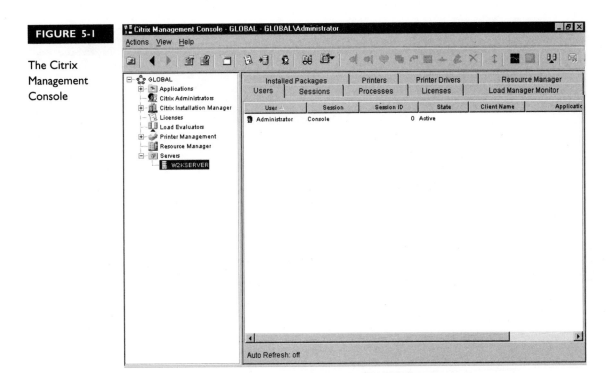

FIGURE 5-1

The Citrix
Management
Console

Citrix Management Console Minimum Requirements

With the Citrix Management Console, administrators are able to manage servers
remotely, without accessing administrative tools through an ICA session. The
MetaFrame XP server can be managed using the CMC in a number of different
ways, and the CMC can run on a variety of platforms independent of the
MetaFrame server farm. This can be useful to helpdesk personnel and remote
administrators who perform administrative functions with the server farm. An
advantage of using the CMC locally to perform management would be the resources
an ICA session running the CMC would use on the server. These are freed up if an
administrator is running the console independently.

Table 5-1 displays the minimum requirements for running the CMC. Notice the
amount of hard disk space and memory required to run the console. It is important
to remember that these numbers are the requirements of the CMC in addition to
the hard disk and memory requirements of the operating system or OS. The CMC
will install and run from any Windows 2000, Windows NT4, or MetaFrame

TABLE 5-1	**Hardware Requirements**	**Software Requirements**
Minimum Installation Requirements of the CMC	Disk Space: 25MB disk space (In addition to the OS)	Any Windows NT 4.0 system Any Windows 2000 system Any MetaFrame server
	Memory: 64MB RAM (In addition to the OS)	JRE: Java Runtime Environment CMC is Java-based and requires Sun JRE v1.3
	Processor: Pentium class or later	

machine. Additionally, the Java Runtime Environment, or JRE, is required for installation of the CMC. Note that the JRE components will be installed automatically during installation of the CMC if they are not already installed on the target machine.

Configuring Data Refresh

By default, automatic refresh of information displayed in the Citrix Management Console is disabled. The reason for this is that most events that occur within the server farm are automatically displayed within the CMC. However, there are some events that do not automatically update the CMC when they occur. Events such as servers coming online and ICA sessions starting do not auto-update the console. Therefore, in order to maintain current information on the status of your Citrix server farm, you can configure the frequency of information updates. Refresh settings for license information are available from the Actions menu, while refresh settings for Citrix servers, folder information, and applications are available from the View menu. The increments for auto-refresh are measured in seconds. You can select from 10, 30, 60, or 90 seconds as your refresh rate. It is important to note that setting auto-refresh on the CMC will cause increased traffic on your network. It may be best to use this setting only when it is imperative you monitor the start of an ICA session or witness a server coming online. Otherwise, manually refreshing the console by pressing the F5 key will accomplish the same goal.

EXERCISE 5-1

Configuring Auto Refresh

To configure Auto Refresh settings on the Citrix Management Console, perform the following steps:

1. From the View menu on the CMC, choose Auto Refresh Settings (as seen in Figure 5-2).

2. The Auto Refresh Settings dialog box should appear (shown in Figure 5-3). Here you can configure refresh settings in increments of seconds. Once you choose to auto refresh servers, server folders, or applications, you may choose from refresh rate options of 10, 30, 60, or 90 seconds in the drop-down box below each selection.

FIGURE 5-2

Auto Refresh Settings option

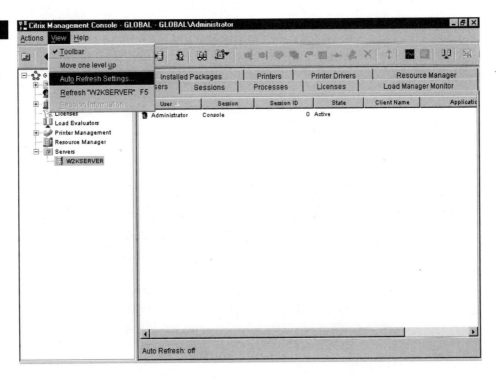

Connectivity

MetaFrame server farms store configuration information such as published applications, users, servers, and printers in a centralized location called the data store. A server farm contains only one data store. During the installation of MetaFrame, you created the database used for the data store (Access, SQL, or Oracle). The next step is to decide whether each server in the farm will access the data store directly or indirectly.

Direct access to the data store requires that you have the proper Open Database Connectivity, or ODBC, drivers to connect the data store database (Access, SQL, or Oracle). Direct access uses Transmission Control Protocol, or TCP port 2513 between the MetaFrame XP server and the data store for communications.

Indirect access to the data store uses another MetaFrame server as an intermediary. The intermediary MetaFrame server has the necessary ODBC drivers installed to make a direct connection to the data store. Indirect access uses TCP port 2512 for communication between MetaFrame servers. If this port is not convenient, it can be changed by altering a registry key on the MetaFrame server containing the data store, as well as all other servers in the farm.

Notice: Be sure to back up your registry before making changes. If you need assistance with the procedure, consult the Microsoft Knowledge Base.

on the **job**

To change the TCP port used for indirect access to the data store:

1. On the MetaFrame XP server containing the data store, change the value of the registry key HKLM\Software\Citrix\IMA\ImaPort to the desired port number.
2. On all other MetaFrame XP servers in the farm, change the value of the registry key HKLM\Software\Citrix\IMA\PsServerPort to the desired port number.

If you chose to use Microsoft Access for your data store, both Windows NT4 Terminal Server Edition or TSE and Windows 2000 servers have the appropriate ODBC drivers within the operating system to support direct access to the data store. Access is a sufficient solution for small server farms (1–50 servers), due to the limitations of Access itself. If you are planning an installation of 40 servers and you expect the size of the server farm to grow, use a robust scaleable database such as SQL or Oracle for your data store.

If SQL or Oracle is the database you chose for your data store, you will need to install the appropriate ODBC drivers to access the data store database on each of the MetaFrame servers that will be configured for direct access. SQL and Oracle are robust, scaleable solutions for any size farm and are the best solution for large to enterprise-sized server farms.

Now that you have a better idea of Connectivity in a MetaFrame server farm, here are some possible scenario questions and their answers:

SCENARIO & SOLUTION

You have a MetaFrame server farm that spans two subnets. Between the two subnets lies a firewall. Some of your users cannot access their published applications. Your MetaFrame servers are set up for indirect access and they are using the default port to access the data store across the firewall. What could cause this?	Either port 2512 (used for indirect access to the data store from MetaFrame servers) or 1494 (used for the ICA Client session to the MetaFrame server) are not open on the firewall.
You have decided on approximately ten MetaFrame XP servers that will act as application servers for your rollout of JDE One World. What is the simplest and most efficient data store you can create for this environment given its size? What type of access options do you have?	Access is the best option in this case, since the server farm is small. Since Access does not require any additional ODBC drivers to be installed, therefore each server, by default, will have direct access to the data store.

CERTIFICATION OBJECTIVE 5.02

Identifying Published Application, Server, and Citrix Administrator Properties

As mentioned in previous sections, the CMC contains many valuable management tools for your server farm. In the following section, we will discuss the options within Published Application, Server, and Citrix Administrator Properties. It is important you be familiar with these settings for your exam.

Application Properties

The Application Properties dialog box allows an administrator to adjust a number of application-specific settings. The tabs displayed within the Application Properties dialog box allow an administrator to "tweak" an application's properties. Any changes made to the properties of an application will affect the properties of that application (when it is accessed through an ICA session) on every server for which it is configured.

Application Name

Use this tab to view or update the reference names and description of the application. This must be a name that uniquely identifies the application in the farm. On this tab you have the option to disable the application. When the application is disabled, no users will be able to access the application. Options displayed on the Application Name tab appear in Figure 5-4.

Application Location

When you choose the Publish Application radio button, the Command Line box within this tab refers to the location of the local executable files for the published application. The Working Directory is the directory where the application's executable file resides. Choosing Publish Desktop here allows the server's entire Windows desktop to be published. When the ICA Client connects to the server, the user sees a desktop interface from which any application installed on that server can be launched. Options displayed on the Application Location tab appear in Figure 5-5.

FIGURE 5-4

The Application
Name tab

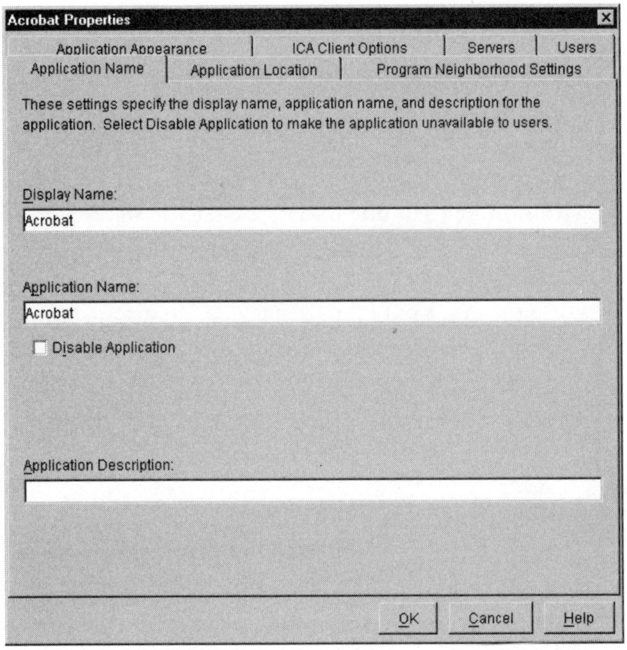

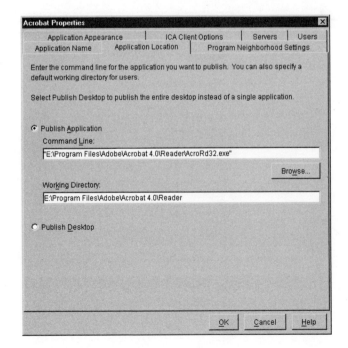

FIGURE 5-5

The Application
Location tab

Program Neighborhood Settings

This tab is used to configure how ICA Clients' applications are displayed within Program Neighborhood. If you would like the application to appear within a directory in Program Neighborhood on the client device, enter the folder name in the Program Neighborhood Folder box. If you would like to nest the application within more than one folder, use backslashes to separate the folders. For example, if your Program Neighborhood folder path is going to be Templates with a subdirectory of Accounting, type **Templates\Accounting** in the Program Neighborhood Folder box. This tab allows the administrator to place an application icon on the client's Start menu and/or desktop. Additionally, the administrator has the option to change the icon displayed for the application. Options displayed on the Program Neighborhood Settings tab are displayed in Figure 5-6.

Application Appearance

Options such as Session Window Size (which can be set to a range of resolutions from 800×600 to full screen) and Color (limited by the server's video adapter, but with 16 color, 256 color, High color, and true color selections) are available to

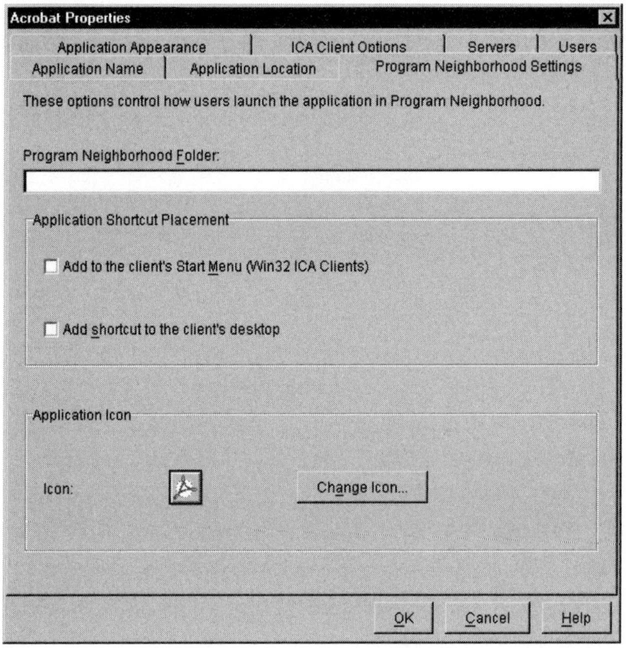

FIGURE 5-6

The Program Neighborhood Settings tab

change the application's appearance. Application Startup Settings include Hide Application Title Bar, which is the Blue Bar at the top of the application that displays the filename and application in use, and Maximize Application At Startup. It is important to note that these settings are ignored for ICA sessions running in seamless mode. Options displayed on the Application Appearance tab are shown in Figure 5-7.

ICA Client Options

This tab is used to configure ICA Client encryption and sound requirements. Options within this tab (shown in Figure 5-8), include Audio On/Off and Encryption Level. Each is explained in the following:

- **Audio Off**   Disables audio support for the application. Users can change this setting on their connection.

- **Audio On**   Enables audio support for the application. If you select Minimum Requirement, users who do not have audio capability will not be able to connect to the application.

FIGURE 5-7

The Application Appearance tab

Acrobat Properties

Application Name | Application Location | Program Neighborhood Settings
Application Appearance | ICA Client Options | Servers | Users

These settings control the application appearance for ICA Clients.

Session Window Size:

Percent of client desktop...

95   Percent

Colors:

256 colors

Application Startup Settings

☐ Hide application title bar

☑ Maximize application at startup

Note: Startup settings are ignored in seamless mode ICA sessions.

OK   Cancel   Help

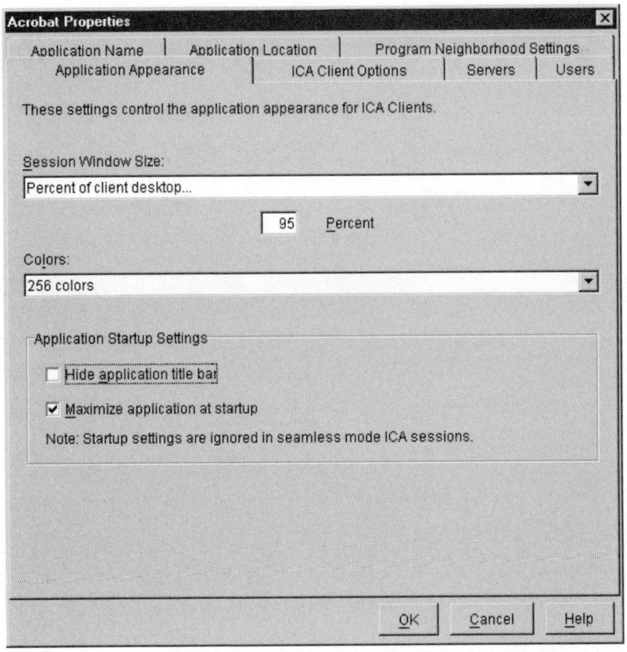

■ **Encryption Level** Encryption requirement for the application. If you select Minimum Requirement, ICA Clients will only be able to connect to the application if they support the specified level of encryption.

Servers

Choose from the list of Available Servers to add another server to the list of those hosting the application. You may also remove a server from the list of Configured Servers by highlighting it and choosing Remove. By selecting a server from the list of Configured Servers and choosing Edit Configuration, you have the option to reconfigure the Command Line and Working Directory of the application on that particular server. Options displayed on the Servers tab appear in Figure 5-9.

Users

Accounts that are allowed to access this application are listed in Configured Accounts. You can add accounts to the list of configured accounts by selecting a

---

FIGURE 5-8

The ICA Client
Options tab

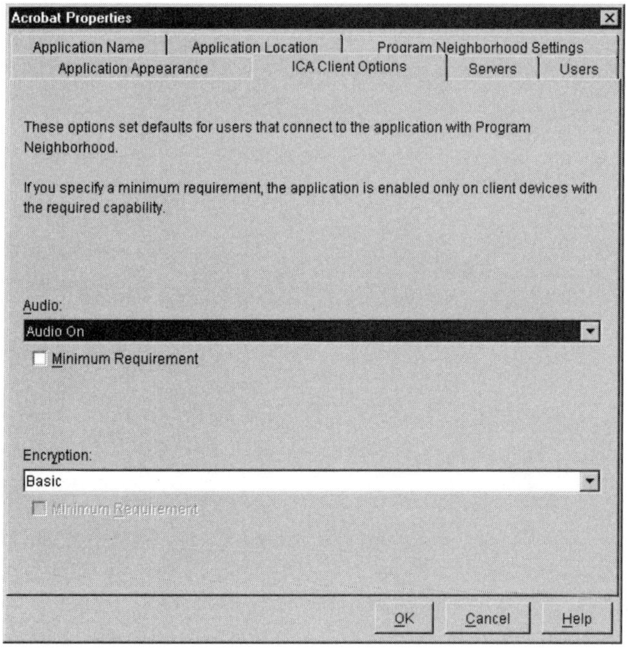

Acrobat Properties

Application Name | Application Location | Program Neighborhood Settings
Application Appearance | ICA Client Options | Servers | Users

These options set defaults for users that connect to the application with Program Neighborhood.

If you specify a minimum requirement, the application is enabled only on client devices with the required capability.

Audio:
Audio On

☐ Minimum Requirement

Encryption:
Basic

☐ Minimum Requirement

OK   Cancel   Help

FIGURE 5-9

The Servers tab

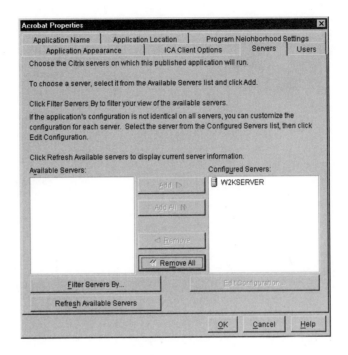

domain or local computer from the drop-down list beneath Domain, then choosing from the list of available accounts. By default, only groups are shown in the list of Available Users until you select the Show Users check box, which will display user accounts in addition to group accounts. Checking the box to allow anonymous access to the application will allow anyone to access this application, whether or not there is a valid account. Options displayed on the Users tab are shown in Figure 5-10.

on the job

Use the Disable Application feature when you have installed an application on a server farm for an upcoming rollout but do not want users to have the ability to connect to it until the rollout of the data.

FIGURE 5-10

The Users tab

FIGURE 5-10

The Users tab

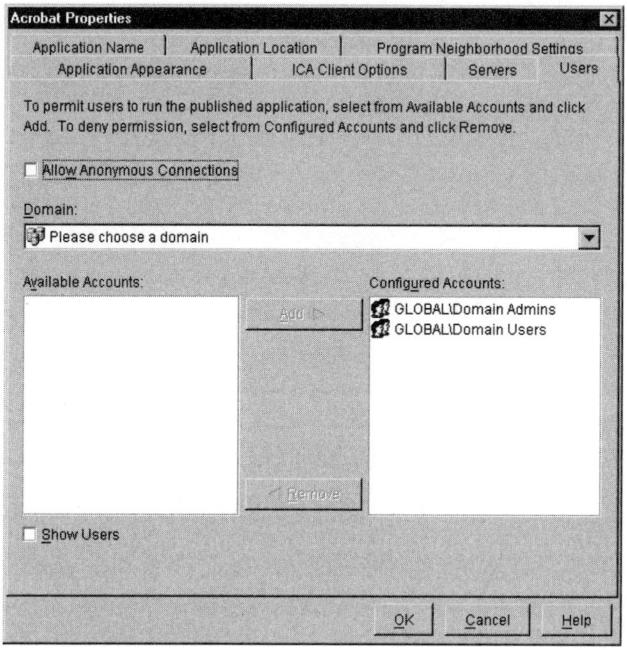

Citrix Administrators

When creating new Citrix Administrators, you have the option to choose from users and groups within the NT4 domain and Active Directory domains.

Once you choose an account, you can assign it read-only or read-write privileges. Read-only privileges allow users to only view the configuration settings within the console. Read-write privileges allow the user to view and make changes to the console settings.

Choosing the Add Local Administrators check box will create an option for the administrators group of your local server within the console.

Figure 5-11 shows the options available when adding a Citrix Administrator to the console.

Server Properties

Server-level management settings are displayed within the Server Properties tab of the CMC. Here you can view and configure settings for servers such as Operating System, TCP/IP address, hotfixes, printer bandwidth, and so on. This allows the administrator to configure server specific settings that vary from one server to the next from the same console. These changes are updated once you click OK in the Server Properties dialog box.

FIGURE 5-11

The Add Citrix
Administrator
dialog box

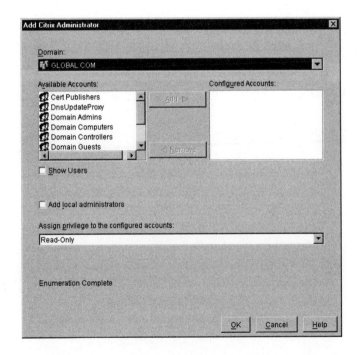

SNMP

If you have an SNMP-based network, you can configure application-based SNMP settings here. By default, the server inherits the Simple Network Management Protocol or SNMP settings placed on the server farm. Options displayed on the SNMP tab appear in Figure 5-12.

Information

Server information, such as operating system, service pack level, installation data, and MetaFrame version, as well as TCP/IP, IPX/SPX, and NetBIOS addresses can be found on the Information tab (shown in Figure 5-13).

Hotfixes

Displays each hotfix installed on the server, the account used to install it, and the date the hotfix was installed. This can be used to verify whether each server in the

---

FIGURE 5-12

The SNMP tab

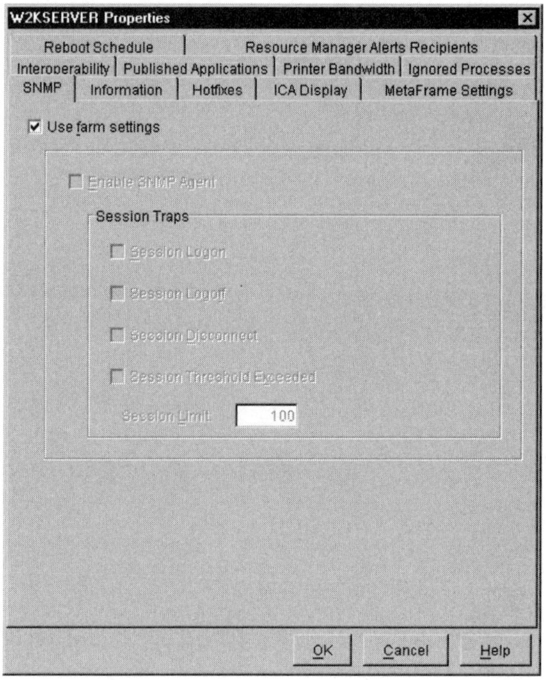

FIGURE 5-13

The Information
tab

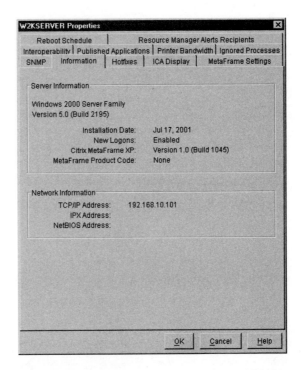

farm has a particular hotfix installed without having to access the registry on each separate MetaFrame server. Options displayed on the Hotfixes tab can be seen in Figure 5-14.

ICA Display

This ICA Display tab includes the same configurable performance options and resource limits as the ICA display on the server farm. By default, the options selected on the server farm apply. This tab is used for setting options for handling graphics over ICA connections on the selected server. The ICA Display tab options can be seen in Figure 5-15. Table 5-2, meanwhile, describes each option to be found there.

MetaFrame Settings

The MetaFrame Settings tab contains ICA browser options (displayed in Table 5-3), such as whether to create a browser listener on UDP, IPX, or NetBIOS networks.

FIGURE 5-15

The ICA Display
tab

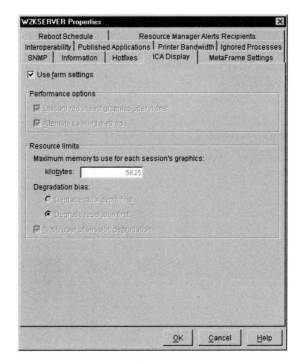

TABLE 5-2 Description of ICA Display Options

Section	Option	Detail
Performance Settings	Discard Redundant Graphics Operations	Discards intermediate graphic rendering to improve bandwidth usage. For example, if an area of the display generates an intermediate image that is immediately replaced by another image, the intermediate image is discarded and never displayed.
	Alternate Caching Method	Uses the updated caching method supported by MetaFrame 1.8 servers.
Resource Limits	Maximum Memory	The maximum memory allowed for use as a buffer by each client connection. The allowed range is 150 to 7500KB
Degradation Bias	Degrade Color Depth First	If the session memory limit is reached, color depth is lowered before resolution is in order to accommodate the buffer limit.
	Degrade Resolution First	If the session memory limit is reached, resolution is lowered before color depth is in order to accommodate the buffer limit.
	Notify User of Session Degradation	Displays a brief explanation when a session is degraded. Possible reasons include exceeding the memory limit, inappropriate licenses, and connecting with an ICA Client unable to support the requested parameters.

TABLE 5-3 The ICA Browser Options Tab

Option	Detail
Do Not Create Listener Port On UDP Network	Prevents the selected server from responding to any ICA browser network packets on UDP networks. Prevents the selected server from responding to any ICA browser network packets on UDP networks.
Do Not Create Listener Port On IPX Network	Prevents the selected server from responding to any ICA browser network packets on IPX networks.
Do Not Create Listener Port On NetBIOS Network	Prevents the selected server from responding to any ICA browser network packets on NetBIOS networks.
Server Responds To ICA Client Broadcast Messages	The selected server responds to ICA client broadcast messages. Note: This option is available only if the server farm is operating in native mode. (There are no MetaFrame 1.8 servers communicating with MetaFrame XP servers in your farm.)

FIGURE 5-16

The MetaFrame
Settings tab

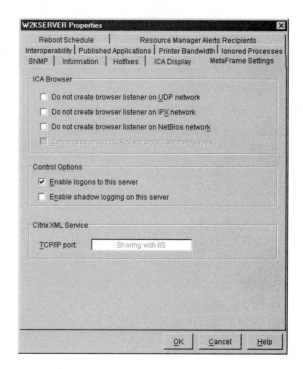

Control options available include enabling logons to the server and enabling shadowing logging on the server. Figure 5-16 shows the MetaFrame Settings tab.

Interoperability

This tab is only available if you choose to interact with MetaFrame 1.8 servers in your farm. The Interoperability tab is displayed in Figure 5-17.

■ **General Settings | Hide From ICA Client's Server List:** Choose this option if you would like users to be allowed to choose from published applications on a particular server but not be able to see that server in the server list.

Published Applications

The Published Applications tab lists the applications published on the server, as well as the details of each. Figure 5-18 displays the Published Applications tab, while Table 5-4 describes each option.

FIGURE 5-17

The
Interoperability
tab

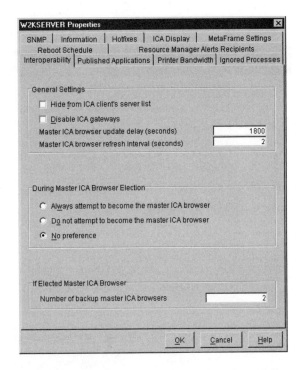

Printer Bandwidth

The Printer Bandwidth tab contains options to limit the bandwidth available for printing. By default, unlimited bandwidth is allowed. The bandwidth limit is the maximum amount of bandwidth a print job can use in a single ICA session. The Printer Bandwidth tab is displayed in Figure 5-19.

FIGURE 5-18

The Published
Applications tab

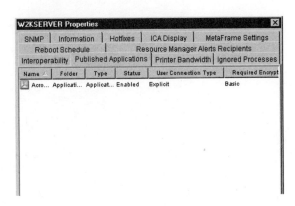

TABLE 5-4	Description of Published Applications Options

Option	Detail
Name	Name of the application that ICA Clients see.
Folder	Folder where the application resides within the CMC.
Type	Either application or desktop, depending on which value was selected on the Application Location tab in the CMC.
Status	Displays whether application is enabled or disabled.
User Connection Type	Either Explicit or Anonymous, meaning you either a valid account and password are required, or the application is configured for anonymous access.
Required Encryption	The encryption level required to connect to the application. Value depends on encryption level selected on the ICA Client Options tab.

FIGURE 5-19

The Printer
Bandwidth tab

Ignored Processes

Ignored Processes are those which Resource Manager, if installed, is configured not to monitor. To stop monitoring a process, choose Add Process and type the exact name of the process. The Ignored Processes tab is displayed in Figure 5-20.

Reboot Schedule

Periodic server reboots can be scheduled using the Reboot Schedule tab for each server. It is a good practice to reboot servers on a regular basis. The reason for this is that applications housed on the server can cause memory leaks that tie up valuable resources on your servers.

on the **Job**

It is best to reboot MetaFrame Servers nightly if you do not run 24/7 application access to your users. Rebooting in the middle of the night is a good practice. Keep your backup job in mind, however, whenever you schedule your server's reboot schedule. You don't want your MetaFrame server rebooting itself in the middle of its backup.

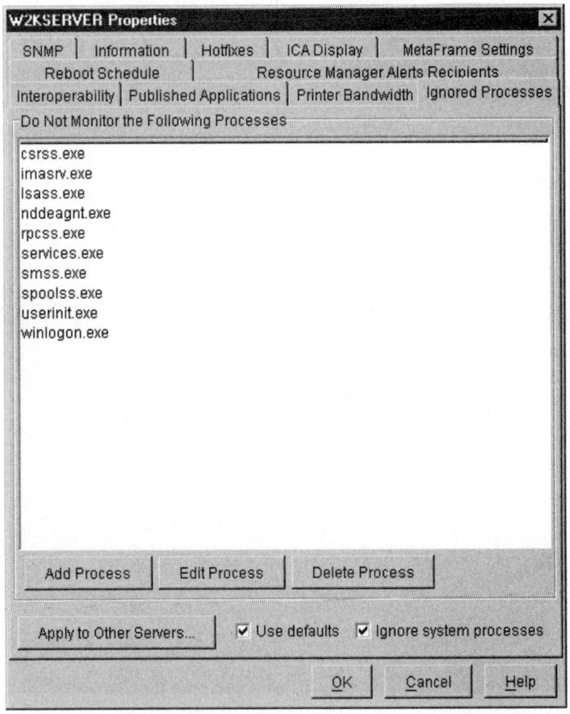

FIGURE 5-20

The Ignored
Processes tab

W2KSERVER Properties

SNMP | Information | Hotfixes | ICA Display | MetaFrame Settings
Reboot Schedule | Resource Manager Alerts Recipients
Interoperability | Published Applications | Printer Bandwidth | Ignored Processes

Do Not Monitor the Following Processes

```
csrss.exe
imasrv.exe
lsass.exe
nddeagnt.exe
rpcss.exe
services.exe
smss.exe
spoolss.exe
userinit.exe
winlogon.exe
```

Add Process | Edit Process | Delete Process

Apply to Other Servers... | ☑ Use defaults | ☑ Ignore system processes

OK | Cancel | Help

Now that you are familiar with the properties of servers and applications, let's take a look at some possible scenarios and solutions:

SCENARIO & SOLUTION

You have published an application that resides on 6 of the servers in your 50 server farm. These 6 servers host only the application you recently published. Users print large reports from this application on a regular basis which seems to be causing bottlenecks on your WAN links when the users running and printing the reports across the WAN link.	Instead of placing a printer bandwidth limit on the farm, begin by limiting the printer bandwidth on the 6 servers hosting the application that generates the large print jobs. This will improve performance of the traffic on the WAN link without affecting the printing performance of the entire farm, only the servers that are causing the bottlenecks. Farm scope printer bandwidth management is configured using the Printer Management object, and server scope bandwidth management is performed on the Printer Bandwidth tab within the Server Properties.
Last night, one of your colleagues updated all of the servers to the latest service pack for Windows 2000. How would you verify the service pack level of each server from the CMC?	Under Server Properties, use the Information tab to display server Operating System and service pack level.

CERTIFICATION OBJECTIVE 5.03

Administering Use of the Citrix Management Console

Administration of XP servers using the CMC is not restricted solely to XP sessions. Instead, the CMC can be installed on, and run from, a variety of connected workstations.

Installing the CMC

By default, the CMC is installed when MetaFrame XP is installed. However, if you are installing the CMC on a non-XP workstation or server that meets the necessary hardware and software requirements, choose the Citrix Management Console Setup option from the installation menu (shown in Figure 5-21).

In this section, we discuss the following administrative tasks performed within the CMC:

- Logging onto the CMC
- Configuring server farm settings
- Printer configuration and management
- Publishing applications and monitor application usage
- Licensing
- ICA Client session management
- Shadowing and sending messages

FIGURE 5-21

The MetaFrame XP installation setup screen

e x a m
ⓦatch
Remember, the CMC can be used to manage ONLY IMA-based MetaFrame
XP servers, not non-IMA-based MetaFrame 1.8 servers.

Logging On to the CMC

Once you launch the CMC, you will be prompted to enter an account and password, which gives you rights to run the CMC. By default, the account you were logged in as when you installed MetaFrame XP is the only account given Citrix Administrator privileges, and thus it is the only account authorized to access the CMC. Once logged on to the CMC, you will have the opportunity to create additional accounts, called Citrix Administrators, with the right to launch and log on to the CMC. Figure 5-22 is an example of a typical CMC logon screen.

e x a m
ⓦatch
Remember, there is ONLY ONE Citrix Administrator account created by
default during the installation of MetaFrame XP.

Configuring Farm and Server Settings

The configuration of server and farm properties is a two-fold endeavor. There are the options you select when XP is installed on the first server, as well as each extra server you add to the farm in addition to the settings. These can be configured on both the server and farm using the CMC.

FIGURE 5-22

The Citrix
Management
Console logon
screen

Log On to Citrix Farm

Enter the name of a server that is in the farm to which you want to connect.

Citrix Server: W2KSERVER

Enter your Citrix Administrator credentials:

User Name: Administrator

Password: ********

Domain: GLOBAL

OK   Cancel   Help

Installation Options

Some configuration options are available only during installation of the XP product. These options are as follows:

- Server farm name
- ICA shadowing restrictions
- Data store configuration

Operating Options

Once METAFRAME XP is installed, you can use the CMC to configure options on both the server farm and server levels. These options include management of ICA sessions, ICA display settings, zone configuration, performance, and 1.8 – XP communication.

Server Farm Settings   The Server Farm node within the CMC expands, displaying the various components of the farm, such as Applications, Citrix Administrators, Licenses, Printer Management, and Servers.

By selecting the server farm within the CMC and choosing the Properties dialog box, you have the option to configure farm-wide settings. Any changes you make within the properties of the server farm will be applied to every server that is a member of the same farm. These settings will be applied when you choose OK. If you make any changes and then click Cancel, the changes are not applied to the server farm.

Five tabs are included in the GLOBAL Properties dialog box (shown in Figure 5-23).

- **ICA Display**   This tab controls the manner in which data is transmitted to the client. The default setting in this section of the server farm properties are optimized for client performance. In most cases, there will be no need to change these settings. However, if you have users who access the farm across low-bandwidth links, you may want to adjust these settings for optimal performance.

    A useful tool when adjusting these settings is the Resource Limits dialog box. Here, you can scale back the amount of memory the ICA session is limited to use. In order to calculate the ICA client desktop size in KB, use the following example: an 800×600 desktop at 24 bits per pixel = 2.25MB.

FIGURE 5-23

The GLOBAL
Properties tab

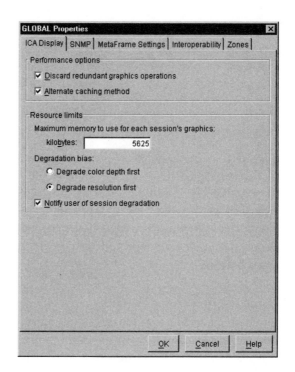

If the amount of memory for the display size is exceeded, the client's
session is either reduced in resolution or in color depth, depending on which
option is selected from the preceding ICA Display properties.

*TWCONFIG is a command-line utility to configure ICA display settings on a
per-server basis. Using TWCONFIG from the command line affects only the
ICA display options on the current server, not the entire farm. To set
farm-wide ICA display options, use the CMC.*

- ■ **SNMP**   If you use an SNMP-based network management product, such as
Tivoli NetView or HP OpenView, and you have the XP SNMP agent
installed, you can configure the SNMP agent to send traps if the percentage
of pooled licenses falls below the threshold you set in this area of the server
farm properties.

- ■ **MetaFrame Settings**   The Broadcast Response box within the MetaFrame
settings tab allows you to configure whether data collectors and RAS servers
in your server farm respond to UDP broadcasts from ICA clients.

Choosing the Data Collectors Respond To ICA Client (UDP) Broadcast Messages check box can be useful when you have older client versions (pre-6.0) that use TCP/IP, instead of TCP/IP+HTTP, to auto-locate resources in the farm using broadcast UDP packets. Additionally, if selecting the UDP response option, you must also have Work With MetaFrame 1.8 Servers checkmarked on the Interoperability tab within the Server Farm Properties dialog box.

The RAS Servers Respond To ICA Client Broadcast Messages option is used when you have ICA Clients who access the network by dialing into a RAS server. Because ICA Clients communicate only with the RAS server, setting the RAS server to respond to broadcast messages allows the client to access resources within the farm from the RAS server.

- **Interoperability**   This tab is used to enable or disable interoperation with MetaFrame 1.8 servers within the same farm. Choosing the option Work With MetaFrame 1.8 Servers In The Farm allows MetaFrame 1.8 servers to be members of the current farm. Selecting this option also makes the Interoperability tab available to each server in the farm.

- **Zones**   All Citrix servers that reside on the same network subnet are members of the same zone, by default. In this tab, you can create additional zones, and rename or delete existing zones. Zones are helpful to improve performance and management in an enterprise server farm where you have geographically diverse servers in the farm. They have the ability to span subnets, and each zone contains one data collector, which is a MetaFrame server that receives information from each MetaFrame server in the zone. Additionally, data collectors act as communication gateways between zones in a server farm.

exam
ⓦatch
Data collectors in MetaFrame XP are similar to ICA Master browsers in MetaFrame 1.8, except that XP servers communicate with each other using TCP/IP, whereas 1.8 servers use UDP for server-to-server communication.

exam
ⓦatch
If there are two XP server farms configured to respond to ICA broadcast messages on the same subnet, ICA Clients will have difficulty browsing for published applications.

Printer Configuration and Management

The CMC offers administrators the ability to manage both local printers (any printer attached to a MetaFrame server) and network printers through the printer management utility within the CMC. To add network print servers to the CMC, right-click the printer management applet in the tree view and choose Import Network Print Server (shown in Figure 5-24). Once you have successfully imported your network printers, you can install and manage the appropriate printer drivers. Printer driver management features include the ability to control auto-replication and auto-update of printer drivers across the farm, a utility for noting incompatible drivers, and a mapping utility that writes directly to the wtsuprn.inf (for those of you who used the manual mapping utility in NT4 TSE). Printer Management options are displayed in Figure 5-24.

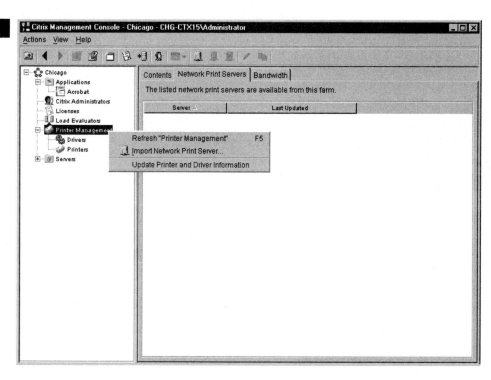

FIGURE 5-24

Printer management options

Shadowing and Sending Messages

Shadowing is a useful tool allowing administrators to monitor and interact with user's sessions. Shadowing an ICA session is similar to using remote control software, like PC Anywhere. It allows the administrator to view and control by remote the full ICA session from their desktop.

When you install MetaFrame XP, you have the option to limit or disable shadowing. The options you choose during installation to enable or disable shadowing on the server are permanent and cannot be changed once MetaFrame is installed.

Sending messages from the CMC allows the administrator to send messages to users, or groups of users, to inform them of upcoming maintenance, system shutdowns, and other events. The message displays as a small dialog box within the user's ICA session.

CertCam 5-2

EXERCISE 5-2

Shadowing a User

To shadow a user perform the following steps:

1. Log on to the CMC and highlight the server that the user is currently logged on to. (See Figure 5-25.) Right-click the user and choose Shadow from the drop-down list that appears.

2. The Start Shadowing dialog box appears. (Figure 5-26).

3. Choose the key sequence you will use to stop shadowing (shown in Figure 5-26) the user; then choose OK. The next screen you see will be the user's ICA session.

Managing ICA Client Sessions

A variety of ICA client management utilities are available within the Users tab of the particular server you are viewing. The following defines and describes the use of each option available.

FIGURE 5-25

Shadowing a user
through the
Citrix
Management
Console

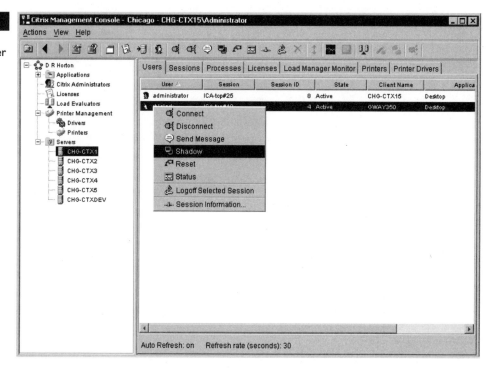

Disconnect

Allows the administrator to disconnect a user from their current session. The session
remains open on the server and the user is able to reconnect to the disconnected
session the next time they log on (provided that the server has not been rebooted).

FIGURE 5-26

The Start
Shadowing dialog
box

Shadow

Allows the administrator to view and remotely control a user's session from the admin desktop. Be aware that shadowing has its limitations. For instance, your server may be configured to ask permission from the user in the ICA session before shadowing can commence. Additionally, the client device you are shadowing from must be capable of supporting the video resolution of the ICA session, otherwise shadowing will terminate.

Logoff

Logs the user off their current session and closes all associated session processes on the server. This option preserves data, as opposed to resetting sessions, which can cause data loss.

Send Message

Allows the administrator to send messages to the users while they are working in their ICA sessions. This can be valuable to remind users of upcoming system maintenance or impending system shutdowns. By default, the date and time will be displayed to users when they receive the messages sent to them within their ICA sessions.

It is best to always send a message out to all users on each MetaFrame server before you restart the server. This gives the user time to save their work and log off before system shutdown.

Reset

Resetting effectively deletes the session and results in loss of data for the user. Only reset a session when it is not responding or has malfunctioned. This is always the last recourse. It is best to use logoff or disconnect to manage user sessions.

Status

View or update the I/O status of a selected session. Table 5-5 displays the options within session status.

TABLE 5-5	Description of Session Status Options	
Option	**Detail**
User	Name of the user account running the session
Session	Type of session, such as ICA-TCP#6, which means the client is running an ICA session over TCP/IP protocol and is connected to TCP port #6 on the MetaFrame server
I/O Status	Displays information on the rates of incoming and outgoing data to the session
Refresh Now	Updates the session information
Reset Counters	Sets the values of the I/O counters in the session to zero

Session Information

View details on the selected session. Details include client name, build number, product ID, hardware ID, address, color depth, buffers, resolution, username, encryption level, client license, server buffers, and modem name.

Licensing

The licensing tool within the CMC allows you to add server and connection licenses to your server, as well as assign licenses. It can also be used to track licensing within the server farm. License Management options are displayed in Figure 5-27.

Using Server and Application Folders

With Citrix Management Console, you can group applications or servers in virtual folders. The grouping of applications or servers makes navigating through their console listings much easier.

By simply right-clicking either the applications or servers folders in the left pane of the CMC and choosing New Folder from the drop-down list, you can create new subfolders that allow an administrator to logically group applications and servers.

exam
ⓦatch

The folder structure within the Applications node is not related to, or reflected in, the folder structure for ICA Clients using Program Neighborhood.

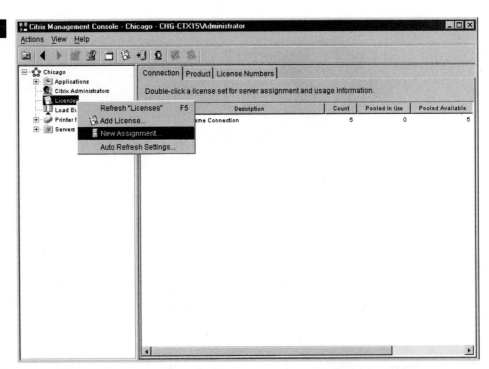

FIGURE 5-27

License
management
options

EXERCISE 5-3

CertCam 5-3

Creating a New Server and Application Folders

Create New Server and Application folders by performing the following steps:

1. Highlight and right-click either the Servers object or the Applications object within the CMC. Choose New Folder from the drop-down list. (See Figures 5-28 and 5-29.)

2. Once you have created and named your folders, simply drag and drop the server or application into them within the CMC.

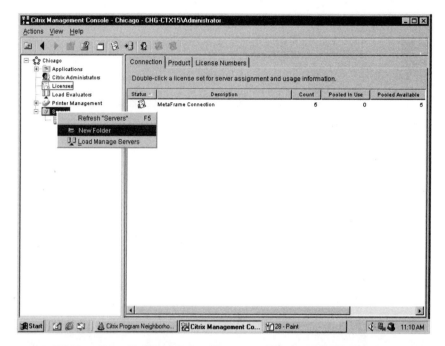

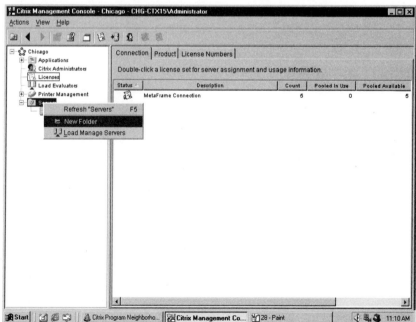

Using Citrix Installation Manager

The Citrix Installation Manager (CIM) is used to install applications on multiple XP servers. There are three key components of the CIM, the CIM plug-in, which resides in the CMC console, the Installer service, which resides on target servers (which don't run on the CMC), and the Packager, which runs on a Windows NT 4.0 TSE Service Pack 5 or later, or a Windows 2000 Server running terminal services in application server mode. When the Citrix Installation Manager is loaded on your server, The Citrix Installation Manager, or CIM, plug-in is displayed in your CMC. Used to manage MSI and ADF packages and install applications on the target servers, the CIM packages are created using the packager component of the CIM on a separate, dedicated MetaFrame XP application server. The CIM plug-in in the CMC is used to manage and schedule package installations across a server farm. Figure 5-30 shows a view of the CIM plug-in within the CMC, as well as the options available.

FIGURE 5-30	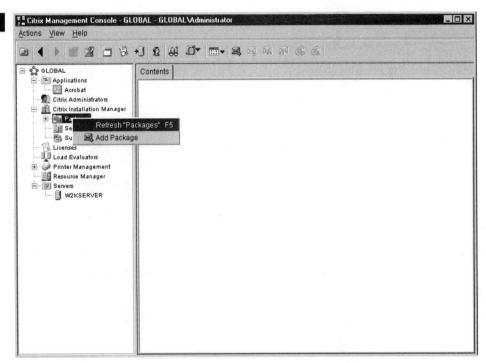

The Installation Manager options

FROM THE CLASSROOM

Potential Exam Questions

Although the exam will cover your knowledge of the entire MetaFrame platform, it is extremely likely you will be asked the following questions. Make sure you know the answers inside and out!

1. What are the minimum installation requirements for the Citrix Management Console?

2. By default, how many Citrix Administrator accounts are created during installation?

3. Is it possible for MetaFrame 1.8 servers to be members of the same farm as MetaFrame XP servers?

4. Is it possible to change the port that the XML service uses, and if so, what command-line utility allows administrators to do so?

5. Can printer bandwidth allocation be set on the farm itself or only on the server properties?

—*Heather Simpson, CCEA, CCA, MCSE*

CERTIFICATION SUMMARY

As you have learned in this chapter, the CMC acts as the primary administrative utility for IMA-based XP server farms. With the ability to configure properties on the server farm, server, and application administration, the CMC serves as a single seat of administration for MetaFrame XP administrators. As you have learned, the robust scalability of the CMC allows for incorporation of management snap-ins, such as Load Manager and Resource Manager.

It is important for the administrator to understand how the CMC works behind the scenes in its communication with the IMA-based servers in the farm. The ports that Citrix MetaFrame XP servers use to communicate with each other and with the client (2512, 2513, and 1494) are valuable facts to know.

✓ TWO-MINUTE DRILL

Understanding the Citrix Management Console

- ❏ The first time you launch the CMC, be sure to log in using the account you used to install MetaFrame.

- ❏ Review the Citrix Management Console minimum requirements.

- ❏ Data refresh is disabled by default on the CMC. Enabling data refresh can cause increased traffic on your network. Additionally, data refresh settings are set on a per-console basis.

- ❏ If you choose to use either SQL or Oracle as your data store, be sure to install the necessary ODBC drivers prior to installing MetaFrame XP.

- ❏ Know the difference between direct access and indirect access as used in the data store and each MetaFrame server.

Identifying Published Application, Server, and Citrix Administrator Properties

- ❏ By default, any configuration set on the Server Farm level will become the default at both the Application and Server levels. However, any settings changed on the Server or Application levels will take precedence.

- ❏ By default, the CMC has only one Citrix Administrator when it is installed. The default account is that which you were logged in as when you installed MetaFrame XP. You can create additional Citrix Admins using the utility in the CMC.

- ❏ Each application name must be unique within the farm.

- ❏ Within the properties of a server, you have the ability to configure scheduled reboots.

- ❏ The Information tab within Server properties offers valuable OS, service pack, and IP addressing information.

Administering Use of the Citrix Management Console

- ❏ The CMC can be installed on a variety of platforms outside the XP console.

❑ During installation, if disabling shadowing on your XP server is configured, it CANNOT be enabled after installation.

❑ Printer management within the CMC allows the administrator to replicate any local printer or imported network printer across the XP servers in the farm.

❑ Bandwidth allocated to printing can be limited.

❑ Useful ICA session management tools include the following: shadowing, disconnect, logoff, send message, reset, and session information.

❑ The Citrix Installation Manager displays package information and deployment schedules for the servers in the farm.

❑ Server and Application folders used within the CMC are for administrative organization only, and are not reflected within the ICA client.

SELF TEST

The following questions will help you measure your understanding of the material presented in this chapter. Read all the choices carefully as there may be more than one correct answer. Choose all correct answers for each question.

Understanding the Citrix Management Console

1. You have the CMC installed on your Windows 2000 professional machine at a WAN site to administer a farm at your corporate data center. You configured your CMC for auto-refresh last week before leaving for vacation. After returning from vacation, you notice your workstation is now locked, with the CMC still running. While you were away, users had been complaining of slow response times within their ICA sessions. What could have caused the sudden decrease in performance?

   A. The CMC was installed on a remote machine across a WAN link.

   B. Having configured data refresh, the normal network traffic is increased when you have your Citrix Management Console open.

   C. Packets are being dropped on your data connection to corporate.

   D. You installed a new domain controller on your network.

2. Which of the following will increase the performance of your servers?

   A. Configuring a reboot schedule on each server

   B. Allowing users to access the CMC

   C. Uninstalling the CMC on all your MetaFrame XP servers

   D. Adding more Citrix Administrator accounts

3. The CMC is a Java-based extensible utility for managing server farms. Which of the following platforms will the CMC NOT run on?

   A. Windows 2000

   B. Windows NT 4.0

   C. Windows 98

   D. MetaFrame servers

4. Which of the following are the minimum requirements of the CMC?

   A. 64MB RAM and 25MB disk space

   B. 64MB RAM and 50MB disk space

    C. 32MB RAM and 50MB disk space

    D. 128MB RAM and 25MB disk space

5. You are planning to install a small five-server farm. Which system or solution is the most efficient and cost-effective way to create the data store necessary for storage of server farm data?

    A. Access

    B. SQL

    C. Oracle

    D. Create an Excel spreadsheet

6. Your server farm's data store is SQL based. You are bringing a new server online next week. You configure its access to the data store as indirect. What is the primary limitation of this type of access?

    A. If the intermediary server which provides indirect access to the data store goes offline, it becomes the single point of failure.

    B. You have to install the proper ODBC drivers on the server, which will indirectly communicate with the data store

    C. A server can only communicate directly with the data store

    D. The CMC must be running in order for the server to communicate with the data store.

Identifying Published Application, Server, and Citrix Administrator Properties

7. Which tab on the server properties allows administrators to disable logons to the server?

    A. Interoperability

    B. Information

    C. MetaFrame Settings

    D. Published Applications

8. Which setting within the CMC allows a Citrix Administrator, user, or group to have only view permissions within the CMC?

    A. Read-Only

    B. Read-Write

    C. No Access

    D. Change access

9. In addition to the ICA display settings on the properties of the server farm, which command-line utility allows the administrator to increase the performance of ICA sessions by tweaking the display settings of ICA clients when they connect to the server farm?

   A. CTXXMLSS

   B. TWCONFIG

   C. CHFARM

   D. CLICENSE

10. You are an administrator of a large MetaFrame server farm. You were out on vacation last week when a patch was applied to the servers to address a printing issue. When you arrive at work this morning, your manager informs you that some users are still having difficulties printing. Your first course of action is to verify that every server in the farm did indeed receive the patch. What tab within Server Properties allows you to view this information from the CMC?

   A. ICA Display

   B. MetaFrame Settings

   C. Hotfixes

   D. Server Farm

11. As the administrator, you want to increase the organization of applications within Program Neighborhood on your clients by using folders. Using elements visible in Program Neighborhood, how can you do this?

   A. Create a new folder under the Applications object within the CMC.

   B. Use the Program Neighborhood Settings tab within Application Properties.

   C. Use the ICA Client Options tab within Application Properties.

   D. Choose Create New Folder within the Folder tab.

Administering the Citrix Management Console

12. You have installed a RAS server to allow users to gain access to the network. You dial into the network via the RAS server to test the user's ability to launch their ICA sessions once they are authenticated to the network. After launching the ICA session, you receive an error that a Citrix server cannot be located. What could be the problem?

   A. The RAS Servers Respond To ICA Client Broadcast Messages check box is not checked on the server farm properties, which would allow the RAS server to respond to ICA Client requests for service.

    B. You must use an account with administrative privileges to log on to the RAS server before the MetaFrame servers will respond to ICA Clients' requests from a RAS server.

    C. You must check the Enable Logons check box on the server you are trying to log on to.

    D. You must use an ICA dial-in in order to access the MetaFrame server farm remotely.

13. When your users who reside in remote offices across WAN links print large print jobs, all users at the remote site end up complaining about poor performance. How can you ensure the performance of ICA sessions across the WAN link and still provide print services?

    A. Add static routes on the router.

    B. Limit the number of users who can connect to the server.

    C. Limit the amount of bandwidth allocated for printing within the CMC.

    D. Replicate the printer driver across the farm.

14. Which of the following tasks allows the administrator to terminate a user's session while closing all processes on the server and freeing up valuable memory resources?

    A. Logoff

    B. Disconnect

    C. Reset

    D. Shadow

15. Which service improves reliability and performance by allowing the administrator to install identically configured applications to each server in the farm?

    A. The Application Publishing utility

    B. Installation Manager

    C. Resource Manager

    D. Replication service

LAB QUESTION

You are called out to do an on-site visit for a company that has a 15-server farm. The administrator at the company was hired after the farm was built and just brought an additional XP server online last week to balance the load of additional users on their network. The new MetaFrame XP server cannot connect to the data store. What could be the problem?

SELF TEST ANSWERS

Understanding the Citrix Management Console

1. ☑ **B.** Setting Data Refresh on your CMC causes a significant increase in traffic on your network. When the console is running, auto-refresh traffic can become cumbersome on the network.

☒ **A** is incorrect because merely having the CMC installed on your machine does not cause an increase in traffic. **C** is incorrect because if packets were being dropped on your network regularly, users would be getting disconnected from their sessions. **D** is incorrect because a new domain controller only affects authentication, not the performance of an ICA session.

2. ☑ **A.** Configuring a reboot schedule on each of your MetaFrame servers will allow the system to free up valuable resources due to memory leaks, as well as increase overall performance of your server farm.

☒ **B** is incorrect because allowing users access to the CMC will not increase the performance of your servers. **C** is incorrect because uninstalling the CMC on each MetaFrame server is impossible and impractical. **D** is incorrect because adding Citrix Administrator accounts will not affect the performance of the servers in the farm.

3. ☑ **C.** The CMC cannot run on a Windows 98 machine.

☒ **A, B,** and **D** are incorrect because the CMC can be installed and run on all Windows 2000, NT4, and MetaFrame servers.

4. ☑ **A.** The CMC requires 64MB of RAM and 25MB of disk space in addition to the operating system requirements.

☒ **B, C,** and **D** are incorrect because it is only necessary to have 32MB RAM and 25MB disk space to install the CMC.

5. ☑ **A.** Using Access is a simple, cost-effective solution, since Access and all its necessary ODBC drivers are components of the base operating system in Windows-based systems.

☒ **B** and **C** are incorrect because SQL and Oracle require additional ODBC drivers to be installed on the server for access to the data store database. Additionally, you would need a dedicated SQL or Oracle server because you cannot install MetaFrame on the same system as an Oracle or SQL install. **D** is incorrect because Excel is not a database, and the data store only supports databases in the form of SQL, Oracle, or Access.

6. ☑ **A.** Although indirect access saves the administrator from having to install the ODBC drivers on each server in the farm, the intermediary server, which acts as the go-between for the data store, becomes the single point of failure in the server farm. If the intermediary goes offline, users will be unable to connect to the servers configured for indirect access.

☒ **B** is incorrect. If you install the ODBC drivers on a MetaFrame server, it can use direct communication with the data store. **C** is incorrect because, although indirect access to the data store is possible, it is not a fault-tolerant solution. **D** is incorrect because it is not necessary for the CMC to be running in order for a server to communicate with the data store.

Identifying Published Application, Server, and Citrix Administrator Properties

7. ☑ **C.** The MetaFrame settings tab on the server properties allows administrators to disable logons to the server. Disabling logons to a particular server is wise when an administrator is installing service packs, applications, or performing any other type of system maintenance on MetaFrame servers. Disabling logons to the server will prevent any users from connecting to the server until maintenance is complete and the administrator unchecks the Disable Logons box, allowing logons to that particular server.

☒ **A** is incorrect because the Interoperability tab is present and used solely for configuring communications between MetaFrame 1.8 and MetaFrame XP servers. **B** is incorrect because the Information tab displays operating system, service pack, MetaFrame version, TCP/IP address, NetBIOS address, and IPX/SPX address information. **D** is incorrect because the Published Applications tab contains a listing of all the applications published on the selected server.

8. ☑ **A:** When configuring Citrix Administrator accounts, you have the option to allow read-only or read-write access to the Citrix Management Console to the account. Read-write access allows Citrix Administrators to make configuration changes within the console, while read-only permission allows Citrix Administrators to view the current configuration, but not to make changes.

☒ **B** is incorrect because it allows administrators to make changes to the settings within the console. **C** and **D** are incorrect because these options do not exist within the CMC.

9. ☑ **B.** TWCONFIG is a command line utility which allows the administrator to make changes to the ICA display settings on each particular server.

☒ **C** is incorrect because the CHFARM command-line utility is used to change the membership of a server from one server farm to another. **A** is incorrect because CTXXMLSS changes the XML service port number. **D** is incorrect because CLICENSE allows administrators to maintain licenses from the command prompt.

10. ☑ C. Each server maintains a list of hotfixes installed, which can be viewed on the Hotfixes tab within Server Properties.

☒ A is incorrect because the ICA Display tab has information related to the appearance of an ICA session. B is incorrect because the MetaFrame Settings tab contains settings for ICA browser, enabling logons, enabling shadowing, and Citrix XML port configuration, not hotfixes. D is incorrect because there is no such tab called Server Farm within the Server Properties.

11. ☑ B. The Program Neighborhood Folder option within the Program Neighborhood Settings tab allows the administrator to place applications within folders that are visible within the Program Neighborhood of the ICA client.

☒ A is incorrect because creating a new folder beneath the Applications object will organize applications in folders, but these folders are visible only to the administrators using the CMC. C is incorrect because the ICA Client Options tab does not contain an option for configuring folders within Program Neighborhood on the ICA Client. D is incorrect because there is no tab named Folders within the CMC.

Administering the Citrix Management Console

12. ☑ A. When the server farm is configured to have RAS servers respond to ICA client broadcasts, users who access the network remotely using pre 6.0 ICA Clients will be able to contact the server farm and connect to published applications. It is not necessary to possess administrative privileges in order to launch an ICA session from a RAS connection. There is no Enable Logons setting.

☒ It is not necessary to log on to a RAS server with an account that has administrative privileges in order to access the server farm, therefore B is incorrect. Although it is necessary to enable logons to the server, the error message stated that a Citrix server could not be located. Therefore, the issue concerns communicating with the server farm, not with authenticating. Thus, C is incorrect. It is possible to remotely access a server farm in a number of ways, including RAS dialing and ICA dial-in, making D incorrect.

13. ☑ C. The CMC offers printer bandwidth management for situations in which ICA clients are experiencing poor performance when large print jobs traverse the WAN link. Printer bandwidth management is on a per-server basis. You can fine-tune the bandwidth allowed per ICA session for printing by using the Printer Bandwidth setting, which can be located by either choosing Printer Management in the left pane and then choosing the Bandwidth Management tab in the right pane or using the Printer Management tab within server properties.

☒ **B** is incorrect because limiting the number of users who can connect to the server will not solve the problem. The bottleneck is on the WAN link, not the server. **A** is incorrect because adding static routes will not solve the problem due to the fact that routing has already been established (or else your users would not be able to connect to the server farm to begin with), and is therefore not an issue. Replicating a printer driver across the farm will not improve overall performance, therefore **D** is incorrect.

14. ☑ **A.** When an administrator chooses to log off a user, all the programs and processes associated with the ICA session are closed in a controlled fashion, and valuable resources used in the ICA session, such as RAM, are recycled.
☒ **B** is incorrect because disconnecting sessions allows administrators to leave the programs and processes of a particular ICA session open on the server so that the user can reconnect to the session at a later time. **C** is incorrect because resetting an ICA session can cause data loss. Therefore, it should be the last course of action, only done when the session cannot be logged off or reset. **D** is incorrect because shadowing a user only allows the administrator to remotely monitor and manage the session.

15. ☑ **B.** Installation Manager is an add-on product that allows the administrator to package preconfigured applications and schedule deployment of the packages to servers within the server farm.
☒ **C** is incorrect because resource Manager is used to keep a count of how many instances of specific applications are running in the server farm. The Application Publishing Utility is used when an administrator initially publishes an application within a server farm. Therefore, **A** is incorrect. **D** is also incorrect because the replication service is not an option within MetaFrame.

LAB ANSWER

Since the administrator is new, and not privy to the details of the install (other than those documented), you should check the registry setting that contains the port where MetaFrame servers connect to the data store. If the value is anything other than the default, 2512, the server will not be able to communicate with the server hosting the data store. You should always check the obvious sources of problems, such as whether the server is plugged into the network, whether the network interface card is functioning, whether the hub or switch is connected to the rest of the network, and so on. The server may also be on a subnet on the other side of a router on which port 2512 is not enabled. This would prevent communication between the server and the data store. Then you should check the default port values to see if the data store requires the new server to be configured with a different value.

6

Additional Management Tools

Over the past decade, Citrix technology has evolved from a simple remote access solution to an enterprise application deployment solution. MetaFrame XP encompasses and builds upon the management utilities that have been included in previous releases of Citrix technology. Citrix administrators will need to have a thorough understanding of the utilities they will use to administrate a Citrix environment. Inherently, the Citrix MetaFrame XP for the Windows Administration Exam (220) will have various questions pertaining to these tools.

The Citrix Server Administration tool and the Citrix Connection Configuration have been an integral part of managing Citrix environments since 1995, when Citrix first released WinFrame. Over the course of time, these utilities have been updated to adapt to the new features of Citrix technology, and several other tools have been added to help Citrix administrators manage their Citrix environments. The Shadow Taskbar was added to provide administrators with more robust shadowing capabilities, while the SpeedScreen Latency Reduction Manager was included to enhance the user experience over slow network connections. Before taking the CCA (Citrix Certified Administrator) test, be sure that you understand the features of each of these tools and the role they will play in managing a Citrix MetaFrame XP environment.

CERTIFICATION OBJECTIVE 6.01

Identifying Features of Citrix Server Administration

The Citrix Server Administration utility provides Citrix administrators a centralized point of management for Citrix servers and users in a Citrix environment. When managing MetaFrame XP or higher servers, it is recommended that administrators use the Citrix Management Console for managing servers and users. However, in a mixed environment, it may be necessary to use the Citrix Server Administration utility to manage WinFrame, MetaFrame, and MetaFrame XP servers from a centralized point of control.

The Citrix Server Administration is a tool that can be used for managing and monitoring users, sessions, and processes on any Citrix server or Terminal Server. With Citrix Server Administration (Figure 6-1) administrators have the ability to

■ View server information

■ View session information

■ View published applications

■ View users and user configuration data

■ View active processes on a server

■ Connect sessions

■ Disconnect sessions

■ Log users off

■ Shadow Citrix sessions

■ Send a message to users

■ Reset Citrix sessions

■ Terminate processes

The Citrix Server Administration tool has been divided into two panes to give administrators an organized view of the Citrix environment. The left pane is referred

FIGURE 6-1

The Citrix Server Administration tool

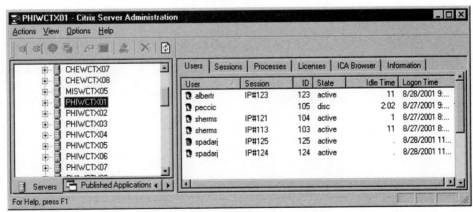

to as the context pane, while the right pane is referred to as the detail pane. You may notice that Citrix Server Administration is organized very much like Windows Explorer. The context pane is used to control the contents of the detail pane. As you change selections in the context pane, the features and contents of the detail pane will change so that you can manage the selected resource. The context pane can be set to view Citrix Servers, Published Applications, or Video Servers.

exam
ⓦatch

The Citrix Server Administration tool is like a "road-map" for managing a Citrix environment. You'll need to know where to manage settings, such as, ICA (Independent Computing Architecture) gateways. More important, you'll need to understand when, why, and how to apply these settings. Try to think of things from a user's perspective and ask yourself how the alteration of these settings will impact ICA clients.

There are several options that can be viewed in the context pane of the Citrix Server Administrator, as shown in Figure 6-2:

- **Servers** This view will show a list of WinFrame, MetaFrame, and Terminal Servers.

- **Published Applications** This view will show a list of published applications and the server farms they are associated with. Published applications that do not belong to a server farm are listed as *Unassociated Applications.*

- **Video Servers** This view will show a list of VideoFrame servers and current information regarding video streams.

FIGURE 6-2

The three options of the context pane

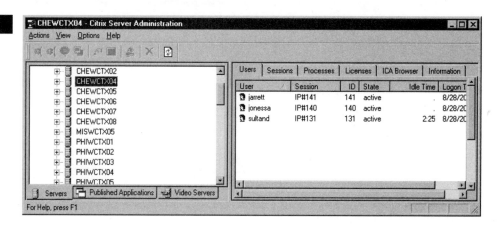

EXERCISE 6-1

Switching Between ICA Sessions and Resetting ICA Sessions from the Citrix Server Administration Tool

1. Using the Citrix ICA client, create two sessions to the same Citrix server, configuring each session with a different screen size.

2. Connect to both sessions and log on with the same administrative account.

3. From the ICA session with the highest configured screen resolution, open up the Citrix Server Administration tool. Expand the server you are logged on to from the context pane so you can see your ICA sessions below the server and also in the detail pane.

4. The ICA session that is colored green is the session you are running the Citrix Server Administration tool from. Right-click the other ICA session and select Connect.

5. You should now be connected to the other ICA session. Open the Citrix Server Administration tool and repeat the process to connect back to your original session.

6. From the bigger ICA session, use the context pane of the Citrix Server Administration tool to locate the other ICA session again. Right-click the session below the server in the context pane and select Reset.

7. The smaller ICA session should now be terminated.

Citrix Server Administration—Managing Servers

Citrix MetaFrame XP is an ideal solution for deploying applications to a large population of users. Load balancing capabilities give administrators the ability to publish applications across hundreds of Citrix servers. MetaFrame XP provides administrators the Citrix Management Console for managing Citrix servers, users, and other resources from a central point of control. However, the Citrix Server Administration tool may also be used to manage these resources.

The Citrix Server Administration tool can be used for managing Citrix MetaFrame servers, as well as Citrix WinFrame servers. By default, the Citrix Server Administration tool will display a list of servers in the context pane and a context-specific list of options in the detail pane. Selecting a Citrix server in the context pane provides access to the following options in the detail pane:

- ■ **Users** This tab provides a list of current users for a selected server, along with detailed session information. Administrators can right-click any of the users in the detail pane for a menu of management options.

- ■ **Sessions** This tab provides a list of active and idle ICA sessions for a selected server. Administrators can right-click a session in the detail pane for a menu of management options.

- ■ **Processes** This tab shows a list of processes that are running on a server and the ICA session that the process is associated with. Administrators have the ability to terminate processes from the detail pane by right-clicking the username to the left of the selected process.

- ■ **License** This tab provides information regarding any licenses that are installed on a selected server. Licensing information can only be seen through this view.

- ■ **ICA Browser** This tab gives administrators a menu of options that can be used to configure ICA settings for a selected server.

- ■ **Information** This tab provides information regarding the operating system, installed services packs, and hotfixes for a selected server.

Citrix servers can be managed from several different views in the context pane of the Citrix Server Administration tool. Depending on what context is set, administrators will have different management options available in the detail pane (Figure 6-3) of the Citrix Server Administration tool. Selecting a domain will show a list of servers in that particular domain, including network address information. Selecting a published application in the context pane will show what servers the application is published on. Selecting the *All Listed Servers* option from the context

FIGURE 6-3

Server options in
the detail pane

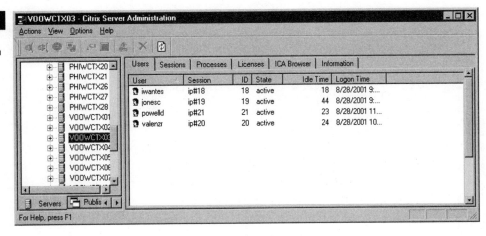

pane shows server information across the enterprise, including ICA gateway information.

In a Citrix environment, there are several Citrix-related settings and parameters that should be applied to each Citrix server. The Citrix Server Administration tool allows Citrix administrators to manage these Citrix-related settings without having to log on to each server one at a time. With the Citrix Server Administration tool, administrators can manage ICA Browser settings, ICA gateways, users, processes, and logons.

Citrix servers communicate with each other through a process known as ICA browsing. It is very important to understand how ICA browsing works and how ICA browser settings can impact a Citrix server or a group of Citrix servers. By default, a Citrix server will be able to communicate with all other Citrix servers on its subnet through ICA browsing. When two or more Citrix servers are on the same subnet, they will perform an ICA browser election, and one of the servers will declare itself the ICA Master browser. This process happens automatically, and there is a set of rules that allow the servers to determine which server will be the ICA Master browser. However, by configuring the ICA browser settings in the Citrix Server Administration utility, administrators can control which servers will participate in the browser elections and which server or servers will become ICA browsers.

FROM THE CLASSROOM

Establishing a Dedicated Master ICA Browser

In a Citrix environment, system uptime includes the ability for ICA clients to establish a connection to a server or application. In a server farm environment, ICA clients may lose the ability to connect to published applications if the Master ICA Browser becomes unavailable. For this reason, Citrix administrators may want to consider deploying a dedicated Master ICA Browser.

One problem you may run into if you're trying to deploy a dedicated Master ICA Browser is deciding what server to use and actually promoting that server to the Master ICA Browser. In a big server farm, you should have a Master Browser server that is used for nothing else. If you do not have a dedicated machine, you should select the server that is being least utilized. Once you have selected a machine to use, you will have to promote the server by altering a few settings in the Citrix Server Administration. If you are working in a production environment, this should be scheduled off-hours, as ICA clients may not be able to connect to the server farm during this process.

Before telling the selected server to become the Master Browser, you should check the current status of the ICA browser by using the QSERVER command from a command line. You should take note of the server that has an M next to its address. This is the current Master ICA Browser. By opening up the Citrix Server Administrator tool and selecting the server that is to become the Master Browser, you can manage the ICA settings of that server. Selecting the ICA Browser tab in the detail pane provides a list of preferences that the server will use during an ICA browser election. You should select the option that tells the server to "Always Attempt To Become The Master ICA Browser" under the *During Master ICA Browser Election* options; then use the Apply button. This will increase the server's chance of becoming a Master ICA Browser, but it may not force the server to become the Master Browser.

In order for the Master ICA Browser to change, an election must occur. In fact, you may have to force an election manually. From a command line, you can use the QSERVER / Election command to force a browser election. After a few minutes, you should be able to run the QSERVER command again and see that the Master ICA Browser is now the server that you configured in the Citrix Server Administration tool. If the server you choose does not become the Master ICA Browser after a few tries, you may have to go a step further.

Using Microsoft's Server Manager, stop the ICA Browser service of every Citrix server except for the server you want to designate as the Master ICA Browser. Once the service has been stopped on all the other servers, you can run the QSERVER /Election command again to force an ICA Browser election. Since the server you selected is the only server with the ICA Browser service running, it should become the Master ICA Browser. Run the QSERVER command again, and you should see that your selected server is the only server in the browse list and has been designated as the Master Browser, noted by the letter M.

From within the Citrix Server Administration tool, you should confirm that no other Citrix servers are configured to attempt to become the Master ICA Browser. Use Server Manager to start the ICA Browser service on the other Citrix servers. Run the QSERVER command again to make sure the server you have selected is still the Master ICA Browser. You have now created a dedicated Master ICA Browser for your subnet. You should make sure your ICA clients have included the address of the new Master Browser in their address list.

—James Spadaro, CCEA, MCSE, CCNA, CNA

ICA browsing is protocol-specific and the browser settings of a particular Citrix server can be managed for each protocol. If a Citrix server is using more than one protocol, it may be participating in multiple browser elections. By selecting a Citrix server from the context pane and then choosing the ICA Browser tab from the detail pane, administrators have direct access to the ICA browser settings of that server. From this view, administrators have the ability to control how the server advertises itself on the network, how the server reacts to an ICA browser election, and how many backup ICA browsers there will be if the server is elected Master ICA Browser.

The ICA Browser tab, shown in Figure 6-4, provides access to the ICA settings of the selected Citrix Server. From this view, administrators have the following options:

- **Hide From ICA Client's Server List** This feature can be used to keep ICA clients from locating a Citrix server. Administrators may have a Citrix server that has a special function. This feature can keep unwanted users from finding the server with their ICA clients.

- **Disable ICA Gateways** This feature would be used to temporarily disable ICA gateways without deleting them. Completely removing an ICA gateway can take several hours, but sometimes administrators may need to restrict Citrix servers from communicating to each other over ICA gateways. By disabling the ICA gateways on a server, administrators can temporarily disable any ICA gateways without having to remove or recreate it.

- **Do Not Participate In TCP Network**   This will keep the server from advertising ICA on a TCP network. Administrators may wish to use this feature if they do not want the server to participate in ICA browsing for TCP/IP.

- **Do Not Participate In IPX Network**   This will keep the server from advertising ICA on an IPX network. Administrators may wish to use this feature if they do not want the server to participate in ICA browsing for IPX.

- **Do Not Participate In NetBIOS Network**   This will keep the server from advertising ICA on a NetBIOS network. Administrators may wish to use this feature if they do not want the server to participate in ICA browsing for NetBIOS.

- **Master ICA Browser Update Delay**   This value, which is set at two seconds by default, controls the time between a client connection, or disconnection, and when the server updates the ICA Master Browser.

FIGURE 6-4

The ICA Browser tab of the Citrix Server Administration tool

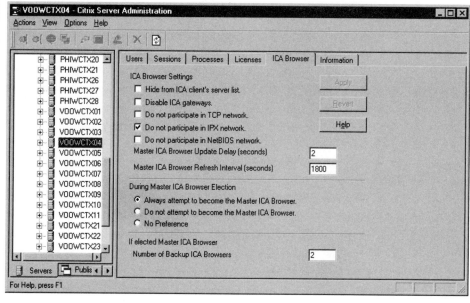

- **Master ICA Browser Refresh Interval** This value, which is set at 1800 seconds by default, controls how often the server updates the ICA Master Browser.

Several of the options shown under the ICA Browser tab of the Citrix Server Administration tool are used to control how a server will react to Master ICA Browser election. This view also provides options for configuring the number of backup browsers if a selected Citrix server is elected as the Master ICA Browser.

- **Always Attempt To Become The Master ICA Browser.** This option would be selected to increase the server's chance of becoming the Master ICA Browser during a Master ICA Browser Election.
- **Do Not Attempt To Become The Master ICA Browser.** This option would be selected to decrease the server's chance of becoming the Master ICA Browser during a Master ICA Browser Election.
- **No Preference** This option, which is set by default, will allow the servers to decide among themselves who will become the Master ICA Browser during a Master ICA Browser election.
- **Number Of Backup ICA Browsers** This feature is set by default so there will be two backup ICA browsers if a server is elected as the Master ICA Browser. Administrators should set this value no lower than two servers to provide fault tolerance in the event the ICA Master Browser becomes unavailable.

Because every Citrix environment is different, there is no standard way to configure ICA settings. Citrix administrators will have to configure the ICA settings that are best suited to their particular Citrix environment. Some Citrix administrators may only have one or two Citrix servers, in which case they may not need to alter the ICA settings of their Citrix servers. Some Citrix administrators, on the other hand, may have hundreds of Citrix servers deployed across multiple subnets, creating a more complicated ICA environment. Typically, the bigger the Citrix environment is, the more important it is to have a good understanding of ICA browsing.

As a Citrix administrator, you will use the Citrix Server Administration tool to manage Citrix servers and users. Here are a few issues that you may see as a Citrix administrator and the configuration settings that would cause these types of issues.

SCENARIO & SOLUTION

Citrix users cannot locate a particular Citrix server with Program Neighborhood. What ICA Browser setting could be used to produce this result?	Hide From ICA Client's Server List has been selected for the server using the ICA Browser tab in the Citrix Server Administration tool.
Running the Qserver command displays the IPX address of the Citrix servers on a subnet. One server running IPX is not displayed in the list. What ICA Browser setting could be used to produce this result?	Do Not Participate In IPX Network has been selected for the server using the ICA Browser tab in the Citrix Server Administration tool.

By default, Citrix servers will only be able to communicate with other Citrix servers that are located on the same subnet. This means that Citrix servers will not share ICA information with other Citrix servers on different subnets. If administrators want Citrix servers on different subnets to communicate with each other, they need to create an ICA gateway between the two subnets. An ICA gateway will allow Citrix servers on different subnets to share ICA information, which is required for allowing the servers to participate in a server farm with each other.

By selecting the *All Listed Servers* icon in the context pane (Figure 6-5), you will be able to establish and/or manage ICA gateways. Administrators will use these options to establish an ICA gateway between Citrix servers on different subnets. One or more Citrix servers can be selected as the local server where the ICA gateway information is stored. Then a server on a different subnet is entered as the remote server, creating an ICA gateway between the two subnets. Once an ICA gateway has been established, ICA Master Browsers will be able to obtain information on Citrix servers, published applications, and server farms from Citrix servers on the other subnet.

Because ICA browser information is protocol-specific, ICA gateways are bound to one protocol. ICA gateways can be set up for TCP/IP, IPX, or both. When a gateway is set up for one protocol, the server will be able to obtain updates from remote servers for that protocol exclusively. The server will only be able to share ICA information with remote Citrix servers for the protocol that the ICA gateway has established.

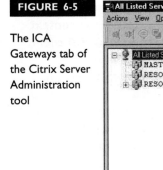

FIGURE 6-5

The ICA Gateways tab of the Citrix Server Administration tool

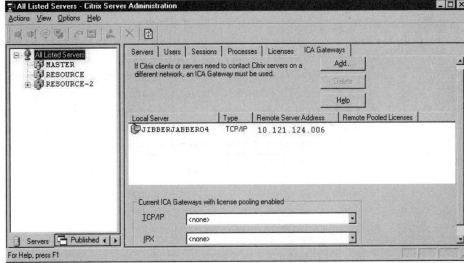

exam
Ⓦatch

The Citrix Server Administration tool has a context pane and a detail pane. Take the time to navigate through the different options in each of these panes. Right-click everything as you go. Make a mental note of the different menus and actions available for different selections.

Citrix Server Administration—Managing Users and Sessions

Many IT professionals will agree that the hardest part of managing any environment is not the technology itself, but the people who are using the technology. Fortunately for Citrix administrators, many of the issues that users have can be resolved without visiting the user's desk. The Citrix Server Administration utility allows Citrix administrators to manage users and sessions across the entire enterprise.

There are several ways to manage users with the Citrix Server Administration tool. The way administrators manage users in a Citrix environment depends on the size and architecture of the Citrix environment. Some administrators may have only one or two Citrix servers, in which case finding a particular Citrix user or session may be relatively easy. In large Citrix environments, administrators may have to navigate through the Citrix Server Administration and utilize the sorting features to locate users and sessions.

on the job

As a Citrix administrator, you will use the Citrix Server Administration tool for many of the support issues you deal with. By selecting a user in the context pane, you can use the Information tab in the detail pane to view ICA client settings for a selected user. This option will not allow you to make any changes to the ICA settings of a client, but viewing the settings of an ICA client is a valuable asset for troubleshooting ICA client issues. You may notice that a particular user who is having printing problems is running an outdated version of the ICA client. If you're a smart Citrix administrator, you'll ask the user to update their Citrix software before investing any more of your time into solving the problem.

There are several ways in which administrators can locate a particular Citrix user through the Citrix Server Administration tool. Users can be located using the following selections from the context pane:

- **All Listed Servers**   This will display a list of all Citrix users on all servers in all the listed domains.
- **Selected Domain**   This will display a list of Citrix users on the selected domain.
- **Selected Server**   This will display a list of Citrix users on the selected server.
- **Published Applications**   This will display a list of Citrix users who are using published applications.
- **Selected Server Farm**   This will display a list of Citrix users who are using the selected server farm.
- **Selected Published Application**   This will display a list of Citrix users who are using the selected published application.

Selecting a server from the context pane of the Citrix Server Administrator will display a list of current users in the detail pane. This list of users can be sorted by username, session name, session ID, session state, idle time, and logon time. This sorting functionality provides Citrix administrators a quick and easy solution for locating exactly what they need in a reasonable timeframe. When managing a Citrix environment, administrators may use these filtering capabilities to locate a hung process or idle sessions.

Once administrators locate the particular user they are searching for, there are several options available to them. By right-clicking a user in the detail pane, as shown in Figure 6-6, administrators will have access to a menu of options.

There are several user management options available by right-clicking on a user in the detail pane of the Citrix Server Administration tool. They include

- **Connect** This option allows you to connect to a different ICA session or re-connect to a disconnected session.

- **Disconnect** This option allows you to disconnect a session without terminating the session. The session will continue to run on the server and can be reconnected to at a later time. Selecting multiple users will allow you to disconnect multiple ICA sessions at once.

- **Send Message** This option allows you to send a message to a selected user; the message will be displayed on the screen on the selected session. Choosing multiple users allows you to send a message to multiple users simultaneously.

- **Shadow** This option allows you to shadow an ICA session and interact with it. An ICA listener can be configured so administrators can completely control a user's ICA session without permission, or it can be configured so the user must give the administrator permission to view or control the session.

- **Reset** This option will immediately terminate an ICA session. It does not give the user a chance to close applications or log off gracefully, but instead simply ends the ICA session. Selecting multiple users will allow you to reset multiple ICA sessions simultaneously.

FIGURE 6-6

Right-clicking a user in the detail pane

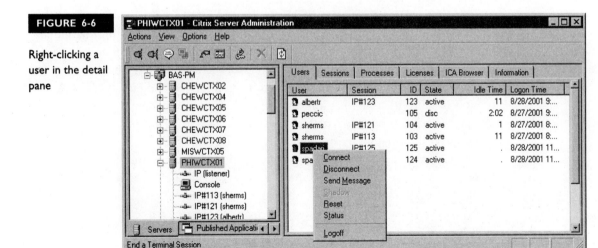

- **Status** This option displays networking information regarding the ICA session. It allows you to monitor bytes and frames of data that are being transmitted to and from and ICA client. Selecting multiple users will allow you to view the status of several users simultaneously.

- **Logoff** This option will gracefully log off a selected user, inherently terminating the ICA session. Selecting multiple users allows you to log off multiple users at the same time.

More detailed information regarding a Citrix user, or an ICA session, can be viewed by expanding a selected server in the context pane of the Citrix Server Administration tool. Once the server has been expanded in the context pane, a list of users and sessions can be located directly beneath the server in the context pane. Highlighting a user in the context pane will provide administrators with a more detailed view that user in the detail pane. When a user is selected in the context pane, the detail pane will have several tabs for viewing user information. The detail pane allows administrators to view process information, client information, client file information, and client cache information. Each of these options has a subset of information pertaining to the selected user.

The *Process* tab shows information regarding the current processes used by the selected ICA session. The ICA session ID, the process state, the process ID number, and the process image or filename are all displayed under the Process tab in the detail pane. By right-clicking a process in the detail pane, administrators have the ability to terminate it.

The *Information* tab (Figure 6-7) shows detailed information regarding the ICA client as well as the session information for a selected user. The user Information tab does not give administrators any management options but is often employed as a starting point for troubleshooting. In this regard, the Information tab allows administrators to see what ICA client version a user has, what directory the ICA client is installed in, and other information critical to troubleshooting Citrix issues.

The *Modules* tab shows what client files a selected ICA client is using. This tab also displays information regarding the version and size of client files.

The *Cache* tab shows information regarding the client cache and the bitmap cache for a selected session. The ICA client relies on caching to provide acceptable application performance across slow network connections. If an ICA client is not configured to cache images properly, users may experience unacceptable performance.

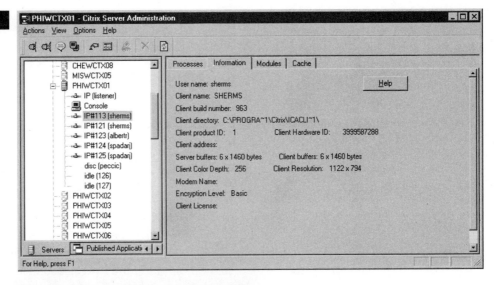

FIGURE 6-7

The user
Information tab
of the Citrix
Server
Administration
tool

CERTIFICATION OBJECTIVE 6.02

Shadowing with the Shadow Taskbar

Undoubtedly, one of the most useful features of Citrix technology is the ability to shadow an ICA session. Shadowing allows administrators to view, or even interact with a user's ICA session. When a Citrix administrator shadows a user session, the administrator and the Citrix user can both see the ICA session at the same time. Logic would dictate that the capability of shadowing an ICA session was originally intended for management and administration. Being able to shadow an ICA session certainly provides administrators with a powerful tool for dealing with those pesky users who keep calling for support, but the shadowing feature lends itself well to a number of different scenarios. Shadowing an ICA session can be the ideal solution for providing users in remote locations with training, presentations, or support.

As the popularity of the shadowing feature increased, so did the scenarios in which people used the feature. Inherently, Citrix added a more robust utility for shadowing ICA sessions known as the Shadow Taskbar. Citrix users can be shadowed from the Citrix Server Administration tool, the Citrix Management Console, or even from a command line. However, using the Shadow Taskbar

FIGURE 6-8

The Shadow
Taskbar

provides a very easy way to shadow users with more robust shadowing capabilities. The Shadow Taskbar also has the ability to shadow ICA sessions from the console of a Citrix server, a capability that the Citrix Server Administration tool lacks.

The Shadow Taskbar (Figure 6-8) uses the ICA client that is installed on the Citrix server where the taskbar is running. When using the Shadow Taskbar, the ICA client on the server creates a separate ICA session for each user the administrator wishes to shadow. By default ICA connections are configured so that the user must grant the administrator permission to shadow his or her session. Using the Citrix Connection Configuration utility, administrators can change these options for a particular ICA connection. Administrators can control the shadowing settings for a particular ICA connection or adjust it for a particular user level. Administrators can configure the following settings for an ICA connection or an individual user:

- **Disable Shadowing** By default, shadowing is enabled for all users and ICA connections.

- **Input On/Off** By default, input is turned on. Administrators can set this option to Off, allowing ICA sessions to only be monitored.

- **Notify On/Off** By default, notification is turned on. By setting this option to Off, Citrix users cannot deny administrators access to an ICA session.

- **Inherit user config** Selecting this option tells the Citrix server to use the shadowing options that have been configured for each particular user in User Manager For Domains.

EXERCISE 6-2

CertCam 6-2

Shadowing Multiple Users with the Shadow Taskbar

1. Log on to a Citrix server with an administrative user account and open the Shadow Taskbar.

2. From a client workstation, create three connections to the Citrix server and log on to all three sessions with any user account.

3. Use the Shadow button from the Shadow Taskbar to open up the Shadow Session dialog box.

4. Locate the three ICA sessions from the list of available users in the left pane of the Shadow Session dialog box. Use the Add button to add the users to the list of shadowed users in the right pane and select OK.

5. An ICA session should now be created for each of the three client connections, allowing you to shadow all three connections simultaneously.

6. Right-click the Shadow Taskbar and select the option to Cascade Shadowed Sessions. This should provide you with a cascaded view of all three sessions.

7. Right-click the Shadow Taskbar again and select the option to End All Shadowed Sessions. This will disconnect you from all sessions you are shadowing.

Additional features available with the Shadow Taskbar include logging capabilities and ICA port selection. Again, these features are not available in the Citrix Server Administration tool. If logging is enabled for the Shadow Taskbar, information regarding shadowed sessions will be stored in a log file that the administrator selects. The shadow log will keep information regarding the start and finish of shadowed sessions. The Shadow Taskbar also allows administrators to select an ICA port, which may be necessary for users who are connecting to an alternate ICA port. Citrix servers listen for ICA connections on TCP port 1494 by default, but this setting can be changed to accept connections on an alternate port, such as, port 80. If this setting has been altered, administrators will have to select the alternate port to shadow users with the Shadow Taskbar.

exam
ⓦatch

There are multiple ways a Citrix administrator can shadow an ICA session. Don't be surprised if you see a few questions about the advantages of using the Shadow Taskbar. Remember that ICA sessions cannot be shadowed from a server console using the Citrix Server Administration tool, but the Shadow Taskbar provides this functionality.

Multiple ICA sessions can be shadowed simultaneously using the Shadow Taskbar from a single location. Shadowing multiple ICA sessions is an ideal solution for training a classroom or monitoring the actions of users. The Shadow Taskbar allows administrators to shadow Citrix users, but non-administrators can also use the utility to have shadowing capabilities over their own ICA sessions. Advanced Citrix users may need to monitor several of their own sessions simultaneously, but administrators may not want them to have access to the Citrix Server Administration tool. Using the Shadow Taskbar solves this issue by providing normal users with limited administration capabilities.

When selecting a user or a group of users to shadow, administrators are presented with a list of available users in the Shadow Session dialog box, as shown in Figure 6-9. Users are organized by server, published application, or username. Administrators can select one or more users from the left pane in the Shadow Session dialog box. Once the user or users have been selected, the Add button is employed to add the user(s) to the list of shadowed users. Likewise, the Remove button removes a user or users from the list of shadowed users. When the administrator clicks the OK button, an ICA session is created for each of the shadowed users, and the administrator is now shadowing the selected users.

FIGURE 6-9

The Shadow Session dialog box

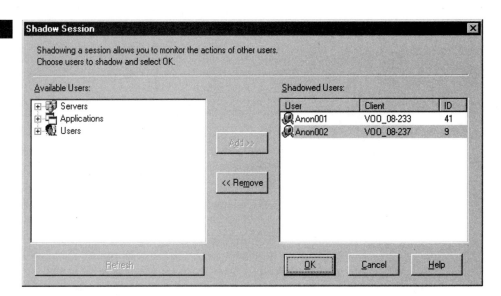

on the
job *ICA sessions can be shadowed from the Citrix Management Console, the Citrix Server Administration tool, or even from a command line. However, you will not be able to use any of these options if you are logged on to the console of a Citrix server. Keep in mind that the Shadow Taskbar will allow you to shadow ICA sessions from an ICA client device, as well as from the console of the server.*

Shadowed sessions are displayed in the form of a button that appears on the Shadow Taskbar. Administrators can move from session to session by simply clicking the desired button from the Shadow Taskbar. When shadowing multiple users, sessions can also be cascaded for easy viewing and navigation. Administrators can disconnect from a session by right-clicking the session or can disconnect from all sessions by right-clicking directly the Shadow Taskbar.

CERTIFICATION OBJECTIVE 6.03

Creating Connections with the Citrix Connection Configuration

When a Citrix user accesses a Citrix server or a published application, three major components are required for the connection. In a very simple overview, an ICA client, a network connection, and a Citrix server are the three components necessary. The ICA client has to know the address of the Citrix server and the type of network connection being used for the connection. On the other hand, the Citrix server has to know what kind of network connection is present, and the server must be configured to accept incoming connections.

The Citrix Connection Configuration utility (Figure 6-10) is a very granular tool that is used to configure and manage server connections. When MetaFrame is installed on a Terminal Server, one ICA connection is created for each network protocol. The Citrix Connection Configuration tool can be used to add more listeners or edit the existing ICA and RDP (Remote Display Protocol) connections. By default, ICA connections do not provide a high level of security, but there are many options for securing a Citrix ICA connection. Some people may refer to ICA and RDP connections as "listeners." In fact, throughout the rest of this section, we will do just that. This way we will not confuse the term with an actual client connection.

FIGURE 6-10

The Citrix
Connection
Configuration
tool

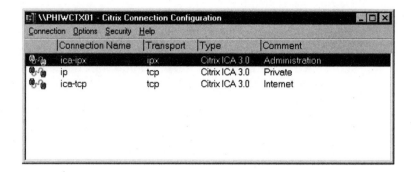

RDP, or Remote Display Protocol, is Microsoft's version of a thin-client protocol. RDP operates on many of the same principles as the ICA protocol. RDP allows users to access and control Windows Terminal Servers remotely, using a minimal amount of resources on the client device. However, the RDP protocol is not as robust as the ICA protocol. The RDP protocol only supports TCP/IP and lacks many of the ICA features that create a seamless user experience for Citrix clients. The ICA protocol also supports a wide range of client devices, and there is an ICA client available for almost every software platform. The client devices and platforms that RDP can support, on the other hand, are somewhat limited.

EXERCISE 6-3

CertCam 6-3

Creating an ICA Connection With the Citrix Connection Configuration tool

1. Open the Citrix Connection Configuration tool and select the New option from the Connection menu.

2. From the New Connection dialog box, name the connection **TEST**.

3. Set the connection type to ICA and select TCP as the transport type.

4. Select the Advanced button and adjust the Timeout settings so that the ICA connection will reset disconnected sessions after two minutes; then select the OK button to return to the New Connection dialog box.

5. Select the Client Settings button and check the option to Disable Audio Mapping; then select the OK button to return to the New Connection dialog box.

6. From the New Connection dialog box, select the OK button again to create the new ICA connection.

7. Open up the Citrix Server Administration tool and locate the Citrix server. Expanding the view of the server should now allow you to see the new listener you created.

Citrix administrators may need to create additional ICA listeners to provide users with connectivity to a Citrix server or published applications. By default, MetaFrame will create an ICA listener for each network protocol that is in use at the time of the MetaFrame installation. Administrators can use the Citrix Connection Configuration tool to edit the listeners that are created during the MetaFrame installation, but they may also want to use this tool to create additional listeners. Opening the Citrix Connection Configuration tool will provide administrators with a list of the existing listeners and the options to create new listeners. Selecting New from the Connection menu brings up the New Connection dialog box (as shown in Figure 6-11).

FIGURE 6-11

Creating a new connection

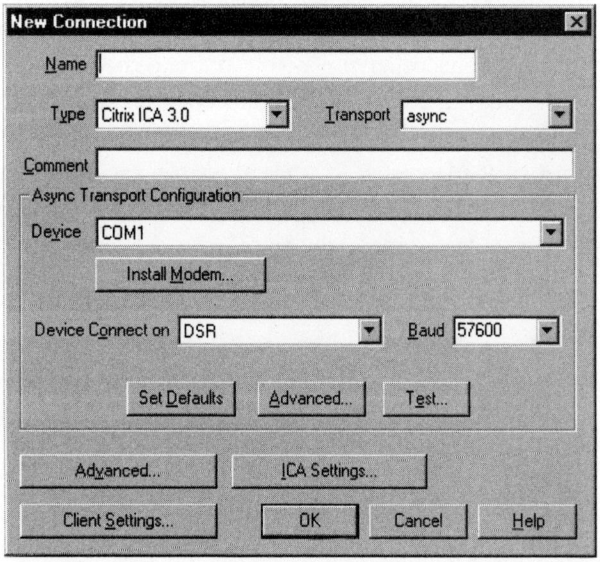

When creating a new connection, administrators will need to select a name for the listener. Each listener on a Citrix server needs to have a unique name. Administrators must also select the connection type and transport for the new listener. The connection type will determine what transport options are available for the connection. If the connection type is set to use RDP, the only transport option that is available will be TCP. Setting the connection type to use ICA will provide more options to select from in the transport field. ICA can be transported over TCP, IPX, SPX, NetBIOS, and async (asynchronous) connections. When a transport option is selected, administrators will see an additional set of transport configuration options in the New Connection dialog box.

on the
Job

Part of your responsibilities as a Citrix administrator will be to ensure that your network is secure and reliable. In a Citrix environment where users need access to Novel resources, you may require IPX on your Citrix servers. When MetaFrame is installed, ICA listeners will be created for each network protocol. If your user population is accessing the Citrix server over TCP/IP, you may want to delete the ICA listeners that were created for IPX.

If the transport option is set to use a network protocol, administrators will see a list of network adapters configured for the selected protocol. By default, the listener will be bound to all the LAN (local area network) adapters that are configured with the selected protocol, and there will be unlimited connections available on the listener. An ICA listener can be restricted to allow a specified number of connections; otherwise, connectivity to the listener is only limited by Citrix licensing. Listeners can be bound to a specific LAN adapter if the Citrix server has multiple network adapters. Administrators may bind different listeners to different network adapters as a means of securing access to a Citrix server. Since each listener has its own set of security options, Citrix administrators can control who connects to a particular listener, how many users can access the listener simultaneously, and what configuration options will be set for those users.

exam
Watch

ICA connections are created with a default set of options. Before taking the CCA test, you should know what the default options are for a new ICA connection, as well as which options can be configured at the user level with User Manager For Domains.

If the transport option is set for asynchronous connections, administrators will see a list of devices that are available for asynchronous connectivity. A list of COM ports and/or modems will be displayed, along with a set of options for the device being used. Async connections have many of the same security features as network connections, but each Async listener is limited to one connection. Asynchronous connections also have additional configuration options not available with network connections. If asynchronous connections are configured for dial-up access, the properties of the selected modem are accessible through the Citrix Connection Configuration tool. Administrators may wish to alter modem settings or configure modem callback using the Citrix Connection Configuration tool.

After creating a new ICA listener, Citrix administrators can use the Citrix Connection Configuration tool to alter the settings of the listener at a later time. Opening the Citrix Connection Configuration tool provides administrators with a list of listeners installed by default, as well as any additional listeners created. Administrators can double-click any of the listeners to access the properties of that particular listener, or highlight the listener and select the Edit option from the Connection menu. Viewing the properties of a selected listener will show the basic configuration information for that listener, along with the following buttons that can be used for managing more detailed configuration options:

- **ICA Settings**   This button provides access to the client audio settings, which can be set to low, medium, or high. Higher audio quality requires more bandwidth.

- **Client Settings**   This button is used for configuring the client settings for a selected listener. Administrators will have access to information, such as client mapping options (as shown in Figure 6-12). Some of these options are available at a user level and can be inherited from a user's configuration.

- **Advanced Settings**   This button allows administrators to manage the advanced options of a selected listener. Administrators can apply a number of different configurations here to secure incoming connections for a selected listener. Many of these options are also available on a user level and can be inherited from a user's configuration.

The Client Settings button, which can be located by editing the properties of an ICA listener, provides access to several settings that are used to restrict access to certain client mappings. By default, a Citrix server will map resources from the Citrix server to an ICA client device to provide a seamless user experience. When an ICA client logs on to a Citrix server, the server will map its own resources to the

FIGURE 6-12

Configuring
Client Settings

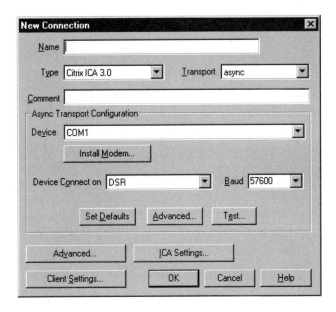

appropriate resource of the client device so the user can utilize local resources from within an ICA session. However, Citrix administrators may want to restrict access to all or some of these local resources.

Now that you are familiar with the Citrix Connection Configuration utility, let's look at some possible scenarios you may run into as a Citrix administrator.

SCENARIO & SOLUTION

Some ICA clients may experience timeout settings when accessing a Citrix server, while other users do not. Other than the Citrix Connection Configuration tool, where can these settings be imposed?	User Manager For Domains provides administrators the capability of imposing timeout settings for individual users. Timeout settings that have been configured for a Citrix server will override user settings.
You have noticed that the user count is not evenly distributed across the Citrix Servers in your server farm. You find out that some users have created custom ICA connections to specific servers. What can be done to resolve this issue?	Within the Citrix Connection Configuration tool, ICA connections can be configured to allow access to published applications only. Using this feature will keep users from creating custom connections to the server.

Using the Citrix Connection Configuration tool, Citrix administrators can disable all or some of the resources mapped by default. This includes ICA client drives, ports, and printers. ICA clients also map to the client's clipboard, so the user can cut and paste between ICA sessions and local applications. Administrators can configure an ICA listener so it does not map these resources at logon. If a resource is not configured to map during a session logon, the resource can be mapped after logging on to the server. If an administrator does not want users to map resources after logging on, the resource mapping must be disabled in the Citrix Connection Configuration tool.

Some of the options in the Citrix Connection Configuration tool are available at the user level using Microsoft's User Manager For Domains or by using the Active Directory Users and Computers utility in Windows 2000. ICA listeners can be configured to use the settings that have been established at a user level or to override any settings that have been applied at a user level. Establishing these settings at a user level provides a higher level of granularity, but also creates more administrative overhead.

Citrix administrators should pay close attention to the configuration of client printers. With such a wide array of client devices and printers, Citrix administrators may find themselves overwhelmed by printing issues. Between technically "challenged" end users and the importance of printing, some administrators may even be tempted to send each user a camera and ask them to take pictures of their screens! On the other hand, a few simple configuration changes may keep the printing problems in check. The Other Options section of the Client Settings has an option for only connecting to a client's default printer. If this option is left unchecked, the Citrix server will attempt to map every printer the client is using. In small Citrix environments, this may not present an issue, but a Citrix server with higher user volume may experience problems.

There are several advanced settings that can be configured for a selected ICA connection. The Advanced button can be found by editing the settings of an ICA connection, and provides administrators with access to the Advanced Connection Settings dialog box, shown in Figure 6-13. From here administrators have several options:

- **Logon Disable/Enable**   This option simply gives Citrix administrators the ability to enable or disable logons for a selected listener. Selecting this option will keep users from connecting to a selected listener without taking the server offline or making serious configuration changes.

- **Timeout Settings** Timeout settings can be configured to terminate connected, disconnected, or idle sessions after a given amount of time elapses. Administrators may wish to use a combination of these settings to keep users from inadvertently wasting server resources. Citrix users may not know the difference between disconnecting from a remote session and logging off from a session, in which case administrators may want to configure timeout settings so that disconnected sessions will be reset.

- **Security Required Encryption** This feature can be used to set the desired level of data encryption for the listener. If the required encryption is set higher than basic encryption, the ICA client must be configured to use a higher level of encryption. This feature also has an option for using Default NT Authentication. If Default NT Authentication is in use, users on the selected connection will be authenticated using the default NT authentication DLL (Dynamic Link Library), regardless of any other authentication packages installed on the server.

- **On Broken Or Timed-Out Connection** This option specifies how the server handles sessions that are erroneously disconnected or timed-out. Broken sessions are configured to disconnect by default, but sessions can be configured to reset if the session is broken or timed-out.

- **Reconnect Session Disconnected** With this feature, Citrix administrators can allow users to reconnect to disconnected sessions from any client device. This option can also be set so users can only reconnect to a disconnected session from the client device that began the session.

- **Shadowing** Shadowing can be enabled or disabled with this feature. It also allows administrators to turn input and prompting on or off for the selected listener.

- **AutoLogon** The AutoLogon option can be configured so all connections to a selected listener automatically log on with a specified user account. However, administrators should carefully consider the security implications of using this option. If this option is used carelessly, administrators may not be able to control who accesses the Citrix server.

- **Initial Program** This feature allows administrators to specify a program that will be run automatically for all sessions that connect to a selected listener. This feature will also give administrators the ability to configure the listener to only allow access to published applications.

- **User Profile Overrides**   This option simply allows administrators to disable wallpaper that is associated with a user's profile. Some users may have graphically intensive wallpaper associated with their mandatory or roaming profile. Disabling wallpaper could provide these users with better performance over slow network connections.

Many of the options found in the Advanced Connection Settings are available in User Manager For Domains. The same options can also be found in the Active Directory Users and Computers utility in Windows 2000. The settings that can be configured on a user level have an option for inheriting the user configuration. Any settings configured for a specific server listener will override settings applied at the user level.

FIGURE 6-13
Configuring Advanced Connection Settings

CERTIFICATION OBJECTIVE 6.04

Configuring the SpeedScreen Latency Reduction Manager

One of the contributing factors to the success of Citrix technology is the performance it provides over slow network connections. The ICA protocol offers exceptional performance over slow network connections by transmitting only keystrokes, mouse clicks, and screen updates. However, users connecting over a slow network or a dial-up connection may experience some degree of latency. During an ICA session, users may experience significant delays between their actions and what appears on their screen. They may, for example, be entering test on their keyboard, but not be able to see the text on their screen for several seconds. In addition to latency with the keyboard, users may experience similar behavior when using their mouse. Users may click their mouse several times before seeing any actions on the screen; such "overclicking" can be very frustrating to users.

Citrix has recognized this issue and responded by creating a new Citrix feature that helps address these types of issues. The SpeedScreen Latency Reduction Manager (Figure 6-14) is a utility that addresses these types of issues by providing local text echoing and mouse click feedback to ICA client devices. The SpeedScreen Latency Reduction Manager is included with MetaFrame XP and can be added to MetaFrame 1.8 with the installation of Feature Release 1 for MetaFrame. The two key features of the SpeedScreen Latency Reduction Manager are

- **Local text echo** This feature provides instant feedback to the screen of an ICA session when a user is entering text from a keyboard.
- **Mouse click feedback** This feature changes the mouse pointer to an hourglass so users will not click multiple times.

SpeedScreen Latency Reduction settings can be applied to servers, applications, and input fields of a specified application. Any settings configured for a specific application will override settings that have been applied to the whole server. Additionally, settings that have been applied server-wide will be used for all the applications on the server. By default, the SpeedScreen settings for a server are set as shown in Figure 6-15. Local text echo is not enabled by default, but mouse click

FIGURE 6-14

The SpeedScreen
Latency
Reduction
Manager

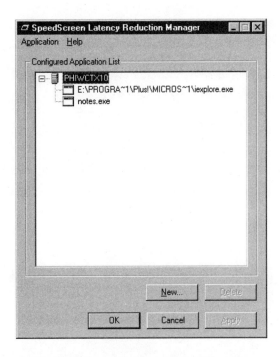

feedback is. Additional server-wide settings include Latency threshold times, which tell the client device when to enable or disable SpeedScreen options. SpeedScreen options at the ICA client device can be turned on or off, or they can be set to auto.

FIGURE 6-15

SpeedScreen
Server Properties

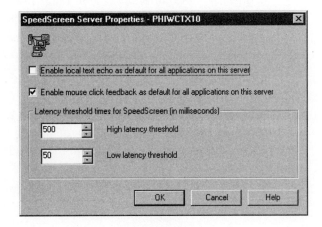

CertCam 6-4

EXERCISE 6-4

Configuring a Citrix Server and an Application with the SpeedScreen Latency Reduction Manager

1. Open the SpeedScreen Latency Reduction Manager.

2. Right-click the Citrix server for access to the SpeedScreen server properties and select the option to enable local text echoing; then select OK.

3. From within the SpeedScreen Latency Reduction Manager, use the New button to define SpeedScreen settings for a specific application.

4. Using the wizard, select Notepad. Notepad.exe should now be listed in the Configured Application List.

5. From the Configured Application List, select Notepad and right-click for access to the application settings.

6. From the Application Settings dialog box, select the option to disable local text echoing. This setting is located under the Application Properties tab.

7. You have now created a set of default SpeedScreen options for a Citrix server, and a set of SpeedScreen options for a specific application. The SpeedScreen settings of the Notepad application will override the server settings.

8. You can test these settings by creating an ICA session to the Citrix server over a slow network connection. By running Notepad alongside Internet Explorer, you should be able to notice the different behavior of text echoing when you type in the applications. Typing in the address bar of Internet Explorer will display text echoing, but typing within Notepad will not.

If the client SpeedScreen options are set to Auto, the client will use the threshold times set for the server to decide when to use SpeedScreen options. If an ICA client detects network latency that is higher than the *High Latency Threshold*, SpeedScreen options will be enabled for the connection. If an ICA client detects network latency that is lower than the *Low Latency Threshold*, SpeedScreen options will be disabled for the connection.

The SpeedScreen Latency Reduction Manager is used to enhance user experience over slow network connections. SpeedScreen settings can be applied to servers, applications, and input fields. If settings are applied in multiple locations, you should know which settings override other settings.

Citrix administrators may wish to configure default SpeedScreen Latency options for a specific server but alter the SpeedScreen behavior for specific applications. From within the SpeedScreen Latency Reduction Manager, administrators can configure the behavior of specific applications by selecting the New button or by selecting New from the Application menu. This option begins a wizard that Citrix administrators use to define the application, or application instance, that they wish to configure. The wizard allows administrators to browse to a selected application or use a drag-and-drop option to define the application. Once it has been defined, administrators can edit the properties of the application in greater detail.

The default view of the SpeedScreen Latency Reduction Manager will display a list of configured applications. Right-clicking a selected application will provide access to the SpeedScreen application settings. The application settings for SpeedScreen behavior are also accessible by highlighting an application and selecting Properties from the Application menu. The Application Settings dialog box is divided into Application Properties (Figure 6-16) and Input Field Configuration (Figure 6-17).

The Application Properties tab will display the name of the application and the path to a specific installation of an application. If there is no path defined for the application, the SpeedScreen settings will be applied to all instances of the application. Local text echo can be disabled for a specific application without interfering with the SpeedScreen behavior of any other applications. Administrators can also use this tab to configure the display of local text echoing for an application. Local text echoing can be displayed in a floating bubble or displayed in place. Displaying text in a floating bubble can help users recognize when SpeedScreen functionality is being used. The *Advanced* button has a single option that can be used to minimize the SpeedScreen functionality of any input fields that have been configured for an application.

The Input Field Configuration tab allows administrators to select specific input fields to configure for a selected application, as shown in Figure 6-17. The SpeedScreen Latency Reduction Manager recognizes input fields by the Windows Class Name of the selected input field of an application. When creating a new input field for an application, the application must be running on the Citrix server. There

FIGURE 6-16

Application
SpeedScreen
Settings

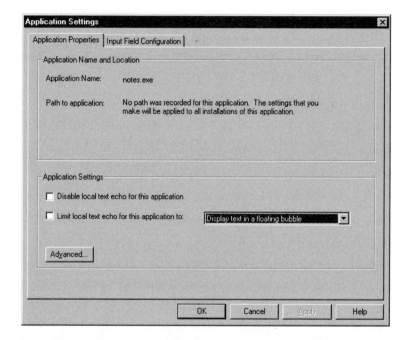

FIGURE 6-17

Application Input
Field settings

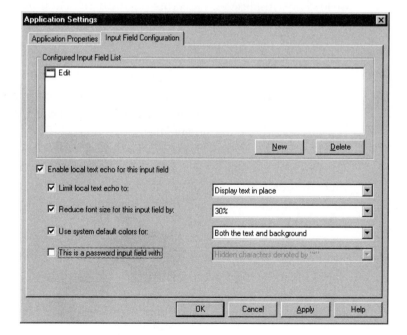

is an Input Field Configuration wizard that allows administrators to drag an icon over the input field of an application. Releasing the mouse over the desired field selects the field class to be configured. Once an input field has been defined, administrators can configure SpeedScreen behavior that will be exhibited for that input field. If local text echoing is enabled for an input field, the following options are available for configuration:

- **Limit Local Text Echo To:** Text can be configured to display in place or in a floating bubble. A floating bubble is more indicative of SpeedScreen usage.

- **Reduce Font Size For This Field By:** Text can be configured so the font size is reduced by 10, 20, or 30 percent. This option may need to be used for non-standard input fields if text echoing is being displayed improperly.

- **Use System Default Colors For:** This option can be set for the background of an input field or for the text and background of an input field. System default colors may need to be used for nonstandard input fields, which may not display text echoing properly.

- **This Is A Password Input Field With:** This option should be configured for all password fields so the local text echoing does not display a password in clear text. If this option is checked, the local text echoing will display spaces or asterisks instead of text.

CERTIFICATION SUMMARY

Citrix MetaFrame XP gives Citrix administrators access to the tools they need to manage a Citrix environment from a centralized point of control. The Citrix Server Administration tool is designed so administrators can monitor and manage Citrix servers and Citrix users from any location. The Citrix Connection Configuration utility also provides administrators with a powerful management tool. The Citrix Connection Configuration tool is used to create and edit ICA and RDP connections for a particular Citrix server. Unlike the Citrix Server Administration tool, the Citrix Connection Configuration tool must be used from the Citrix server that is being managed.

Some MetaFrame features are intended for management purposes, while other features are simply designed to provide users with acceptable performance. The Shadow Taskbar is only one of several ways in which a Citrix administrator can shadow an ICA session. Although shadowing is available in other Citrix utilities, the Shadow Taskbar provides functionality that some other utilities lack. The SpeedScreen Latency Reduction Manager is a feature of Citrix that administrators can use to address latency issues. SpeedScreen settings can be applied to a Citrix server or application, providing local text echo and mouse click feedback to users over slow network connections.

✓ TWO-MINUTE DRILL

Identifying Features of Citrix Server Administration

❑ The Citrix Server Administration tool is used to manage ICA settings, ICA gateways, and processes of Citrix servers.

❑ ICA sessions can be viewed, reset, disconnected, logged off, shadowed, and connected to from within the Citrix Server Administration tool.

❑ The context pane of the Citrix Server Administration tool controls the contents of the detail pane.

Shadowing with the Shadow Taskbar

❑ The Shadow Taskbar can shadow multiple ICA sessions simultaneously.

❑ Citrix administrators can use the Shadow Taskbar to shadow sessions from the console of a Citrix server.

❑ The ICA client on the Citrix server creates a separate ICA session for each user that is being shadowed.

❑ The Shadow Taskbar can be configured for shadowing ICA sessions over alternate ICA ports.

Creating Connections with the Citrix Connection Configuration

❑ ICA and RDP connections can be created, viewed, and edited using the Citrix Connection Configuration tool.

❑ The Citrix Connection Configuration tool can be used for restricting the number of sessions allowed by a connection.

❑ Control the security and encryption settings of ICA and RDP connections.

Configuring the SpeedScreen Latency Reduction Manager

❑ The SpeedScreen Latency Reduction Manager is used to enhance user experience over slow network connections.

❑ SpeedScreen settings can be configured for Citrix servers, applications, and input fields of applications.

❑ SpeedScreen settings configured for an application will override any settings that have been configured for a Citrix server.

❑ By default, local text echoing is turned off, and mouse click feedback is turned on.

SELF TEST

The following questions will help you measure your understanding of the material presented in this chapter. Read all the choices carefully as there may be more than one correct answer. Choose all correct answers for each question.

Identifying Features of Citrix Server Administration

1. The ABC Company wants to create a single server farm to provide users access to a customized application. As the Citrix administrator, you have been asked to create this server farm. Your Citrix environment consists of six MetaFrame XP servers in New York and five MetaFrame 1.8 servers in San Francisco. There is a WAN link between the two offices, and each office has only one subnet. What is your best strategy for creating this server farm?

   A. Establish an ICA gateway between the two subnets using the Citrix Server Administration tool and create the server farm using the Published Application Manager.

   B. Move all the servers in New York to San Francisco and create the server farm using the Published Application Manager.

   C. Move all the servers in San Francisco to New York and create the server farm using the Published Application Manager.

   D. Install RMS on all servers.

2. The Citrix Server Administration tool allows administrators to alter all but which of the following features?

   A. ICA gateways

   B. ICA client settings

   C. ICA browser election preferences

   D. Published Application settings

3. A Citrix user in your company is having problems printing to a network printer from their ICA client device. Other Citrix users with the same client devices can print to the same printer without any problems. Where is the best place to look in the Citrix Server Administrator to begin troubleshooting this issue?

   A. Right-click the server from the context pane.

   B. Right-click the user from the context pane

   C. Select the server from the context pane and then the Information tab in the detail pane.

   D. Select the user from the context pane and then the Information tab in the detail pane.

4. What server always maintains an ICA browse list?

   A. The XML (Extensible Markup Language) gateway server

   B. The primary domain controller

   C. The ICA Master browser

   D. The backup domain controller

Shadowing with the Shadow Taskbar

5. What are some advantages of using the Shadow Taskbar instead of the Citrix Server Administration tool to shadow ICA sessions.

   A. Administrators can change ICA settings of a Citrix server with the Shadow Taskbar.

   B. The Shadow Taskbar allows administrators to shadow an ICA session from the console of a Citrix server.

   C. The Shadow Taskbar can be installed on Windows 95, 98, or NT.

   D. The Shadow Taskbar supports shadowing multiple sessions simultaneously.

6. Which of the following Citrix utilities will allow administrators to shadow an ICA session?

   A. The Citrix Server Administration utility

   B. The Citrix Management Console

   C. The Shadow Taskbar

   D. All of the above

7. The Shadow Taskbar creates a separate ICA session for each user session being shadowed. What technology is used for creating these sessions?

   A. Java Beans

   B. The ICA client

   C. ICA gateways

   D. The ICA browse list

8. Using the Citrix Server Administration tool, you are shadowing an ICA session to troubleshoot an issue. Several other users are having the same issue and you would like to shadow all the users simultaneously. What is the best way to do this?

   A. From the command line of the server.

   B. Right-click Multiple Users from the detail pane of the Citrix Server Administration tool and select Shadow.

C. Right-click Multiple Users from the context pane of the Citrix Server Administration tool and select Shadow.

D. Exit the Citrix Server Administration tool and use the Shadow Taskbar.

9. The Shadow Taskbar supports all but which of the following capabilities?

A. Shadowing ICA sessions from a server console

B. Shadowing multiple ICA sessions simultaneously

C. Shadowing ICA sessions over alternate TCP ports

D. Shadowing the console session of a Citrix server

Creating Connections with the Citrix Connection Configuration

10. You have a MetaFrame XP server running TCP/IP and IPX to provide clients with access to published applications over the Internet. You want to provide clients with ten concurrent connections. You also want to connect to the server from your workstation without consuming a client connection. What is the easiest way to accomplish this?

A. Disable the ICA connections from the Citrix Connection Configuration tool.

B. Install a second network adapter card on the Citrix server.

C. Limit the ICA-TCP connection to ten connections and create an ICA-IPX connection for management.

D. Restrict connectivity to the server by using the Licensing Manager.

11. Within the Citrix Connection Configuration tool you have configured Timeout settings to inherit any settings configured at a user level. One particular user keeps complaining she is being disconnected from the server after ten minutes of inactivity. What is a possible cause of this problem?

A. Timeout settings have been configured for the specific user to reset idle sessions after ten minutes.

B. Timeout settings have been configured for the specific user to reset connected sessions after ten minutes.

C. Timeout settings have been configured for the Citrix server to reset idle sessions after ten minutes.

D. Timeout settings have been configured for the Citrix sever to reset disconnected sessions after ten minutes.

12. RDP connections are supported over which network protocols?

A. IPX

B. ICA

C. SPX

D. TCP

13. Your company has established connectivity to a Citrix server at a customer location for access to their payroll system. To simplify firewall rules, you have decided to connect your users to a Citrix server on your network. From your Citrix server, users have an ICA file for accessing the remote Citrix server at the customer location. The Citrix administrator at the customer location notices that there are hundreds of printers configured for your users. What should you do to prevent unnecessary printers from being created on your customer's Citrix server?

A. Delete all current printers from you local server.

B. Use the Citrix Connection Configuration tool to configure ICA connections to only connect to a client's main printer.

C. Upgrade the print drivers on your client workstations.

D. Use the Citrix Connection Configuration tool to disable Windows Printer mapping.

14. How can a specific ICA connection be disabled?

A. Disable the ICA connection using the Citrix Connection Configuration tool.

B. Highlight the server in the Citrix Server Administration utility and select disable logons.

C. Use the Qserver command from a command line.

D. Create an RDP connection from the Citrix Connection Configuration tool.

15. How many ICA connections are created by default during the installation of MetaFrame?

A. One for each RDP connection

B. One for each network protocol

C. One for each active user

D. None of the above

16. ICA connections support which of the following network protocols?

A. IPX

B. SPX

C. TCP

D. All of the above

Configuring the SpeedScreen Latency Reduction Manager

17. The SpeedScreen Latency Reduction Manager can be configured to provide SpeedScreen options at which of the following levels?

A. Server

B. User

C. Application

D. Process

18. You are the administrator of a Citrix MetaFrame environment that provides access to published applications over dial-up networking connections. You have configured server-wide SpeedScreen settings for local text echo and mouse click feedback. Some of the nonstandard applications are not displaying text echo properly. What would be the best solution to this issue?

A. Disable mouse click feedback for the specified application.

B. Disable local text echo for the server.

C. Disable local text echo for the application.

D. All of the above.

19. You have imposed several settings to a Citrix server using the SpeedScreen Latency Reduction Manager to improve performance for dial-up networking users. What must be done to an ICA client before it will take advantage of these settings?

A. The ICA client must be configured for a full-screen connection.

B. The appsrv.ini file must be deleted from the user profile directory.

C. The ICA client must be configured to use 256 colors.

D. None of the above.

20. Your company has a group of users who connect to published applications over slow network connections. You have enabled SpeedScreen settings for some of the applications. Your boss has informed you that the users are upset because the text echo feature is displaying passwords for password input fields of a specific application. Using the SpeedScreen Latency Reduction Manager, what can you do to fix this problem?

A. Disable text echo for the application.

B. Disable text echo for the password-input fields.

C. Set the password-input option to hide characters for the password-input fields.

D. All of the above.

LAB QUESTION

You have recently become the administrator of a large Citrix environment that is distributed across four different geographical locations. Each location has between 20 and 30 Citrix servers that are used for access to client data. Each location houses data for different clients, and all the users in your company need access to client data at each location. In addition to internal users, clients will need to access their own data using Citrix.

The consultants who deployed the Citrix solution for your company created server farms in each of the four locations. A customer server farm and an employee server farm were created in each of the four locations, for a total of eight Citrix server farms. Being a new Citrix administrator in this environment, you notice a few problems right away. Users cannot figure out which server farm to use for which clients. In addition, your helpdesk does not know which server farm people are using when they call in with support issues.

You want to improve this environment and make it more supportable by providing all Citrix users with a standard client configuration that allows them to access client data at each of the four locations. You also want to give the helpdesk a standard way of emulating users who call for support. How will you go about implementing these improvements?

SELF TEST ANSWERS

Identifying Features of Citrix Server Administration

1. ☑ A is correct. Establishing an ICA gateway between two subnets allows the ICA browsers to obtain updates from servers on both subnets. This functionality is required to create a server farm across multiple subnets.

☒ B and C would solve the problem, but this is not the best option. As for D, RMS is not an integral part of creating a server farm.

2. ☑ B and D are correct. ICA client settings and published application settings cannot be altered through the Citrix Server Administration tool.

☒ A and C are incorrect because these settings can be managed using the Citrix Server Administration tool.

3. ☑ D is correct. Selecting a user from the context pane provides an Information tab in the detail pane that can be used for viewing detailed information regarding the user's ICA session.

☒ A, B, and C are incorrect because they will not provide you with any information regarding the user's ICA client or session.

4. ☑ C is correct. The ICA Master browser maintains a list of servers, farms, applications, and load data for the entire subnet.

☒ A is incorrect because the XML gateway, which is used with NFuse, may or may not be an ICA Master browser. B and D are incorrect because MetaFrame should not be installed on a domain controller.

Shadowing with the Shadow Taskbar

5. ☑ B and D are correct. The Shadow Taskbar uses the ICA client installed on a Citrix Server to create a separate ICA session for each user being shadowed. This functionality allows administrators to shadow several users at once from an ICA session or from the console of a Citrix server.

☒ A is incorrect because ICA settings are altered through the Citrix Server Administration tool. C is incorrect because the Shadow Taskbar is a feature of MetaFrame that cannot be installed on a non-Citrix platform.

6. ☑ D is correct. ICA sessions can be shadowed from all of the utilities mentioned.

7. ☑ B is correct. The Shadow Taskbar uses the ICA client on the Citrix server to create a separate ICA session for each user being shadowed.

☒   **A, C,** and **D** are incorrect because the Shadow Taskbar does not use these technologies for creating ICA sessions.

8.   ☑   **D** is correct because the Shadow Taskbar will allow you to shadow several users simultaneously.
☒   **A** is incorrect because shadowing from a command line only allows you to shadow one user at a time. **B** and **C** are incorrect because the Citrix Server Administration tool only allows you to shadow one user at a time as well.

9.   ☑   **D** is correct because the console session of a Citrix server cannot be shadowed.
☒   **A, B,** and **C** are incorrect because the Shadow Taskbar supports all of these capabilities.

Creating Connections with the Citrix Connection Configuration

10.   ☑   **C** is correct because it is a quick configuration change.
☒   **A** is incorrect because it will disable access to the server altogether. **B** is incorrect because installing a network adapter does not change the attributes of ICA connections. **D** is incorrect because you cannot restrict connectivity for specific ICA connections using the Licensing Manager.

11.   ☑   **A** is the correct answer because the user is experiencing disconnects after a period of inactivity.
☒   **B, C,** and **D** are incorrect because these settings do not apply to session inactivity.

12.   ☑   **D** is correct. RDP is only supported over TCP.
☒   **A, B,** and **C** are incorrect because RDP cannot be transported over these protocols.

13.   ☑   **B** is correct because you only want to remove printers that are unnecessary.
☒   **A** is incorrect because the printers will be re-created when the users log back on to the server. **C** is incorrect because client print drivers will not prevent a Citrix server from mapping to all the client's printers. **D** is incorrect because it will completely disable printing.

14.   ☑   **A** is correct. ICA connections can be disabled from within the Citrix Connection Configuration tool.
☒   **B** is incorrect because it will disable logons to the entire server, not just a specific ICA connection. **C** is incorrect because the Qserver command will not disable an ICA connection. **D** is incorrect because creating an RDP connection will not alter the attributes of the existing ICA connections.

15.   ☑   **B** is correct. One ICA connection is created for each network protocol during the MetaFrame installation process.
☒   **A** and **C** are incorrect because these options are not taken into consideration when the ICA connections are being created by the MetaFrame installation process.

16. ☑ D is correct. ICA is supported over TCP, IPX, SPX, and NetBIOS.

Configuring the SpeedScreen Latency Reduction Manager

17. ☑ A and C are correct. The SpeedScreen Latency Reduction Manager can configure SpeedScreen settings for a Citrix server, an application, or input fields within an application.
    ☒ B and D are incorrect because SpeedScreen settings cannot be applied at a user or process level.

18. ☑ C is correct because application settings will override any server settings that have been configured in the SpeedScreen Latency Reduction Manager.
    ☒ A is incorrect because mouse click feedback does not provide local text echoing. **B** is incorrect because it is not the best solution to the problem, this option would disable text echo for all applications on the server.

19. ☑ D is correct. None of these options will enable the SpeedScreen settings on the client. The connection must have SpeedScreen options turned to On or Auto for the ICA client to use SpeedScreen functionality.
    ☒ A, B, and C are incorrect because they do not alter SpeedScreen settings for the ICA client.

20. ☑ D is correct. All of these solutions will address the issue. However, you may want to leave text echo enabled for as many resources as you can. In which case, the best solution would be **C**.

LAB ANSWER

The first thing you will need to do is create ICA gateways to and from each location so that the Citrix servers in each spot can communicate with the servers from the other three locations. Keep in mind that ICA gateways are not transitive, so you will have to create three gateways at each location. Once all the Citrix servers can communicate with each other, they can be consolidated into one server farm. If you create a single server farm that spans all four locations, you can allow users to access resources in all those locations by creating a connection to only one server farm. Using the features of load balancing, you can create published applications that exist only on the servers in the location of the client's data. If all Citrix users are accessing the same server farm, your helpdesk will be able to provide a higher level of support. By creating a connection to the single server farm, helpdesk staff can emulate any user's environment by simply logging onto the farm with the user's credentials.

7

Load Management and Security

S ecurity and load management are two of the most important features in MetaFrame XP. The load management feature of MetaFrame XP comes with the XPe or Xpa versions. XPs does not have load management capabilities. As the administrator of a MetaFrame server farm, you must understand the entire load management system. This process starts with the creation of load evaluators and ends with your users being routed to the least busy server hosting your applications.

However, as an administrator, you must also understand each of your security options. How each piece of the security puzzle is configured, how it works, and when to use it are keys to a successful deployment. Security, as described in this chapter, affects all revisions of MetaFrame XP, including XPs.

The exam is sure to test your knowledge on both of these topics. Do not focus your attention more on one part of this chapter than the other. Both are equally important.

CERTIFICATION OBJECTIVE 7.01

Analyzing Load with Load Manager

When using Citrix's load management feature, you first must understand what it was intended for and how it actually works. Load management, or load balancing, is intended to route new client connections to the least busy server in the farm. It determines which server is the least busy by using a set of configurable rules called load evaluators.

Load evaluators are extremely flexible load balancing criteria. MetaFrame XP installs with two evaluators: Default and Advanced. You will learn how to configure and use load evaluators as you progress through this chapter.

Load Management

At its basic level, a Citrix server will calculate its load based on the number of users logged into the server. This load is then sent to the zone's data collector as a numeric value called a load index. The data collector stores this load information for each server in the zone.

When a client attempts to make a connection to a published application, the data collector sorts through the load information from each server, then routes the client connection to the server with the lowest load index. This load balancing happens only during the initial connection of a MetaFrame client. No dynamic rebalancing takes place between MetaFrame servers. If a MetaFrame server fails while users are logged on, these sessions are not dynamically transferred to another server. Instead, the sessions are terminated, and the user must reconnect to another server in the farm. This makes load balancing a high-availability solution, but not a fault-tolerant solution.

Figure 7-1 shows a common connection sequence in a load-balanced environment. The client will request to run a published application. The zone data collector will respond to the client with the address of the least busy server hosting that application. The client will then connect to that server and launch the application.

FIGURE 7-1   Example of a connection to a load-balanced application

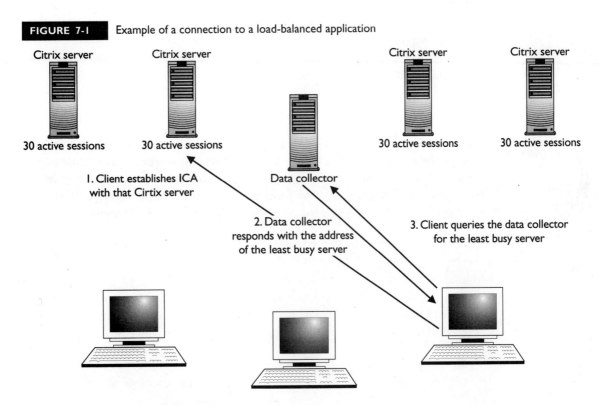

Load index numbers are generated at the individual MetaFrame server. The MetaFrame servers use load evaluators to determine what their current load is. When the load for a server changes, whether it increases or decreases, this new information is sent to the zone data collector. This means all new client connections are routed through the data collector.

During the exam you must remember that load balancing only occurs during the initial client connection. Active client sessions are not dynamically rebalanced to other servers in the event that the server they are connected to goes down. They will be able to reconnect to another MetaFrame server, but all work they had open and unsaved in their previous session will be lost.

Load Evaluators

A load evaluator is a set of rules used to calculate load on a MetaFrame server in your farm. These load evaluators can be assigned to specific servers or to published applications in the MetaFrame farm.

Each rule within a load evaluator consists of an identifier, a description of the rule and threshold settings that can be adjusted on a rule-by-rule basis. A load evaluator can consist of only one rule or use many in concert. When several rules are used, the load management system uses the rules together to determine the overall load of the server.

An example of a single rule Evaluator would be an Evaluator that will only look at the current number of users logged into the server when calculating load, such as the Default evaluator. These evaluators will work just fine in small environments, but as your farm grows, it may be necessary to "tweak" your evaluators to look at your hardware bottlenecks more closely.

Load evaluators can be created, customized, deleted, and duplicated. They can also be assigned to published applications and to servers, all using the Citrix Management Console when using MetaFrame XP*a* or XP*e.*

Two evaluators, Default and Advanced, are installed with MetaFrame XP*a* or XP*e.* The Default evaluator is assigned to every Citrix MetaFrame server in the farm at install. These two evaluators can be copied and viewed but not edited or modified.

■ The Default evaluator is a single-rule evaluator based on the Server User Load rule. This rule is configured for a maximum user load of 100 simultaneous users. When the user count for a server reaches 100 user sessions, the load management system on that server will report full load and not allow any more connections.

■ The Advanced evaluator is a multiple-rule evaluator based on three rules: CPU utilization, memory usage, and page swap. The server that has this evaluator assigned to it will constantly monitor these three metrics and their predefined thresholds. If any one of the rules report full load, the server is considered at full load, and user connections are routed to another server.

Citrix recommends that all servers in the farm use the same load evaluator and that a threshold for a rule should never be set to the absolute maximum value that a server can handle. Example: You have baselined your servers and determined that they can handle 50 users. Above 50 users the performance drops dramatically. It is recommended that you set your rule, in this case, user count, to a little below 50, say 48 or 49. This will help to keep servers from becoming overwhelmed in the event the server is at full load, but a connection is routed to the server before the data collector is updated with the new load information.

Some environments may run a mix of hardware in their MetaFrame server farm. This may include dual and quad processor servers mixed together, or all of the servers could have the same number of processors with some having 1GHz and others running 400MHz processors. In these situations the default evaluator's performance may not be acceptable. The faster servers can handle more user load than the slower servers, but the load rules in the Default evaluator will route an even number of connections to each type of server. This can quickly overwhelm the slower machines and leave the faster servers underutilized. In this scenario, the Advanced evaluator can be applied to each of the servers. Since it monitors hardware performance and not the number of active sessions, load will be distributed evenly based on hardware utilization, not user count.

on the
ⓘo b

Assigning the same evaluator to every server in the farm will work for most MetaFrame environments, but if you are running a farm that has mixed hardware, this can be problematic. Let's say you have four quad processor servers capable of 100 users each. You also have four dual processor servers capable of 50 users each. In this case, assigning the default evaluator to every server may overload the duals because the load management system sees the duals and quads as the same and routes users equally to them. In a case like this, you may want to make two different evaluators, one for the smaller server and one for the larger servers, and assign them accordingly.

To create a new load evaluator, we can right-click the Load Evaluators node in the Management Console and select New Load Evaluator (see Figure 7-2), or we can select an existing load evaluator from the node. Then from the pop-up menu, select Duplicate. This will allow us to work with the existing rules in that evaluator.

In the New Evaluator dialog box, we are able to select our rules from the list of available rules on the left and add them to the list of configured rules on the right (see Figure 7-3). Once a rule is added to the configured list, it can then be edited to change its high or low thresholds. Then when you are finished creating the evaluator, you can save your changes by clicking OK.

Each rule within the evaluator has its own thresholds that can be configured by the administrator. These thresholds help you as the Citrix administrator to load-balance your servers with a mind on performance bottlenecks and the actual number of users your servers can handle. When any one of the rules reports full load the server is considered 100 percent busy and will accept no more client sessions.

FIGURE 7-2	
New Load Evaluator	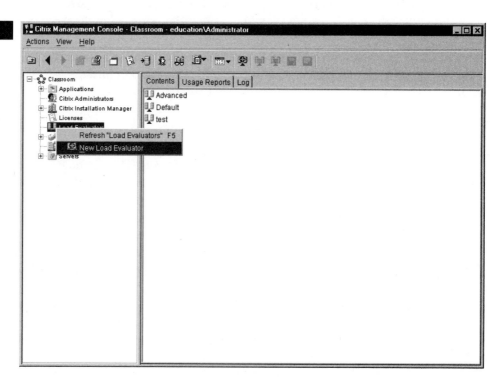

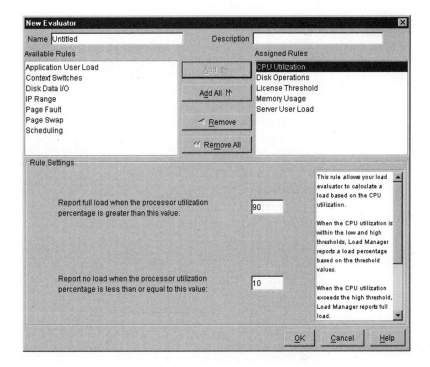

FIGURE 7-3

The New Load Evaluator dialog box

When the server is below 100 percent utilization, it will use all the rules assigned to the evaluator to determine how busy it is and to send that information to the zone's data collector.

Table 7-1 lists rules that are available for load evaluators.

TABLE 7-1 Assignable Rules for Load Evaluators

Application User Load	By default, reports full load when the number of users using a selected application is greater than 100. (Only works with MetaFrame XP; will not function in Mixed mode.)
Context Switches	Monitors the number of context switches on the server. By default, this will report full load when the number of context switches is greater than 16,000 per second and will report no load when the number of context switches is less than 900 per second.

TABLE 7-1	Assignable Rules for Load Evaluators *(continued)*
CPU Utilization	Monitors overall processor utilization. This rule, by default, will report full load when processor utilization is greater than 90 percent and will report no load when processor utilization is less than 10 percent.
Disk Data I/O	Monitors Disk I/O per second in kilobytes. This rule, by default, will report full load when the total disk I/O in kilobytes per second is greater than 32,767 and will report no load when the disk I/O in kilobytes per second is equal to 0.
Disk Operations	Monitors Disk reads/writes per second. This rule, by default, will report full load when the number of disk operations are greater than 100 per second and will report no load when the disk operations are equal to 0.
IP Range	This rule monitors the Client's Transmission Control Protocol/Internet Protocol (TCP/IP) address. Within this rule, you are able to allow or disallow one, or several, ranges of IP addresses.
License Threshold	Monitors both assigned and pooled MetaFrame XP connection licenses in use on the server. This rule, by default, will report full load when either the number of assigned licenses in use is greater than 10 or the number of pooled licenses in use is greater than 50. By default, it will also report no load when either of these counts is equal to 0.
Memory Usage	Monitors the percentage of physical memory in use. This rule, by default, will report full load when the memory in use is greater than 90 percent and will report no load when the memory in use is less than 10 percent.
Page Fault	Monitors the number of page faults per second. This rule, by default, will report full load when the number of page faults a second are greater than 100 and will report no load when the number of page faults a second are equal to 0.
Page Swap	Monitors number of page swap operations per second. This rule, by default, will report full load when the number of page swaps are greater than 100 and will report no load when the number of page swaps a second are equal to 0.
Scheduling	This rule allows an administrator to schedule a time at which the server will report full or no load. It will also allow or deny access to a server or published applications on that server during certain hours.
Server User Load	Monitors the number of active client sessions on the server. This rule, by default, will report full load when the user load reaches 100 and will report no load when the user load is equal to 0.

Now that you have a better idea of load management, here are some possible scenario questions and their answers:

SCENARIO & SOLUTION

You have three servers. All three support 50 users each. You notice though that when one server goes down performance on the other two servers suffers greatly. What is going on?	Load balancing is allowing the users that were dropped to reconnect to the remaining two servers. This is obviously overloading those servers and could possibly cause a domino effect, where each server may come down in turn. To resolve this, change the load evaluator for all three servers to allow only the number of users on the server that it can support.
You have recently created a new load evaluator that will limit the number of users who can log on to your server. You then wait a day and notice that the user count has not been limited to your amount and it is actually a lot higher than what you specified. What is the problem?	By just creating an evaluator you have done nothing more than build a set of rules. You must assign that evaluator to your servers in order for your rules to take effect.
You notice that several users have just logged off one of your servers, decreasing the load significantly. You wait several minutes, but none of your existing users are being routed to that server. What is the problem?	There is no problem. Load balancing only takes place at login. New users will be routed to this server, but existing connections will remain where they are currently.

EXERCISE 7-1

CertCam 7-1

Creating a Load Evaluator

1. Open the Citrix Management Console and locate the Load Evaluator node.

2. Right-click the Load Evaluator icon and select New Load Evaluator.

3. Name your evaluator LAB TEST.

4. Add in the following rules:

   ■ CPU Utilization

   ■ Memory Usage

   ■ Server User Load

5. Edit the threshold for Server User Load and set it to 15.

6. Save your load evaluator and ensure it is now displayed in the Load Evaluators node in the Citrix Management Console.

The larger your farm is the more likely you are to have several evaluators. Citrix has made it easy for you to track which evaluators are being used by applications and servers with the Usage Reports tab in the Load Evaluators node (see Figure 7-4). By selecting this tab, you are able to see a list of evaluators and sort through their usage by application, server, or by the evaluator's name. This report can come in handy when you are trying to delete an evaluator, and the Management Console continues to report that it is in use. A simple sort by evaluator in this report will allow you to find the server or application that has had the evaluator assigned.

FIGURE 7-4

Load evaluator usage reports

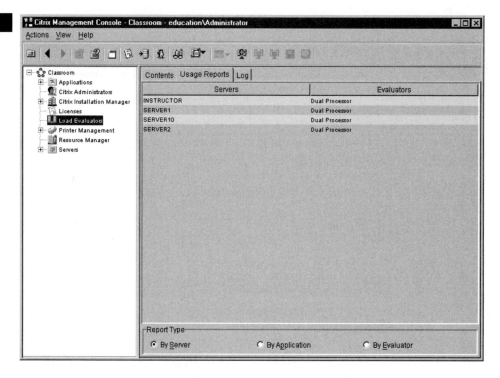

Calculating Load Values

Once your load evaluators are configured, you must now decide how to use them in the farm. Generally, you will define a need first, then create a load evaluator, but here we needed you to have a better understanding of what an evaluator was before you started assigning these evaluators to servers and applications.

In the preceding lab, you created a load evaluator. You have defined rules, and thresholds for those rules, but even though it appears in the Citrix Management Console, it is not currently being used by any server or application in the farm. It is merely a set of rules waiting to be assigned to a server or an application.

A load evaluator can be assigned to a specific server by right-clicking the server in the Servers node and selecting Load Manage Server. Then, in the Load Manage Server dialog box, you are able to select from the list of available evaluators and assign one to this server (see Figure 7-5). The server will immediately begin calculating load using the new evaluator. To verify this, you can return to the Load Evaluators node and use the Usage Reports tab to view your assignment.

FIGURE 7-5

The Load Manage Server dialog box

EXERCISE 7-2

Assigning a Load Evaluator to a MetaFrame Server

1. Select your server in the Citrix Management Console in the Servers node.

2. Select Load Manage Server by right-clicking on your server.

3. Select the load evaluator you created in the previous lab.

4. Close the Load Manage server dialog box.

5. In the Citrix Management Console, choose the Load Evaluators node; then select the Usage Reports tab.

6. Sort this list by load evaluator and verify that your server is using the proper evaluator.

Most load-balancing needs can be met by simply assigning an evaluator to your servers in the farm, but in some situations it may be beneficial to assign a load evaluator to a specific published application. A load evaluator can be assigned to a specific published application by right-clicking that application in the Applications node and selecting Load Manage Application. (See Figure 7-6.)

In the Load Manage Application dialog box, you can assign a different load evaluator to that application for every server on which it is load-balanced (see Figure 7-7). Generally, the same evaluator is assigned to each server load balancing the application, since multiple evaluators for one published application can be extremely difficult to track and manage.

Once you are load-balancing your applications, you will need to ensure that servers are utilized most efficiently. This will include tracking your servers' performance and determining whether your load evaluators are keeping them from being fully utilized. Using the load Manage Monitor, you can view the activity or rules assigned to the evaluator for the server. This monitor will show you the overall utilization based on the evaluator and will show you activity of each rule within the evaluator.

The Monitor is in a chart form, with the top of the chart representing 100 percent utilization or full load and the bottom of the chart being no utilization or no load. (see Figure 7-8). This graph will quickly allow you to identify which of your rules are most active or closest to full load.

FIGURE 7-6

The Load Manage Application dialog box

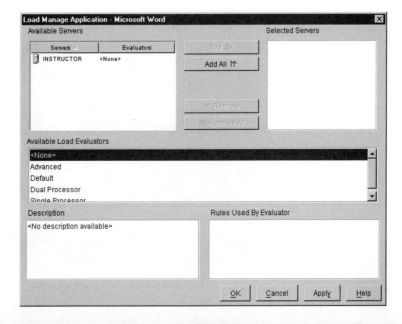

FIGURE 7-7

Load evaluator usage reports

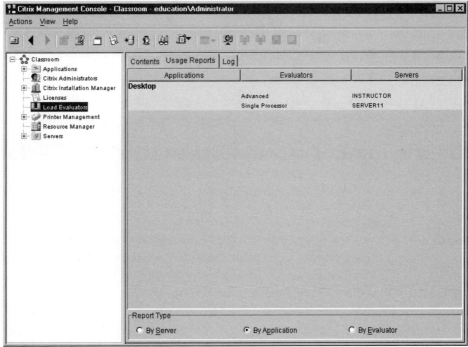

FIGURE 7-8

Load Manager
Monitor

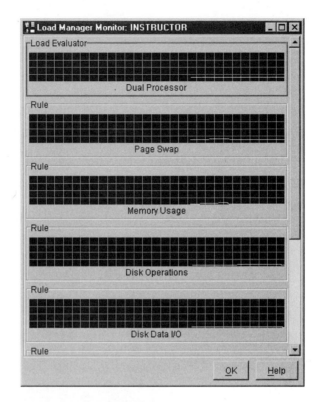

CERTIFICATION OBJECTIVE 7.02

Identifying Encryption Strengths and Performance

When looking at security, there are many things you must take into account. As an administrator, you have to deal with share and file permissions, login restrictions, password length, and change enforcement. However, as a Citrix administrator, you will have to deal with securing the ICA data stream and possibly your NFuse Web site.

MetaFrame XP has much of what you need to secure your system already built in. MetaFrame supports three levels of encryption for the ICA connection, 40-, 56-, and 128-bit encryption. It has multiple client support, including the Web Clients, and it has enforceable encryptions levels that can be set per connection and per published application.

Understanding Encryption

Encryption has become extremely common in today's Web-enabled world. Companies need to secure their data so that it is only read by the intended recipient. Encryption generally comes in two forms:

- **Public Key-Private Key** This type of encryption uses one key to encrypt the data, and one key to decrypt the data. The public key is used during the encryption process. Once the data is encrypted, it is sent to the recipient who then uses the private key to decrypt the data. The public key in this scenario can be transmitted freely across public lines. No data is contained in the public key that can compromise the private key. If an unauthorized user was to obtain the public key, they could only encrypt data, not decrypt it. This means that since the private key is used to decrypt your data, it must be kept secure at all times. The drawback to Public Key-Private Key is its speed. Though it is considered more secure than symmetric key encryption, it is also slower.

- **Symmetric Key** This encryption is a little different. It uses the same key to both encrypt and decrypt the message we are sending. While this encryption method is generally faster than Public Key-Private Key it also depends on the symmetric key remaining totally secure and never being compromised. This means that the symmetric key must be sent over a secure channel or hand delivered to the parties involved in the communication.

Another way to rate encryption is by the length of the key encrypting the data. A key that has only 8 bits would have 256 possible combinations. Trying each one of the combinations on a modern computer would take less than a second. But a key that has 128 bits would have 2^{128} possible keys. It is estimated that a modern parallel processing computer like a Cray would take 10^{18} years to try every combination in a 128-bit key.

MetaFrame XP uses both of these encryption methods in its technology. MetaFrame uses the RC5 algorithm to encrypt data sent between the MetaFrame server and its ICA client. The RC5 algorithm was developed by RSA security and is a Symmetric Key algorithm, meaning the symmetric key must be delivered to the participants in a secure manor. For this, MetaFrame uses a Public Key-Private Key algorithm called the Diffie-Hellman key agreement algorithm.

The Diffie-Hellman key agreement algorithm was designed to allow two computers to exchange information that would allow both to arrive at the same exact symmetric key without ever transmitting data in the communication that would compromise the symmetric key used in that session.

The MetaFrame server runs an encryption service that generates two numbers at random intervals. These numbers, called Diffie-Hellman parameters, are used during key negotiation. When a secure ICA client establishes an encrypted session, the MetaFrame server and client use a public key algorithm to pass public keys and these parameters over the communication path. Using these parameters, the client and server's private and public keys, both the client and the server arrive at the same unique symmetric key. This symmetric key is 1024 bits long and unique for every client connection.

exam
ⓦatch

The exam is sure to test your knowledge of the two different encryption methods and how MetaFrame uses each. You should understand how they work and what the name of each algorithm is.

MetaFrame XP also supports three levels of encryption above Basic: 40-bit, 56-bit, and 128-bit. In addition to these three levels of encryption, MetaFrame also offers the following security features:

- 128-bit encryption during user authentication.

- Compatibility with the latest ICA clients for DOS, Win16, Win32, Web Clients, Windows CE, and Linux x86 clients. (The Linux ARM client is not supported.) These clients ship with MetaFrame XP (version 6.01.xxx) and support encryption. Earlier MetaFrame clients that were not distributed with Secure ICA may not support encryption.

- Enforceable minimum encryption levels that can be specified by Connection type using Citrix Connection Configuration or by Published Application using the Citrix Management Console.

- Dynamic key generation for each new ICA session.

When a user connects to a MetaFrame server, the entire ICA packet (except for a small encryption header) is encrypted. All ICA data between the client and the MetaFrame server are transmitted securely. This includes the following:

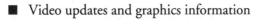

- Video updates and graphics information
- Keystrokes and mouse movements
- Client drive information
- Client printer data
- Client audio data

 exam **Ⓦatch** *Be sure to know what data is encrypted when using Citrix encryption. The exam is sure to test your knowledge of this.*

Now that you have a better understanding of encryption, here are some possible scenario questions and their answers:

SCENARIO & SOLUTION	
You have just increased the required encryption level for your TCP connection. You then receive calls from several users stating that they can no longer connect to the MetaFrame server. After investigation, you find that all these users have a Mac client operating system. What can be done to resolve this issue?	You must reset the required encryption level to Basic if the Mac users are to connect. The Mac client does not support encryption above Basic.
You are contacted by one of your users, who asks if his data is encrypted when he saves it. He has been saving data from his Citrix session to a remote share on a file server.	Citrix does not encrypt this communication path. ICA encryption would encrypt communication between his Citrix session and his local client device, but not a file save to a remote server.
You are tasked to deploy Citrix in the most secure manner possible. You decide every connection should require 128-bit encryption. You audit you local client base and find that it contains the following OSs: Windows 9x, Windows 3.1, and Linux. Will you be able to encrypt all ICA traffic?	If the Linux clients are on Intel x86 platforms, yes. There are secure clients for Win32, Win16, and Linux x86.

figuring Encryption on a MetaFrame XP Server

There are two basic ways to configure security in your MetaFrame XP farm. You can enforce the encryption level at the connection the users use to connect to the MetaFrame server, or you can force the encryption level for specific published applications.

To configure a connection for minimum encryption, open Citrix Connection Configuration, edit the properties of the connection, and under the Advanced Connection Settings change the required encryption level to the one you wish to enforce. (See Figure 7-9.)

FIGURE 7-9

Advanced Connection Settings under Citrix Connection Properties

---

EXERCISE 7-3

Configuring a Connection to Use Encryption

1. Using Citrix Connection Configuration, edit the properties of the connection you use to connect to your server (e.g., ICA-TCP).

2. Edit the Advanced Properties of this connection by selecting the Advanced button in the Connection Properties window.

3. Set the required encryption level to 56-bit.

4. Save your changes to the connection.

5. Using the ICA client, create a connection to the server that uses 40-bit encryption.

6. Execute this connection and verify that you receive a message stating "You do not have the proper encryption level to access this session."

7. Select OK on the message.

8. Change the connection you created in step 5 to use 56-bit encryption.

9. Attempt to connect to the Citrix server now. You should connect successfully.

---

on the job

When using NFuse and forcing encryption at the connection level, you may experience problems where users have a secure client, launch an application via NFuse, but still receive the message that they do not meet the required encryption level. The easiest way to fix this, if you do not mind running encryption for every session (which you must not, since you set it at the connection level), is to set each application to use the encryption level you forced at the connection level. This information will be included in the ICA file when users connect to the NFuse site to launch applications, and their session will begin with the required encryption.

To configure an application to use encryption, we must change its default settings in the Citrix Management Console (see Figure 7-10). Do so by editing the properties of the published application. Go to the ICA Client Options tab and change the encryption level using the pull-down menu.

FIGURE 7-10

ICA client
options within
the properties of
a published
application

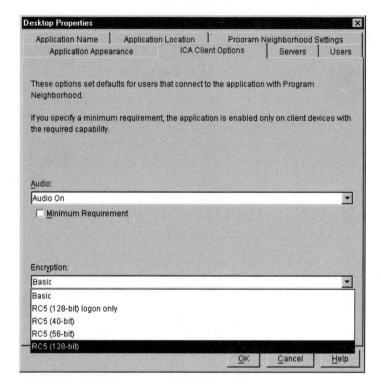

Security and NFuse

When using NFuse to allow users access to your farm via the Internet, there are several security questions that need to be taken into consideration. Some of these include these:

- How do I secure my user credentials between the client browser and my Web server?

- Is the information sent between my Web server and my MetaFrame server secure? If not, how can I secure it?

- Is the ICA session encryption taken care of by the Web server?

- What is placed in the ICA file that could be compromised?

The following security mechanisms have been put in place to address each of these items individually:

■ Secure Hypertext Transfer Protocol (HTTPS). This is a secure version of HTTP used on the internet. It uses Secure Sockets Layer (SSL) to secure data passed through it. The NFuse Web pages should be configured to use HTTPS (see Figure 7-11) in order to guarantee that the user credentials are encrypted when they are passed from the client browser to the Web server. (See your Web server's admin guide on how to configure SSL).

SSL relay also uses the SSL protocol, but the SSL relay encrypts the data between the Web server and the back-end MetaFrame server. Without the SSL relay being used, application information and user credentials are passed between the MetaFrame server and the Web server as clear text. (See the Citrix SSL Relay Configuration later in this chapter).

■ ICA encryption (RC5) is used to secure the session information just as it would be in a normal session not using NFuse. This will encrypt all data sent between the ICA client and the MetaFrame server.

■ Authentication tickets are used to keep the user's credentials secure in the ICA file downloaded to the user. The ICA file, by default, contains the user's username and domain name in clear text. The password is "scrambled" in the

The Directory Security tab for the default Web site on an Internet Information Server version 5

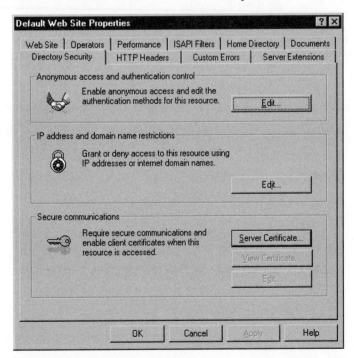

ICA file. If the ICA file was captured, these credentials can be cut and pasted into a new ICA file and reused over and over. An authentication ticket is issued to the user and used in place of the user's credentials. This ticket is encrypted and good for only one use or 200 seconds. Once it has been used, or the timeout has expired, the ticket will no longer be accepted by the MetaFrame servers. (See Figure 7-12 and 7-13.)

exam
ⓦatch

In order to pass the exam, you must know each of the security functions for NFuse. HTTPS for login credentials, SSL Relay for Web server to MetaFrame server security, ticketing for securing ICA file user credentials, and RC5 for securing the ICA data stream.

Citrix SSL Relay Configuration

This tool is used to configure secure communications between your Web server and the back-end MetaFrame server. It can be accessed under the Citrix Program group and has three major tabs: Relay credentials, Connections, and Ciphersuites. (See Figure 7-14.) At the top of each tab is a small box that will indicate whether the information in that tab has been saved to the registry or not. A green check mark indicates the information is stored in the registry, while a red X indicates that the information has not been written to the registry yet.

FIGURE 7-12

Typical NFuse
ICA file not using
authentication
tickets

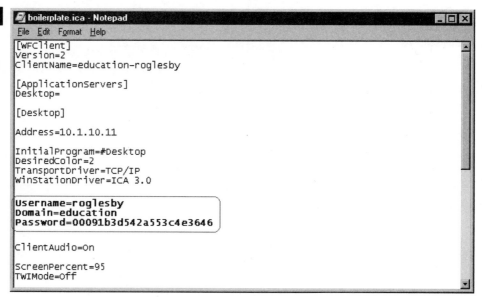

```
[WFClient]
Version=2
ClientName=education-roglesby

[ApplicationServers]
Desktop=

[Desktop]

Address=10.1.10.11

InitialProgram=#Desktop
DesiredColor=2
TransportDriver=TCP/IP
WinStationDriver=ICA 3.0

Username=roglesby
Domain=education
Password=00091b3d542a553c4e3646

ClientAudio=On

ScreenPercent=95
TWIMode=Off
```

FIGURE 7-13

NFuse ICA file using authentication ticketing

```
[WFClient]
Version=2
ClientName=education-roglesby

[ApplicationServers]
Desktop=

[Desktop]

Address=10.1.5.4

InitialProgram=#Desktop
DesiredColor=2
TransportDriver=TCP/IP
WinStationDriver=ICA 3.0

AutologonAllowed=ON

Username=roglesby⌷Domain=\EA4B1F834724A2C0⌷
ClearPassword=328BFBA66F16AA⌷

ClientAudio=On

ScreenPercent=95
TWIMode=Off


[EncRC5-0]
DriverNameWin16=pdc0w.dll
DriverNameWin32=pdc0n.dll
```

FIGURE 7-14

The Relay Credentials tab of the Citrix SSL Relay Configuration tool

Citrix SSL Relay Configuration

☑ Relay Credentials | ☑ Connection | ☑ Ciphersuites |

Key Store Location: c:\winnt\SSLRelay\keystore   Browse...

Display Friendly Name: ☑

Server Certificate:

Password:

OK   Cancel   Apply   Help

FROM THE CLASSROOM

NFuse Communication and Security

One of the toughest things to teach a new Citrix administrator is security as it relates to NFuse. The main reason for this is the new administrator's lack of understanding regarding how NFuse itself works.

The best way to learn these features is to first draw out how NFuse functions without concern for security. Draw out the following objects and their communications paths:

■ Client Web browser communicates with the Web server, passing user credentials to the Web server.

■ The Web server communicates with the MetaFrame XP server on behalf of the client, passing the user's credentials to an Extensible Markup Language (XML) service on the MetaFrame server and receiving back a list of applications.

■ The Web server issues an ICA file to the client that contains connection information for the server.

■ Client establishes an ICA session with the MetaFrame server.

Now that you have the communication paths drawn out, you can see everything that needs to be secured. We can see that the client to Web server communication path needs to be a secure (HTTPS connection). The data sent between the Web server and the MetaFrame server needs to be secured (SSL Relay). The ICA file contains the username and domain in clear text, along with just a lightly scrambled password that can be used over and over (authentication tickets). And the ICA stream itself needs to be secure (RC5).

—Ron Oglesby MCSE, CCEA, CCI, CSA

The Relay Credentials tab contains the following information (see Figure 7-14):

■ **Key Store Location**   This specifies which directory on the server contains the certificate used to present the relay's identity to the NFuse Web servers. The default location for this certificate is %SYSTEMROOT%\SSLRelay\keystore.

■ **Display Friendly Name**   This will display the Certificate's friendly name instead of its common name (generally the server name).

■ **Server Certificate**   Specifies the server certificate used to identify the SSL Relay.

■ **Password**   Specifies the password used by the selected server certificate.

The Connection tab contains configuration settings for the listener port and specifies the destinations for the SSL Relay (see Figure 7-15).

- **Relay Listening Port** Specifies the port over which your Web server will communicate with the SSL Relay. This uses the default SSL port of TCP 443. If you change the port number for the SSL relay, you must also change the port number on your Web server.

- **Server IP Address** Shows the IP addresses of the MetaFrame XP servers to which decrypted packets will be sent. By default, only the server hosting the SSL Relay is listed, but other MetaFrame server can be added for redundancy.

- **Ports** Specifies which TCP port is being used for the XML service. The default for this port is 80, but this can be changed during install or later using a command-line utility.

- **New** Allows you to add additional MetaFrame XP server to the relay destination list. You will need to configure the target server's IP address, the port number in which the XML service is running, and the source address for the packets.

FIGURE 7-15

The Connection tab in the Citrix SSL Relay Configuration dialog box

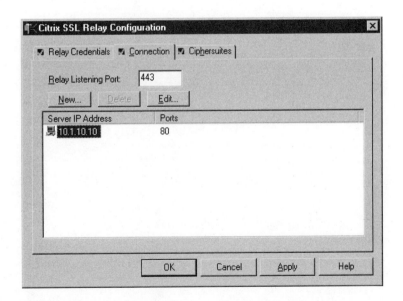

The Ciphersuites tab contains the settings that configure which ciphersuites the SSL relay will accept from the Web server. A ciphersuite is an encryption/decryption algorithm. This tab contains a list of all Citrix supported ciphersuites. From the list of available ciphersuites, you may select which ciphersuites you wish to use. The Add button moves the selected ciphersuite from the list of available ciphersuites to the list of selected ciphersuites. The Delete button removes a selected ciphersuite (see Figure 7-16).

In order to configure an SSL relay, you must obtain a server certificate from a Certificate Authority such as Verisign (www.verisign.com). This certificate must then be copied into the Keystore directory; the default is %SYSTEMROOT%\SSLRelay\Keystore\certs. You must keep the original file extension of the certificate file sent to you and use the KEY extension for the private key file. Once this is installed, use the Citrix SSL Relay Configuration tool to configure the certificate and the servers you will relay to.

FIGURE 7-16

The Ciphersuites tab in the Citrix SSL Relay Configuration tools

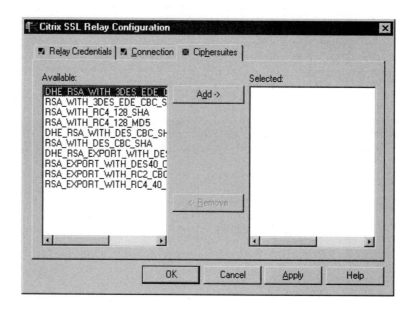

Now that you understand how to configure encryption for the server and security for NFuse, here are some possible scenario questions and their answers:

SCENARIO & SOLUTION

You have deployed NFuse to the Internet to allow your users to access their applications from home. Your company hires a consultant to perform a security audit, and he finds that he can capture the username, domain name, and password of any user logging in to this Web site. What security feature needs to be put in place to correct this?	HTTPS should be configured to secure the username and password transmission to the Web server. The security consultant has most likely captured the data between clients and your Web server.
You have decided to place your IIS server outside the firewall, but are worried about the server-to-server communication between the IIS server and the MetaFrame server. How can you secure this communications?	Configure your MetaFrame server to use an SSL Relay. This will allow for secure communication between your Web server and the MetaFrame server.

CERTIFICATION SUMMARY

Load management and security will be two of the most important items on your exam. Understanding how these systems function, as well as why they function the way they do can help you pass the exam.

Experienced administrators may find this chapter simple, but to pass the exam you must understand the details of these systems. Once you are past the exam, you will also find these features are used every day in a Citrix environment. Knowing how to configure load balancing properly will prevent overtaxed servers from unneeded downtime. With that in mind, learning how to secure your connections and NFuse sites will reduce the danger of hacker attacks.

TWO-MINUTE DRILL

Analyzing Load with Load Manager

❑ The load management feature only comes with MetaFrame XP*a* or XP*e*.

❑ MetaFrame installs with two evaluators: default and advanced.

❑ The default evaluator is assigned to all servers during their installation.

❑ The default evaluator monitors Server User Load and sets its threshold at 100 users.

❑ The advanced evaluator monitors Processor Utilization, Memory Utilization, and Page Swap.

❑ The default and advanced evaluators cannot be edited.

❑ Load balancing occurs at login. It is not dynamic.

❑ By default, no evaluator is assigned to published applications.

Identifying Encryption Strengths and Performance

❑ Public key-private key encryption uses one key to encrypt data and another to decrypt data.

❑ Symmetric key encryption uses the same key to encrypt and decrypt data.

❑ MetaFrame supports 40-, 56-, and 128-bit encryption.

❑ RSA's RC5 algorithm is a symmetric key algorithm, used to secure the ICA data stream.

❑ Diffie-Hellman is a public key-private key algorithm used to negotiate the symmetric key for ICA data encryption.

❑ Minimum encryption levels can be set at the connection level using Citrix Connection Configuration or per published application using the Citrix Management Console.

❑ DOS, Win16, Win32, Linux x86, and the Web clients support encryption.

❑ HTTPS is used to secure user credentials between the client and the Web server, while SSL Relay is used to secure the XML data connection between the Web server and the MetaFrame Server.

SELF TEST

The following questions will help you measure your understanding of the material presented in this chapter. Read all the choices carefully, as there may be more than one correct answer. Choose all correct answers for each question.

Analyzing Load with Load Manager

1. Which of the following is NOT a rule that can be assigned to a load evaluator?

A. Server User Load

B. Application User Load

C. Disk Data I/O

D. Specified Users

2. Which load evaluator is assigned to MetaFrame servers during their installation?

A. The advanced evaluator.

B. The default evaluator.

C. No evaluator is assigned.

D. A Custom evaluator defined by the administrator.

3. You have baselined your servers using Performance Monitor. You have determined that the maximum number of users you can support on your hardware is 45. Above 45 users and performance starts to decline dramatically. You have created a new load evaluator based on Server User Load. What should you set the Server User Load threshold at?

A. 45, the number of users the server can host.

B. 47 to 50 to allow room for growth.

C. 43 to 44, a little less than the maximum.

D. 100. You should never change the default value.

4. You have two MetaFrame XP*a* servers load balancing a common desktop. During the middle of the workday, server number 2 crashes. How will this affect the users currently logged on to server number 2?

A. No effect to the end users. User sessions will fail over to the first server.

B. The users will lose their current unsaved work but will be able to reconnect to the first server.

C. The end user will be disconnected from server 2, but when they are reconnected to server 1, they will reconnect right where they left off.

D. The end users will be disconnected from server 2, but once it is rebooted, they will be able to reconnect to it and continue working with no loss of data.

5. What evaluator is assigned to published applications by default?

A. The advanced evaluator if it is an application and not a published desktop.

B. The default evaluator if it is a published desktop.

C. The application evaluator.

D. No evaluator is assigned to published applications by default.

6. You wish to create a load evaluator that will monitor active sessions on your server. You also wish to limit the number of sessions to 50. Which of the following answers will allow you to do this? (Choose all that apply.)

A. Copy the default evaluator and change the threshold settings.

B. Copy the advanced evaluator and change the threshold settings.

C. Create a new evaluator using only the Server User Load rule and set its threshold at 50.

D. Create a new evaluator using only the Application User Load rule and set its value at 50.

7. The advanced evaluator monitors which of the following rules? (Choose all that apply.)

A. CPU Utilization

B. Page Faults

C. Page Swaps

D. Memory Usage

8. You have published a load-balanced desktop across three MetaFrame servers on your network using the default parameters for both the servers and the application. After tracking the performance of your servers, you notice that while each server has the same number of active sessions, two of the servers are underutilized, but the remaining server is running at almost 100 percent utilization. What adjustments can be made to remedy this problem? (Select the best answer.)

A. Change the default evaluator on each server to handle the appropriate number of active sessions.

B. Create a new evaluator that better reflects the number of users each server can handle; then assign them appropriately.

C. Assign the advanced evaluator to each server so that only the hardware utilization is analyzed and not the User Load.

D. Configure each server's connection settings to limit the number of active sessions to what you feel the server can handle.

9. After creating a new load evaluator which of the following is true? (Choose all that apply.)

A. The load evaluator can remain unused

B. The load evaluator can be assigned to a server

C. The load evaluator can be assigned to a published application

D. The load evaluator can be assigned to every server in the farm

10. You have just created a new load evaluator and assigned it to several servers in your farm. You wish to view the activity for the rules within the load evaluator. Which utility would you use to do this?

A. Load evaluator usage reports.

B. Load evaluator status reports.

C. Load Manager Monitor in the Load Evaluators node.

D. Load Manager Monitor from the server you wish to view.

Identifying Encryption Strengths and Performance

11. Which of the following describes public key-private key encryption? (Choose all that apply.)

A. A single key is used to encrypt and decrypt data.

B. The private key must be kept secret.

C. The public key can be distributed freely.

D. It is faster than symmetric key encryption.

12. You have several types of client Operating Systems on your network. They include Windows 98, Windows 2000, DOS, Linux x86, and Sun Solaris 2.7 (Unix). All clients use Citrix MetaFrame to host user applications. You are considering enabling encryption on your Citrix servers and forcing a minimum level of 128 bits for every connection. What effect will this have on your client connections? (Choose all that apply.)

A. Windows 98 and Windows 2000 clients will be able to connect to the encryption sessions.

B. DOS clients will not be able to connect because they do not support encryption.

    C. The Linux clients will be able to connect to the encryption sessions.

    D. The Sun Solaris clients will not be able to connect using encryption.

13. Which of the following is true about Citrix encryption? (Choose all that apply.)

    A. A new symmetric key is generated for every client connection.

    B. A public key-private key algorithm is used to generate the symmetric key at login.

    C. MetaFrame supports 40-, 56-, 128-, and 168-bit encryption levels.

    D. Both Web clients support encryption.

14. During the key negotiation algorithm, a symmetric key is generated. This key is how many bits long?

    A. 128 bits

    B. 256 bits

    C. 512 bits

    D. 1024 bits

15. Which of the following is encrypted during an ICA session? (Choose all that apply.)

    A. Client drive information

    B. Client printer data

    C. Video updates and graphic information

    D. Key strokes and mouse movement

16. You wish to require that every connection made to your MetaFrame server be encrypted at a minimum level of 128 bits. Which utility would you use to prevent users from connecting to your server without 128-bit encryption enabled?

    A. The Citrix Management Console

    B. Citrix Connection Configuration

    C. Citrix Server Administration

    D. Citrix SSL Relay Configuration

17. When implementing NFuse, you wish to ensure that your user credentials are passed securely across the Internet when using the NFuse Web site. What should you use to secure these passwords?

    A. Use the SSL Relay Configuration tool to configure SSL encryption for client to Web server communication.

    B. Configure SSL on your Web server and require that the NFuse pages use encryption.

    C. Configure ICA encryption at the connection level. This will encrypt the user logon.

    D. Nothing. The passwords are sent securely by default.

18. While troubleshooting a client connection problem with NFuse, you notice that the ICA file the client is being downloaded has the username and domain name in clear text. You are then able to cut and paste this into other ICA files and use this user's login several times. How can you configure the NFuse Web site so these credentials are more secure?

    A. Enable ticketing on the MetaFrame XP data store.

    B. Enable ticketing on the NFuse Web pages.

    C. Configure and enable the SSL Relay.

    D. Configure SSL on the Web server.

19. The SSL Relay Configuration is used to secure what communication path?

    A. Communication between the client and the MetaFrame server.

    B. Communication between the data collector and the MetaFrame server.

    C. Communication between the NFuse Web server and the MetaFrame server.

    D. Communication between the client and the Web server.

20. What is the default location for the key store in the SSL Relay Configuration?

    A. Program Files\Citrix\IMA\SSLRelay\Keystore

    B. %SYSTEMROOT%\Keystore

    C. %SYSTEMDRIVE%\Keystore

    D. %SYSTEMROOT%\SSLRelay\Keystore

LAB QUESTION

You are about to deploy Citrix MetaFrame using Citrix's NFuse via the internet. All of your clients are Win32 and will access your applications using an external Web server. You wish to do this as securely as possible. You must come up with a basic design and description of how you will secure all the data paths.

    Describe your design.

SELF TEST ANSWERS

Analyzing Load with Load Manager

1. ☑ D is the correct answer. Specified Users is not a valid rule for a load evaluator.
   ☒ A, B, and C are incorrect because they are valid load evaluator rules.

2. ☑ B is correct. The default evaluator is assigned at installation.
   ☒ A, C, and D are incorrect. A is a valid evaluator, but not assigned by default. Since the default evaluator is assigned at installation, C and D are also incorrect.

3. ☑ C is the correct answer. You should never set the value for a threshold at the maximum a server can handle.
   ☒ A is incorrect, since we are not setting it at its maximum. B is incorrect since it is above the maximum. C is also incorrect, since you should change this to reflect your environment.

4. ☑ B is correct. Load balancing is not like clustering. Any unsaved work will be lost, and the users will not be able to re-establish a connection to their previous sessions.
   ☒ This makes A, C, and D incorrect.

5. ☑ D is correct. No evaluator is assigned to published applications by default.
   ☒ A, B, and C are incorrect, since no load evaluator is assigned to published applications by default.

6. ☑ A and C are correct. The default evaluator monitors only Server User Load. This evaluator can be copied, or a new one created to monitor the same rule. Setting the threshold to 50 will limit the number of active sessions to 50.
   ☒ B is incorrect, since the advanced evaluator does not monitor Server User Load, and D is incorrect, since Application User Load will only monitor the number of specific sessions running a specific application, not the entire number of sessions on the server.

7. ☑ A, C, and D are correct. The advanced evaluator monitors CPU Utilization, Page Swaps, and Memory Usage.
   ☒ B is incorrect, since Page Faults is not monitored.

8. ☑ C is correct. Assigning the advanced evaluator to the server will make the evaluators take hardware usage into consideration instead of straight user load.
   ☒ A is incorrect because the default evaluator cannot be edited. B is incorrect because, while this may work, it is easier to create a single evaluator for all three servers than it is to create and

manage three separate evaluators. **D** is incorrect because this will limit the number of logons to the server but does not affect the load-balancing mechanism.

9. ☑ **A**, **B**, **C**, and **D** are all correct.

10. ☑ **D** is correct. To view the activity of the load evaluator, you must select the server it is assigned to and view the Load Manager Monitor.

☒ **A** is incorrect because these show which evaluators are assigned to applications and servers, but not their activity. **B** is incorrect because it also does not show activity, and **C** is incorrect because this utility does not exist in the Load Evaluators node.

Identifying Encryption Strengths and Performance

11. ☑ **B** and **C** are correct. Public key-private key encryption uses two keys. The public key used to encrypt data can be distributed freely. The private key must be kept secure, since it is used to decrypt the data

☒ **A** is incorrect because a single key algorithm is called symmetric key encryption. **D** is incorrect because symmetric key encryption is faster than public key-private key encryption.

12. ☑ **A**, **C**, and **D** are correct. Windows 98 and Windows 2000 both use the Citrix Win32 client, which does support encryption. The Linux x86 client also supports encryption and will be able to connect. The Sun Solaris systems use a Unix client, which does not support ICA encryption.

☒ **B** is incorrect, since the DOS client does support ICA encryption.

13. ☑ **A**, **B**, and **D** are correct. The Diffie-Hellman, public key-private key, and key agreement algorithm is used at logon to create a new symmetric key for each session. Both the Netscape Plug-in and Internet Explorer ActiveX control support ICA encryption.

☒ **C** is incorrect, since MetaFrame supports only 40-, 56-, and 128-bit encryption.

14. ☑ **D** is the correct answer. The algorithm establishes a 1024-bit key at each login, but only the first 256 bits of the key is used.

☒ **A**, **B**, and **C** are incorrect.

15. ☑ **A**, **B**, **C**, and **D** are all correct. These are all encrypted in the ICA session.

16. ☑ **B** is correct. Using Citrix Connection Configuration, you can configure the required encryption for every connection. A user connecting without the required encryption level will not be allowed to log on.

☒ **A** is incorrect because while you can configure it for each application individually, this, by itself, does not stop a user from connecting to a specific server without encryption. **C** is incorrect because there are no encryption settings within Citrix server Administration, and **D** is incorrect because the SSL Relay Configuration configures SSL encryption for NFuse.

17. ☑ **B** is correct. In order to secure browser to Web server security, you will need to set up SSL encryption for your NFuse Web pages.
☒ **A** is incorrect, since the SSL Relay Configuration does not configure client-side SSL. **C** is incorrect because ICA encryption does not protect passwords entered into an NFuse Web site. **D** is incorrect, since the passwords are passed to the Web server in clear text when not using SSL.

18. ☑ **B** is correct. Ticketing will encrypt the domain name and password and replace them with a "ticket." This ticket is only good for one use or 200 seconds.
☒ **A** is incorrect because the data store has no ticketing function. **C** is incorrect, since the SSL Relay has nothing to do with ticketing. **D** is incorrect because this is used to secure the client username and password when transmitted to the Web server.

19. ☑ **C** is correct. The SSL Relay is used to encrypt the XML communication between the Web server and the MetaFrame server.
☒ **A** is incorrect because this is handled by RC5 ICA encryption. **B** is incorrect because this communication does not require external encryption. And **D** is incorrect, since SSL on the Web server is used for browser to Web server communication.

20. ☑ **D** is correct. This is the default location for the key store.
☒ **A**, **B**, and **C** are incorrect directories for the default location.

LAB ANSWER

You should use the following security measure to secure the NFuse site:

1. Obtain a server certificate for your Web server and configure the Web server to use SSL encryption to protect usernames and passwords within the NFuse pages.

2. Obtain a server certificate for the back-end MetaFrame server. Then configure an SSL relay between the Web server and the MetaFrame server. This will protect the XML communication between these two servers.

3. Configure the NFuse Web pages to use authentication ticketing. This will reduce the amount of risk involved if a hacker intercepts the ICA file as it is downloaded to the end user.

4. Enable encryption on all published applications. This will protect the ICA data stream and will allow for each application launched via the NFuse page to run encrypted.

8

Applications

Application management and configuration are crucial elements of Citrix MetaFrame administration. At the end of this chapter, you should have a firm understanding of how to install and configure applications, application publishing, and the Citrix Installation Manager.

CERTIFICATION OBJECTIVE 8.01

Installing Applications

Most application setup procedures provide no way to propagate private application settings (either INI files or profile settings) to users other than the installation user on MetaFrame. Citrix introduced different installation modes so that application installation and configuration could be tracked, if required, to enable propagation of private settings to any user running the application.

Managing Sessions During Application Installation

Applications should NEVER be installed while you have remote users logged on to the system. When users are logged on, it is possible for their session to have open file handles to files the application is attempting to overwrite.

Always disable logins either by disabling the Enable Logon To This Server check box in the MetaFrame Settings tab of the server in the Citrix Management Console (see Figure 8-1) or by using the command: change logon /disable. Also use the Citrix Management Console to verify that no users have existing sessions open on the MetaFrame server BEFORE installing applications. Once an application has been installed and configured, logins can be re-enabled.

exam
⍟atch

Be sure to know that logons must be disabled and no users logged on prior to installing applications.

How Modes Affect the Installation

There are two different modes of application execution:

1. Installation mode
2. Execute mode

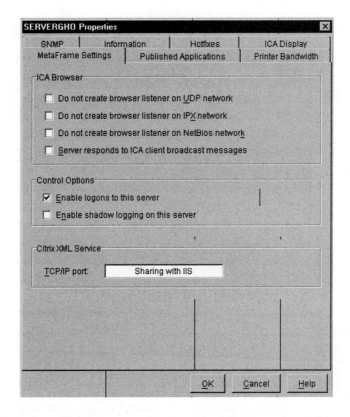

FIGURE 8-1

The MetaFrame
Settings tab in the
Citrix
Management
Console

A server is normally always in execute mode, where %windir% points to an individual users' %homedrive%homepath%\windows (or %userprofile%\.dows, if a home drive hasn't been defined). The install mode can be enabled either by using the Add/Remove Programs applet in the Control Panel, and choosing Install Application For Multiple Users, or by running the command, change user /install, at the DOS prompt (see Figure 8-2). The Install mode enables applications to be installed and configured so settings and INI files will be distributed on a per-user basis.

Before we define what each mode does, there are a number of system variables and abbreviations that have to be defined. These are listed in Table 8-1.

Install mode does the following:

1. Sets %windir% to %systemroot% instead of the execute mode default of %homedrive%%homepath\Windows.

FIGURE 8-2

Changing to
installation mode
via the command
prompt

FIGURE 8-2

Changing to installation mode via the command prompt

2. Registers any application INI files for later automatic distribution under HKLM\Software\Microsoft\Windows NT\CurrentVersion\Terminal Server\ Install\IniFile Times.

3. Links HKCU\Software with HKLM\Software\Microsoft\Windows NT\ CurrentVersion\Terminal Server\Install\Software.

4. Tracks changes of HKLM in HKLM\Software\Microsoft\Windows NT\ CurrentVersion\Terminal Server\Install\Machine.

TABLE 8-1   Commonly Used Variables

Abbreviation or Variable	Description
%systemroot%	Operating system directory on system drive
%homedrive%	User's home drive
%homepath%	User's home folder off %homedrive%
%windir%	Pointer to functional Windows directory
%winsysdir%	%windir%\system32
%userprofile%	Location of user's profile while logged on, for example, c:\wtsrv\profiles\ %username% (NT 4.0) or c:\documents and settings\%username% (Win2K)
%appinstalldisk%	Disk drive used for application installs by IM 2.0
%username%	User's login name
HKLM	HKEY_LOCAL_MACHINE
HKCU	HKEY_CURRENT_USER

on the **Job**

Even printer drivers and fonts should be installed in install mode, or they could be copied to the wrong location. Good evidence that install mode hasn't been used properly is the presence of DLLs and programs in the install user's home Windows directory or fonts installed to the home Windows\fonts directory.

Once users log on in execute mode, the application install tracking ensures that when a user now tries to run a correctly installed application the following actions occur:

1. For install mode-installed applications that use INI files, if the INI file doesn't exist in the user's home Windows directory (%windir% in execute mode), it is copied there from %systemroot%. If the INI file in the home Windows directory exists but is older than the file in %systemroot%, it is renamed to inifilename.CTX and replaced with the newer file.

2. For applications that store settings in the user's profile, when the application is run the first time, it creates application-specific registry entries under HKCU. If the newly-created registry key exists under HKLM\Software\ Microsoft\Windows NT\CurrentVersion\Terminal Server\Install\Software, then the contents of the key are copied into the user's profile (HKCU\ Software).

This way, any settings are automatically replicated to users when they first run a new application. When using Add/Remove Programs, never let an installation program reboot the system until Finish has been selected. This allows the system to finish its application tracking and safely record the changes. In Windows 2000 Server (Application Server), if you attempt to install an application any way except via the Add/Remove Programs applet in the Control Panel, the installation will fail unless you are in install mode.

exam **Watch**

The exam is sure to test your knowledge of install mode. Be sure you understand how to change modes.

Application Compatibility Scripts

Many applications require post-setup modifications to enable them to run properly for multiple users in a MetaFrame XP environment. These modifications can be made using application compatibility scripts, located under %systemroot%\

Application Compatibility Scripts. There are three types of scripts, located in three directories (see Figure 8-3):

- **Install** Makes any registry or other configuration changes necessary for the application to be multiuser after installation.

- **Logon** Copies nonshareable files; also makes profiles or other user-specific changes needed for an application on login.

- **Uninstall** Removes references to a script added using an install script.

In normal usage, install scripts are run once after the installation of an application, while logon scripts are run each time a user logs on by being called via the system login script: %systemroot%\system32\usrlogon.cmd.

Not all applications have compatibility scripts, although more are being made available either by Citrix (http://www.citrix.com/support) or Microsoft (see http://www.microsoft.com/windows2000/docs/W2kTSApCmpt.doc).

on the job *Application compatibility install scripts can be run automatically after an application is installed by using Citrix Installation Manager.*

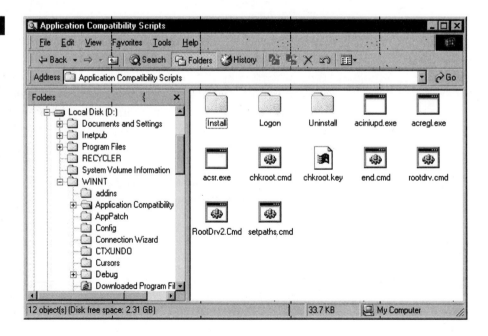

FIGURE 8-3

The Application Compatibility Scripts directory located in %systemroot%

Now that you have a better understanding of how to install applications, here are some possible real-world issues and their solutions.

SCENARIO & SOLUTION

You have just installed an application and its icons and INI files only appear for the user that installed it.	It is possible that the application was not installed in install mode. Uninstall the app as that user, then reinstall it in install mode.
You are about to install an application that requires you do so from the command line. What is the easiest way to change into install mode?	Execute the command: change user /install
You are now finished installing the example application. How do you change back into execute mode?	Execute the command: change user /execute

EXERCISE 8-1

CertCam 8-1

Installing Microsoft Word 2000

In order to complete this lab, you must have a copy of Microsoft Office 2000 and the Microsoft MST for installing Office in a Terminal Services Environment. This MST file (a Windows Installed Template) is named TERMSRVR.MST and can be downloaded from Microsoft's Web site or is included with the Office resource kit.

1. Log on to your MetaFrame XP server as Administrator.

2. Access the Add/Remove Programs applet in the Control Panel.

3. Choose the appropriate option to install a new application.

4. Browse to the setup.exe on the root of the Office 2000 CD.

5. Assuming your E:\ is the CD-ROM drive, the setup command line should look like this: E:\setup.exe

6. Modify the preceding command line so it includes the path to the TERMSRVR.MST, making the command line look like this: E:\SETUP.EXE /Transforms=C:\temp\termsrvr.mst (This assumes you have downloaded the MST file to your C:\temp directory. If not, specify the correct path.)

7. Install the components of MS Office you wish to use.

8. Once the install is complete, do not reboot. Make sure to return to the Add/Remove Programs window and click Next, then Finish.

Uninstalling Applications

Applications have to be uninstalled the same way they were installed. Logins should be disabled, and logged in users should be logged out BEFORE uninstalling an application. If any users are logged on and using the application, the executables and DLLs will be in use and will not be removed.

A manual uninstallation can then be completed either by using the Add/Remove Programs applet in the Control Panel or by implementing the Change User /Install command before running the application's uninstaller. Logins can then be re-enabled.

exam
Ⓦatсh

Applications installed using Installation Manager should never be uninstalled using either Add/Remove Programs or the application's uninstaller.

Citrix Installation Manager 2.0 Overview

Citrix Installation Manager 2.0 is an integral part of the MetaFrame XP*e* Enterprise solution. It is a sophisticated software deployment tool that can be used to automate the installation of applications, files, registry changes, hotfixes and service packs across a server farm or an enterprise (WAN-connected farms). The features of the Installation Manager include these:

■ An improved Packager that has a rollback capability

■ Deployment of multiple application packages

■ Comprehensive logging of the application deployment process

■ Scheduling of application deployment, including intelligent (no users logged on) and postponed timing

■ Installation of MSI packages, as well as ADF (application deployment files) packages

- Installation of ADF packages from MetaFrame 1.8 Installation Management Services 1.0

- Centralized management of deployment to individual servers and groups of servers (generally in zones) across an enterprise

Installation Manager 2.0 consists of three components: the Packager, an Installation Manager 2.0 plug-in for the Citrix Management Console, and the Installer. Implementation of Installation Manager 2.0 requires the following:

- A workstation or server to host the Citrix Management Console

- A valid MetaFrame XP*e* license for the farm (or an eval XP*e* license for each of the servers if in a pilot)

- A network share point to accommodate the ADF and MSI deployment packages

- MetaFrame Xp*e* servers participating in an Independent Management Architecture (IMA) farm

- An application packager system

exam
ⓦatch   *Be sure to know the three components of Citrix Installation Management Services.*

The Packager

The Citrix Installation Manager 2.0 packager can be used to package one or more applications, application compatibility scripts, MSI packages, and files into a single project or package to be deployed to servers in the farm. Important packager usage considerations are

- The installer system configuration has to be similar to the MetaFrame XP*e* systems that will get the deployment packages. This includes operating system, service packs, hotfixes, MetaFrame hotfixes, but not necessarily the same hardware.

- Separate packages must be made for each version of the operating system on servers in the farm. Use separate partitions (or machines) for different operating system versions.

- Many Microsoft applications require that Internet Explorer (at least version 4 SP2) is present, or the installation will fail.

- The package requires a network mount point to store the packages. Create a directory for a new package before running the packager.

If you intend to use Installation Manager 2.0 to distribute Windows NT (4.0 or Windows 2000) service packs or hotfixes, the installer system hardware MUST be identical to the target systems.

Packager output is controlled by parameters in the packager initialization file: \Program Files\Citrix\IM\Packager\packager.ini. You can edit packager.ini to modify which objects and actions are included in the finished package or project.

One very important function of packager.ini is that it defines exclusions, files, directories, and registry changes that will NOT be recorded. These include *.tmp files, the TEMP directory and HKLM\Software\Microsoft\Windows NT\ CurrentVersion\Terminal Server\Install. The latter exclusion means that default packager-deployed applications will not support propagation of user registry settings to other users unless you include appropriate application compatibility scripts in the package.

The packaging process starts with a new project that can consist of one or more recordings of application installations, upgrades, service packs, MSI packages, or hotfixes. An example in which multiple recordings would be of use is a database client application project, which could include the database client and the application that uses it. You can either start a new project, open an existing project, or launch the Project Wizard. (See Figure 8-4). A project can consist of seven sections:

- **Project Entries**   Lists project inputs including installation recordings, compatibility scripts, file collections, and so on (modifiable)

- **Applications**   Applications installed as a result of the project entries (read-only)

- **Symbols**   Lists symbols used by the package installer (modifiable)

- **File System Changes**   File system changes resulting from the project entries (read-only)

- **Registry Changes**   Registry changes resulting from the project entries(read-only)

■ **History Log**   Lists the actions taken on this project

■ **Installation Sequence**   Optional section; only invoked when installation includes disabling and enabling services

If an application doesn't use the Windows installer (MSI package), then the usual way to build the package is to add a recording and specify the full path to the installation program. The normal setup or installation program is then executed. The recording logs all aspects of an application's installation. These include

■ Any changes made to the registry

■ Any changes made to INI files

■ The copying of any files like executables and dynamic link libraries (DLL)

While you have to let the installation complete before ending the recording, don't let the application reboot the packager system. Cancel the reboot and then end the recording by selecting Done. Stopping the reboot from occurring allows the Citrix Packager to complete its recording process. A reboot during the recording process will cause packaging to fail.

FIGURE 8-4

Citrix Packager
Project Wizard

The recording allows the package deployment to behave almost exactly like the applications setup program. Any additional components and application compatibility scripts will need to be added to the package before it is built.

To add registry changes to a project, create a .reg file that makes appropriate registry changes and then execute the regfile while recording. This is extremely useful for setting application preferences stored in the registry but not available as options during the install. You can also use this feature to deploy standard registry changes, such as increasing the number of idle sessions, configuring the Second Level Data Cache, and tuning the user's desktop environment to reduce the amount of screen updates during a session.

Once the project is completed, the bottom window in the Citrix Packager utility allows you to view logs created during the packaging/project building operation. Three tabs in the window allow you to select what you would like to view. History, Build, and Post are your available logs.

When you build the package, the packager will copy any included files to the application's package share point directory—for example, \\FP01\ctxpkg$\ project98—and then compile an installation script or ADF file (with WFS extension). The ADF file is a text file in the INI file format that can be edited if necessary to modify the installation conditions, such as the installation target directory. (See Figure 8-5.)

An example in which this could be necessary is when installing Office 97-based applications (such as Project 98 or Publisher 98) on to systems that were already running Office XP. Normal behavior of the Office XP setup looks like this: if an Office 97 product exists in \Microsoft Office\Office\, Office XP will install into

FIGURE 8-5

Typical directory containing the Application Deployment File (ADF) Package

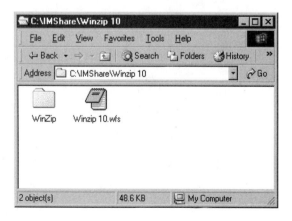

\Microsoft Office\Office10\ to avoid overwriting essential Office 97 components. However, if we are doing the opposite, then a global search and replace of \ Microsoft Office\Office\ for \Microsoft Office\Office8\ in the ADF file would be needed to keep the Office DLL versions separate.

If you edit the ADF file, it's a good idea to check the file syntax by running the ADFverfw utility against the ADF file.

The Rollback function in the packager lets you remove any application install changes and get the system back into a "clean" condition for the next project.

on the
Ⓙob *If a project consists of several different recordings, you have to remove them, using rollback, in the reverse order they were recorded.*

exam
Ⓦatch *Make sure you know the Packager is NOT installed on a production system. Instead, it is installed on a system dedicated to packaging with an OS that matches the target servers.*

The Installer

Software deployment on servers in a MetaFrame XP*e* farm is carried out by the Installation Manager Installer. The Installer needs to be loaded on every server in the farm and consists of three components:

- **The ADF Installer service**   Installs ADF packages and invokes the MSI installer as required
- **The MSI installer**   Installs MSI packages
- **Independent Management Architecture**   Sends and receives scheduling and configuration information to the ADF installer

The Installer service requires a user account to function. This account must have read access to the share point that the packages are stored in. It also must have rights to install applications on the MetaFrame servers in the farm. You can configure this account by right-clicking the Installation manager icon in the Citrix Management Console and selecting Properties. Once in the Configuration tab, select the Edit button to browse for the network account and supply the account's password (see Figure 8-6).

FIGURE 8-6

Configuring the
Network
Account for
Installation
Manager

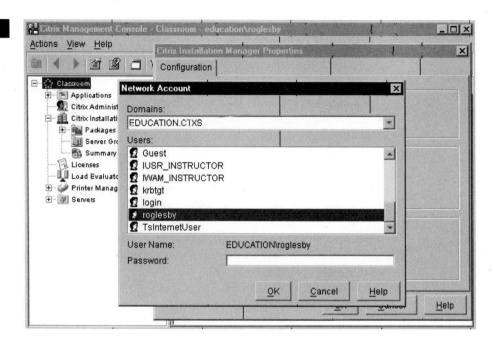

Deploying Applications to a Server Farm

Building the package creates the files necessary for the application to be installed on
the MetaFrame servers. Using the Citrix Management Console's Installation
Manager (IM) plug-in, you can add the package to the MetaFrame XP farm by
right-clicking the Packages icon in the Installation Manager node and selecting Add
Package. You will then browse to find the Package's script file (WFS extension) or a
Microsoft Installer File (MSI extension). (See Figure 8-7.)

Once the package is added to the data store, you have the ability to install the
package by right-clicking the package's icon in the Citrix Management Console and
selecting Install Package. You will be prompted with two options. The first concerns
which servers to install the package on. The list of available servers will only show
MetaFrame servers with the IM Installer service installed. The second, and perhaps
most important, is scheduling. The scheduler allows administrators to schedule
package installation during off-peak hours, reducing downtime. (See Figure 8-8.)

Once the installation has been scheduled, you can monitor the status of that
installation by selecting the application package in the Citrix Management Console
and then viewing the jobs tab for that package. (See Figure 8-9.) The Jobs tab will
show you all pending and completed installations, along with their status. Once the

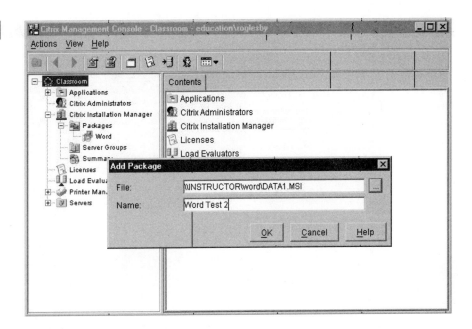

FIGURE 8-7

Using the Citrix Management Console to browse for an MSI or ADF package

installation has completed successfully the application looks and functions like any application installed manually.

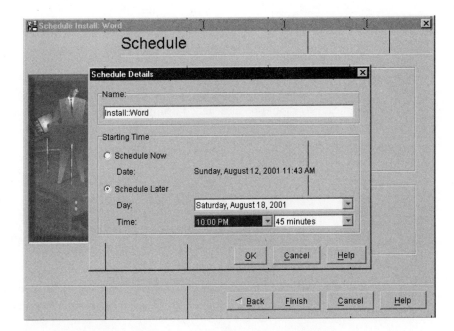

FIGURE 8-8

Scheduling an application package

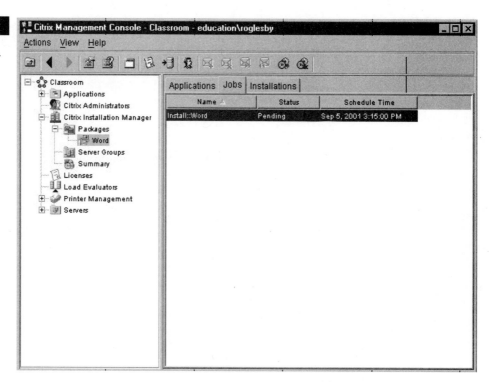

Removing Applications

When deciding how to remove an application from a MetaFrame server, you must consider how the application was installed. An application installed using the Citrix Installation Manager should not be removed using Add/Remove Programs. These applications should be uninstalled using the Installation Manager utilities. An application installed manually using Add/Remove Programs should be removed the way it was installed, using Add/Remove Programs.

Uninstalling an application that was installed using IM should be done through the Citrix Management Console. In the Installation Manager node, you should select the package's Installations tab. Here you will be presented with a list of every MetaFrame server that has installed the package. By right-clicking the proper server and selecting Uninstall Package, you will remove that program and all its associated files.

on the job *Just like with the application installations, you should ensure this is done during off hours, or during a period when no users have active sessions to the server.*

To uninstall an application that was manually installed, you should remove it using the Add/Remove Programs applet in the Control Panel. If the application you are removing has an application compatibility script, you should determine if an uninstall compatibility script exists. If so, this script should be executed as well. If no uninstall script exists, then you must verify that all calls for logon compatibility scripts are removed from Usrlogn2.cmd in %systemroot%\system32 directory.

Now that you have a better understanding of Installation Manager, here are a few real-world issues and their solutions.

SCENARIO & SOLUTION

After installing several packages to your farm using the Citrix Installer, you find that you want to remove two of them from one of the servers. What is the easiest and most proper way to accomplish this?	Use the Citrix Installation Manager Plug-in in the Citrix Management Console to remove the packages from the target server.
You have a mix of different hardware on your network, but the same operating systems. Is it possible to deploy Windows Service Packs using Installation Management Services?	No. Your hardware should be exactly the same if you are deploying service packs.

CERTIFICATION OBJECTIVE 8.02

Configuring Applications for Use in a MetaFrame Environment

After the application is installed, you have to configure the application to make it available to the end user and to make it function properly in this environment. In this section, you will first learn how to "publish" the application and then how to correct certain application problems unique to this environment.

One of the most challenging aspects of MetaFrame XP administration is to get badly written legacy applications, which were designed to run on a single-user system, working properly in a multiuser environment. Fortunately, there are a number of tools available to make this possible. These tools fall into two broad categories, debugging tools to find out what's wrong, and configuration tools to fix the problems.

Publishing Applications

In order to load-balance an application, or make an application available to a Program Neighborhood or NFuse client, the application must be published. Publishing an application allows an administrator to control user access, determine minimum client requirements, configure application settings, set required encryption levels, and choose which server the application is load-balanced on.

Applications are published and managed using the Citrix Management Console's Applications node. Within this node you can change, add, delete, or copy published applications within the MetaFrame XP farm.

To publish an application in the MetaFrame farm, right-click the Applications node in the Citrix Management Console and select publish application. You will then be presented with the Application Publishing Wizard, which will walk you though your configuration. (See Figure 8-10.) The wizard will prompt you for information pertaining to the applications configuration. Table 8-2 lists the information required when publishing an application.

FIGURE 8-10

The Application Publishing Wizard

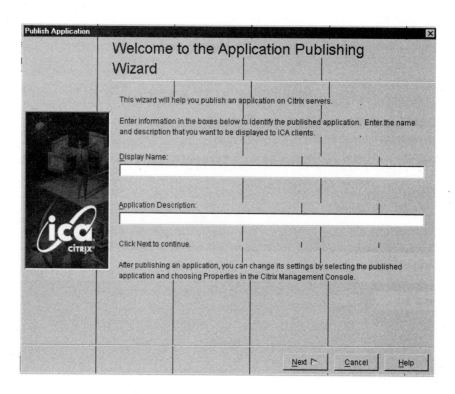

TABLE 8-2 Available Options Within the Published Application Wizard

Field Name	Description
Display Name (required)	Published Application name that clients will see when using NFuse and Program Neighborhood, or when browsing for Citrix published applications.
Application Description	Detailed description of the application being published.
Published Application Command Line & Working Directory (required if not publishing a desktop)	Command line executable and working directory for the application. The executable listed will launch when a user selects that application.
Published Desktop (radio button)	Used to publish a load-balanced desktop instead of a specific executable.
Program Neighborhood Folder	Used for Program Neighborhood and NFuse clients. Will create a folder in the Program Neighborhood interface for sorting applications.
Application Shortcut Placement (Start Menu and Desktop)	Allows an administrator to put an icon for the application on the user's Start menu or on their desktop. (Win32 Program Neighborhood clients only)
Window Size and Colors	Configures minimum settings for application to launch.
Audio	Allows an administrator to configure audio to be on or off for the application. This can also be set as a minimum requirement.
Encryption	Allows an administrator to configure the encryption level for this application. This can also be set as a minimum requirement.
Specify Servers	Allows you to configure which servers will host the application.
Specify Users (required unless anonymous connections are used)	Allows the administrator to specify which users or groups have access to that published application.

One important facet is the ability to publish applications "anonymously." While Citrix documentation will lead you to believe that a user can launch applications without authentication, this is not the case. Due to Windows NT and Windows 2000's need to remain C2 security-compliant, it is impossible to launch an application or a session to a Windows server without some type of authentication. So to work around this security, Citrix creates several local anonymous user accounts during the installation of MetaFrame. When a connection to an anonymous application is launched, the server will use one of the local anonymous accounts to authenticate the user (see Figure 8-11). So, while the user is not required to "log in" with their own credentials, they are still being authenticated using these local accounts. This type of application is often used with programs that have their own authentication built in, with no need for domain resources.

While this may seem like a very convenient way to publish applications it does have a couple of drawbacks:

■ No access to domain resources. Since the accounts used to authenticate are local to the server, they do not have access to domain resources.

■ User-specific application information normally stored in the user's profile is not unique to each user. Since a user never knows which local account they are using, their applications settings are lost at logoff.

Because of both of these drawbacks, applications like Microsoft Outlook, which requires both domain resources and user profile settings, do not lend themselves well to anonymous publishing.

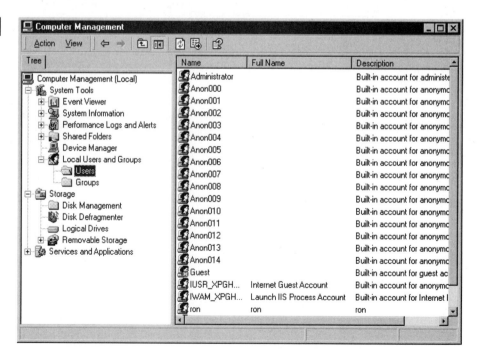

FIGURE 8-11

Local Computer Management, Local Anonymous Users

on the **Job**

In certain situations, you may find you wish to publish an application anonymously, but wish the anonymous connection to have access to a Windows shared folder. This was common with older database applications that used a flat database like DB3 or FoxPro. In this case, all the anonymous connection may require is a mapped drive to a network share point. This can still be accomplished, though it does pose some security risk.

By placing a Net Use command in a script that runs at login, these anon accounts can accomplish this. You will need to create a domain account with access to the share you want to map to, then use this account in the command line that follows.

```
NET USE X: \\Servername\Sharename /user:Domainname\username password
```

Placing this command in the USRLOGN2.CMD in the %systemroot%\ system32, or any files that it calls will map this drive for everyone connecting to that server (anonymous or not). The /user switch will authenticate to the share using the credentials that follow it. Replace Domainname with your domain name. Username should be replaced with the account name you created, and password should be replaced with the password for the generated account.

EXERCISE 8-2

CertCam 8-2

Publishing Microsoft Word 2000

1. Log on to your server as Administrator.

2. Log on to the Citrix Management Console.

3. Right-click the Applications node and select Publish Application.

4. Name the application **word test**.

5. Using the Browse button, browse to winword.exe, where you installed Office. The default is Program Files\Microsoft Office\Office\winword.exe.

6. The working directory should default to the proper directory. Click Next.

7. Select Add Shortcut To Client's Desktop. Click Next.

8. Select Maximize application at startup. Click Next.

9. Add your server to the list of configured servers. Click Next.

10. Add domain users into the list of configured users. Click Finish.

The exam is sure to test your knowledge of publishing applications. Make sure you know which utility to use and the available options.

Debugging Tools

Finding out why an application is generating dumps is generally a logical progression comprised of the following steps:

1. Monitor file system level activity by the application. What DLLs, INI files, and temporary scratch areas are being accessed; are there any access denied errors?

2. Monitor registry access by the application. Are there any missing registry settings, or access denied errors? Are the value settings logical?

FROM THE CLASSROOM

Troubleshooting Permissions-Related Problems

Teaching students how to use Filemon from www.sysinternals.com is extremely simple, but often overlooked during class. I have found that one of the easiest ways to teach this utility is done after installing Microsoft Office. When installation is complete, I remove Domain Users from the permissions list on the MS09.DLL in the Office directory. Then,

as an Admin, I log in and use Word and Excel. The students then log in using standard domain user accounts and try to run the same applications.

Once the application fails, I have them run Filemon while launching the application, afterward viewing the results to find the Access Denied on the MS09.DLL.

—*Ron Oglesby MCSE, CCEA, CCI, CSA*

Optimizing Application Performance

Optimizing application performance means something special on multiuser systems. Normally, the intention is to tune systems and applications to run as fast as possible, but on multiuser systems, the strategy has to change, tuning applications so they run adequately for as many users as possible.

An additional factor to consider when tuning is that in NT 4.0 TSE and Windows 2000 terminal services, the operating system is application-aware. If an application uses the system message queue too heavily, it can be flagged as a "bad" application and will typically run much slower than normal. Once this happens, you will have to tune the application to make it run at an acceptable speed.

Application Compatibility Settings

Some applications have special requirements to enable them to work properly on MetaFrame XP. These requirements may include memory size restriction, CPU usage modification, special handling of INI files, and system naming modifications. One method of modifying application behavior is to use application compatibility flags and values.

These are located under HKLM\Software\Microsoft\Windows NT\ CurrentVersion\Terminal Server\Compatibility\Applications. Three CPU utilization settings exist: FirstCountMsgQPeeksSleepBadApp, MsgQBadAppSleepTimeInMillisec, and NthCountMsgQPeeksSleepBadApp, as well as a flags value that is the sum of the wanted application compatibility flags.

To "register" an application and begin with default compatibility settings, create a new key under the Applications key using the application name. For example, for Prowin32.exe, create a key named PROWIN32. A good starting point is to copy the values under the MSACCESS key. The resulting key is shown next.

Tuning CPU Utilization

Copying the MSACESS key values for your application gives you a starting point for bad application tuning. The basic strategy in tuning a bad application, after creating the application key and settings, is to define a time-measurable task for the application, run up Performance Monitor and then modify the application compatibility values.

The new values take effect immediately on restarting the application, so the tuning process is quite fast. Measure the task completion time versus CPU utilization for each new setting.

The idea is to get acceptable performance with the least amount of impact to the CPU. The best strategy is to start by setting MsgQBadAppSleepTimeInMillisec to 0. This allows the application to run with no restrictions. If it doesn't run any faster, your slow speed problem is due to something else. If it does run faster, then the next step is to set MsgQBadAppSleepTimeInMillisec back to 1, and slowly increase the FirstCountMsgQPeeksSleepBadApp value until the times are acceptable.

More detailed information on application compatibility settings is provided in Table 8-3 and Table 8-4 that follow.

on the Job *There are times when you will be using every tool you can find to reduce the amount of processor used by an application. At such moments, either processor utilization will not decrease, or it will decrease in such a way that the application will slow to a crawl.*
When this happens, you may have to look at an application change. Most applications can be tuned to work in this environment, but you should be aware that there are applications that will not work correctly, no matter how many tools you throw at them.

TABLE 8-3 Description of Application Compatibility Settings

Value Name	Description
FirstCountMsgQPeeksSleepBadApp	Number of times the application can query the message queue before it is put to sleep. Increase this to make the application faster.
MsgQBadAppSleepTimeInMillisec	Number of milliseconds the application is suspended. Setting this to zero turns off bad app detection.
NthCountMsgQPeeksSleepBadApp	Number of times the application can query the message queue before it is suspended again. Increase this to make the application faster.
Flags	See Table 8-4 that follows.

TABLE 8-4	Application Compatibility Settings—Flags and Actions

"Flags" Value (Hex)	Action
0×1	DOS application
0×2	OS/2 application
0×4	Windows 16-bit application
0×8	Windows 32-bit application
0×10	Return username instead of computername
0×20	Return Citrix build number
0×100	Disable registry mapping for this application
0×400	Not substitute user Windows directory for %systemroot% directory
0×800	Limit physical memory reported to app to 32MB
0×1000	Log object creations to %citrix_compat_logpath%

Note: the easiest way to modify the application compatibility values is with the free tool: CMPTMAN.EXE. There are separate NT 4.0 TSE and Windows 2000 versions of this utility available from Citrix. (See Figure 8-12.)

FIGURE 8-12

The CMPTMAN.EXE user interface

Now that you have a better understanding of how to configure applications, here are some real world problems and their solutions.

SCENARIO & SOLUTION

You need to make an application available to any user on your network. The application is sensitive and does not require any per user configuration settings. What is the simplest way to deploy this app so everyone can use it?	Using the Citrix Management Console will publish the application anonymously.
In trying to determine why one of your servers has extremely high utilization, you discover that a DOS application is consuming an enormous amount of CPU time. What possible utilities can you use to fix this?	DOSKBD can be used with NT 4.0 Terminal Server. TAME and DPAKBD can be used with Windows 2000.

Modifying INI File Handling

While the normal execute mode INI file distribution mechanism works very well, there are a number of applications that use personalized INI files that shouldn't be updated. A couple of examples of these are the Lotus Notes client and SAP GUI client. The normal behavior, updating from %systemroot%, can be modified by registering the INI files as exceptions under the key HKLM\Software\Microsoft\ Windows NT\CurrentVersion\Terminal Server\Compatibility\IniFiles, with values having the name of the INI file, less extension and data corresponding to the flags, shown next in Table 8-5.

TABLE 8-5	Flag Value (Hex)	Action
Inifilename Values	0×4	Windows 16-bit application.
	0×8	Windows 32-bit application.
	0×40	Synchronize user INI file to system version.
	0×80	Do not substitute user Windows directory.

Other Application Tuning Tools

DOS applications can use excessive CPU time if the DOS application has uncontrolled keyboard polling. While the application compatibility settings provide a way to tune 16- and 32-bit Windows applications, these will not work effectively for DOS applications. While NTVDM.EXE could be registered as a "bad" application to control the CPU utilization of misbehaving DOS applications, this would adversely affect all DOS applications on the server. A far more effective way is to use DOSKBD for NT 4.0 TSE, a TSR that can control keyboard polling behavior.

Microsoft does not provide or support any tools such as DOSKBD for controlling DOS applications on Windows 2000. However, DPAKBD (ftp://ftp.citrix.com/utilities/dpakbd.zip) has been used with some success and version 4.0 of TAME (http://www.mindspring.com/~dgthomas/tame.htm) is excellent for managing DOS applications on Windows 2000.

CERTIFICATION SUMMARY

While the Citrix Certified Administrator exam may not cover the installation management features in depth, it is sure to cover some of that information on the exam. Be sure to understand the concepts defined in this chapter, such as install and execute mode, the options available when publishing an application, what components make up Installation Manager, and how IM works.

TWO-MINUTE DRILL

Installing Applications

❑ Install mode is used to install applications in a MetaFrame environment.

❑ Install mode can be accessed two ways: through the command line with Change User /Install, or through Add/Remove Programs.

❑ Logons should be disabled prior to installing applications, and no users should have sessions active on the server.

❑ When uninstalling applications that were manually installed, use Add/Remove Programs.

❑ When uninstalling applications that were installed using Installation Manager, use the Installation Manager plug-in for the Citrix Management Console.

❑ Application registry settings and INI files are configured for a user either at logon or when they first use the application.

❑ Application compatibility scripts are used to correct application problems in a multiuser environment.

❑ Citrix's Installation Manager has three components: the Packager, the Installer, the IM Plug-in for the Citrix Management Console.

Configuring Applications for Use in a MetaFrame Environment

❑ Anonymous applications use local user accounts and do not have access to domain resources.

❑ You can configure minimum encryption levels for specific applications using the Citrix Management Console.

❑ Only published applications (including published desktops) can be load-balanced.

❑ When publishing an application, users and groups can be specified as "configured" users to restrict application access.

❑ Applications that run for administrators but not regular users are generally related to file permissions.

❑ Applications can be tuned using application compatibility keys in the registry.

❑ CMPTMAN.EXE is a utility provided by Citrix for tuning applications.

❑ DOSKDB is used with NT 4.0 TSE to control CPU usage of DOS applications. TAME and DPAKBD are two third-party apps available in Windows 2000.

SELF TEST

The following questions will help you measure your understanding of the material presented in this chapter. Read all the choices carefully, as there may be more than one correct answer. Choose all correct answers for each question.

Installing Applications

1. Before installing an application, which of the following must be accomplished? (Choose all that apply.)

   A. Logons must be disabled.

   B. The application must be installed in install mode.

   C. Users who will utilize the application should be logged on to the server.

   D. The IMA service should be stopped.

2. What is the command line used to disable logons?

   A. Change user /disable

   B. Disable /Logon

   C. Change Logon /disable

   D. Change user /logondisable

3. A new application has been installed in install mode. This application uses an INI file for user settings. When users log on, they automatically receive a copy of the INI in their Home directory. Where is this INI file copied from?

   A. The Application Compatibility Scripts directory

   B. The user's profile

   C. The %systemroot% directory

   D. The application's working directory

4. You have an application that you must install using Installation Manager. You do not want this to affect the operations of your servers during the day. How can you install this application without interrupting the service of your servers?

   A. Publish the application using the Citrix Management Console.

   B. Use a Windows AT command to schedule the install.

    C. Use the scheduling option included with the Installation Manager plug-in.

    D. Publish the load scheduling utility.

5. You wish to remove an application that was manually installed using Add/Remove Programs and had a compatibility script. How would you accomplish this?

    A. Right-click the Applications node in the CMC and select delete published application.

    B. Remove the application using Installation Manager.

    C. Use Add/Remove Programs and run the uninstall compatibility script.

    D. Delete the application program files from the server.

6. Some applications require post-setup modifications in order for them to run properly in a terminal server environment. What is used for these post-setup modifications?

    A. CMPTMAN.EXE

    B. Filemon from http://www.sysinternals.com

    C. Application compatibility scripts

    D. Custom EXEs and DLLs from Microsoft

7. You plan on removing several applications from your servers. These applications were installed using Citrix Installation Manager. How should the applications be removed?

    A. By using Add/Remove Programs on each server

    B. By using Add/Remove Programs on the server in which the applications were packaged

    C. Manually, by deleting their program files and registry entries

    D. By using the Installation Manager Plug-in in the Citrix Management Console to remove the applications from the target servers.

8. Installation Manager consists of three components. What are they? (Choose all that apply.)

    A. Citrix Packager

    B. Citrix Installer

    C. Citrix ADF files

    D. Citrix Management Console Plug-in

9. Which of the following can be installed using the Citrix Installation Manager? (Choose all that apply.)

    A. 32 Windows applications

    B. Operating System service packs

C. Operating system hotfixes

D. Application upgrades

10. Which of the following are true about the Citrix Installer? (Choose all that apply.)

   A. It requires a user account to access the network share point and to install the applications.

   B. It is installed on the production MetaFrame servers.

   C. It supports MSI and ADF files.

   D. It can install applications that were scheduled for a later date.

Configuring Applications for Use in a MetaFrame Environment

11. In order to load-balance an application you must... (Choose all that apply.)

   A. Publish the application using the Citrix Management Console

   B. Select multiple servers in the Published application's properties

   C. Have the application installed on each of the selected servers

   D. Publish the load-balancing utility

12. You wish to sort your published applications using folders so that when a client uses NFuse they will access Microsoft Word by opening the Office folder. How can you accomplish this?

   A. Right-click the Applications node in the CMC and select Add Folder.

   B. In the Published Application's properties, enter the word **Office** in the Program Neighborhood Folder.

   C. Create a folder on the client side and copy the icons into the folder.

   D. Copy the application icons from the server to the client desktop.

13. Which of the following can be published on a MetaFrame XP server? (Choose all that apply.)

   A. Applications

   B. Citrix utilities

   C. Server desktops

   D. Server farms

14. You have added a new accounting application to one of the servers in your farm. This application will be used for your users to access the accounting package via the Internet. You wish to ensure that this application is only run with ICA encryption turned on and set to 128-bit encryption. What is the easiest way to do this?

A. By setting the encryption level to 128 under the Advanced button of the ICA connection.

B. By changing the connection to the published application on the client side to 128-bit encryption.

C. By changing the Application Set Properties on the client side to 128-bit encryption.

D. By changing the properties of the published application and setting required encryption to 128-bit.

15. Which of the following are true regarding published applications? (Choose all that apply.)

A. Publishing an application in the server farm requires that at least one server host the application.

B. You can have a mix of anonymous and explicit applications in your server farm.

C. Applications that require domain credentials should not be published anonymously.

D. A published application can only reside on one server.

16. Which types of applications may use excessive CPU cycles and can be tuned using TAME or DSOKBD?

A. OS/2 applications

B. Windows 32-bit applications

C. DOS applications

D. Windows 16-bit applications

17. Where in the registry would you find the compatibility flags for tuning windows applications?

A. HKLM\Software\Microsoft\Windows\Current Version\Terminal Server\Compatibility\Applications

B. HKCU\Software\Microsoft\Windows\Current Version\Terminal Server\Compatibility\Applications

C. HKCU\Software\Microsoft\Windows NT\Current Version\Terminal Server\Compatibility\Applications

D. HKLM\Software\Microsoft\Windows NT\Current Version\Terminal Server\Compatibility\Applications

18. What utility does Citrix provide for creating application compatibility keys for applications?

A. CMPTMAN.EXE

B. Application compatibility scripts

    C. DOSKBD

    D. TAME 4.0

19. Which utility is used to publish applications on a MetaFrame XP server?

    A. Citrix Server Administration

    B. Citrix Published Application Manager

    C. The Citrix Management Console

    D. The Citrix WinStation Configuration

20. Deleting a published application from the Citrix Management Console has which of the following effects? (Choose all that apply.)

    A. It removes the application from the server.

    B. The application will no longer be available to Citrix clients for load balancing.

    C. The application will no longer be available to NFuse or Program Neighborhood clients.

    D. The application will still be installed on the server.

LAB QUESTION

You are faced with the following situation:

You have four servers and four applications. You have found that one of the applications performs extremely poorly and often requires so many resources that it brings the performance of other applications to a crawl. You have a need to support 100 total users and your server can handle 40 users each when using the "well-behaved" applications. You wish to publish the applications in such a way that this "bad" application will not affect the other applications on the farm, since only a handful of people use it.

How can you publish the applications so this "bad" app does not affect the performance of other applications in the farm?

SELF TEST ANSWERS

Installing Applications

1. ☑ A and B are correct. Logons should be disabled, and the application must be installed in install mode.

☒ Since logons must be disabled, C is therefore incorrect. The IMA service does not need to be stopped, so D is incorrect as well.

2. ☑ C is the correct command line.

☒ A, B, and D are incorrect.

3. ☑ C is the correct location. The user's INIs are synched with the system's INI.

☒ This makes A, B, and D incorrect.

4. ☑ C is correct. The scheduling option allows you to schedule installs during off hours.

☒ A, B, and D are all incorrect.

5. ☑ C is correct. The program should be removed the same way it was installed, and if an uninstall script exists, it should be run.

☒ A is incorrect, since this deletes the published application but not the application itself. B is incorrect, since this will only work if you installed it using Installation Manager. D is incorrect, since this is never the correct way to uninstall an application.

6. ☑ C is correct. Application compatibility scripts correct problems with applications in a multiuser environment.

☒ A and B are incorrect because these are both utilities used to find problems or tune an application. D is incorrect because Microsoft does not have problems. They are built-in features.

7. ☑ D is correct. Installation packages should only be removed using the Installation Manager in the Citrix Management Console.

☒ A, B, and C are incorrect.

8. ☑ A, B, and D are correct. IM consists of the Packager, the Installer, and the Plug-in.

☒ C is incorrect because ADF files are supported but not necessary.

9. ☑ A, B, C, and D are all correct. All of these can be installed using Installation Manager

10. ☑ A, B, C, and D are all correct.

Configuring Applications for Use in a MetaFrame Environment

11. ☑ **A, B, and C** are correct. Using the CMC, you should select all the servers you wish to load-balance the application across. The application must be installed on each of the servers.
    ☒ **D** is incorrect because there is no such utility or requirement.

12. ☑ **B** is correct. By entering the Folder name as the Program Neighborhood folder, any application with an identical folder name will be sorted together in the same folder.
    ☒ **A, C, and D** are incorrect.

13. ☑ **A, B, and C** are correct. Applications can be published from a MetaFrame server, and so can Citrix utilities (such as the Citrix Admin toolbar), which are just normal windows executables. Selecting the Published Desktop radio button in the Published applications properties can also publish desktops.
    ☒ **D** is incorrect, since a server farm is a group of servers and cannot be published.

14. ☑ **D** is the correct answer. While the other answers may work, D is the easiest way to set encryption for that application.
    ☒ **A** is incorrect, since it is a global change. It will meet the required encryption, but will require every connection to the server to run encryption, not just connections, to that application. **B and C** are incorrect, since it is much easier to change the application properties on the server side than to make the change at each client.

15. ☑ **A, B, and C** are correct. An application must be on at least one server in the farm to be published. You can have a mix of anonymous and explicit applications in your farm, and if an application requires domain credentials or user-specific settings, it should not be run anonymously.
    ☒ **D** is incorrect, since you can publish a single application to multiple servers to provide for load balancing and some fault tolerance.

16. ☑ **C** is correct. DOS applications tend to use excessive amounts of CPU due to unchecked keyboard polling.
    ☒ **A, B, and D** are incorrect, since they are tuned using the compatibility flags in the registry.

17. ☑ **D** is the correct location for application compatibility flags.
    ☒ **A** is incorrect because it specifies the "Windows" key instead of Windows NT. **B and C** are incorrect because they specify HKEY_Current_User. Compatibility flags are never stored in the User's profile.

18. ☑ **A** is correct. CMPTMAN.EXE is a GUI base utility provided by Citrix Systems to create the compatibility flags for applications.

☒ **B** is incorrect because compatibility script are used for port setup modifications to the application, but do not create these flags. **C** and **D** are incorrect, since these utilities are not for creating compatibility flags.

19. ☑ **C** is correct because with MetaFrame XP the Citrix Management Console has replaced the Published Application Manager.

☒ **B** and **A** are incorrect, since they are used to manage MetaFrame 1.X servers and not MetaFrame XP servers. **D** is incorrect, since this utility was used in WinFrame for connection configurations.

20. ☑ **B, C,** and **D** are correct. Deleting the published application does not remove the app from the server. Instead, it removes it from the list of available published applications (load-balanced or not).

☒ **A** is incorrect, since the application itself is not removed unless it is uninstalled.

LAB ANSWER

Given that you can handle enough users on three of the servers, by running the other three "well-behaved" applications we can isolate the bad application to its own server.

The first three servers in the farm will load-balance the well-behaved applications, while the fourth server in the farm will be dedicated to the "bad" application. This will keep its resource hogging isolated on its own server where it cannot adversely affect the other applications in the farm.

9

Citrix ICA Client Software

The Citrix Independent Computer Architecture Client software allows multiple platforms access to the MetaFrame XP server. This software also permits clients to access local resources mapped to the server. During this chapter, you will learn deployment methods of the Citrix Client Software, different requirements and features of the Citrix clients, and preconfiguration of Citrix clients.

CERTIFICATION OBJECTIVE 9.01

Installing the Citrix ICA Client Software

The ICA client software has three different deployment methods, but careful consideration is needed when choosing a deployment method, as each has its strengths and weaknesses. The three deployment methods are

- Client installation disks
- Network share-based
- Web-based

Care needs to also be given to what client is needed, as well as the application delivery method. These deployment methods, except for the Web-based install, are only for the DOS, Windows 9*x*/ME/NT and Windows 3.11 clients.

Remember, Mac, Unix, and Windows CE clients require manual installation the first time they're installed.

Client Installation Disks

Installation diskettes—probably the easiest of all deployment methods—are created from the Independent Computing Architecture (ICA) Client Creator in the Citrix toolbar. This is also the most tedious and time-consuming method of distributing the ICA client. The client installation disk method of deployment is mostly for smaller companies that do not want to set up a network share point, or remote locations that need to be sent disks when installing over a wide area network (WAN) line is too costly or too slow to be practical. Obviously this method requires touching every machine you want the client on, so distributing clients this way is pretty labor intensive. This method is recommended if you want to put the client on only a few machines, or, as mentioned earlier, you need to send the disks to a remote location. This is the way to distribute the ICA DOS client, as the files on the ICA Client CD are broken into individual disks. Although all these files can be copied to a share point and installed, it really is preferable to install the DOS client manually.

Network Share Point

Deploying from a network share point is usually the best method to get the clients the appropriate files. To deploy using a share point, create a directory on a shared network drive or volume. Into this directory, copy the ICA client installation files. (Note: This method again only works for the Windows 9*x*/ME/NT and Windows 3.11 clients.) The client files will be in the directory X:\icaweb*language*, where X is your CD drive. Copy the files over to the share point, and point your users to this point. The users then double-click on the file to install the client.

FROM THE CLASSROOM

Deploying from a Network Share Point

Understanding how to deploy a Citrix client using a network share point is key to successfully deploying Citrix. The following steps will take you through setting up your share properly.

1. Log in to a file server with administrative permissions.

2. Create a directory on a drive on the server (e.g., D:\clients).

3. Copy the files from X:\icaweb\language over to this directory. X: is your CD drive, so for an English install, it would be E:\icaweb\en.

4. Share this directory and give users permissions to it.

5. Have your users (or IT staff) go to this directory. There they will find the appropriate client. Double-click the client to install.

That's the procedure. Not only is it easy, but it is a massive time-saver compared to doing a manual install. Remember, though, this is only for Windows clients. All other clients have to be installed by hand.

—*Kevin Wing, MCSE, CCEA, CCNA*

Web-Based Install

Web-based install is the best deployment method if you're using NFuse in your enterprise. When the client connects to an NFuse enabled Web page, the server will check its system for the appropriate client. If the client does not exist on the system, it will analyze their platform and present the client for install. To enable this, copy the contents of the icaweb directory on the ICA Client CD to a directory named Citrix in the NFuse server's root directory. For example, c:\wwwroot\citrix. You must copy the entire directory structure of icaweb to the server for this to work. An NFuse-enabled Web page uses the following code to check for an ICA client:

```
// if (noClientDetect == -1) {
// ### Open ICA Client Install popup web page at 380x440px.
// var icaPopUpWindow =
window.open("icaclient.asp?initCheck=true","icaPopUp","toolbar=no,location=no,
directories=no,status=no,menubar=no,resizable=no,width=380,height=440");
// icaPopUpWindow.focus();
// }
```

Even if you have not implemented NFuse in your organization, you can still do a Web-based installation. Set up a directory on a file server to hold the client images, copy the icaweb directory over to it, and create a Web page that links to the setup file of the client. The client will not be automatically detected or installed as in the NFuse installation, but it does allow Web links to the installation point.

Now that we've discussed the deployment methods, let's look at some scenarios of when you would use these different methods.

SCENARIO & SOLUTION

You need to deploy the client to hundreds of users on your LAN.	Use network share-based installation
You have DOS clients that need to access MetaFrame.	Use client installation disks
You run NFuse.	Use web-based install
You have remote users.	Use client installation disks
You want easy access to a share point.	Use web-based install
You need to automatically install Macintosh clients.	Use web-based install

EXERCISE 9-1

CertCam 9-1

Create Client Installation Disks

This exercise will take you through the steps required to create the Citrix ICA client diskettes.

1. Click on the ICA Client Creator and the Make Installation Disk Set dialog box will appear.

2. Choose the appropriate client. (Note: Only the client for DOS, Windows 9x/ME/NT, and Windows 3.11 clients can be created from the ICA Client Creator, as shown in Figure 9-1).

3. Select the floppy drive you want the client to be copied to (it should be autoselected to A:), and check the Format Disks box if you want the floppies to be formatted before writing.

4. Click OK and follow the instructions on the screen. This method requires three floppies.

FIGURE 9-1

The Citrix
Installation Disk
creator

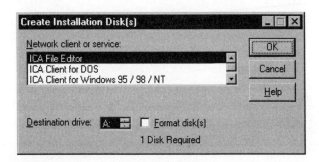

Using Server Auto-Location and Server Groups

When a Citrix client is not configured with a specified server, it will attempt to auto-locate the nearest Citrix server. This is handled by sending broadcasts out through the network, depending on the protocol the client is configured with. For example, with TCP/IP, a broadcast is made to UDP port 1604. This broadcast is read by the Citrix master browser, which returns the server location to the client. The client then connects to the server through TCP port 1494. By using broadcasts, this obviously increases the load on the network. This can be eliminated by configuring the client with a server. Click Add in the address list, as shown in Figure 9-2, type the server address, click OK, and the server will be listed. When refreshing an application set, the client will contact that server to get the list of applications available to the user.

Server groups can also be defined so as to contain several servers to contact, in case the main server cannot be reached. The server groups built into the client are Primary, Backup 1, and Backup 2. These can be renamed if needed. Each one of these groups can hold up to five server addresses. The groups are then queried in order to try to create a Citrix session. A packet is sent to all the servers in the

FIGURE 9-2

The client server configuration screen

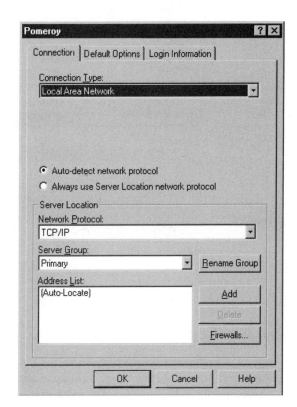

Primary list, then through each of the servers in the Backup groups. If at any time one of the servers responds, all subsequent attempts are aborted, and the client creates the normal ICA connection.

Another piece of the configuration at this point is firewall information. The Citrix client can connect to Citrix servers located behind a firewall as long as the server has an alternate address configured for the firewall. Simply check the box to activate the alternate address setting, which is displayed in Figure 9-3. The address for a SOCKS proxy can also be entered here.

exam
ⓦatch

Expect a question dealing with alternate addresses for firewalls. Remember, simply configuring the address on the server is not enough; the client must be configured for this as well.

Windows 9x and Windows ME

There are two different clients for Windows 9*x* and ME. One is the graphical Program Neighborhood client; the other is the Web-based client. Where these clients should be used depends upon the needs of the organization. If Citrix is mainly used for published applications on a LAN and there are few or no Web connections, then the Program Neighborhood client would be the correct client to install. If most of the connections come from a Web page and the client needs to embed inside that page, then the Web client would make more sense. Both have many of the same features and requirements.

FIGURE 9-3

The firewall
configuration
screen

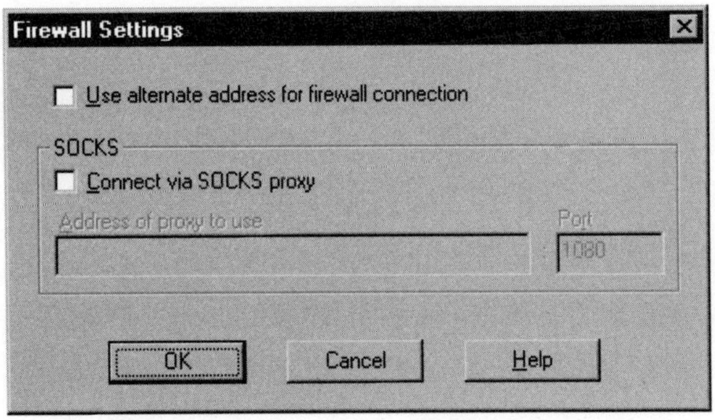

Program Neighborhood Client

The Citrix Win32 Program Neighborhood client allows graphical access to applications published on a Citrix server. Users can browse the Program Neighborhood (as shown in Figure 9-4) to access application sets that have been configured on the Citrix server. They can then launch the application from the Program Neighborhood window. This client can also be used with NFuse to run applications configured to launch a separate window. Application icons can be pushed to the client desktop or the Start menu, allowing the user to run the application without opening the client program.

The Win32 Program Neighborhood has also the following features.

TAPI Support

The Win32 client works with TAPI (Telephony Application Programming Interface) compliant modems to allow dial-up access to Citrix servers. The standard Windows modem support is integrated into the client. If a non-TAPI modem is

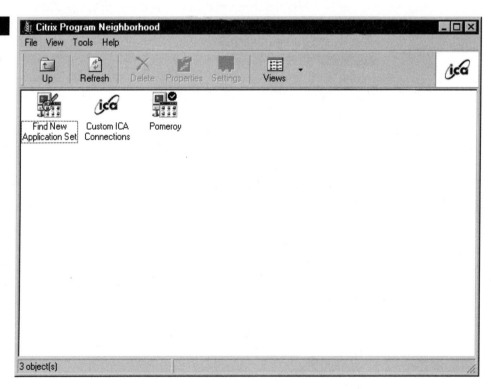

FIGURE 9-4

The Win32 ICA Program Neighborhood client

installed, the client can still load and configure the modem for Citrix access. This allows direct dial-up access to a Citrix server. It does not use the Remote Access Service (RAS) inside Windows and does not allow dial-up connections to a RAS server. It only permits connections to a Citrix server that has modems configured for direct dial-up access.

Seamless Windows

The Win32 client supports the seamless integration of local and remote application windows. Full mouse and keyboard, including clipboard integration and wheel-mouse support is incorporated in the client. The user can switch between local and remote applications using standard keyboard shortcuts, cut and paste items between local and remote windows, and tile and cascade local and remote application windows. Cutting and pasting between local and remote sessions is handled as if the remote sessions are local to the desktop. Users can also drag and drop information from either window.

If clipboard mapping needs to be disabled, the client connection properties need to be configured. Click the Client Connection button on the MetaFrame toolbar. Select the connection, and go to its properties. Click the Settings button. Check the box marked Disable Client Clipboard Mapping. This will disable the feature.

Client Device Mapping

The Win32 client supports client device mapping during a Citrix session. This allows local drives, printers, and COM ports to be accessed while running remote applications. Client drive mapping also allows remote drives to be mapped to local drives on a user's computer. For example, a home directory on a server can be mapped to the user's C: drive. The drive can then be accessed by all standard file tools. Printer mapping allows clients to use their local printers in remote applications, just like they would with local applications. COM port mapping permits almost any peripheral that connects through the COM port to be accessed in a Citrix application session. (Note: These features are not available when connecting to MetaFrame Unix servers.)

Client drive, printer, and COM port mapping can all be disabled from the server. Click the Client Connection button on the MetaFrame Toolbar. Select the appropriate connection and go to its properties. Click the client settings button. Choose the check box next to the feature that is to be disabled. Printer and drive mappings are automatic, by default. To disable this automatic mapping, uncheck the Inherit User Config box, then uncheck the box marked Connect Client Drives At Logon For Drive Mappings, or Connect Client Printers For Printer Mappings.

Printer mappings can also be forced to the default printer on the client by checking the box labeled Default To Main Client Printer. To prevent every printer on every client from being auto-created on the server, check the box named Connect Only The Client's Main Printer. The default printer on the client will be the only printer auto-created on the server.

COM ports must be manually mapped to the server. When connected to a Citrix session, open up a command prompt. From the prompt, type **net use com***x*: **\\clientname\com***z*, where *x* is the COM port on the server, and *z* is the COM port on the client that needed to be mapped.

Client drives are mapped to accessible drive letters. Table 9-1 provides the drive mappings.

The letters on the Citrix server can be remapped to not interfere with the local client drives. The user then sees their local drives by the local drive letters (C stays C). The server drives can be mapped to any drive letter to prevent conflicts with mapped network drives. The letters follow the pattern of C: drive on server mapped to letter, all subsequent drives are the next letter. For example, if C: is mapped to M:, drive D: on the server is mapped to N:, and so on. This mapping is set during the initial installation of MetaFrame and cannot be changed after setup.

Sound Support

Win32 client sound support allows users with a compatible sound card to play sound files on the server and hear them through their local computer sound system. The sound files can be compressed to meet bandwidth requirements for the network. Sound support can be managed on the client side from the settings of the application set. Select the application set, and click Settings. Click the Default Options tab, and enable sound. Choose a sound quality option. There are three:

TABLE 9-1	Client Drive Letter	Accessed in a Citrix Session as
Default Drive Mappings of Client Drives	A	A
	B	B
	C	V
	D	U

high, medium, and low. Sound quality options depend on bandwidth. High quality sound requires 1.3Mbps to play clearly. This will eat up bandwidth and processor time, so only use this option if clear sound is an absolute necessity. Medium quality sound uses 64Kbps, which is fine for most local area network connections, while Low quality uses 16Kbps, providing sound support for most modem connections. Client audio mapping can be disabled in the Client Connection Properties, just like drive and printer mapping. The quality of sound can also be controlled from the server. Click on the ICA Settings tab of the connection properties. There is a drop-down list specifying the audio quality.

on the **!**
Üob

Client sound support is more important than one might think. Although sound is usually fairly trivial in most applications, for some users it is vital. Enabling sound support for users helps with political issues surrounding a Citrix roll-out, especially if the user's local desktop is being totally replaced with a Citrix session. The impact on the network can be minimized by compressing the audio to its lowest level. This allows the user to still get sound, but doesn't beat up the network too much.

Client Auto-Update

Client auto-update allows users to connect to the Citrix server and download the latest Citrix client. This frees the administrator from having to touch every machine when a new client becomes available. Clients are stored in the central Client Update Database. New clients can be added to the database using the Client Distribution Wizard on the MetaFrame Toolbar. Click the wizard and provide the path to the new client. The client will then be added to the database, allowing users to auto-update on their next connection. When a Citrix client connects to the server, its version is compared to the version on the server. If a newer client is available, the server informs the users and allows them to download the latest client. Should they choose to download it, they simply wait for it to upgrade before beginning their session, or they can have it download in the background and then update after their session is over. Client auto-update can be disabled from Tools | ICA Settings. Uncheck the box labeled Allow Automatic Client Updates.

Disk Caching and Compression

Disk caching and compression allows the Win32 client to work well over low speed links, whether they are asynchronous or WAN links. To manage the amount of caching and files stored on the local machine, select the Application set; then click Tools | ICA Settings. Select the Bitmap Cache tab. From here, the amount of drive space given over to caching can be modified (the default is one percent), the cache directory can be chosen, and the minimum size bitmap to be cached can be configured. To disable bitmap caching, right-click the Application set, choose Properties, and select the Options tab. Uncheck the box marked Use Disk Cache For Bitmaps.

TCP/IP+HTTP Server Location

This feature allows ICA clients to find Citrix servers without using UDP (User Datagram Protocol) broadcasts. Some networks restrict UDP packets, and most routers are configured to filter out broadcasts. The client transmits XML (eXtensible Markup Language) information in HTTP (Hypertext Transfer Protocol) packets to port 80 (by default) on the server. This functionality can be used with or without NFuse.

exam
Watch

Although it may look like questions on TCP/IP+HTTP server location properly belong on an NFuse exam, this is a new feature of the clients, and will be tested.

Per-User Time Zones

Clients logging into a MetaFrame XP server in a different time zone can have their Citrix session reflect local time zones. This is a new feature with MetaFrame XP.

Encryption

The Win32 ICA Web client includes encryption levels of 40-, 56-, or 128-bit. Published applications and Citrix sessions can require a specific encryption level from the client. If encryption is not set, the client will not be able to connect. The encryption requirement can be set on either the application, or applied to an entire connection. The choices of Basic, 40-, 56-, 128-bit (Logon Only), or 128-bit are available. To configure the connection, click the Connection Properties button on the ICA toolbar. Click the desired connection, and select Properties. Click the Advanced button. Select the desired encryption level. To require the encryption, click the button for Minimum Requirement. To configure at the published application level, select the application; then choose Properties. On the Application tab, select the encryption level and click the button marked Minimum Requirement. This can also be configured when the program is initially published.

Now that encryption does not require a separate add-on to the Citrix server to function, more IT departments are requiring it on their clients. Expect it to be tested.

Encryption in Citrix once required the Secure ICA add-on pack, which was separately licensed and installed. It is now part of the MetaFrame XP package. All clients, version 6 and later, now support encryption. Although encryption may not necessarily be required in every organization, the performance hit associated with 128-bit encryption is minor. Most users will not be able to tell the difference between the encrypted and unencrypted sessions. It may be a good idea to go ahead and require at least some level of encryption on all connections.

Pass-Through Authentication

Pass-through authentication allows local usernames and passwords to be automatically forwarded to servers to allow users to log in to their applications. This reduces the number of logon windows a user will face. The main drawback of this feature is that automatic client update will not work. To enable pass-through authentication, right-click the Application Set, and select Properties. Under the tab marked Logon Information, enter the username, password, and domain for the Application Set. If the password is to be saved, check the box labeled Save Password.

While pass-through authentication does reduce the amount of logon screens the client sees, losing the ability to auto-update the client is a significant drawback. Although you may hear users complain about all the logon screens they see, that may be preferable than hand-installing every new client update.

Installing the Win32 Program Neighborhood Client

Installing the Program Neighborhood client depends upon the deployment method used. If being deployed from the client disks created on the server:

1. Insert Disk 1. Double-click "My Computer," then the floppy drive. Double-click setup.exe.

2. The setup program will then search the computer for any previously installed versions of the client software. If one is found, a screen will ask if the client is to be upgraded, or to be installed in a separate instance. If no previous client is found, it will skip to the Choose Destination Location screen.

3. The default path is C:\Program Files\Citrix\ICA Client. This can be customized to any location.

4. The Select Program Folder dialog box will appear. The default group is Citrix ICA client. It will be created if it doesn't exist.

5. The next screen asks for the ICA client name. Each ICA client needs a unique name to identify itself to the server. If names are repeated, the mapping of devices will not work properly.

6. The files will be copied to the hard drive. The installation program will prompt for the next disk when needed.

Installation from a network share point is the same process, except that all the files needed are in the same directory.

The Win32 Web Client

The Win32 ICA Web client allows connections to applications through an NFuse server using a Web browser. The ICA session is embedded in the web browser window. The Win32 Web client replaces the Active-X controls and Netscape Plug-In clients. The size of the installation executable is much smaller than the full Program Neighborhood client, allowing for faster installation and downloads. While the Win32 Web client supports most of the same features as the Program Neighborhood client; it does not support TAPI or any modem connections. The Web client can also be configured for silent installation and deployment.

System Requirements

System requirements for the Win32 ICA Program Neighborhood client are as follows:

- 386 or above
- Window 9*x*, 2000, ME or NT 3.5 and later

- 8MB of RAM for Windows 9*x*; 16 MB of RAM for NT 3.5 or later/2000
- Approximately 6.5MB of hard drive space (more may be required for caching)
- VGA or SVGA video card with monitor
- For dial-up connections, either an internal or external modem
- For network connections, a network interface card configured for the appropriate network transport. Transports supported are TCP/IP, IPX, SPX, and NetBIOS

System requirements for the Win32 ICA Web client are the same, except that Internet Explorer 4 or later, or Netscape Navigator 4 is required.

exam
ⓦatch

Expect a question dealing with standalone kiosks or terminals.

Now that you know more about the Win32 clients, let's look at why you would choose one client over another, depending on the situation.

SCENARIO & SOLUTION

If your setup consists of all users on a local network	Use program Neighborhood client
If your setup consists of an Application Server Provider	Use Web client
If your setup consists of a LAN with many subnets	Use program Neighborhood client
If your setup consists of Standalone kiosk or terminal	Use Web client

DOS

The ICA DOS client allows access to Citrix server and published applications from DOS. This client comes in two flavors, 16-bit and 32-bit. The DOS client supports many of the same features as the other clients, with the obvious lack of Windows graphical features. Most of the graphical elements of published applications will show up on the DOS client.

System Requirements

The system requirements for the ICA DOS client are:

- 286 or later (16-bit client); 386 or later (32-bit)
- 2MB of RAM or greater
- XMS memory (16-bit client)
- Microsoft mouse or 100 percent compatible
- Sound Blaster 16 or compatible for sound support (optional)
- VGA or SVGA video card and monitor
- DOS 4.0 or later
- Internal/External modem for dial-up connections
- Network interface card with appropriate drivers for the network transport

To install the ICA DOS client, run the install.exe from Disk one of the client diskettes, or from the Client CD. The MetaFrame XP client CD only contains the DOS 32 client. The DOS 32 client is recommended for connections to an XP server.

Windows 3.1*x*

The ICA Win16 client allows 16-bit Windows PCs to connect to a Citrix server and published applications. The Win16 client allows up to three concurrent ICA sessions. It has the same features as the Win32 clients, and the same system requirements.

Mac

The ICA Macintosh client enables Macintosh computers to run Windows-based programs on their desktops. The local Macintosh drives, printers, and communication ports can also be mapped to the server to allow user access during a Citrix session.

System Requirements

The system requirements for the ICA Macintosh client are

- 68030/40 or PowerPC processor
- System 7.1 or later
- 8MB of RAM
- 3MB of disk space
- 16 color or better display
- Open Transport TCP/IP version 1.1.1 or later
- Internal/external modem for dial-up connections
- Network interface card with the appropriate network drivers

The ICA Macintosh client, since it is a Mac program, is a bit different than the DOS and Windows clients. The Macintosh client, although it supports published applications, does not support the Program Neighborhood. Citrix connections are configured through the ICA Client Editor. A server address is entered and can be configured to either launch the server desktop or a specific published application. Multiple connections can be configured to give the "feel" of Program Neighborhood, allowing the Mac clients to have multiple connections on their desktop. Every time a new application is added to the server, a new connection will have to be created on the Mac client. The Mac will not automatically poll the server for new applications, as with the Program Neighborhood clients. The Macintosh client does support Windows keyboard mappings, allowing Mac users to still enter Windows key combinations using their keyboard. Macintosh clients also have to be installed manually the first time, but can be auto-updated from the server after initial installation.

Unix

The ICA Unix clients come in two different versions. Version 6 of the client, which supports all the latest features of the ICA client, runs on Linux, AIX, and Sun Solaris (SPARC). Version 3 of the client supports SGI IRIX, Tru-64 Unix, SunOS,

Solaris(X86), SCO, and HP-UX. Most of the features available to the version 6 clients are also available on version 3. The features not replicated are

- COM port mapping
- Audio mapping
- Encryption
- SpeedScreen
- Increased color support
- Seamless Windows

The Unix client supports the features of the clients for other platforms, but, as with the Mac client, it lacks two key features. It does not support Program Neighborhood (though it does support running an application automatically at start), and it does not have a way to install other than manually. Once installed, it can take advantage of the client auto-update feature.

Linux

The ICA Linux client allows connections to Citrix servers from Red Hat, SuSE, Caldera, and Slackware Linux platforms. It supports all of the features of version 6 of the ICA client for Unix. When a new workstation is to be set up with the Citrix client, it must be installed manually the first time. To install the Linux client, insert the Client CD into the CD-ROM drive on the PC. Mount the CD onto the system. Switch to the icainst/*language*/icaunix directory. Run the setup script by typing **./setupwfc**. A menu of options will appear on the screen, choose 1 to install the ICA client. The installation program will prompt for the program directory (default is /usr/lib/ICAClient). The license agreement screen will come up; type **Y** to accept the license. The installation will proceed. When finished, the menu will reappear. To exit the menu, type **3**. To start the ICA Unix client, at a prompt type **/usr/lib/ICAClient/wfcmgr**.

Deploying Multiple ICA Clients with Identical Configurations

When deploying ICA clients, sometimes it is advantageous to be able to preconfigure them before making them available. This way, multiple clients can be deployed with the same configuration, server lists, and firewall settings without the IT staff having to touch the individual client machines. There are four files inside the client distribution package. They are appsrv.src, module.src, pn.src, and wfclient.src. These files can be extracted from the package using any compression utility and changed to meet the needs of the organization. They can then be recompressed and distributed. All the settings that can be configured through running the ICA client can be preconfigured inside these four files. Table 9-2 gives an idea of when you should preconfigure a client setup.

| TABLE 9-2 | Pre-configuring a Client Setup |

Client setup	Preconfigure or Not
A few local clients	Configure at the desktop
MAC/Unix clients	Configure at the desktop
Multiple Win32 clients on a network	Preconfigure
Multiple Windows client needing firewall settings	Preconfigure
Multiple Windows clients connecting to one server	Configure at the desktop

CERTIFICATION SUMMARY

Citrix clients control all access to the Citrix server from the local desktop. This alone makes them an important part of the Citrix environment. Like any desktop software, care and planning needs to go into a Citrix client rollout. The needs of the organization and the capacity of the network require study before clients are installed on the network. The deployment methods for the Win32 client, for example, can put tremendous strain on the network if not planned in advance. Multiple users all connecting to a shared drive and installing software at the same time can cause many networks to groan under the strain.

As we've seen, most computer platforms are covered by one of the Citrix clients. The Unix and Macintosh clients allow Windows applications to be run on their desktop without the need for different binaries or server configurations. They can run the same applications that Windows users are running at the same time. All of the clients can be configured to replace the local desktop if need be. The user still has access to their printers, drives, and COM ports, but everything is on the server. This allows more control for the administrator and lower support costs.

The Citrix client is the user's view of the Citrix server. It is what the user interacts with on their desktop. Proper planning and care when deploying the client will allow a smooth user experience.

TWO-MINUTE DRILL

Installing the Citrix ICA Client Software

❏ Windows clients can be deployed three ways: installation disks, network share point, and Web-based.

❏ Only the Windows clients can be deployed remotely.

❏ All clients support mapping of local drives and printers.

❏ Server auto-location can put a strain on the network through its use of broadcast traffic.

❏ Citrix servers can be configured as server groups for the client. The client will query these servers in order.

❏ There are two clients that run on Windows 32-bit platforms: the graphical Program Neighborhood client and the Web-based client.

❏ The client must be configured to use firewall addresses.

❏ The DOS client must be installed locally on each desktop.

❏ The user's drive letters will be remapped so as not to conflict with the server drives.

❏ The Macintosh and Unix clients support published applications, but they do not support Program Neighborhood.

❏ Clients can be preconfigured by editing the files appsrv.src, module.src, pn.src, and wfclient.src.

❏ Citrix clients can auto-update when connecting to a server that contains a newer version of the client.

❏ Encryption is now included with version 6 of the Citrix client.

❏ Audio support allows audio files from the server to be played in a Citrix session.

❏ Creating installation disks is the longest and most tedious way to install the Citrix client.

SELF TEST

The following questions will help you measure your understanding of the material presented in this chapter. Read all the choices carefully, as there may be more than one correct answer. Choose all correct answers for each question.

Installing the Citrix ICA Client Software

1. Your company has multiple Citrix servers running across several subnets. Users complain that they cannot access Citrix servers that are not local to their floor, but they can access other resources across the network. Each floor is separated by a router, and you are using server auto-location. What could be the problem?

   A. They don't have permissions to the other Citrix servers.

   B. Your routers are filtering out broadcasts.

   C. The network is having connectivity problems.

   D. They are using outdated clients.

2. What drive letter is the client CD drive remapped to, assuming the server drives (floppy drive, one hard drive, one CD drive, no network shares) have not been remapped?

   A. B

   B. D

   C. U

   D. V

3. You need to access a Citrix server behind a firewall. The server is set with an alternate address for firewall translation. What else needs to be done?

   A. Configure the client to use the alternate address.

   B. Nothing, this will work fine.

   C. Make sure the Citrix client has a public IP address.

   D. Update the Citrix client.

4. You need to deploy multiple clients over a network share point. You have several Mac users that cannot install from the share point. They can see the files inside the directory, but cannot install the client. What is wrong?

   A. They don't have the correct permissions.

   B. They have the wrong version of their system OS.

C. Macintosh clients cannot be deployed remotely.

D. They need the Windows client.

5. How much RAM does the NT version of the Win32 client require?

A. 8MB

B. 32MB

C. 4MB

D. 16MB

6. Which version of DOS do you need to be running for the ICA DOS client to function?

A. 3.3

B. 4.0

C. 5.0

D. 6.0

7. You are using pass-through authentication with your Citrix clients. You update the Citrix client on the server, expecting the client to be auto-updated. You then notice that none of the clients have been updated. What is the problem?

A. Pass-through authentication doesn't allow auto-updating.

B. The clients aren't connecting to the server.

C. The clients aren't configured to auto-update.

D. The clients are Mac clients.

8. What is the server group order that the client should check for an available server?

A. Primary, Secondary, Backup

B. Primary, Backup, Standby

C. Primary, Backup1, Backup2

D. Primary, Backup2, Backup1

9. You need to set up a DOS client. From the Citrix server, how would you deploy the proper client?

A. Create a share point; copy the DOS install files over to it.

B. Create client diskettes from the Client Diskettes Creator window on the MetaFrame toolbar.

C. Push the client out to the DOS computer.

D. None of the above. You have to take the Client CD to the client to install.

10. Which clients cannot be created in the Client Diskettes creator window?

    A. Win32

    B. DOS

    C. Linux

    D. Win16

11. You have just set up a brand new Citrix XP server. It is located behind a router, so you know the router will filter out the broadcasts. You do not want to set up a server list on the client, as the server's address may change. How would you configure the client to auto-locate the server?

    A. Use IPX

    B. Use TCP/IP+HTTP

    C. Use AppleTalk

    D. Nothing needs to be changed.

12. Which network protocol is not supported by MetaFrame?

    A. VINES

    B. TCP/IP

    C. IPX

    D. NetBIOS

13. You support a base of installed Citrix Win32 clients, all running the Program Neighborhood client. You have started using NFuse in your organization. What must you do with these installed clients?

    A. Remove them; then install the Web client instead.

    B. Update them to the latest version.

    C. Nothing. The Win32 client will work with NFuse Web pages.

    D. Install the Web client over the Win32 Client.

14. Which clients support Program Neighborhood?

    A. Win32

    B. Win16

    C. Mac

    D. Unix

    E. All of the above

15. You are running Citrix clients on several Solaris(x86) machines. The clients have a bar-coding gun that hooks up to their COM port. None of their Citrix applications can access the gun, but their regular applications can. What is the problem?

  A. The client for Solaris(x86) does not support COM port mapping.

  B. The COM ports need to be manually mapped.

  C. Version 6 of the client needs to be installed.

  D. The bar-coding gun is not compatible with their systems.

16. You want to set up dial-up connections for your Citrix clients. You currently use the Win32 Web client, but find that you cannot configure any type of dial-up connection. What is wrong?

  A. The Web client needs to be updated.

  B. You need to install a modem.

  C. You need to set up TAPI-compliant drivers.

  D. The Web client does not support dial-up connections.

17. Which TCP port does the ICA client use to connect to the server by default?

  A. 1494

  B. 1604

  C. 1023

  D. 9999

18. You need to set up multiple applications for a Win16 client. The user contacts you and says he gets an error when running many applications. You check and find out he is trying to run five applications at the same time. Why is he getting an error?

  A. He needs to update his client.

  B. The server is having problems.

  C. The Win16 client can only have three application windows at a time.

  D. He has incorrect credentials for his applications.

19. Which file is one of the four that can be edited to preconfigure clients?

  A. pn.src

  B. client.ini

  C. system.ini

  D. win.src

20. Which client would usually be run on a standalone kiosk or terminal?

    A. Win32 Program Neighborhood

    B. DOS32

    C. Win16

    D. Win32 Web client.

LAB QUESTION

You have recently implemented MetaFrame XP in your network. You have around 200 clients locally, plus you also support about 40 remote users. These remote users will require access to Citrix applications. None of your users have an ICA client installed, and you're trying to decide the best method for implementing the client on your system. Remotely, all your users are running Windows 95 machines, which connect through a 256Kbps WAN link. Locally, most of your users are running Windows 2000 machines; however, you do have an Art department with 10 Macintosh systems. All of your local users need access to the Citrix server. The application that you've published supports sound, but you do not want your WAN bandwidth taken up by sound support, as sound is not necessary for the local users. How would you deploy the ICA client to the local and remote users, and how would you manage sound support on the remote users?

SELF TEST ANSWERS

Installing the Citrix ICA Client Software

1. ☑ **B.** Citrix clients that use server auto-location send a broadcast packet to find the nearest Citrix server. If the server is located on another subnet, the router between will filter out the broadcasts. Enter the server addresses in a server group for these users.
   ☒ **A** is incorrect, as this will respond with a credentials error. **C** is incorrect because other resources can still be accessed. **D** is incorrect because the server would attempt to auto-update their client.

2. ☑ **C.** U is the drive that the Citrix client's CD drive is remapped to.
   ☒ **A** is incorrect because that is the client's floppy drive. **B** is incorrect because the server would be using drive D as its CD drive. **D** is incorrect because that is what the client's hard drive is mapped to.

3. ☑ **A.** The Citrix client must also be configured to use the alternate address. Simply check the box marked Alternate Address For Firewalls under the firewall section of the server configuration screen.
   ☒ **B** is incorrect because you must configure the client. **C** is incorrect because the Citrix client does not require a public IP address to work. **D** is incorrect because the client doesn't necessarily need to be updated to connect.

4. ☑ **C.** Macintosh clients need to be installed locally on the client the first time. After this initial install, they can be updated from the server.
   ☒ **A** is incorrect because they can see files in the directory. **B** is incorrect because they would get an error stating they have the wrong OS version. **D** is incorrect because they use the Macintosh client.

5. ☑ **D.** The Win32 client requires 16MB of RAM or higher.
   ☒ **A, B,** and **C** are incorrect because the NT version of the Win32 client requires 16MB of RAM or higher.

6. ☑ **B.** DOS 4.0 is required.
   ☒ **A, C,** and **D** are incorrect because DOS 4.0 is required for the ICA DOS client to function.

7. ☑ **A.** Pass-through authentication blocks auto-updating. It also reduces the amount of login screens the users sees.
   ☒ **B** is incorrect; they've been running their Citrix sessions correctly. **C** is incorrect because all Citrix clients check for updates. **D** is incorrect because the Mac client will auto-update.

8. ☑ C. Primary, Backup1, Backup2 is the correct order.
   ☒ A, B, and D are incorrect because the correct server group order that the client should check for an available server is Primary, Backup 1, Backup 2.

9. ☑ B. Creating client diskettes from the Client Diskettes window is the proper way to deploy the client. You still have to take the diskettes to the local client and install them, of course.
   ☒ A is incorrect; the DOS files should be installed locally by hand from created diskettes. C is incorrect because you cannot push the client. D is incorrect because, although you can install this way, you can create diskettes on the server.

10. ☑ C. Linux diskettes cannot be created on the server.
    ☒ A, B, and D are incorrect because only Linux diskettes cannot be created on the server.

11. ☑ B is correct. TCP/IP+HTTP encapsulates an XML packet inside an HTTP packet to find a server. These packets will pass through routers, as they aren't broadcast.
    ☒ A is incorrect; IPX still uses broadcasts to find servers. C is incorrect because the Citrix client doesn't support AppleTalk. D is incorrect, as the router will filter out any broadcast packets.

12. ☑ A. MetaFrame does not support Banyan VINES protocol.
    ☒ B, C, and D are incorrect because Banyan VINES protocol is the only network protocol listed that is not supported by MetaFrame.

13. ☑ C is correct. The Win32 supports launching applications from an NFuse Web page.
    ☒ A, B, and D are incorrect because you do not have to do anything with these installed clients. The Win32 client will work with Nfuse Web pages.

14. ☑ A and B. Win32 and Win16 support Program Neighborhood.
    ☒ C, D, and E are incorrect because the Mac and Unix clients support published applications, but they do not support the actual Program Neighborhood.

15. ☑ A. The Solaris(x86) client does not support COM port mapping.
    ☒ B is incorrect because the ports cannot be mapped. C is incorrect; the highest client for this OS is version 3. D is incorrect, since local applications can access the gun.

16. ☑ D is correct. The Web client is for network only connections, as it connects through an opened browser window.
    ☒ A is incorrect because updating will not change this. B and C are correct for the Win32 Program Neighborhood client only.

17. ☑ **A** is correct. The ICA client connects to the server over TCP port 1494. It uses UDP port 1604 to search for Citrix servers.
    ☒ **B, C,** and **D** are incorrect because the ICS client uses TCP port 1494 to connect to the server by default.

18. ☑ **C** is correct. The Win16 client can only have three application windows open at one time, along with the Remote Application Manager window.
    ☒ **A, B,** and **D** are incorrect because the reason the user is getting an error is that he is trying to run too many applications at one time.

19. ☑ **A** is the correct answer.
    ☒ **B, C,** and **D** are incorrect because the pn.src file is one of the four that can be edited to preconfigure clients.

20. ☑ **D** is correct. You can run the Win32 Web client kiosk or terminal.
    ☒ **A** is incorrect because, although you can run Wind 32 Program Neighborhood on a kiosk, these are usually configured to run embedded applications in a Web browser. **B** and **C** are incorrect because you would not normally run DOS32 or Win16 on a standalone kiosk or terminal.

LAB ANSWER

The local Windows 2000 clients should be deployed from a network share point. Create a shared drive on a fileserver; then copy the Win32 ICA client files to that drive. At the client machine, double-click the folder that contains the files; then run setup.exe. This will install the ICA Win32 Program Neighborhood client.

The Macintosh clients will have to be installed by hand. Remember, only the Win32/Win16 clients can be installed from a network share point. Take the Citrix Client CD to each Mac and install the Mac client.

The remote users can be installed in one of two ways. The most tedious method is, of course, to create client diskettes from the ICA Client Creator window on the server and send the diskettes to the remote office. Each user, or a local staff member, will then have to install the client by hand on their machine. The other method would be for them to install from the previously configured network share point. The drawback to this method is bandwidth. If all 40 users decide to install at the same time, the link could become saturated fairly quickly, therefore staggering the installs would be the best method.

The best way to take care of the sound issue is to simply disable client audio mapping on the Citrix connection. To disable it for only the WAN users, this would have to be set at the client level, which would require someone touching each client machine. Since audio support is not mandatory for the local users, it would be easier to simply disable all audio mapping. Click on the Citrix Connection button on the ICA toolbar, select the appropriate connection, and choose Properties. Click the ICA Settings button and check the box next to Disable Client Audio Mapping. This will turn the audio off for all users on this Citrix connection.

CITRIX® CERTIFIED ADMINISTRATOR

10

Citrix Program Neighborhood

T his chapter focuses on features and functions of Program Neighborhood (PN), also referred to as the Citrix ICA Client. The primary purpose of Program Neighborhood is to connect client devices to MetaFrame servers or published applications. Program Neighborhood is designed to be device independent, that is, it provides connectivity for a variety of client devices and operating systems.

We will also be focusing on PN configuration and customization. We will learn the basic levels of the PN interface, as well as connectivity and client customization for specific applications. In addition, we'll cover what each view provides the user and the capabilities of each, and then learn the menu functions and toolbar buttons in detail.

Finally, we will discuss how to publish applications to specific or anonymous users, and see how application publishing affects the way users see published application sets.

CERTIFICATION OBJECTIVE 10.01

Customizing the Program Neighborhood Interface and Recognizing ICA Toolbar Icons

Program Neighborhood is the client-side software that allows Independent Computing Architecture (ICA) connectivity through a variety of client devices to connect published applications and MetaFrame servers. Currently, the list of supported devices includes

- 32-bit Windows-based PCs
- 16-bit Windows-based PCs
- Windows CE, Linux, and Windows NT Embedded thin client devices
- Personal Digital Assistants (PDAs)
- DOS-based PCs
- IBM OS/2–based PCs
- Apple Macintosh computers
- Java clients

■ EPOC/Symbian Operating System (OS) clients

■ Unix

For the remainder of this chapter, we will focus on the Win32 Program Neighborhood unless otherwise specified. The minimum requirements for the Win32 client are

■ An Intel or compatible 386 CPU or better (OS requirement)

■ An Intel or compatible 133 MHz Pentium CPU for Windows 2000 (OS requirement)

■ A Win32 OS (Windows 9x, Windows ME, Windows NT 3.5x, Windows NT 4.0, Windows 2000)

■ 8MB of RAM for Windows 9x

■ 16MB of RAM for Windows NT

■ 64MB of RAM for Windows 2000

■ A mouse

■ A VGA or SVGA video adapter

■ A 1.44MB floppy drive

■ A hard drive with available space for client

■ Optional sound card for audio

■ Optional Network Interface Card (NIC) for network connections with appropriate protocols installed

■ Optional internal or external modem for dial-up connections

Program Neighborhood Views

Program Neighborhood consists of three distinct views: Application Set Manager, Default, and Custom ICA Connections.

Application Set Manager View

The Application Set Manager view (Figure 10-1) lists existing farm connections, and it allows the user to connect to new application sets (server farms). The user can also

FROM THE CLASSROOM

Get Exposure

You should get exposure to as many different ICA clients as you can. DOS, Win16, and Win32 clients may be easier to come by; but if possible, practice installing and configuring the Java, MAC, CE and Unix clients. Note what features are not available in the non-Win32 and Java clients, such as connections to a server farm.

Remember, many handheld devices run Windows CE, so you can have full Windows NT or 2000 functionality on a handheld device. However, there is no PALM OS client, so these devices will not work. Practice using the various color depths, screen sizes, and seamless windows, and note how each behaves.

—Joel W. Stolk, CCA, CCNA, MCSE

select a default view, the initial view seen when PN is launched. The default view can either be a server farm or the Custom ICA Connections view.

Find New Application Set   This icon launches the Find New Application Set Wizard (see Figure 10-2).

FIGURE 10-1

The Application Set Manager view

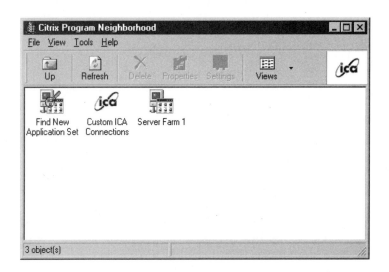

FIGURE 10-2

The Find New
Application Set
Wizard

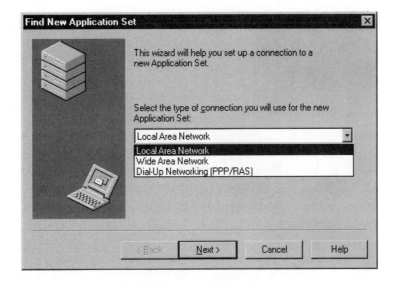

This screen asks you to select from the following options: Local Area Network, Wide Area Network, and Dial-Up Networking (PPP/RAS). Local Area Network will send out a broadcast for the ICA Master Browser for a list of server farms. Wide Area Network performs the same action as the Local Area Network, with the only difference being that this will turn on bitmap caching. Bitmap caching stores commonly used bitmaps and graphics on the local hard drive, and helps speed up slower connections. Bitmap caching is enabled by default on Dial-Up Networking (PPP/RAS) connections. Dial-Up Networking connections are direct connections over a modem, ISDN, DSL, or other type of WAN connection. Choosing a Dial-Up Networking (PPP/RAS) connection will allow you to launch Dial-Up Networking on the client device and allow you to choose an existing dial-up connection.

The next screen in the wizard (Figure 10-3) allows for the connection to the farm itself. The description will be the same as your server farm by default. If your server farm is on your subnet it will appear when you click the drop-down arrow. Program Neighborhood sends a broadcast packet and listens for the nearest ICA browser to respond. Once this happens, the client will request a list of farms from the ICA Browser. If you need to make a connection to a remote server farm or want to specify a server or protocol, you need modify connection properties by clicking the Server Location button.

The Locate New Application Set (Figure 10-4) lets you specify the connection protocol and server(s) to which you need to connect for ICA browsing. The

FIGURE 10-3

The Find New
Application Set
Wizard, Screen 2

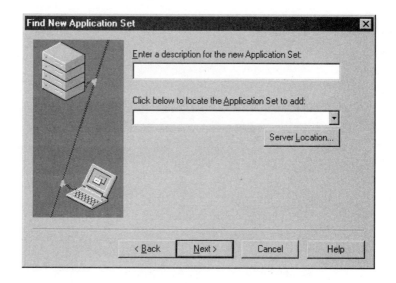

available protocols are TCP/IP, TCP/IP+HTTP, IPX/SPX and NetBIOS. When
using a TCP/IP+HTTP connection, you must have a Citrix server on your network
mapped to the default name of ica.*yourdomain*, or specify an address.

FIGURE 10-4

The Locate New
Application Set
dialog box

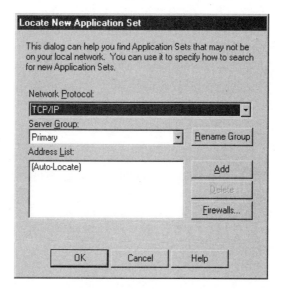

The Server Group lets you specify up to three address groups to which you can connect. The groups are used in the following order:

1. Primary
2. Backup
3. Backup2

The client will attempt connection to servers in the Primary group. If no connection is made after five seconds, the Backup group will be selected, and so on. These groups can be renamed with the Rename Group button. Servers can be added or deleted from groups in the address list box. When using TCP/IP+HTTP, you can specify a port, but the default is 80.

When you click the Firewalls… button, the screen in Figure 10-5 appears.

The Use Alternate Address For Firewall Connection check box allows you to connect to the public address if your ICA browser is inside a firewall.

e x a m
ⓦatch

The program altaddr.exe specifies an alternate address on a Citrix server. This is the external address specified on a router when using Network Address Translation (NAT) on a private network. The format for altaddr.exe is

```
servername /SET AlternateAddress (to set an external address)
servername /DELETE AdapterAddress (to delete an external address)
```

The check box Connect Via SOCKS Proxy will allow the client to connect to a remote ICA browser when the client is inside a SOCKS firewall. You must specify the IP of the SOCKS proxy and its port.

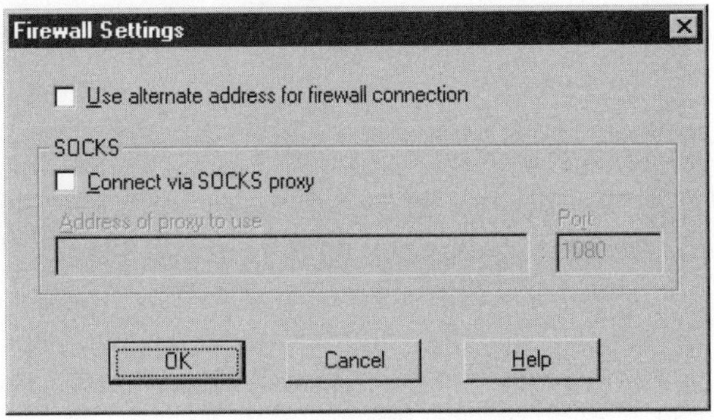

FIGURE 10-5

The Firewall
Settings dialog
box

After you have made your connection to your Application Set (Farm), you have the option to configure how the connections will be presented on the next screen (Figure 10-6). The Enable Sound For This Application Set check box will turn client audio mapping on if selected. Under the Windows Colors drop-down menu, you can choose between 16 Colors, 256 Colors, High Color (16-bit), and True Color (24-bit). Under Window Size, we have the following options:

- 640×480
- 800×600
- 1024×768
- 1280×1024
- 1600×1200
- Custom (in pixels)
- Percent of Screen Size (up to 100%)
- Full Screen
- Seamless Window

The first six options let us specify the size of the connection window in pixels. These first six options will also dictate the amount of bandwidth to be consumed

FIGURE 10-6

Application Set settings

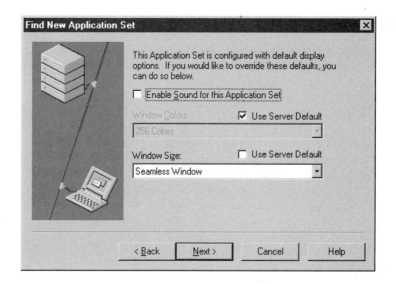

for graphics, as will the numbers of colors. When trying to enhance performance, the least amount of pixels and colors should be used in a session. The Percent Of Screen Size option will size the connection window as a percentage of the client's screen size. A full screen window will fill the entire client screen with the connection window. A Seamless Window will have no window around the session. It will appear as if the session is running on the local client machine. The user will have to press ALT-DEL to return to the local client window.

Once your application set has been created, you can right-click the icon and select from several options (see Figure 10-7).

If you select Set As Default, this will specify the application set to be the Default view, which is discussed in the next section. Create Desktop Shortcut will create an icon on the desktop that will allow connection to the Application Set without going through Program Neighborhood. Duplicate, or F8, will make a copy of the application set. Choosing Delete, or DEL, will delete the application set from this view. Rename, or F2, will allow you to rename the application set. Application Set Settings brings up the following tabs:

The Connection tab options (Figure 10-8) allow us to set all of the settings, such as the Server Location… button mentioned earlier, with the addition of one option: Auto-detect Network Protocol. When this is selected, the Server Location entries are circumvented, and the ICA client searches for the ICA browser automatically on the local subnet.

FIGURE 10-7

Application Set
options

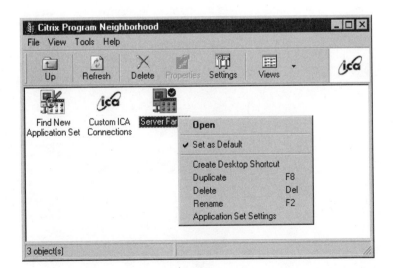

The Default Options tab (Figure 10-9) lets you specify several settings for this connection. Data compression reduces the amount of bandwidth needed for the connection, at the expense of additional processor utilization. It is recommended for slower connections. The Use Disk Cache For Bitmaps option turns bitmap caching on or off. Queuing mouse movements and keystrokes reduces bandwidth by waiting longer to send this information to the server, but also slows responsiveness within an ICA session. It should be used only on very slow connections. Turning off desktop integration will prevent the set from creating icons on the desktop. This helps if you have a rogue administrator who likes to flood your desktop with ICA shortcuts to published applications. Select the Enable Sound check 2box to enable client audio remapping. You can choose from the following options:

■ **High**   Best sound quality (up to 1.3 Mbps); can use a lot of bandwidth

■ **Medium**   Compressed sound up to 64 Kbps; good for LAN connections

■ **Low**   Compressed sound up to 16 Kbps; good for slower LANs and RAS connections

FIGURE 10-8

The Connection tab

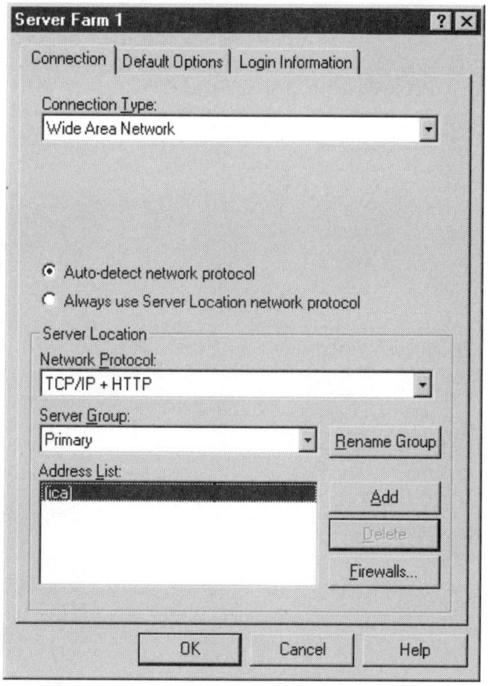

FIGURE 10-9

The Default
Options tab

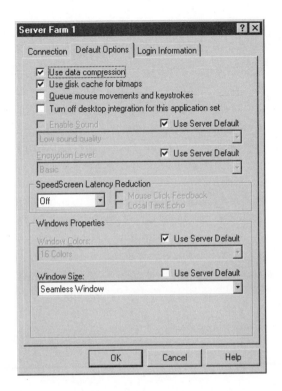

Client audio remapping should be disabled unless absolutely necessary. It uses a lot of unnecessary bandwidth, especially over dial-up connections. The easiest way to disable this is on the server side, which will override the client settings. Whenever remapping client ports and devices, the advantages and disadvantages of such actions should be weighed. Advantages concern things like functionality, while disadvantages include losing bandwidth and slowing down the login process.

The encryption level, also referred to as SecureICA, is also selected in this tab. The client-side encryption levels are as follows (from lowest to highest security):

■ Basic (default minimal ICA encryption)

■ 128-bit Logons Only (session is encrypted during the logon process only)

■ 40-bit (all of the session is encrypted at this bit rate)

■ 56-bit (all of the session is encrypted at this bit rate)

■ 128-bit (all of the session is encrypted at this bit rate)

If your client-side encryption is set lower than the Citrix server's minimum requirement for a published application, the user will not be able to connect. It's best to leave this setting as Use Server Default.

SpeedScreen latency has three settings: Off (default), On, and Auto. When this setting is set to On or Auto, you can turn on Mouse Click Feedback and Local Text Echo. This gives low-bandwidth users instant feedback and makes their session appear to be running faster. This should be turned off on LAN connections. The Auto setting is used when you are unsure of your bandwidth. The last part of this tab concerns the window size and colors we covered earlier.

The last tab on the application set settings is the Login Information tab (Figure 10-10). This lets us specify login information for the domain to which we are connecting. This tab should be used with great caution, as it could pose a security risk if a user walks away from their computer. The Don't Use Local Username And Password Option is grayed out. This option is available when the Program Neighborhood software is installed, and in this instance it has been turned off.

FIGURE 10-10

The Login
Information tab

Server Farm 1	? ☒

Connection | Default Options | Login Information

Application Set Name:

☐ Don't use local username and password

Ｕser name:

Password:

Ｄomain:

☐ Save password

| OK | Cancel | Help |

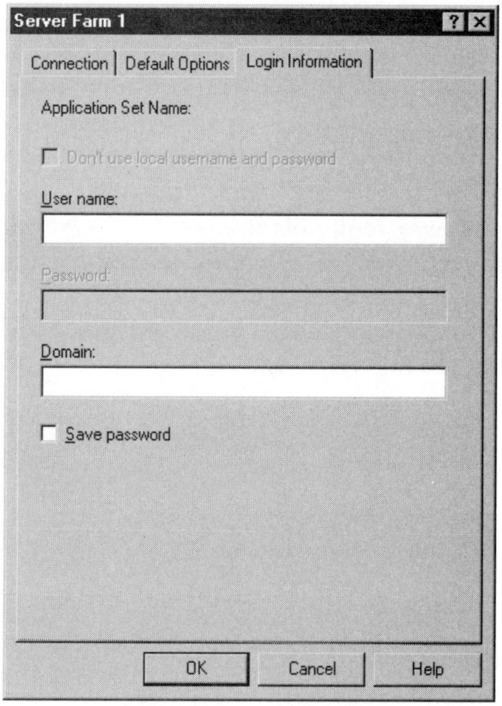

Default View

The Default view is the initial view displayed when Program Neighborhood is launched and is selected from within the Application Set Manager view. When a default view is chosen, a check box appears on the top right of the icon.

Custom ICA Connections View

The Custom ICA Connections view (Figure 10-11) allows the user to create direct connections to specific MetaFrame servers, or connect directly to a published application. If applications are published to an NT domain instead of a farm, custom connections will need to be created for each published application to which the users need to connect.

exam
ⓦatch

Only the Windows 32-bit and Java clients support the Application Set Manager. However, this can be circumvented by publishing PN as an application using ICA PassThrough.

ICA PassThrough

ICA PassThrough is essentially publishing Program Neighborhood to ICA clients that do not support connecting to server farms. ICA PassThrough is installed on a MetaFrame XP server by default and resides on the server in the subfolder

FIGURE 10-11

The Custom ICA
Connections view

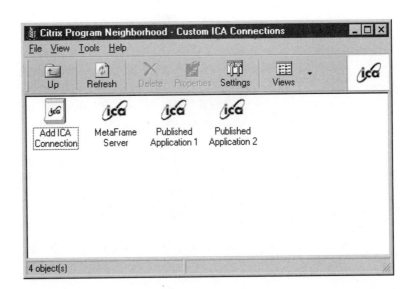

%systemroot%\system32\ICA PassThrough. To enable ICA PassThrough, publish PN.EXE in an NT domain scope, and create a custom connection to the published application. Essentially, this type of connection is an ICA session within an ICA session, but special modifications to ICA PassThrough increase the overall performance.

exam
Ⓦatch

Client LPT and COM port mapping is not supported when using ICA PassThrough. However, it does support drive, printer queue, and audio mapping.

Let's look at some examples of when we would use the Application Set Manager, Custom Connections, and Default views.

SCENARIO & SOLUTION

Application Set Manager view	Use this view when connecting to one or more Application Sets or farms.
Custom Connections view	Use this view when connecting to a specific published application or server.
Default view	Use this view when you want a specific application set to appear when a user first launches Program Neighborhood.

Add ICA Connection   The Add ICA Connection icon launches a wizard to create your custom connection. The wizard screens are as follows:

The first screen in the Add New ICA Connection Wizard (Figure 10-12) lets you specify your connection type. The only new connection type we see here is the ICA Dial-in. An ICA Dial-in connection allows you to connect directly to a modem or modem pool connected to the Citrix server, and can be used instead of a Dial-Up Networking (PPP/RAS) connection. An ICA Dial-in differs from a RAS connection in that you're authenticated within the session instead of making a network connection outside of the session beforehand.

exam
Ⓦatch

You can configure your server for ICA Dial-in or RAS, but not both. You must use one or the other for dial-up connections.

The Add New
ICA Connection
Wizard

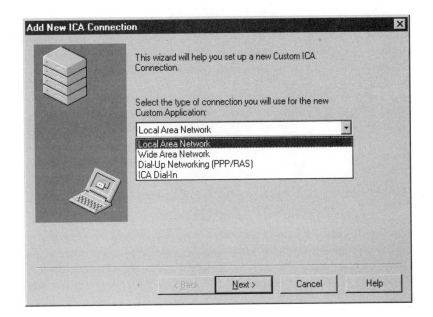

Add New ICA Connection

This wizard will help you set up a new Custom ICA Connection.

Select the type of connection you will use for the new Custom Application:

Local Area Network

Local Area Network
Wide Area Network
Dial-Up Networking (PPP/RAS)
ICA Dial-In

< Back   Next >   Cancel   Help

This screen is similar to the Application Set Wizard (Figure 10-13), but now we have the option to connect either directly to a Citrix server, or to a Published Application. The available protocols are TCP/IP, TCP/IP+HTTP, IPX, SPX, and NetBIOS. Again, we can use the Server Location… button to create a custom connection configuration.

Configuring the connection here is the same as in the Application Set Wizard (Figure 10-4 and Figure 10-5), so we won't rehash it. If your connection has been configured, you should select either a server or published application to which you want to connect (Figure 10-14). If you have contacted the ICA browser, the drop-down menu will display a list of servers or applications to which you can connect.

Connecting to a Published Application   If you are making a connection to a published application, the next screen in the wizard will prompt you to select either a seamless window or a remote desktop window (Figure 10-15).

Again, a seamless window will make the application appear to be running on the local client machine, and a remote desktop window will run the application inside of a window.

FIGURE 10-13

The Add New
ICA Connection
Wizard, Screen 2

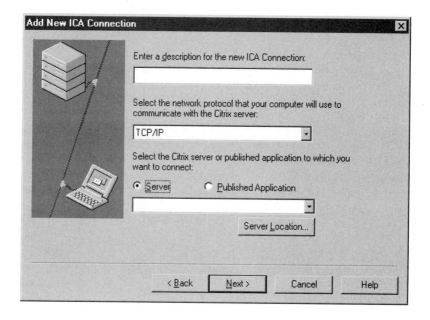

The next wizard screen will prompt you to select an encryption level for this connection (see Figure 10-16). These encryption options will be the same as if we were connecting to an application group. Select the Use Default check box if you want the server to determine the encryption level for this connection.

FIGURE 10-14

The Locate
Server or
Published
Application
dialog box

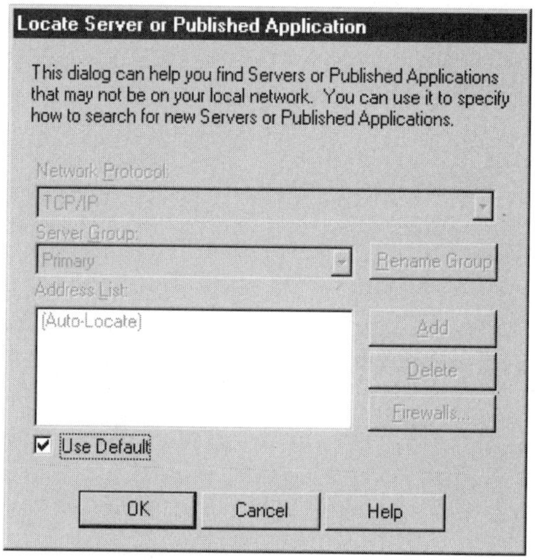

Connecting
to a Published
Application

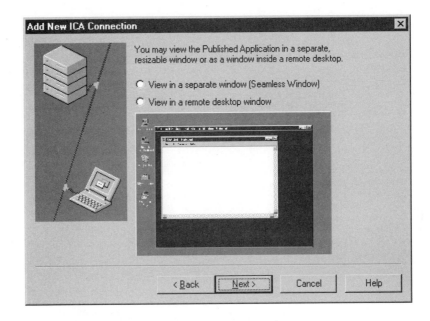

The next screen will prompt you to enter domain logon information to be saved with this session (see Figure 10-17). This is similar to the screen we saw for an

Encryption
settings

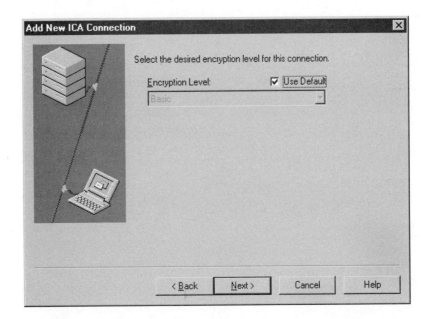

application group (Figure 10-10). Be cautious when entering information here, as it will be saved on the client machine—albeit lightly encrypted. The Use Local User Name And Password is grayed out here because this option was not turned on when the Program Neighborhood client software was installed.

The last noteworthy screen in this wizard concerns selecting the color depth and screen size. If you selected seamless window, you will see the options listed next (see Figure 10-18). If you selected a remote desktop window, you will have the additional option of selecting the window size. If you leave the Use Default check box selected, the server on which the application is published will determine these settings. Decreasing the color depth of the ICA connection will reduce the amount of bandwidth used on the ICA connection, and it will speed up slower sessions.

Connecting to a Server   The wizard screens differ a bit when connecting to a server. The next screen you will see after adding the server connection (Figure 10-13) will be the encryption settings (Figure 10-16). The screen after that in the wizard will be the logon information (Figure 10-17), followed by both the screen options and the window size option (Figure 10-18).

The last noteworthy screen in the wizard is a new one. This screen allows you to specify an application to run once the connection is made to the server (Figure 10-19).

FIGURE 10-17

Connection
Logon
Information

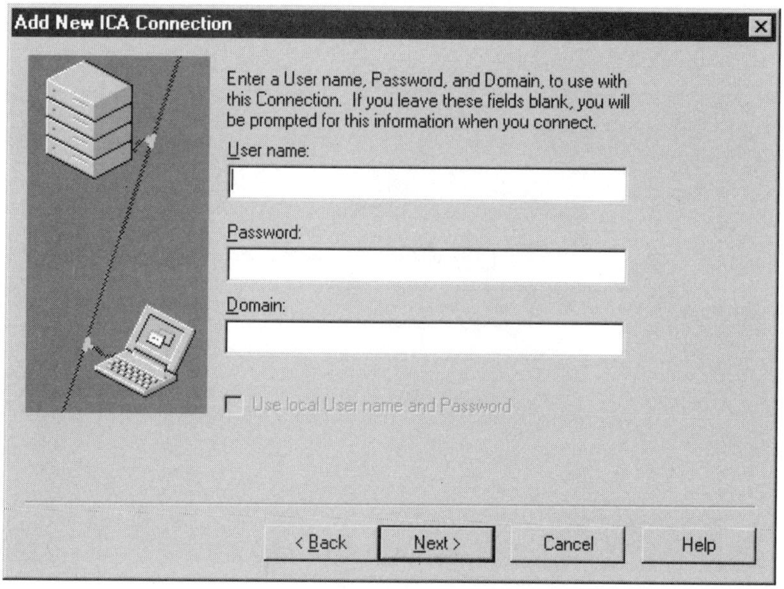

FIGURE 10-18

Published application screen options

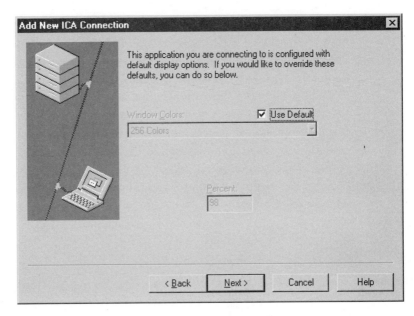

The working directory should be the working directory of the application you will be running. By default, you should leave these options blank if you want to simply make a connection to an Explorer window.

FIGURE 10-19

Choosing an application

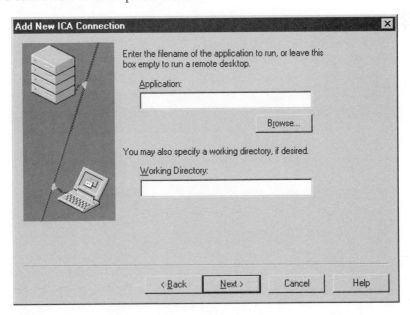

Custom Connection Properties   When you right-click an icon in the Custom ICA Connection view, you see the same options as when you right-click an icon in the Application Set Manager view (Figure 10-7). The only option you do not have is to set a custom connection as the Default view. This is because the Default view can only be an application set. When we select Custom Connection Settings from this context menu, the connection options will see two tabs, Connection and Default Options. The Connection tab will display and allow us to change the connection settings seen in the wizard (Figure 10-14).

The Default Options tab (Figure 10-20) will allow us to configure the session settings, specifically the sound, encryption, and video settings for this custom connection.

The Default
Options tab

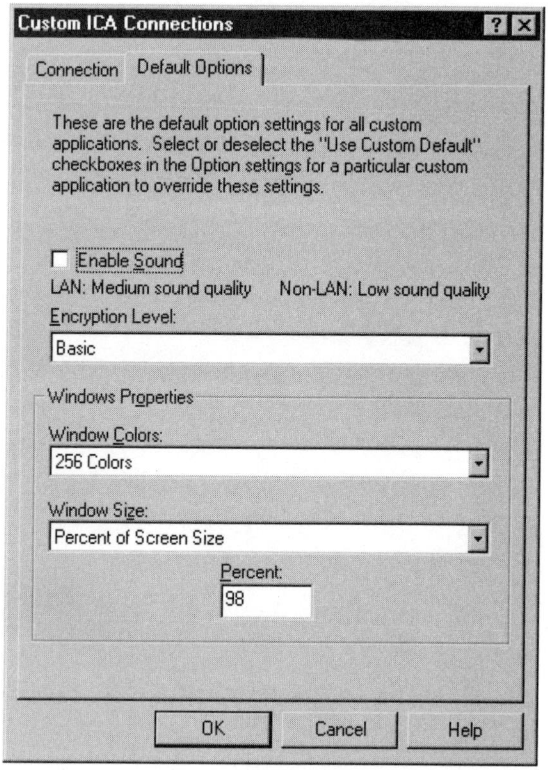

FIGURE 10-21

The ICA Toolbar

The ICA Toolbar

The ICA Toolbar is an integral part of Program Neighborhood. You can perform most or all of PN's functions from this toolbar, including many of the menu options and context menus.

Program Neighborhood Toolbar Buttons

Program Neighborhood has several buttons (see Figure 10-21). Table 10-1 explains what each one does. Many of these features are available from the right-click context menus within Program Neighborhood (explained in the previous section).

Many administrators do not want end users to have access to many of these features. It is best that they be disabled when users are running Program Neighborhood on a published desktop or direct server connection, or when Program Neighborhood is published using an ICA PassThrough. A restricted (gray) Program Neighborhood can be downloaded from http:// www.thethin.net.

TABLE 10-1   Explanations of ICA Toolbar Buttons

Icon	Function
Up	Allows the user to change view from Custom ICA Connections to Application Set Manager, or from Application Set Manager to the default view. When this icon is grayed out, the user is at the topmost view.
Refresh	Queries the ICA Master Browser for the latest information or application set.
Delete	When an item or items are selected, this icon will delete the item(s).
Properties	Displays the properties of a selected custom connection or a published application.
Settings	Displays the connection settings and options of a custom connection, published application, or application group.
Views	Switches the current PN view between Large Icons, Small Icons, List, and Details.

Program Neighborhood Menu Items

There are four menus within Program Neighborhood:

- File
- View
- Tools
- Help

The File menu allows users to open a connection or close the program. In the Application Set Manager view or Custom Connections view, right-click context menu items are added to this menu (see Figure 10-7).

The View menu allows customization of the Program Neighborhood menus and icons, which can also be found by right-clicking the toolbar itself or using the Views button. You can remove the toolbar buttons or text; change the icon size; or refresh the current view, which is the same as clicking the Refresh button.

The Tools menu is the most important, as it allows customization of the client itself. These are the three menu items on the Tools menu:

- ICA Settings...
- Modems...
- Serial Devices...

ICA Settings   The ICA Settings menu item shows four tabs (Figure 10-22): General, Bitmap Cache, Hotkeys, and Event Logging.

The General tab allows you to set the following items:

- **Client Name**   A unique identifier for the client. This must be unique because Citrix uses this identifier to map client devices. By default, this will be filled in by the local computer name. This name is stored in the file %HOMEDRIVE%\wfname.ini.

- **Serial Number**   This field is normally left blank unless you are using a client from a Citrix PC Client Pack.

- **Keyboard Layout**   This is set by default to the local client machine's keyboard layout. You can change this to another language layout if necessary.

- **Keyboard Type**   This is set, by default, to the local client machine's keyboard type. You can change this to another language type if necessary.

FIGURE 10-22

The General tab

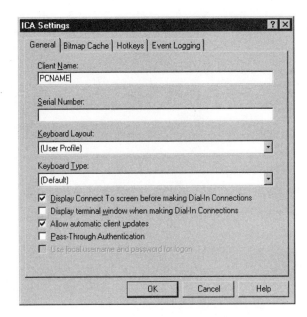

- **Display Connect To Screen Before Making Dial-In Connections** Selecting this check box shows the Connecting To screen when a connection is attempted.

- **Display Terminal Window When Making Dial-In Connections** Selecting this check box will show an ASCII terminal screen when a dial-in connection is made.

- **Allow Automatic Client Updates** Select this check box to allow the client to be automatically updated on the Citrix server.

- **Pass-Through Authentication** Select this check box to enable authentication information to be "passed through" to other sessions.

- **Use Local Username And Password For Logon** When this option is selected during Program Neighborhood installation, select this check box to use the local client login information when connecting to a session or application set.

The Bitmap Cache tab, meanwhile, lets you set the following items (see Figure 10-23):

- **Amount Of Disk Space To Use** Specifies the percentage of disk that will be used for bitmap caching.

FIGURE 10-23

The Bitmap
Cache tab

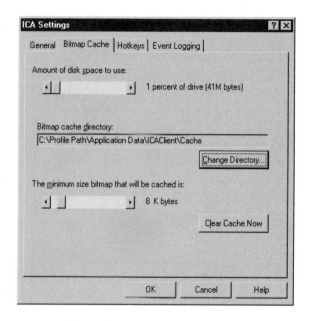

- **Bitmap Cache Directory**   Specifies the path to which the bitmaps will be cached. By default, this will be in the user's profile path.

- **Change Directory**   Use this button to change the bitmap cache directory location.

- **The Minimum Size Bitmap That Will Be Cached**   Defines the minimum size bitmap allowed for caching.

- **Clear Cache Now**   Clears the bitmap cache.

The Hotkeys tab (Figure 10-24) allows you to change the mapped out hotkeys within a session. This is useful when applications have hard-coded hotkeys that cannot be changed. These hotkeys are set by default to not interfere with local client Windows hotkeys.

On the Event Logging tab (Figure 10-25), you can set the following items:

- **Event Log File**   Here, you can specify the path to Program Neighborhood's event log, and whether or not you want it to overwrite or append the log each time PN is run. By default, this log file is located in the local user's profile path.

- **Log Events**   This section specifies which events will be logged.

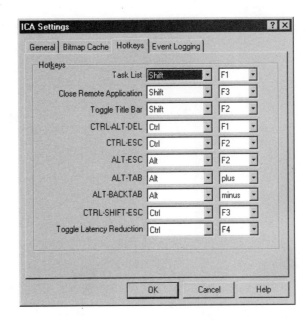

FIGURE 10-24

The Hotkeys tab

Modems   The Modems item in the Tools menu brings up the TAPI (Telephone Application Programming Interface) from the local computer (Figure 10-26). This is the same interface that can be accessed from the Control Panel and can be used to

FIGURE 10-25

The Event
Logging tab

FIGURE 10-26

TAPI

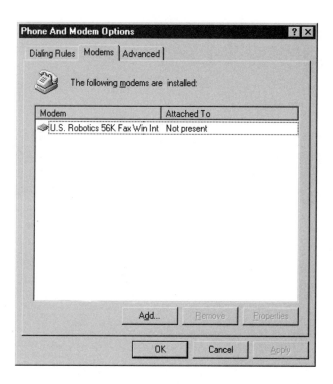

add and delete modems, set dialing rules, and configure TAPI service providers. It is not an interface specific to Program Neighborhood. DOS and Win16 clients have built-in TAPI emulation support.

Serial Devices   The Serial Devices item on the Tools menu allows configuration of direct connections to a Citrix server through a COM port (see Figure 10-27).

FIGURE 10-27

Serial Devices

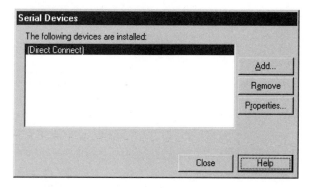

Although this configuration is rarely seen, it is still supported by Program Neighborhood. Here you can add, remove, and configure COM ports for a direct connection.

Now that you understand the difference between Custom Connections and Application Sets, let's look at some examples of when to use each.

SCENARIO & SOLUTION

You need to log on to a particular server in your load-balanced farm for administrator tasks.	A custom connection would be better because connecting to a load-balanced published desktop may connect you to an unintended server.
A user needs to use a published Office XP suite.	An application set would be best because the user would only have to make one connection to get all their applications.
You have one MetaFrame server that users connect to for a remote desktop.	Either a custom connection or application set would work. However, an application set would allow for future growth of the farm.

Preconfiguring Program Neighborhood

Program Neighborhood allows for custom preconfiguration of the client. Preconfiguration is also called creating "ready connect" clients. This is done by first extracting the client installation package and editing the following text files:

- Appsrv.src
- Module.src
- Pn.src
- Wfclient.src

After these files are edited with a text editor, you can repackage your installation and roll out your preconfigured client to your users. When installed, the .src extension will become an .ini extension. Alternatively, you can install the client on a machine and configure it the way you want for the users. After this is done, you can rename the .ini files to .src and copy over the .src files in your package. This is an easier way to get the changes you want if you do not know or understand the parameters of the .src files.

Appsrv.src will allow you to edit parameters relating to custom ICA connections, specifically application servers and the client settings seen in the Custom ICA Connections view. You can use this file to restrict users to a particular view and remove icons you do not want them to use. Module.src contains information about network protocols and transports, including COM ports. Pn.src configures settings in relation to application sets and contains two sections: Program Neighborhood and Application Set. The Program Neighborhood section defines the application sets. The Application Set section defines all configuration information for those defined sets. Wfclient.src defines general PN client configuration, including keyboard settings and video defaults.

exam
🕲 a t c h   ***Be sure to remember all four of these filenames.***

EXERCISE 10-1

CertCam 10-1

Creating Custom Client Diskettes Using the ICA Client Creator

You should practice creating custom client diskettes because this situation is likely to come up on the job. Perhaps you have a remote group of users who have no local support, and who need to connect to a MetaFrame XP server with no hassles. Sending a custom client diskette set would be the best option.

To complete this exercise, you need a Win32 computer and two blank floppies.

1. On the server, go to the ICA Client Creator under the Start menu by choosing Programs | MetaFrame XP | ICA Client Creator.

2. When you see the Make Installation Set window, select the appropriate client set. This dialog box will let you know how many disks are required for the ICA client set.

3. After the disks are created, open Disk 2. You'll notice the .src files are located here.

4. Install the client (not necessarily from the disk set) onto a Win32 computer, and then customize the client as if it were for a remote user.

5. Set up an ICA dial-in connection, or alternatively, set up a connection to the Internet.

6. Create an application set connection. Make the application set you connect to the Default view.

7. Rename and copy Appsrv.ini, Module.ini, Pn.ini, and Wfclient.ini to Appsrv.src, Module.src, Pn.src, and Wfclient.src. Remember to copy and overwrite the files on disk 2 of the custom client set.

8. Uninstall the client on the Win32 machine and reinstall using the disk set. You should have exactly the same configuration you did before the uninstall, and the application set should start as the Default view.

Enabling Applications for Specific Groups

In order to deliver the applications we want, to the users we want, we need to publish the applications using the Citrix Management Console (CMC) on the MetaFrame XP server (Figure 10-28).

FIGURE 10-28

The Citrix Management Console

Applications are published using the Applications folder within the CMC. Here we can have a published application (Notepad), a published desktop (Remote Desktop), and Program Neighborhood folders. Program Neighborhood folders allow us to publish applications in a logical folder structure, similar to the logical layout of a hard drive partition. We can group common applications in their own folders, so when a user connects to an application set, they can more easily navigate the list of published applications. These applications and folders will show up in the Application Set Manager view or Default view (if a server farm has been set as default). However, users will only see the applications and folders published to them, either explicitly or anonymously.

Anonymous Users

When MetaFrame is installed, 15 anonymous user accounts are installed on the local computer in a local group called Anonymous. This is so you can publish applications that do not require a username or password to connect. These accounts will be guest access accounts and will have the name Anon*XXX,* where *XXX* is a number from 000 to 014. These accounts will have the following restricted access rights: 10-minute idle timeout on sessions, broken or timed-out sessions will be logged off, no password required, and users will not be able to change their password. However an administrator can change the properties of these accounts.

The fact that there are 15 accounts is related to the original 15 licenses that are installed with the base MetaFrame. If you add licenses, you may wish to increase the number of anonymous accounts.

The server will not save any user profile information when an anonymous user logs off the session.

exam
ⓦatch
Anonymous user accounts will only be created on servers that are not domain controllers.

Explicit Users

Explicit users are, by definition, normal user accounts. These can be domain accounts, or local user accounts if no domain is present. You should always use explicit users when security is important. Explicit users will use their normal logon credentials when connecting to an application set or custom connection, and unlike anonymous accounts, their user profile information will be saved when the explicit user logs off.

Let's look at some examples of when to use Anonymous versus Explicit users:

SCENARIO & SOLUTION	
You need to set up a kiosk in a mall for public use of a Web browser.	Anonymous: Logins are unwanted.
You are publishing an accounting application to a group of remote employees.	Explicit: Security is important.
You need to set up a product demo in your office lobby so guests can demo your software.	Anonymous: Security is not an issue. Ease of use is more important.
You are rolling out a published desktop to all your users in your domain.	Explicit: Security and profiles are necessary.
Your CEO requests touchscreen thin client devices running a published MP3 player application in the executive bathrooms.	Anonymous: Ease of use is most important.

Roaming Users

Utilizing explicit applications will allow you to deliver the correct applications to users, regardless of what device they use to connect. When you publish an explicit application, you select which users you want to see that application when they make a connection to that application set. When a user moves from one computer to another, all the user has to do is create a connection to their server farm in the Application Set Manager view, and their applications will appear. For users that move from Win32 or Java clients to other non-Program Neighborhood clients, it is important to publish Program Neighborhood using an ICA PassThrough.

CERTIFICATION SUMMARY

Program Neighborhood allows a wide variety of clients to connect to Citrix servers. Among these are DOS, Win16, Win32, Java, Unix, Macintosh and OS/2 clients providing true platform independence. This chapter focused on the Win32 client and its feature set. The Win32 and Java clients are the only Citrix ICA clients that support Program Neighborhood.

The three main views in Program Neighborhood we discussed were the Application Set Manager, Custom Connection Settings, and Default views. The Application Set Manager view allows clients to connect to published application sets, or farms. The Custom Connections Settings view allows for connection to specific published applications or directly to a server. The Default view is the initial application set a user connects to when launching. Program Neighborhood, and it is set in the Application Set Manager view. We also covered how to configure icons in these views.

Later, the Program Neighborhood toolbar was introduced, which includes seven buttons: Up, Refresh, Delete, Properties, Settings, and Views. Each was explained. Also, we covered the PN menu items, which allow for customization of the client software.

Last, we covered application publishing from the Citrix Management Console, and how to provide the correct applications to the users. We described the two types of users, Anonymous and Explicit, and how they affect PN delivery and security. We also saw that, no matter where you go, you will always get the right set of applications.

TWO-MINUTE DRILL

Customizing the Program Neighborhood Interface and Recognizing ICA Toolbar Icons

❑ The three views in Program Neighborhood are the Application Set Manager, Custom Connection, and Default views.

❑ The Default View is set by right-clicking an Application Set and selecting Set As Default.

❑ Use Bitmap Caching to speed up slow connections.

❑ The available protocols in PN are TCP/IP, TCP/IP+HTTP, IPX/SPX, and NetBIOS.

❑ The Use Alternate Address For Firewall Connection check box allows you to connect Citrix server behind a firewall.

❑ Use altaddr.exe to set an alternate (public) address on a server.

❑ Data compression reduces the amount of bandwidth, but increases processor utilization.

❑ The encryption options in PN are Basic, 128-bit Logons Only, 40-bit, 56-bit, and 128-bit.

❑ Only Win32 and Java clients support the Application Set Manager.

❑ Use an ICA PassThrough to publish PN to non-PN clients.

❑ Client LPT and COM port mapping is not supported when using ICA PassThrough.

❑ A seamless window will make the application appear to be running on the local client machine, and a remote desktop window will run the application inside a window.

❑ The Up toolbar button allows the user to change views from Custom ICA Connections to Application Set Manager, or from Application Set Manager to the default view.

❑ The Refresh toolbar button queries the ICA Master Browser for the latest information or application set.

❑ The Delete toolbar button will delete the selected item(s).

❑ The Properties toolbar button displays the properties of a selected custom connection or a published application.

❑ The Settings toolbar button displays the connection settings and options of a custom connection, published application, or application group.

❑ The Views toolbar button switches the current PN view between Large Icons, Small Icons, List, and Details.

SELF TEST

The following questions will help you measure your understanding of the material presented in this chapter. Read all the choices carefully as there may be more than one correct answer. Choose all correct answers for each question.

Customizing the Program Neighborhood Interface and Recognizing ICA Toolbar Icons

1. What encryption levels are included in the ICA client? (Choose all that apply.)

   A. Basic

   B. 40-bit

   C. 56-bit

   D. 64-bit

   E. 128-bit

2. Which of the following is not a supported platform for the ICA client?

   A. Microsoft Windows 3.1

   B. Apple Macintosh

   C. Palm OS

   D. Microsoft DOS

   E. BEOS

3. Your company has a MetaFrame XP farm with several remote sites that use dial-up connections. One user, Juan, has been complaining that his session seems slow to respond. What could you check or change in Program Neighborhood to ensure that Juan's connection is more efficient or appears to be faster?

   A. Make sure bitmap caching is turned on for Juan's under ICA Settings… in the Tools menu.

   B. Increase the color depth of the Application Set.

   C. Reduce the settings of or turn off audio remapping in the properties of the Application Set.

   D. Enable SpeedScreen Latency Reduction.

4. Which of the following clients can use Program Neighborhood? (Choose all that apply.)

   A. Unix clients

   B. Win32 clients

   C. Macintosh clients

   D. Java clients

   E. Win16 clients

5. Greg is a remote MetaFrame user in San Francisco, CA. He dials up to the Internet and tries to connect to a server farm in Austin, TX. When he tries to connect, though, he gets an error message that states "Cannot connect to the Citrix server: There is no Citrix Server configured on the specified address." What could be wrong?

   A. In the properties for the server farm, the check box Use Alternate Address For Firewall Connection is not selected.

   B. The client name in the file wfname.ini is a duplicate.

   C. Greg's encryption settings are too low.

   D. Client audio remapping has been turned off.

6. A user named Amy is complaining that when she launches Microsoft Word, which is a published application, she gets an annoying window around the program that distracts her from her job. Her connection in Program Neighborhood is a custom connection. How could you help Amy get rid of this window on her computer?

   A. Edit her appsrv.ini file and add the line SetOutsideWindow=0ff.

   B. Have Amy click the Refresh button on her Program Neighborhood toolbar.

   C. Edit the properties of the published application on the server to be a seamless window.

   D. Edit the properties of the published application on the client to be a seamless window.

7. If your client audio is set to High, what is the maximum amount of bandwidth the remapped audio can use?

   A. 16 Kbps

   B. 32 Kbps

   C. 64 Kbps

   D. 1.3 Mbps

   E. 128 Mbps

8. You just published Microsoft Access to the users in the Dallas farm. Bob calls and complains that he cannot see the Microsoft Access icon in his application set. What would you do to correct this problem?

    A. Delete the application set, and create a new connection to the Dallas farm in the Application Set Manager view.

    B. Have Bob reboot the machine.

    C. Tell Bob to press the Refresh button on the Program Neighborhood toolbar.

    D. Have Bob edit the server farm properties and reduce the session screen size.

9. Your human resources department has just given you a new application to publish on your server farm. They have stressed that security is critical, because the application includes the personal records of every employee. How would you publish this application to the users in a secure manner?

    A. Add the human resources global group to the local anonymous group on your server, and then publish the application anonymously.

    B. Publish the application explicitly to the human resources global group.

    C. Publish the application explicitly to the Everyone group.

    D. Publish the application anonymously.

10. Which of the following protocols is not valid when making a Program Neighborhood connection?

    A. TCP/IP

    B. TCP/IP+HTTP

    C. RDP

    D. IPX/SPX

    E. NetBIOS

11. You have been given the task to publish Microsoft Office XP, five accounting applications and three marketing applications to all of your users. How would you publish the applications so that the users would not get confused when they connect to the application set?

    A. Create global groups for each application group and publish them explicitly to each group.

    B. Create global groups for each application and publish them anonymously to each group.

    C. Create Program Neighborhood folders in CMC for each set of applications and then publish all of the applications to your users.

12. Where would you change the bitmap cache settings in Program Neighborhood?

   A. Tools menu, ICA Settings, Bitmap Cache tab

   B. Properties on the application set

   C. Tools menu, Client Settings, Bitmap Cache tab

   D. Tools menu, General tab

13. One of your users, Andy, calls to say that he is having problems in his terminal emulation application on Citrix. Andy says that when he presses SHIFT-F2 to print in the application, his title bar goes away. When he tries it again, his title bar returns. What is Andy's problem?

   A. Andy suffers from working too much and is making the wrong keystrokes.

   B. Andy should just use the File | Print menu options.

   C. Andy should configure the hotkey for Toggle Title Bar under the Tools | ICA Settings | Hotkeys tab to be something other than SHIFT-F2.

14. Mike is a user on your local LAN. He complains that when he listens to Internet radio stations on the MetaFrame server, the sound quality is very poor, making it difficult to dance to when he is on breaks. How can we fix this?

   A. Turn off client audio remapping.

   B. Decrease his client audio settings to Low.

   C. Increase his client audio settings to Medium.

   D. Increase his client audio settings to High.

15. You just imaged three new PCs and sent them out to your users. Your users call you and complain that when they try to connect to the Citrix farm, only one user at a time can log on, while the other two get error messages. How can you correct this problem? (Choose all that apply.)

   A. Rename the computer names under Network in the Control Panel.

   B. Edit the wfcname.ini on the machines and change the CLIENTNAME to be unique on each machine.

   C. Choose Tools menu | ICA Settings | General tab, and then make the Client Name entry unique on each machine.

   D. Make sure the login names for each user are unique.

16. The installation path for the ICA PassThrough client on a MetaFrame server is

    A. %systemroot%\system32\ICA PassThrough

    B. %homedrive%\system 32\ICA PassThrough

    C. %systemroot%\ICA PassThrough

    D. %systemdrive%\system\ICA PassThrough

17. The term TAPI refers to what?

    A. The WinSock protocol

    B. The Telephone Application Programming Interface found under the Modems item in the Tools menu

    C. The Telephone Action Programming Interface found in the Properties dialog box of a custom connection

    D. The feeling you get after too much coffee

18. A user named Bruce in the Graphics department just bought a new iMac and set it up on the LAN. He downloads and installs the latest Macintosh PN client for the machine. However, he now is complaining that he can't see his application set. What is the problem?

    A. Bruce is not using the Application Set Manager view.

    B. Bruce does not have his firewall settings configured correctly.

    C. Bruce is not using a compatible protocol.

    D. Bruce is not using a client that supports application sets.

19. Which ICA clients have built-in TAPI emulation support? (Choose all that apply.)

    A. DOS

    B. Win16

    C. Win32

20. Which color depths does Program Neighborhood support? (Choose all that apply.)

    A. 640×480

    B. 800×600

    C. 1024×768

    D. 1280×1024

    E. 1600×1200

LAB QUESTION

You are the administrator of a farm in Memphis consisting of five servers. You have just installed Microsoft Office 2000 on your servers, and the application is load-balanced across all of them. You want to roll out the application to a new group of users in Rhode Island, and you want to ensure that they see this application in their Default view when the Program Neighborhood client is installed.

Your servers are located behind a firewall on your local LAN in Memphis. Your users will be dialing up to the Internet, and then connecting to the server farm. You will be having the local administrator in Rhode Island install Program Neighborhood on the users' Windows 2000–based PCs. Configure the client software so that after installing the client, there will be no problems connecting to the application set when the end users launch Program Neighborhood for the first time.

SELF TEST ANSWERS

Customizing the Program Neighborhood Interface and Recognizing ICA Toolbar Icons

1. ☑ A, B, C, and E are all valid encryption levels.
   ☒ D is incorrect because 64-bit is not an available encryption level.

2. ☑ D is correct because there is no Citrix ICA client written for these platforms.
   ☒ A, B, C, and E are incorrect as all have valid Citrix ICA clients.

3. ☑ A is correct because bitmap caching helps speed up a connection by caching commonly used bitmaps to the local hard drive.
   ☒ B is the incorrect answer because increasing the color depth of the Application Set would cause more information to be sent over the connection. You should reduce the color depth to help speed up a slow connection. C is incorrect because turning audio remapping off will speed up a connection by eliminating the need to send audio information. D is incorrect because SpeedScreen Latency Reduction gives the user instant feedback for mouse strokes and keyboard entry, thus making the session appear to run faster.

4. ☑ A, B, C, D, and E can all use Program Neighborhood. Win32 and Java clients use Program Neighborhood natively, and all other clients can use Program Neighborhood through an ICA PassThrough connection.

5. ☑ A is correct because Greg is unable to connect to the public address of the ICA browser. When this option is checked, the client will use the alternate address configured on the server. This option is set using the altaddr.exe command.
   ☒ B is incorrect because although this would cause an error message, the client would still be able to contact the Citrix server. C is incorrect because encryption settings that are too low would not keep the client from connecting, but could restrict the user from using a session if the minimum encryption required for that application set was not met. D is incorrect because turning off client device mapping would not stop a user from connecting to a Citrix server.

6. ☑ D is correct because we need to edit the properties of the custom connection to change it to a seamless window. When a custom connection is configured, we have the option of using a remote window or a seamless window. When a seamless window is used, the application appears to be running on the local machine and does not have a windowed box around the application.
   ☒ A is incorrect because there is no value SetOutsideWindow in appsrv.ini. B is incorrect

because refreshing the Program Neighborhood window will not change the settings of the connections. **C** is incorrect because client settings would override the server settings. Also, the question asked what you could change on the local machine.

7. ☑ **D** is correct. Audio remapping set to High can use up to 1.3 Mbps of bandwidth.
   ☒ **A, B, C,** and **E** are incorrect because the High setting could use more or less than these answers.

8. ☑ **C** is correct because this would cause the ICA client to request an update to the Dallas farm from the ICA browser, showing the new published application in the farm when the request was completed.
   ☒ **A** is incorrect because this may refresh the application set icons, but it is not the most efficient method of getting a new list of applications. **B** is incorrect because, although this would probably refresh the application set the next time the user logs in to Program Neighborhood, it is not the best answer. **D** is also incorrect because session screen size has no impact on application set connections.

9. ☑ **B** is correct. When security is important, you should always publish to Explicit users. Explicitly published applications require domain authentication before a user connects to a session. Anonymously published applications do not require a logon to connect.
   ☒ **A** is incorrect because this would not tighten security or require domain authentication. **C** is incorrect because this would allow anyone in the domain access to the application. **D** is incorrect because it would not require a logon.

10. ☑ **C** is not a valid protocol. RDP is used with the Microsoft Windows Terminal Services client software.
    ☒ **A, B, D,** and **E** are all valid PN protocols.

11. ☑ **C** is correct because using PN folders is the easiest way to manage a large number of applications. For example, you could create an Office folder, an Accounting folder, and a Marketing folder.
    ☒ **A** and **B** are incorrect because publishing the applications to different groups would not separate the applications logically in PN.

12. ☑ **A** is the correct location to set the bitmap cache settings.
    ☒ **B, C,** and **D** are all invalid locations.

13. ☑ **C** is correct. Under this tab, we can change the hotkeys if they conflict with an application. The disappearing title bar Andy experienced was due to this hotkey being set to Toggle Title

Bar on the application by default.

☒ **A** and **B** are incorrect because this would not fix Andy's problems with keystrokes.

14. ☑ **D** would be the correct setting for LAN usage, which is up to 1.3 Mbps of bandwidth for high quality audio. This setting should be used with caution, as several users with this setting could bog down the network, and should not be used for low speed connections.

☒ **A, B,** and **C** are incorrect because these would not improve the audio quality on Mike's session.

15. ☑ **B** and **C** are correct. The client names for each client must be unique when connecting to a Citrix server. This can be changed in either of these two places with the same result. If two or more PN client names are the same, an error will occur when more than one user tries to log in.

☒ **A** and **D** are wrong because this will have no effect on the PN client name.

16. ☑ **A** is the correct path for the ICA PassThrough Client.

☒ **B, C,** and **D** are all invalid installation paths.

17. ☑ **B** is the correct answer. The TAPI interface lets you configure modems and telephony settings for dial-up connections.

☒ **A, C,** and **D** are invalid answers because they do not correctly describe the term.

18. ☑ **D** is correct because only Win32 and Java clients can use the Application Set Manager view. Alternatively, you could publish PN on the server using ICA PassThrough and have Bruce set up a custom connection to this published app; or you could install and run the Java client on the iMac.

☒ **A, B,** and **C** are all incorrect because these solutions will not allow Bruce to connect to an application set.

19. ☑ **C** is correct because Win32 clients support TAPI natively so no emulation is required.

☒ **A** and **B** are incorrect since these clients do not support TAPI natively on the OS, TAPI must be emulated by the ICA client.

20. ☑ **A, B, C, D,** and **E** are all supported resolutions in Program Neighborhood.

LAB ANSWER

This scenario poses several problems: ensuring connectivity through the firewall, making sure the client connections are efficient for dial-up, and setting the Default view to the new Application Set.

The easiest way to configure a custom PN client is to first install the client on a similar client machine, customize the client, and then copy the appropriate .ini files to the installation source. After you have installed the client on a Windows 2000 machine, create a connection to the new application set. A good way to emulate the situation in Rhode Island would be to use a dial-up connection to the Internet on the machine you will be configuring. That way, you will know if the connection works or not.

When you configure your connection to the application set, you will need to select your protocol, which will be TCP/IP or TCP/IP+HTTP if you are connecting using the Citrix XML service on port 80. Remember, you will need to set an alternate address on your ICA browser using the altaddr.exe command and configuring your firewall to recognize this address if you are using NAT. After you have entered your ICA browser or browsers in the Address list using the Servers… button in the wizard, you will need to click the check box for Use Alternate Address For Firewall Connection, which can be found under the Firewalls… button.

You will want to make sure data compression, bitmap caching, and possibly SpeedScreen is turned on for the new application set by checking the properties. SpeedScreen can be used with very slow dial-up connections to make the session appear to be faster. Turn off client audio remapping unless absolutely necessary.

After you have set up the connection, you will need to right-click the Application Set icon in the Application Set Manager view and select Set As Default. This will ensure that this application set will be their Default view when they launch the program for the first time.

When your configuration is complete, you will need to copy the four files from your client installation to your installation source for your Rhode Island administrator. These files will be Appsrv.ini, Module.ini, Pn.ini, and Wfclient.ini. You will need to rename the .ini extensions to .src for your installation set.

When this is complete, uninstall Program Neighborhood from your client machine and install your newly created custom client. It is always good to test your settings before you roll it out. This way you know if everything is working properly or if you need to make any changes.

CCA
CITRIX® CERTIFIED ADMINISTRATOR

11

Web
Connectivity

C itrix MetaFrame XP now includes a Web interface to Program Neighborhood called NFuse that allows users to access applications via the Internet or an intranet. NFuse offers all of the same management capabilities that come standard with MetaFrame XP but allows administrators to completely customize the interface through a Web browser. Web sites that dynamically generate application sets based upon user credentials can be created by administrators and Web developers alike using a wizard or the application programming interface (API).

CERTIFICATION OBJECTIVE 11.01

Recognizing Citrix Web Components

A key to success in a corporate portal is bringing applications to users through a Web interface. Typical Web-enabled applications that make use of Hypertext Markup Language (HTML), Java, or a scripting language can be time consuming to create, modify, and maintain, and may require major client-side resources to run. With Citrix NFuse, however, any application that will run in a Terminal Server environment can be Web enabled without rewriting a single line of code. There are three essential Citrix Web components that NFuse requires:

- Citrix server farm
- Web server
- Independent Computing Architecture (ICA) Client device with a Web browser

exam
ⓌatchW
Make sure you know what the three Citrix Web components are: a Citrix server farm, a Web server, and an ICA Client device.

The Citrix Server Farm

The Citrix server farm component is a single or group of MetaFrame servers that provide published applications that users can access explicitly or anonymously. Server farms capable of participating with NFuse are Citrix MetaFrame servers for Windows and Citrix MetaFrame servers for Unix Operating Systems. Table 11-1 shows the Citrix MetaFrame products and their supported platforms, each of which is NFuse capable.

TABLE 11-1	Supported Citrix MetaFrame Products and Their Supported Platforms

Citrix MetaFrame Product	Platform
Citrix MetaFrame XP for Windows version 1.0	Windows NT 4.0 Terminal Server Edition, the Windows 2000 Server family
Citrix MetaFrame for Windows version 1.8 with Service Pack 2 and Feature Release 1	Windows NT 4.0 Terminal Server Edition, the Windows 2000 Server family
Citrix MetaFrame for Unix Operating Systems version 1.1	Solaris 2.6 (Sparc), Solaris 7 (Intel and Sparc), Solaris 8 (Intel and SPARC), HP-UX 11.x, AIX 4.3.3

on the
job

A Citrix WinFrame server, though it can be managed in the same Citrix server farm as a Citrix MetaFrame server, cannot participate in the NFuse technology.

Citrix MetaFrame 1.8 and WinFrame 1.8 server farms were the first versions to introduce the concept of published applications. Published applications provided an automated way for users to view all of the applications they had access to without browsing for specific applications. Employing Program Neighborhood, users could authenticate to a supported server farm and receive the published applications they had access to, or receive their application set. NFuse is simply a Web-enabled version of Program Neighborhood, providing users with their application set information through a Web page (see Figure 11-1).

exam
Watch

It is important to know that NFuse is a Web-enabled interface for Program Neighborhood.

The Citrix server farm performs the following roles within an NFuse system:

- Provides the Web server with application set information when a user authenticates through NFuse
- Hosts the published applications

The MetaFrame servers that participate with an NFuse system use the Citrix Extensible Markup Language (XML) Service to provide published application information to both users and Web servers via the Transmission Control Protocol/Internet Protocol (TCP/IP). MetaFrame servers capable of running this service are Citrix MetaFrame XP for Windows version 1.0, Citrix MetaFrame for Windows

FIGURE 11-1

An example
NFuse Web site
showing an
application set

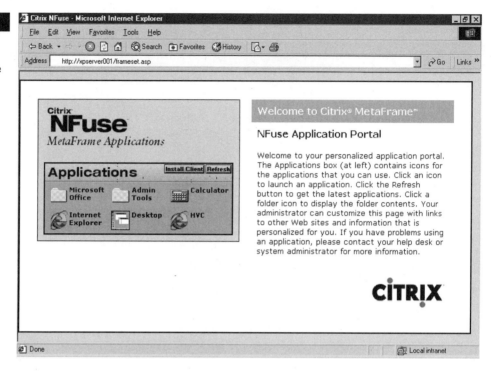

version 1.8 with Service Pack 2 (SP2) and Feature Release 1 (FR1), and Citrix
MetaFrame for Unix Operating Systems version 1.1.

Make sure you know the two roles the Citrix server performs within an NFuse system: provide the Web server with application set information when users authenticate and host the published applications.

Web Server

The Web server hosts the NFuse Java objects and Web server-side scripts. The
NFuse Web pages include the server-side scripts that then call the NFuse Java
objects to perform the following functions:

- Authenticate users to a Citrix server farm
- Generate application sets for authenticated users
- Modify the properties of individual applications before they are presented
  to the user

■ Create and send Independent Computing Architecture (ICA) files to client devices that can then launch an ICA sessions

The NFuse Java objects are added to the Web server through the Citrix NFuse Web Server Extension installation executable. The installation program also includes sample Web sites that can be used to implement advanced NFuse features such as multiple server farm display and cookie data encryption (see Figure 11-2).

exam
ⓦatch

It is important to know when the NFuse Java objects are installed and what functions they perform.

An additional executable, the NFuse Web Site Wizard is included on the NFuse CD as part of the NFuse package, but is not installed with the NFuse Web Server Extensions. The Web Site Wizard can create customized Web sites including sites based upon Microsoft's Active Server Pages (ASP), Sun Microsystems' Java Server Pages (JSP) and Citrix's own proprietary Hypertext Markup Language (HTML) extensions.

FIGURE 11-2

Web page that describes and demonstrates advanced NFuse capabilities

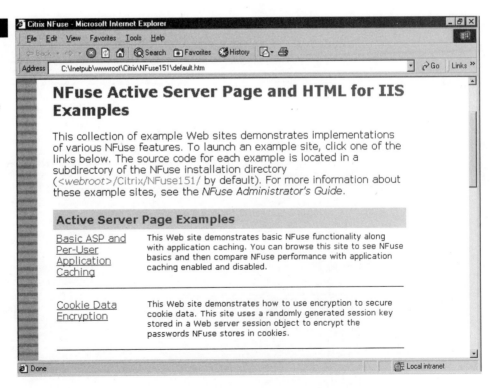

NFuse Active Server Page and HTML for IIS Examples

This collection of example Web sites demonstrates implementations of various NFuse features. To launch an example site, click one of the links below. The source code for each example is located in a subdirectory of the NFuse installation directory (*<webroot>*/Citrix/NFuse151/ by default). For more information about these example sites, see the *NFuse Administrator's Guide*.

Active Server Page Examples

Basic ASP and Per-User Application Caching	This Web site demonstrates basic NFuse functionality along with application caching. You can browse this site to see NFuse basics and then compare NFuse performance with application caching enabled and disabled.
Cookie Data Encryption	This Web site demonstrates how to use encryption to secure cookie data. This site uses a randomly generated session key stored in a Web server session object to encrypt the passwords NFuse stores in cookies.

NFuse has incorporated Web-based ICA Client installation. Essentially, this is a Web browser-based method of installing ICA Clients. During the Web Server Extension installation, the setup program prompts for the ICA Client CD or a CD image. Setup copies the contents of the CD's ICAWEB directory called NFuseClients to the Web server's wwwroot folder. This code, by default, is included with any site created with the Web Site Wizard. When visiting the NFuse Web sites, Web-based ICA Client Installation code detects the device and Web browser types and will prompt the user to install the appropriate ICA Client, as can be seen in Figure 11-3.

If the NFuseClients folder does not exist in the root of the wwwroot folder, Web-based ICA Client installations will fail.

The Web-based ICA Client installation code can correctly identify the following platforms successfully: 32-bit Windows, 16-bit Windows, Macintosh, Solaris, SunOS, SGI, HP/UX, IBM/AIX, SCO, Dec/Tru64, and Linux. For platforms it cannot identify, the Web-based ICA Client installation recommends the ICA Java Client application.

FIGURE 11-3

The Web-based ICA Client installation

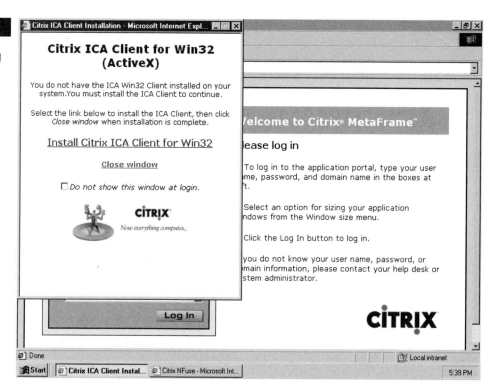

The Web-based ICA Client installation code can only identify successfully the presence of an ICA client on either a 32-bit or 16-bit Windows platform. Therefore, for all other devices, the Web-based ICA Client installation code will always offer the user the opportunity to install an ICA Client until the "Do not show this window at login" check box has been checked.

EXERCISE 11-1

CertCam 11-1

Create a Custom NFuse Web Page

This exercise will demonstrate how to create a custom NFuse Web site using the NFuse Web Site Wizard. The Web Site Wizard is a 32-bit application and may be installed on any 32-bit Windows machine on the network. The Web Site Wizard presents the following options when creating a custom Web site:

- How the Web server will communicate with the Citrix servers
- How the Web site will appear
- How to access the NFuse Java objects on the Web server
- How users view applications
- How users authenticate

Follow these steps to create a custom NFuse Web site using the NFuse Web Site Wizard:

1. Launch the NFuse Web Site Wizard from Start | Programs | Citrix | NFuse | Web Site Wizard. This will begin the process of creating a set of Web pages for your Web site (see Figure 11-4).

2. Click Next.

3. Page 2 of the Citrix Web Site Wizard (Figure 11-5) shows the options to choose from regarding how the Web server will communicate with the Citrix server. Click Next to keep all defaults.

4. The choice of how Web pages will appear is shown in Figure 11-6. Make sure Standard is selected under Web Site Scheme and click Next.

5. Here, the options for how the Web server will access the Java objects are presented. (See Figure 11-7.) Select the Active Server Pages (Scripting Based) button and click Next.

Step 1 of 8 in the custom Web site configuration process

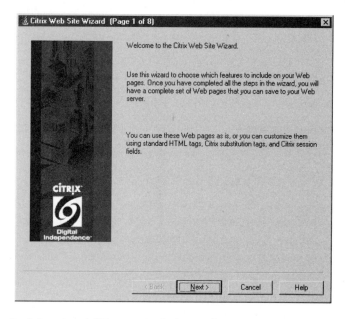

6. Page 5 of the wizard (Figure 11-8) shows the options available regarding how users will view their applications. Make certain the Launched In Separate Window button is selected and that both the Use Seamless If Available check box and that for Enable Ticketing are checked.

Step 2 of 8 in the custom Web site configuration process

FIGURE II-6

Step 3 of 8 in the
custom Web site
configuration
process

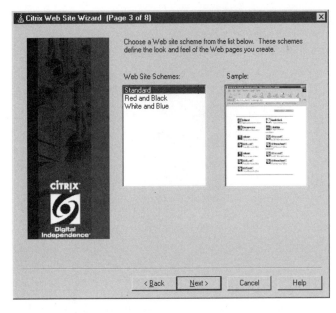

***If the Enable Ticketing check box is to be used, all Citrix servers in the farm
must have the Citrix XML Service running on the same port.***

7. Additional options on how the Web site will appear are presented on Page 6
of the wizard (seen in Figure 11-9). Accept the defaults and click Next.

FIGURE II-7

Step 4 of 8 in the
custom Web site
configuration
process

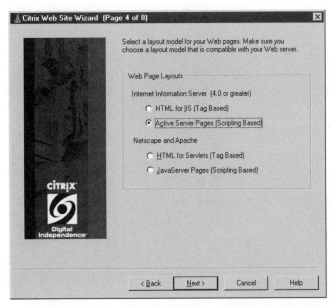

Step 5 of 8 in the custom Web site configuration process

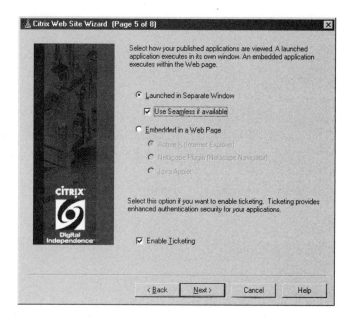

8. The choices presented in this next step allow several different ways for users to authenticate to the application set (see Figure 11-10). Accept the defaults and click Next.

Step 6 of 8 in the custom Web site configuration process

FIGURE 11-10

Step 7 of 8 in the
custom Web site
configuration
process

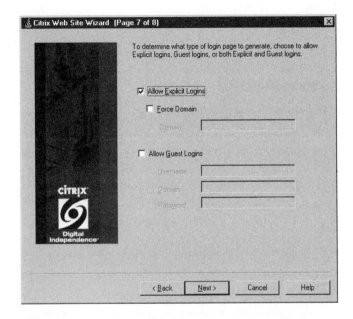

9. Save the Web site to a location and click Finish (see Figure 11-11).

FIGURE 11-11

Step 8 of 8 in the
custom Web site
configuration
process

exam
ⓦatch *Make certain you know what properties you can customize during the process of creating a Web site with the Web Site Wizard.*

The ICA Client Device

The ICA Client device component is defined within an NFuse system as any computing device capable of launching an ICA session and a Web browser. Several examples include personal computers (PCs), Net appliances such as personal digital assistants (PDAs) or thin client terminals, and Unix workstations.

The ICA Client device works together with the Web browser and the ICA Client as a two-part system. The Web browser is capable of viewing the application set and downloading the ICA files, while the ICA Client acts as the engine to launch the ICA sessions.

After providing details on all three Citrix server components, here are some questions and answers to review:

SCENARIO & SOLUTION	
What program will create customized NFuse Web sites?	The NFuse Web Site Wizard
NFuse Java objects are installed with what executable?	The NFuse Web Server Extensions
What two items make up an ICA Client device?	A Web browser and an ICA Client

How NFuse Works

The following steps explain the interaction between the Citrix server farm, Web server, and ICA Client device when using NFuse.

1. An ICA Client device visits the Citrix NFuse login page and enters the user credentials. The client Web browser, meanwhile, sends this authentication information, via the Hypertext Transfer Protocol (HTTP) protocol, to the Web server.

2. The Web server, using its NFuse Java objects, forwards the authentication information to a designated Citrix server via the Citrix Extensible Markup Language (XML) Service.

3. The MetaFrame server using the Citrix XML Service retrieves from the farm a list of the applications the user has access to (their application set) and returns this information to the Web server.

   - MetaFrame XP servers retrieve application set information from the Independent Management Architecture (IMA) system.

   - MetaFrame 1.8 servers retrieve application set information from the Program Neighborhood service.

   - MetaFrame for Unix Operating System servers retrieve application set information from the ICA Browser and the local NFuse configuration file.

4. The Web server, using Java objects, generates a Web page containing links to the applications in the authenticated user's application set. Each link in the Web page points to a template ICA file located on the Web server.

   - An ICA file uses an .ica extension except that it is formatted identically to a Windows .ini file. This ICA file contains parameters needed by the ICA client to launch an ICA session. Parameters included are authentication information, the name of the published application, and the address of the server.

5. By clicking one of the hyperlinks associated with an application, the Web browser sends a request to the Web server to retrieve an ICA file for the selected application. The Web server passes the request to the Java objects, which locates the template ICA file, template.ica (see Figure 11-12).

   Located within the template ICA file are substitution tags that the Java objects parse, replacing the tags with specific information pertaining to the user and the application (see Figure 11-13).

6. The Web server's Java objects pass the customized ICA file to the Web browser.

7. The Web browser sends the ICA file to the ICA Client.

8. The ICA Client then launches an ICA session based upon the parameters specified in the ICA file.

An overview of this entire process can be seen in Figure 11-14.

exam
ⓦatch

Be sure to understand each step of how NFuse works.

```
🖼 template_noticket.ica - Notepad                                          _ 🗗 ✕
File  Edit  Format  Help
<[NFuse_setSessionField NFuse_ContentType=application/x-ica]>
<[NFuse_setSessionField NFuse_windowType=seamless]>

[WFClient]
Version=2
ClientName=[NFuse_ClientName]

[ApplicationServers]
[NFuse_AppName]=

[[NFuse_AppName]]
Address=[NFuse_IPV4Address]
InitialProgram=#[NFuse_AppName]
DesiredColor=[NFuse_windowColors]
TransportDriver=TCP/IP
WinStationDriver=ICA 3.0

AutologonAllowed=ON
Username=[NFuse_User]
Domain=[NFuse_Domain]
Password=[NFuse_PasswordScrambled]

<[NFuse_IFSESSIONFIELD sessionfield="NFUSE_SOUNDTYPE" value="basic"]>
ClientAudio=On
<[/NFuse_IFSESSIONFIELD]>
<[NFuse_IFSESSIONFIELD sessionfield="NFUSE_windowType" value="launch"]>
ScreenPercent=0
<[/NFuse_IFSESSIONFIELD]>
[NFuse_IcaWindow]

[NFuse_IcaEncryption]

[EncRC5-0]
DriverNameWin16=pdc0w.dll
DriverNameWin32=pdc0n.dll

[EncRC5-40]
DriverNameWin16=pdc40w.dll
DriverNameWin32=pdc40n.dll
```

```
🖼 launch.ica - Notepad                                                    _ 🗗 ✕
File  Edit  Format  Help
[WFClient]
Version=2
ClientName=MW-luchtcm

[ApplicationServers]
Internet Explorer=

[Internet Explorer]
Address=192.168.0.192
InitialProgram=#Internet Explorer
DesiredColor=8
TransportDriver=TCP/IP
WinStationDriver=ICA 3.0

AutologonAllowed=ON
Username=luchtcm
Domain=MW
Password=00083848134332592553


DesiredHRES=640
DesiredVRES=480
TWIMode=On



[EncRC5-0]
DriverNameWin16=pdc0w.dll
DriverNameWin32=pdc0n.dll

[EncRC5-40]
DriverNameWin16=pdc40w.dll
DriverNameWin32=pdc40n.dll

[EncRC5-56]
DriverNameWin16=pdc56w.dll
DriverNameWin32=pdc56n.dll
```

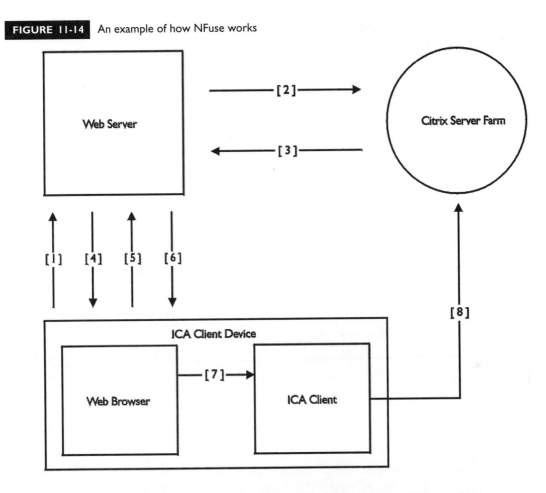

FIGURE 11-14 An example of how NFuse works

Now that you have been through the steps on how NFuse works, here are a couple of scenario questions and answers to review:

SCENARIO & SOLUTION	
Which NFuse component creates customized ICA files?	The Web server using its Java objects.
Which NFuse component is responsible for providing application set data?	The Citrix server farm using the Citrix XML Service.

CERTIFICATION OBJECTIVE 11.02

Identifying NFuse Features and Components

NFuse must demonstrate it can overcome several hurdles, including secure access to corporate applications through a public network, providing support for a wide variety of client devices and server platforms and providing a single point of access for all users.

NFuse provides some industry standard techniques for securing information across communication channels in addition to providing added security of its own, allowing secure communication between all three tiers. NFuse also provides a large number of client devices and server platforms to participate within this Web-enabled technology. In addition, server-side scripting and configuration can create a single point of access for all users connecting to NFuse.

Designing Three-tiered Solutions

Two important considerations that an administrator must consider before publishing applications via an Internet or intranet site are security and design. Designing a three-tiered solution should allow for efficient and secure access to published applications.

Security

Using industry-standard security practices in addition to some Citrix-provided safeguards, administrators can provide robust security for all three communication tiers.

Web Browser to Web Server Security: Secure HTML (HTTPS)

Many secure Web servers rely on a technology developed by Netscape Communications called Secure Sockets Layer (SSL). SSL is an open, non-proprietary, industry-standard Web protocol designed to provide secure server authentication, data encryption, message integrity, and optional client authentication. By combining the SSL technology with HTML, HTTPS was created. SSL and therefore HTTPS use the TCP port 443, by default, for its communications.

With NFuse, HTTPS can create a secure tunnel in which users can pass credentials posted in the NFuse login page. All items passed between the Web server and Web browser travel through this secure tunnel, including ICA files, cookie information, and HTML data.

Virtually all Web servers and Web browsers are optimized to use HTTPS. The use of HTTPS is transparent to both NFuse and the Web browser, so no special configuration is required. For more information on how to implement HTTPS on a Web server, visit: http://www.verisign.com.

Web Browser to Web Server and Citrix Server Security: Ticketing

Previous versions of NFuse, by default, placed user credential information within the ICA file it sent to the ICA Client devices. An attacker, able to intercept the file, would be able to use the ICA file to gain access to a Citrix server. Enabling the ticketing technology eliminates this risk. By default, all custom Web sites built with the Web Site Wizard have ticketing enabled.

All Citrix MetaFrame XP for Windows 1.0 servers support the ticketing technology. All Citrix MetaFrame for Windows 1.8 must have SP2 and FR1 licensed and activated for ticketing to function. Citrix MetaFrame for Unix Operating Systems 1.1 does not support ticketing at this time. In order for ticketing to work, all servers in the server farm must have ticketing support.

Ticketing works like this:

1. When a user selects an application to run from the NFuse application set page, the Web servers NFuse Java objects request from the server farm a ticket for that user. (A ticket is a 30-character string generated by the server farm that correlates the user to their credentials but does not contain the credentials themselves. Tickets have a configurable expiration time and are valid only for a single ICA session.)

2. The server farm passes this ticket to the Web server.

3. The Web server places this ticket in the ICA file sent to the ICA Client device.

4. The ICA Client authenticates itself to the server farm using the ticket.

5. The server farm compares the ticket to the user's actual credentials and if it matches, will log the user in.

Web Server to Citrix Server Security: SSL Relay

SSL Relay works much the same as the SSL technology enabled between a Web server and a Web browser except that now the secure tunnel is being passed between the Web server and a Citrix server farm. SSL Relay is a default component of Citrix MetaFrame XP for Windows 1.0 and Citrix MetaFrame 1.8 with SP2 and FR1 licensed and activated. By default, SSL Relay uses TCP port 443 for its SSL communication.

To install and configure SSL Relay on a Citrix server, use the Citrix SSL Relay Configuration Tool. On a Web server, a Web site must be configured to use SSL Relay. This information is configurable when creating a custom Web site with the Web Site Wizard.

SSL Relay works like this:

1. The Web server first verifies the identity of the SSL Relay server by checking the SSL Relay server's certificate against a list of trusted certificate authorities.

2. Once this has completed, the Web server and the SSL Relay server negotiate an encryption method for the session.

3. The Web server then sends all information requests to the SSL Relay server encrypted.

4. The SSL Relay server decrypts the requests and passes them to a configured Citrix server.

5. The Citrix server passes all information requested back to the SSL Relay server.

6. The SSL Relay server passes all request information back to the Web server for decryption.

ICA Client Device to Citrix Server: RC5 Encryption   RC5 is an encryption algorithm that Citrix employs to encrypt session information from ICA Client devices to Citrix MetaFrame for Windows servers. RC5 encryption uses the RC5 encryption algorithm developed by RSA Data Security, Inc. and the Diffie-Hellman key agreement with a 1024-bit key to generate RC5 public and private keys. RC5 encryption supports 40-, 56-, and 128-bit encryption that can be enforced by Citrix administrators on a per-connection basis. In addition, minimum encryption levels can be used to enforce encryption if a connection is to be made.

Clients that support RC5 encryption include: all version 6.0 clients or later, ActiveX Control, 16-bit Plug-in, 32-bit Plug-in, DOS32 and DOS16.

ICA Client Device to Citrix Server and Web Server: Implementing a Firewall   A firewall is a security system installed within a network. It prohibits any kind of information that is not authorized to pass from one network to another, chiefly the public Internet and a private network.

To use Citrix, several ports must be opened on a firewall for certain communication to work. Commonly, port 80 for HTTP traffic, port 443 for HTTPS traffic and port 1494 for ICA session traffic are all opened on a firewall for inbound access.

exam
Watch

Make sure you know the ports that need to be opened up on a firewall for proper communication to work

ICA Client Device to Citrix Server and Web Server: Network Address Translation   Most firewalls have the ability to use a technology called Network Address Translation (NAT). Using NAT with Citrix, each MetaFrame server receives an alternate IP address. Only ICA Clients that know the alternate address will pass through the firewall. In addition, only those ICA Clients that request the alternate address will be able to connect successfully.

To assign an alternate address, the command *altaddr* is used. For example: altaddr/set 4.60.224.251.

Design

Designing the three tiers effectively can result in better performance when it comes to running applications remotely.

Bandwidth: Web Server to Citrix Server Farm   The bandwidth requirements between a Web server and a Citrix server farm are generally not heavy, but can make a difference in overall performance. If possible, have the Web server and the Citrix server farm running on the same local area network (LAN). If the Web server and Citrix server farm must be separated by a wide area network (WAN) link, ensure that the link speed is at least 128K, allotting a minimum 64K of the bandwidth for ICA connection traffic.

Bandwidth: ICA Client Device to Web Server and Citrix Server Farm
The bandwidth requirements between an ICA Client device and either a Web server or Citrix server farm are minimal. A 14.4k modem is required, but a 56K connection or better is recommended.

on the
Job

Frame Relay, DSL, or ISDN operating at the same 56k speed as a modem will be far faster due to the 12–15 percent overhead that 56K dial-up users may experience.

Utilization: Running NFuse on a Citrix Server   When possible, dedicate a separate server to act as the Web server. Citrix servers are designed to host applications with as little unnecessary overhead as possible, and by running the Web services on the Citrix server, precious resources are being used.

Small Implementation

This first design scenario concerns a small implementation that hosts applications via an NFuse Web site on their Intranet. Because of money constraints, this is a single server solution, where the Web server and Citrix MetaFrame XP for Windows 1.0 server have been installed on the same machine (see Figure 11-15).

FIGURE 11-15 An example of a small NFuse deployment

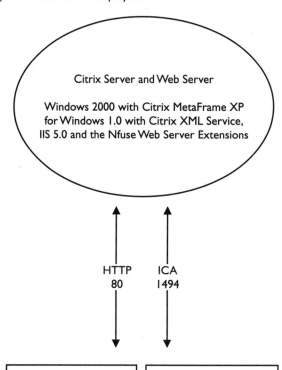

Citrix Server and Web Server

Windows 2000 with Citrix MetaFrame XP
for Windows 1.0 with Citrix XML Service,
IIS 5.0 and the Nfuse Web Server Extensions

HTTP   ICA
80   1494

ICA Client Device	ICA Client Device	ICA Client Device	ICA Client Device
Windows 95 with Netscape Navigator 4.01 and Netscape ICA Client Plug-in	Windows 98 with Internet Explorer 4.0 and ActiveX ICA Client	Windows 2000 Professional with Internet Explorer 5.0 and ActiveX ICA Client	Windows 2000 Professional with Internet Explorer 5.0 and ActiveX ICA Client

Security Considerations   All traffic is passed on the LAN. No special security considerations are necessary in this configuration.

Design Considerations   The Citrix server will have more overhead introduced onto it because the Web server is also hosted on the same machine. No special bandwidth considerations are needed because all traffic is kept within the LAN.

Medium Implementation

The second design scenario has been built to host published applications via an NFuse Internet site. Within this scenario, ten Citrix MetaFrame XP for Windows 1.0 servers comprise a single farm on the same LAN as a single Web server running IIS 5.0 with the NFuse Web Extensions and an SSL digital certificate (see Figure 11-16).

Security Considerations   Traffic passing between remote locations through the public Internet and the corporate LAN are a reason to implement a firewall in this scenario. Ports on the firewall that will need to be opened for inbound communication are TCP ports 80 for HTTP, 443 for SSL, and 1494 for ICA traffic. In addition, to ensuring secure communications between the ICA Client device and the Citrix servers, RC5 encryption will be used.

Design Considerations   A separate Web server has been introduced to take the burden off a Citrix server from incurring the overhead introduced. All traffic between the Web server and Citrix servers is on the LAN, so no bandwidth concerns are introduced.

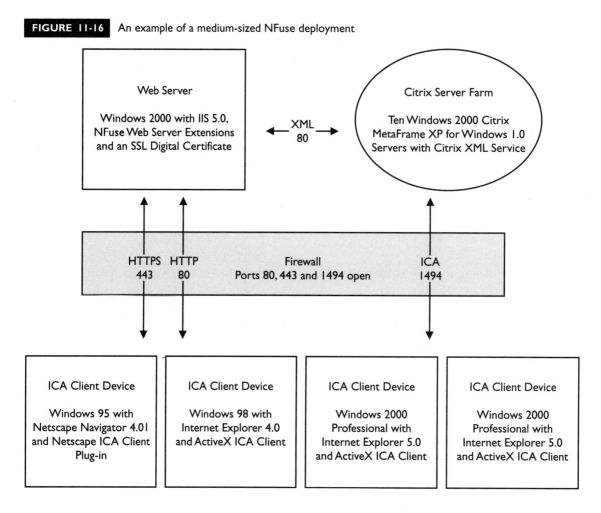

An example of a medium-sized NFuse deployment

Large Implementation

In this final scenario, published applications will be presented via an NFuse page for remote connectivity through the public Internet. On the back end, a single Web server runs Windows 2000 with IIS 5.0 and the NFuse Web Server Extensions, while an SSL digital certificate resides on the same LAN as two separate twenty-server Citrix server farms running Window 2000 with Citrix MetaFrame XP for Windows 1.0. The NFuse Web site has been configured to allow the application sets of two farms to appear in one page (see Figure 11-17).

FIGURE 11-17 An example of a large NFuse deployment

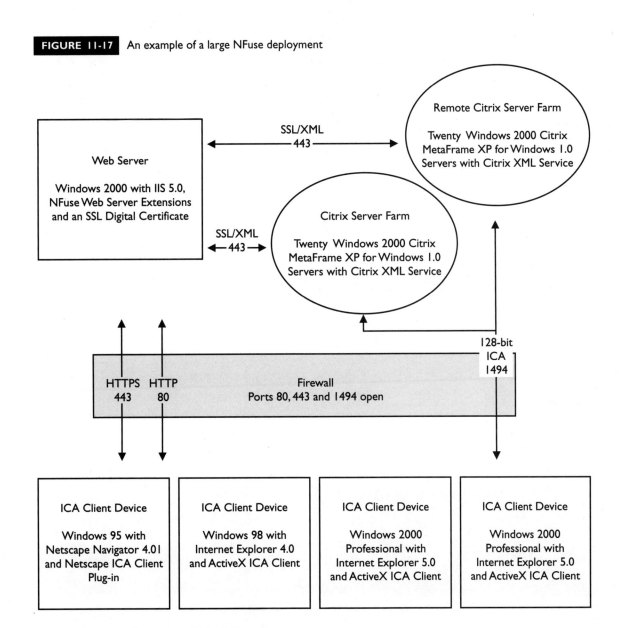

Security Considerations

■ An SSL digital certificate has been installed on the Web server to allow secure traffic between the ICA Client devices and the Web server.

- A firewall has been installed to further secure all communication between remote clients and the corporate LAN. Ports open on the firewall are TCP ports 80 for HTML, 443 for SSL, and 1494 for ICA traffic.

- NAT is being used for additional firewall security.

- Between the Web server and the Citrix servers, an SSL Relay server has been configured on both server farms, enabling encryption between the Web server and the Citrix servers.

- Ticketing has been built into the Web site so secure authentication information can be passed between all three tiers.

- 128-bit encryption has been set as a minimum requirement for all ICA communication between the ICA Client devices and the Citrix servers.

Design considerations

- A separate Web server has been installed to take the burden off a Citrix server from incurring the overhead that would be introduced from the HTTP and SSL traffic.

- Two Citrix server farms exist, one local to the Web server and one remote. The traffic that will pass between the Web server and remote Citrix server farm has created the need for a WAN link. The WAN link used in this scenario is 384K to allow for expansion.

- To allow for secure communication between the Web server and the two server farms, especially the remote server farm, a single SSL Relay server has been set up on each of the Citrix server farms.

SCENARIO & SOLUTION

In order for SSL to work through a firewall, what port must be opened?	TCP port 443
HTTP (Web) traffic uses what port by default?	TCP port 80
What program do you run to configure the SSL Relay on a Citrix server?	Citrix SSL Relay Configuration Tool

Now that designing the three tiers has been covered, here are some possible scenario questions and their answers:

Minimum Requirements to Install NFuse

One of the benefits of the Citrix NFuse technology is that it can be run on nearly any device on virtually every platform. The following section lists the minimum requirements for each of the three Citrix Web components.

Minimum Requirements for the Citrix Server Farm Component

NFuse supports the following MetaFrame platforms:

- Citrix MetaFrame XP for Windows version 1.0
- Citrix MetaFrame for Windows version 1.8
- Citrix MetaFrame for Unix Operating Systems version 1.1

Additional software requirements for Citrix MetaFrame for Windows version 1.8 servers:

- Citrix MetaFrame 1.8 servers must have SP2 installed
- Citrix MetaFrame 1.8 servers must have an installed and activated Feature Release 1 (FR1) license

Additional software requirements for Citrix MetaFrame for Unix Operating Systems version 1.1:

- The Citrix XML Service for Unix Operating Systems must be installed on at least one server in the farm. This server will act as the primary contact point between the Web server and the server farm
- Optionally, additional servers may have the Citrix XML Service installed. These will act as backups for the primary server.

General requirements:

- Citrix MetaFrame servers must be a part of a server farm.
- They must have published applications that are created in the server farm management scope.

on the **Job**   *During installation, the option to install NFuse on the Citrix server is presented. This will only install, however, if the server is running IIS 4.0 or IIS 5.0 and the Microsoft Java Virtual Machine (JVM).*

Minimum Requirements for the Web Server Component

NFuse is supported on the following Web server/platform combinations as seen in Table 11-2.

This is a list that contains all tested and supported Web server/platform combinations. It may be possible, however, to use other Web servers that support Java servlets and/or JavaServer Pages.

Minimum Requirements for the ICA Client Device Component

To use NFuse, the ICA Client device must be using a supported Web browser in combination with a supported ICA Client. All ICA Clients that ship on the ICA Client CD are supported, with the exception of ICA Clients that cannot be launched with a Web browser (an example would be any of the ICA DOS clients).

Additionally, some previously released ICA Clients are capable of running NFuse. Table 11-3 lists all the ICA Clients and Web browsers supported.

TABLE 11-2   NFuse-supported Web Servers and Their Supported Platform Configurations

Web Server	Platform
Microsoft Internet Information Server 4.0	Windows NT 4.0 Server, Windows NT 4.0 Terminal Server Edition
Microsoft Internet Information Server 5.0	The Windows 2000 Server family
Netscape Enterprise Server 3.6	Solaris 7, Solaris 8
iPlanet Web Server 4.0 with Service Pack 4	Solaris 7, Solaris 8
iPlanet Web Server 4.1	Solaris 7, Solaris 8
Apache Server 1.3.9	Red Hat Linux 6.0, Solaris 7 and Solaris 8 using Sun Java Development Kit 1.2.2, Apache Jserv 1.1, and GNUJSP 1.0

| TABLE 11-3 | A List of All Supported ICA Clients and the Web Browsers They May Be Configured with |

ICA Client	Version	Supported Web browsers
Win32	4.21.779 and later	Netscape Navigator 4.01 and later, Internet Explorer 4.0 and later
Unix	3.0 and later	Netscape Navigator 4.01 and later, Netscape Communicator 4.61 and later
Linux	3.0 and later	Netscape Navigator 4.01 and later, Netscape Communicator 4.61 and later
ActiveX Control	4.21.779 and later	Netscape Navigator 4.01 and later, Internet Explorer 4.0 and later
Netscape Plug-in	4.21.779 and later	Netscape Navigator 4.01 and later, Internet Explorer 4.01 and later
Win16	4.21.779 and later	Netscape Navigator 4.08 and later, Internet Explorer 4.01 and later
Java—Applet	4.11 and later	Netscape Navigator 4.01 and later, Internet Explorer 4.0 and later
Java—Application	4.11 and later	Netscape Navigator 4.01 and later, Internet Explorer 4.0 and later
Macintosh	4.10.23 and later	Netscape Navigator 4.01 and later, Netscape Communicator 4.61 and later

Single Point of Access

Providing users with a single Web page from which they can access their applications has many benefits; one of which is a single point of access for published applications. With NFuse, Web server-side scripting can allow all ICA Client options to be configured using server-side scripts and custom-created ICA files. Users with local ICA Clients no longer need to configure server location information to access their application sets.

Example 1: Local Area Network Connectivity

To allow users to connect to published applications via the LAN through an NFuse Web site, no special configuration is needed with any of the three NFuse components. In this example, an ICA Client device connects to a single server running both the NFuse Web component and the Citrix server component (see Figure 11-18).

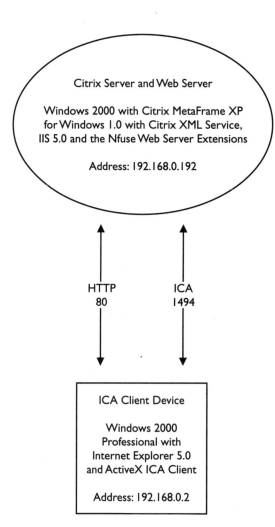

Citrix Server and Web Server

Windows 2000 with Citrix MetaFrame XP
for Windows 1.0 with Citrix XML Service,
IIS 5.0 and the NFuse Web Server Extensions

Address: 192.168.0.192

HTTP
80

ICA
1494

ICA Client Device

Windows 2000
Professional with
Internet Explorer 5.0
and ActiveX ICA Client

Address: 192.168.0.2

By creating a custom Web site using the NFuse Web Site Wizard, with no special configuration being done on either the Web side or Citrix server side, the following ICA file is presented to the ICA Client device to initiate an ICA session (see Figure 11-19).

Example 2: Remote Location Connectivity without NAT

In this second example, an ICA Client device connects to a remote NFuse Web site through a firewall where it receives its published application information (see Figure 11-20). Security is a concern in this scenario, so the administrator has required a minimum of 128-bit encryption for any published application to be launched.

FIGURE 11-19	
The customized ICA file for a single server deployment	

```
[WFClient]
Version=2
ClientName=MW-luchtcm

[ApplicationServers]
Internet Explorer=

[Internet Explorer]
Address=192.168.0.192
InitialProgram=#Internet Explorer
DesiredColor=8
TransportDriver=TCP/IP
WinStationDriver=ICA 3.0

AutologonAllowed=ON
Username=luchtcm
Domain=MW
Password=00083848134332592553


DesiredHRES=640
DesiredVRES=480
TWIMode=On



[EncRC5-0]
DriverNamewin16=pdc0w.dll
DriverNamewin32=pdc0n.dll

[EncRC5-40]
DriverNamewin16=pdc40w.dll
DriverNamewin32=pdc40n.dll

[EncRC5-56]
DriverNamewin16=pdc56w.dll
DriverNamewin32=pdc56n.dll
```

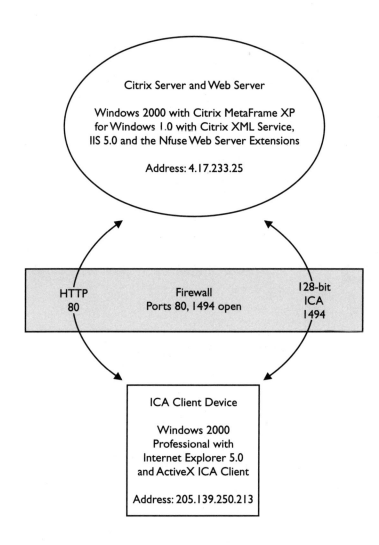

FIGURE 11-20

An example of a single server deployment through a firewall without NAT

As can be seen in Figure 11-21, the ICA file passed to the user in this scenario contains the external address of the server, 4.17.233.25, in addition to adding a new ICA parameter, EncryptionLevelSession=EncRC5-128.

FIGURE 11-21

A customized
ICA file requiring
128-bit
encryption

```
launch.ica - Notepad                                              _ B X
File  Edit  Format  Help
[WFClient]
Version=2
ClientName=MW-luchtcm

[ApplicationServers]
Internet Explorer=

[Internet Explorer]
Address=4.17.233.25
InitialProgram=#Internet Explorer
DesiredColor=8
TransportDriver=TCP/IP
WinStationDriver=ICA 3.0

AutologonAllowed=ON
Username=luchtcm
Domain=MW
Password=0008f7c450cf71d566df



DesiredHRES=640
DesiredVRES=480
TWIMode=On


EncryptionLevelSession=EncRC5-128

[EncRC5-0]
DriverNameWin16=pdc0w.dll
DriverNameWin32=pdc0n.dll

[EncRC5-40]
DriverNameWin16=pdc40w.dll
DriverNameWin32=pdc40n.dll

[EncRC5-56]
DriverNameWin16=pdc56w.dll
DriverNameWin32=pdc56n.dll
```

Example 3: Remote Location Connectivity with NAT

In the third scenario, an ICA Client device connects to a remote NFuse Web site through a firewall using NAT. All applications have been configured to require 128-bit encryption as a minimum (see Figure 11-22).

For the ICA Client device to communicate successfully with the Citrix server, the ICA Client must request the alternate address of the Citrix server. Should the ICA Client not request the alternate address, the Web server would create an ICA file that would identify the Citrix server at 192.168.0.192. This is a non-routable IP address, and the connection would fail. Instead, if the ICA Client were to request the alternate address to be given, the Web server would generate an ICA file with

An example of a single server deployment through a firewall with NAT

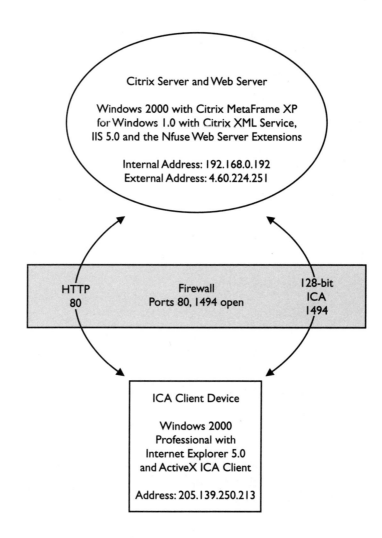

the Citrix server's alternate address, and communication between the two would be successful.

A change must be made to the template.ica file within the NFuse Web site to force ICA Client devices to request alternate addresses. Replace the line: Address=[NFuse_IPV4Address] with Address=[NFuse_IPV4AddressAlternate].

CertCam 11-2

EXERCISE 11-2

Configuring NFuse to Use an Alternate Address

This exercise will demonstrate how to configure NFuse to specify an alternate address for remote ICA Client devices.

1. Run the altaddr command on the Citrix server to specify an alternate address. The syntax is: altaddr /set *AlternateIPAddress* (see Figure 11-23).

2. Locate and edit the template.ica file within your NFuse Web site.

3. Locate the line that reads: Address=[NFuse_IPV4Address] (as seen in Figure 11-24).

4. Replace it with: Address=[NFuse_IPV4AddressAlternate] (as seen in Figure 11-25).

exam
ⓌⒶtch

It is important to know how, why, and when you would need to specify an alternate address.

FIGURE 11-23

Running the altaddr command

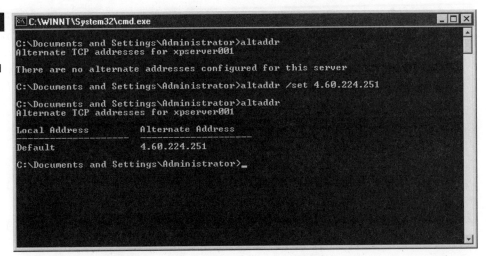

The template ICA
file before
alternate address
support

```
template.ica - Notepad
File  Edit  Format  Help
<[NFuse_setSessionField NFuse_ContentType=application/x-ica]>
<[NFuse_setSessionField NFuse_windowType=seamless]>

[WFClient]
Version=2
ClientName=[NFuse_ClientName]

[ApplicationServers]
[NFuse_AppName]=

[[NFuse_AppName]]
Address=[NFuse_IPV4Address]
InitialProgram=#[NFuse_AppName]
DesiredColor=[NFuse_windowColors]
TransportDriver=TCP/IP
WinStationDriver=ICA 3.0

AutologonAllowed=ON
[NFuse_Ticket]

<[NFuse_IFSESSIONFIELD sessionfield="NFUSE_SOUNDTYPE" value="basic"]>
ClientAudio=On
<[/NFuse_IFSESSIONFIELD]>
<[NFuse_IFSESSIONFIELD sessionfield="NFUSE_windowType" value="launch"]>
ScreenPercent=0
<[/NFuse_IFSESSIONFIELD]>
[NFuse_IcaWindow]

[NFuse_IcaEncryption]

[EncRC5-0]
DriverNameWin16=pdc0w.dll
DriverNameWin32=pdc0n.dll

[EncRC5-40]
DriverNameWin16=pdc40w.dll
DriverNameWin32=pdc40n.dll

[EncRC5-56]
```

The template ICA
file after alternate
address support

```
template.ica - Notepad
File  Edit  Format  Help
<[NFuse_setSessionField NFuse_ContentType=application/x-ica]>
<[NFuse_setSessionField NFuse_windowType=seamless]>

[WFClient]
Version=2
ClientName=[NFuse_ClientName]

[ApplicationServers]
[NFuse_AppName]=

[[NFuse_AppName]]
Address=[NFuse_IPV4AddressAlternate]
InitialProgram=#[NFuse_AppName]
DesiredColor=[NFuse_windowColors]
TransportDriver=TCP/IP
WinStationDriver=ICA 3.0

AutologonAllowed=ON
[NFuse_Ticket]

<[NFuse_IFSESSIONFIELD sessionfield="NFUSE_SOUNDTYPE" value="basic"]>
ClientAudio=On
<[/NFuse_IFSESSIONFIELD]>
<[NFuse_IFSESSIONFIELD sessionfield="NFUSE_windowType" value="launch"]>
ScreenPercent=0
<[/NFuse_IFSESSIONFIELD]>
[NFuse_IcaWindow]

[NFuse_IcaEncryption]

[EncRC5-0]
DriverNameWin16=pdc0w.dll
DriverNameWin32=pdc0n.dll

[EncRC5-40]
DriverNameWin16=pdc40w.dll
DriverNameWin32=pdc40n.dll

[EncRC5-56]
```

Java Objects

The NFuse objects are Java objects that are Component Object Model (COM) compliant. COM is a method for different software components to communicate with one another, regardless of hardware, operating system, or language being used.

Java objects perform the following tasks:

- Authenticate users to a Citrix server farm
- Retrieve application set data from a server farm per-user
- Provide the capability of modifying properties of any published application before presenting them to users.
- Create dynamic Web pages with application set information and hyperlinks to allow the ICA Client device to launch ICA sessions.

Table 11-4 lists the NFuse Java objects and their corresponding functions:

TABLE 11-4   The NFuse Java Objects and Their Functions

Java Object	Description
CitrixWireGateway	Creates a communication link between the Web page requesting a user's application information and the server farm containing the applications.
ClearTextCredentials	Encapsulates user credentials for transference to the server farm.
GroupCredentials	Contains a list of group names with an associated domain for use in retrieving applications for user groups.
AppEnumerator	Provides an interface for accessing a user's application set information.
App	Represents a single application in the application set and contains the properties of an application.
AppSettings	Represents an application property container that allows property modifications to be made.
AppDataList	Contains a list of App objects that can be quickly accessed to determine application set lists for users.
AppListCache	Caches AppDataList objects on a Web server so the Citrix server farm does not need to be repeatedly contacted.
TemplateParser	Performs the substitution tag processing on text files. This allows for the customizing of ICA files before being presented to users.

FROM THE CLASSROOM

The Benefits of Deploying NFuse

The two most common questions I hear regarding Citrix MetaFrame are: What is NFuse, and What are the benefits of using it? With the robust features of NFuse combined with the solid foundation of the Citrix MetaFrame technology, most new (and current) MetaFrame deployments should take a hard look at what NFuse can do for them.

- One of the largest and perhaps most important feature of NFuse in my mind is the consistency of the environment. In a mixed computing environment where Unix workstations, desktop PCs running DOS, 16- and 32-bit Windows, and Macintoshes reside, with NFuse deployed, you have a single, consistent portal to access all of your applications no matter where you are. The single largest praise I have heard about NFuse to date has been that accessing the applications from home in the same manner as in at work is an absolute blessing.

- Web-based ICA Client installation is another large factor in the ease of using the environment. Little to no work is needed on nearly every platform supported to get up and running with your published applications in little time.

- The ease of use ties in with the consistency of the environment. Most people know how to surf the Internet. Because of this, they need little to no additional training to run their applications from any device capable of supporting NFuse.

- Secure, quick responding applications for remote access users. With all of the security features that can be tied in with all three tiers of the NFuse model, gaining access to your applications from anywhere, with very little threat of compromising corporate data, is another large plus for NFuse.

- For large enterprises, the need for Web-enabling many of the existing applications becomes a moot point. Corporations no longer need to spend thousands of dollars and man-hours working to rewrite applications for Web access.

- It's free! If you already operate a Citrix MetaFrame environment that is running under a supported platform, NFuse can be easily integrated at no additional cost!

- NFuse has support for many additional advanced functions. The most popular implementation of one of these advanced features is the multiple farm display. A single NFuse page can combine application data from multiple farms.

These benefits, I believe, justify NFuse to be used in almost every situation of any new MetaFrame deployment. With all of the current capabilities of NFuse, this free technology alone can make a very strong point for deploying Citrix MetaFrame in any environment, and it's only going to get better.

—Craig Luchtefeld, MCSE, MCP+I, CCEA

CERTIFICATION SUMMARY

The ability for corporations to publish applications via an intranet or the Internet provides some new and highly sought-after functionality. NFuse essentially replaces Program Neighborhood as a Web-enabled portal to a user's application set data.

Among the many benefits of NFuse is the capability to create custom Web sites that include a wide range of functionality via the NFuse Web Site Wizard. Another such benefit is the wide range of supported client and server platforms that can participate within an NFuse system.

Security is a large factor when it comes to publishing corporate applications via the public Internet. NFuse and MetaFrame offer a wide range of technologies that cover all three tiers of communication. NFuse also offers a single point of access for all supported clients. This includes downloading and installing an ICA client and creating customized ICA files for users so that no configuration is necessary on their end.

✓ TWO-MINUTE DRILL

Recognizing Citrix Web Components

❑ The three tiers (or components) of NFuse are a Web server, a Citrix server farm, and an ICA Client device.

❑ NFuse is essentially a Web-enabled Program Neighborhood.

❑ Only those applications published in the Farm Management Scope will appear in NFuse.

❑ The NFuse Web Extensions are what install the NFuse Java objects.

❑ The Web Site Wizard will help create a customized Web site to fit a company's needs.

❑ All Web sites created with the Web Site Wizard include code for Web-based ICA Client installation.

❑ An ICA Client device is comprised of a Web browser and an ICA Client.

❑ An ICA file contains parameters needed by the ICA client to launch an ICA session.

Identifying NFuse Features and Components

❑ On a firewall, the following inbound TCP ports need to be open for communication to occur for: 80 for HTTP, 443 for SSL, and 1494 for ICA sessions.

❑ To specify an alternate address on a Citrix server, you must run the altaddr command.

❑ To specify an alternate address on a Web server, you must replace the substitution tag [NFuse_IPV4Address] with [NFuse_IPV4AddressAlternate].

❑ NAT is used in conjunction with alternate addresses.

❑ Ticketing allows authentication to occur without passing credentials within an ICA file.

❑ SSL Relay is a secure communication created between the Web server and the Citrix server farm.

❑ NFuse Java objects are COM compliant.

❑ 128-bit RC5 encryption allows secure communication to occur from the ICA Client device to the Citrix server farm.

SELF TEST

The following questions will help you measure your understanding of the material presented in this chapter. Read all the choices carefully, as there may be more than one correct answer. Choose all correct answers for each question.

Recognizing Citrix Web Components

1. Define NFuse.

   A. A Citrix portal software that allows users to access published applications via Program Neighborhood.

   B. A Citrix portal software that allows administrators to create server farms.

   C. A Microsoft add-on product that allows Program Neighborhood to be Web-enabled.

   D. A Citrix portal software that allows users to access published applications via the Web.

2. You have just created a custom NFuse Web site using the Web Site Wizard. On a new desktop PC running Windows 2000, you browse to the NFuse Web site using Internet Explorer 5.0. The Web-based ICA Client installation pop-up window appears stating that you do not have the latest ICA Client. However, when you click the link to install the ICA Client, it brings up a Page Not Found notice. What could be the cause of this?

   A. Internet Explorer 5.0 is not supported and needs to be upgraded to version 5.5.

   B. The Web server cannot communicate with the Citrix server.

   C. You did not select "ICA Client Detection" when creating your custom NFuse Web site.

   D. The NFuseClients folder does not exist in the wwwroot folder on the Web server.

3. What are the components that make up the three tiers of NFuse?

   A. A Web browser

   B. An ICA Client device

   C. A Citrix server farm

   D. A Web server

4. NFuse is a Web-enabled version of what program?

   A. Program Neighborhood

   B. The Citrix ICA Client

   C. Citrix Management Console

   D. Published Application Manager

5. You have created a custom Web site using the Web Site Wizard. Your Unix users are complaining that they get the Web-based ICA Client Installation window every time they return to the NFuse login page. What can you do to fix this problem?

   A. Install the Web-based ICA Client

   B. Remove the NFuseClients folder from the wwwroot on your Web server.

   C. On the Web-based ICA Client installation pop-up window, check the box labeled Do Not Show This Window At Login.

   D. By design, this cannot be fixed.

6. The NFuse Web Site Wizard installation is not installed with the NFuse Web Server Extensions. Where can this executable be found?

   A. It can only be downloaded from the Citrix Web site.

   B. It resides on the NFuse CD and must be installed separate from the NFuse Web Server Extensions installation.

   C. On the Web server, this executable may be found under the NFuseClients folder in the wwwroot folder.

   D. It can be found on any 32-bit Windows machine running the ICA Client.

7. What Web server component will authenticate users to a Citrix server farm?

   A. NFuse Java objects

   B. Web Site Wizard

   C. Program Neighborhood

   D. Microsoft ASP or Sun JSP scripting

8. What three items can you use to call and use NFuse Java objects?

   A. JavaServer Pages

   B. Active Server Pages

   C. Notepad

   D. Citrix proprietary substitution tags

9. Your company has two Citrix server farms that they want to be integrated into one NFuse page. Both Citrix server farms reside in the same domain. What two ways could you enable the NFuse page to force domain authentication information?

   A. Configure the Citrix XML Service to pass only the domain information you request.

   B. Using the NFuse Web Site Wizard, create a custom Web site to force the domain name for explicit logins.

   C. Using the NFuse Web Site Wizard, create a custom Web site to allow guest logins.

   D. Configure the user's local ICA Clients to only log in to a specific domain.

10. Which of the following are functions of the Citrix server farm with an NFuse system?

    A. Hosts published applications.

    B. Provides the Web server with application set data for authenticating users.

    C. Hosts the NFuse Java objects.

    D. Passes customized ICA files to ICA Client devices.

Identifying NFuse Features and Components

11. What TCP port is used by default for SSL communication?

    A. 1494

    B. 2513

    C. 443

    D. 80

12. Which of the following ICA Clients are capable of supporting 128-bit encryption?

    A. Unix

    B. Win32

    C. Win16

    D. WinCE

13. Your company wants to implement an NFuse Web site that will bring the published application information from two server farms, a MetaFrame XP 1.0 farm and a MetaFrame 1.8 farm, together on a single page. How would you create this Web site to allow for ticketing?

    A. Create a custom Web site using the Web Site Wizard that allows for ticketing.

    B. Create a custom Web site using the Web Site Wizard that allows for ticketing. Install and activate Feature Release 1 on all of the MetaFrame XP 1.0 servers.

    C. Create a custom Web site using the Web Site Wizard that allows for ticketing. Install and activate Feature Release 1 on a single MetaFrame 1.8 server.

    D. Create a custom Web site using the Web Site Wizard that allows for ticketing. Install and activate Feature Release 1 on all MetaFrame 1.8 servers.

14. You just installed a Citrix MetaFrame XP for Windows 1.0 server farm with all of the default ports left intact and created a custom NFuse Web site to publish your applications via the Internet. On your firewall, you opened ports 80 for HTTP traffic and 443 for ICA communication. When testing connectivity through the NFuse site locally, everything works fine, though your remote users get no connectivity through the firewall. What do you need to do to fix the problem?

    A. Require that all your published applications have a 128-bit encryption ICA session to connect.

    B. Enable ticketing on the custom created NFuse Web site.

    C. Open port 1494 for ICA communication on your firewall instead of port 443.

    D. Instruct your remote users to download the latest Citrix ICA Client.

15. Which of the following is NOT a function performed by the NFuse Java objects? (Choose all that apply.)

    A. Encrypts all data from the Web browser to the Web server.

    B. Authenticate users to a Citrix server farm.

    C. Retrieve application set data from a server farm on a per-user basis.

    D. Create dynamic Web pages that have application set information with hyperlinks to allow the ICA Client device to launch ICA sessions.

16. You are the administrator of a MetaFrame XP server farm. Your company wants you to create an NFuse Web site allowing for secure communications between the Web server and the Citrix server farm. Which of the following must you do to accomplish this?

    A. Create a custom Web site using the Web Site Wizard that allows for ticketing. Nothing needs to be done on the MetaFrame XP servers, since these can use the ticketing technology by default.

    B. Create a custom Web site using the Web Site Wizard. Install a digital certificate on the Web server to allow for HTTPS communication between the Web server and the Citrix server farm.

C. Configure a Citrix server to allow SSL Relay by running the Citrix SSL Relay Configuration Tool. Create a custom Web site using the Web Site Wizard.

D. Configure a Citrix server to allow SSL Relay by running the Citrix SSL Relay Configuration Tool. Create a custom Web site using the Web Site Wizard that contains the SSL Relay information of the Citrix server.

17. You are using NAT on your firewall and have configured an alternate address on your Citrix server to allow for remote connectivity. You find that your remote users cannot connect when entering through the NFuse Web site. On your firewall, you have opened TCP ports 80 and 1494 to allow for Web and ICA traffic. What else could be the problem?

A. TCP port 443 needs to be open for SSL communication.

B. The NFuse Web site must change the substitution tag [NFuse_IPV4Address] with [NFuse_IPV4AddressAlternate] in the template.ica file.

C. The NFuse Web site must change the substitution tag [NFuse_IPV4Address] with [NFuse_IPV4AddressAlternate] in the launch.ica file.

D. The NFuse Web site must change the substitution tag [NFuse_IPV4Address] with [NFuse_IPV4AlternateAddress] in the launch.ica file.

18. You are the administrator of a single server implementation of a Web server running NFuse with Citrix MetaFrame XP. Your single server is accessible via the Internet. Your company does not have a firewall and can spend no more additional dollars on this project. What should you do to secure your single server as best you can?

A. Create a custom NFuse Web Site using the Web Site Wizard that will allow for ticketing.

B. Create a custom NFuse Web Site using the Web Site Wizard that will disable ticketing.

C. Enable NAT on your Citrix server.

D. Publish each application with a minimum requirement of 128-bit encryption for all ICA sessions.

19. Which of the following are not supported platforms for an NFuse web server? (Choose all that apply.)

A. Windows NT 4.0

B. Lotus Domino Server

C. Citrix WinFrame 1.8

D. The Microsoft Windows 2000 Server family

20. NFuse objects are Java objects that are _____ compliant?

    A. JSP

    B. COM

    C. XML

    D. ASP

LAB QUESTION

You are the MetaFrame administrator for ABC Manufacturing, Inc. ABC has two Citrix server farms, a Citrix MetaFrame for Windows 1.8 farm and a Citrix MetaFrame XP for Windows 1.0 farm, both residing within the same domain. They would like both of these farms to be accessible via the Internet with maximum security from the ICA Client device to the Web server and Citrix server. In addition, they wish to force all domain-specific information for their users. Design a plan to present to the board how this can be accomplished.

SELF TEST ANSWERS

Recognizing Citrix Web Components

1. ☑ **D** is the correct answer. NFuse is a portal software that allows users to access published applications through an Internet or intranet Web site.
   ☒ **A** is incorrect because applications are accessed through a Web browser and not through Program Neighborhood. **B** is wrong because NFuse does not allow administrators to create server farms. **C** is incorrect because NFuse is not a Microsoft technology.

2. ☑ **D** is correct. If during the NFuse Web Server Extensions setup you did not supply an ICA Client CD or copy the contents of the CD's ICAWEB folder to the NFuseClients folder, the Web-based ICA Client installation will fail.
   ☒ **A** is wrong because Internet Explorer 5.0 is supported. **B** is wrong because the Web server hasn't reached a point where it would need to contact a Citrix server. **C** is incorrect because this isn't an option using the Web Site Wizard.

3. ☑ **B, C,** and **D** are correct. All three make up the three tiers that NFuse requires.
   ☒ **A** is incorrect because it is not a component of NFuse; it is a component of the ICA Client device.

4. ☑ **A** is correct. NFuse is essentially a Web-enabled version of Program Neighborhood.
   ☒ **B** is wrong because the ICA Client device uses the Citrix ICA Client to initiate ICA sessions to the Citrix servers. **C** and **D** are simply incorrect.

5. ☑ **C** is correct. The Web-based ICA Client Installation piece can correctly detect the presence of the ICA Client on only the 32-bit and 16-bit Windows platforms. For all other platforms, this window will pop up until the Do Not Show This Window At Login check box has been marked.
   ☒ **A** is wrong because even if you do install the Web-based ICA Client, the Web-based ICA Client Installation code cannot correctly detect the presence of an ICA Client on the Unix platform. **B** is incorrect because even if you remove the NFuseClients folder from the wwwroot on the Web server, this pop-up box will remain. **D** is wrong because placing a check in the check box will stop the page from popping up on subsequent visits to the login page.

6. ☑ **B** is correct. The NFuse Web Site Wizard is a separate installation from the NFuse Web Server Extensions and may be installed on any 32-bit Windows machine.
   ☒ **A** is wrong because not only can it be downloaded from the Citrix Web site, but it also can be found on the NFuse CD. **C** is wrong because the Web-based ICA Clients reside under the

NFuseClients folder under the wwwroot on the Web server. **D** is incorrect because it does not install with the ICA Client program.

7. ☑ **A** is correct. The NFuse Java objects perform several functions, one of which is assisting in authenticating users to a Citrix server farm.
    ☒ **B** is incorrect because the Web Site Wizard plays no part in Citrix server farm authentication. **C** is wrong because Program Neighborhood is an ICA Client device component, not a Web server component. **D** is incorrect because these are examples of two Web-server side scripts that will call NFuse Java objects but do not perform the function of authentication.

8. ☑ **A, B,** and **D** are correct. These three items allow an administrator to call and execute NFuse Java objects.
    ☒ **C** is incorrect because Notepad cannot be used to make NFuse Java object calls.

9. ☑ **B** and **C** are correct. During the custom Web site creation process using the NFuse Web Site Wizard, you have the ability to force domain information for explicit logins and allow guest logins where the domain is specified.
    ☒ **A** is incorrect because the Citrix XML Service cannot be configured to pass specific domain information for authentication purposes. **D** is incorrect because all connection information used through NFuse is passed through the ICA file customized for the ICA Client, not the ICA Clients local settings.

10. ☑ **A** and **B** are correct. The Citrix server farm's role within an NFuse system is to host the published applications and provide the Web server application set information for users authenticating themselves.
    ☒ **C** and **D** are incorrect because these are roles of the Web server with an NFuse system.

Identifying NFuse Features and Components

11. ☑ **C** is correct. By default, all SSL communication is done through TCP port 443.
    ☒ **A** is wrong because it is the default port for ICA session communication. **B** is incorrect because it is the port for Citrix Management Console-to-MetaFrame XP server communication. **D** is wrong because it is the default port for HTTP, or Web, traffic.

12. ☑ **B, C,** and **D** are correct. These three clients are all capable of using 128-bit encryption.
    ☒ **A** is incorrect because Unix does not have 128-bit RC5 encryption support.

13. ☑ **D** is correct. A custom Web site created using the Web Site Wizard that allows for ticketing will enable the Web server for ticketing. All Citrix MetaFrame XP 1.0 servers have

the capability of using ticketing by default, but Citrix MetaFrame 1.8 servers must have FR1 installed and licensed on all servers participating in the farm.

☒   A is incorrect because SP2 and FR1 need to be installed and activated on the MetaFrame 1.8 server farm. B is incorrect because FR1 needs to be installed on the MetaFrame 1.8 servers, not the XP servers. C is incorrect because FR1 needs to be installed on all servers in the farm, not just one.

14.   ☑   C is the correct answer. Local users have no problem connecting to the NFuse Web site and running their applications, which is an indication that both the Web server and Citrix servers are functioning properly. To have allowed users to connect initially, only port 80 for HTTP traffic and 1494 for ICA traffic needed to be opened. Port 443 is used for SSL communication.

☒   A, B, and D are all incorrect because if port 1494 is not opened on the firewall, no ICA session can be established. Though incorrect, each one is a good idea of things to do once connectivity has been established.

15.   ☑   A is correct in that it is not a function of the NFuse Java objects. This is an example of what SSL encryption on a Web server can provide.

☒   B, C, and D are incorrect because they are all functions that NFuse Java objects perform.

16.   ☑   D is correct. To allow for secure, encrypted communication between the Web server and the Citrix server farm, a single Citrix server must be configured as an SSL Relay server. In addition, the SSL Relay server information must be entered in when creating a custom Web site using the Web Site Wizard.

☒   A is incorrect because ticketing allows for secure authentication information between all three tiers. B is incorrect because HTTPS communication exists between the Web server and the Web browser. C is wrong because the SSL Relay server information needs to be entered into the custom Web site for SSL Relay to work.

17.   ☑   B is correct. The remote users must specify the alternate address of the Citrix server to connect through the firewall running NAT. In this scenario, the Citrix server will return its internal IP address which the users will not be able to connect to.

☒   A is incorrect because TCP port 443 is not needed in this scenario. C is incorrect because substitution tags only exist in the template ICA files, not the customized ones passed down to the ICA Client device. D is incorrect because the syntax for the substitution tag is wrong.

18.   ☑   A and D are correct. By allowing ticketing, authentication information is not passed through the ICA file. In addition, publishing all applications to require 128-bit encryption will allow for secure communications over the ICA connection between your ICA Client device and your Citrix server.

☒　B is wrong because ticketing would be a benefit in this scenario. C is incorrect because NAT is a feature of a firewall, not a Citrix server.

19.　☑　B and C are correct in that they are not a supported platform for an NFuse Web server.

☒　A and D are incorrect because they are supported platforms for an NFuse Web server.

20.　☑　B is correct. Java objects are Component Object Model (COM) compliant. COM is a method in which different software components can communicate with one another, regardless of hardware, operating system, or language being used.

☒　A is incorrect because JSP is a form of Web-side scripting. C is wrong because the XML service is used in conjunction with Java objects. D is incorrect because it is also a form of Web-side scripting.

LAB ANSWER

The following steps will need to be performed to maximize secure communications between the ICA Client device and the Web server and Citrix server and create an NFuse Web site capable of supporting these technologies.

1. Ticketing will allow all secure authentication without passing them through the customized ICA files. The Citrix MetaFrame XP for Windows servers support this by default. The Citrix MetaFrame for Windows 1.8 servers will need Feature Release 1 licensed and activated in order for ticketing to work.

2. 128-bit encryption as a minimum requirement on all published applications will ensure that the ICA session is as secure as possible.

3. Enable HTTPS communication on the Web server. HTTPS requires only a digital certificate to be installed on the Web server. Virtually all Web servers and Web browsers support this technology seamlessly.

4. Install a firewall to allow only inbound Web traffic and ICA session communication. The following TCP ports will need to be opened for inbound communication: 80 for HTTP traffic, 443 for HTTPS traffic, and 1494 for ICA session traffic.

5. Enable NAT on the firewall. NAT enables the MetaFrame server internally to have an internal, nonpublic, nonroutable IP address (not accessible through the Internet) and an alternate address that is reachable for remote communications.

6. Using the Web Site Wizard, create a custom NFuse Web site that will allow for ASP scripting, ticketing, and explicit login domain information. Once complete, the template ICA file will need to be modified to force remote users to specify the alternate address of the Citrix server.

7. Following the instructions on the NFuse ASP Examples Web page that installs with the NFuse Web Server Extensions, integrate into the custom-built NFuse Web site support for multiple farm display.

12

Printing

T he printing system in a MetaFrame XP environment is often one of the most challenging systems a new Citrix administrator must learn. Most problems lie in the fact that the new administrator fails to understand that there are multiple ways to print in a MetaFrame environment. In order to pass the test and successfully administer printers, you must be able to differentiate between the three types of printers available.

While printing in a thin-client or MetaFrame XP environment can be a challenge, most printing problems can be overcome simply by understanding how the process works.

The Citrix Certified Administrator test for MetaFrame XP is sure to cover all the printing fundamentals. You must make sure you understand all available options thoroughly and how to implement them.

CERTIFICATION OBJECTIVE 12.01

Creating Client, Network, and Local Printers

To understand the printing options in MetaFrame XP, you first must define the three types of printers available. When designing a MetaFrame environment, you must also decide which of these three (or combination thereof) you are going to support. Your three choices are: client printers, network printers, and local printers. There are some commonalities to each type, including

- **A printer** The Windows icon you see in the Printers applet in the Control Panel. This icon is a logical reference to a print device attached to the local system bus via a communications port.

- **A print driver** The software used by the operating system to interpret an application's print commands and convert these into a language that the printer will use to produce a print job.

- **A print device** The physical printer that produces the print jobs. A print job is the binary translation of the file you are printing into a language the printer understands.

- **A print queue** The holding area for print jobs waiting to be printed on a print device. These queues are generally located on a print server and accessed in Windows environments by a printer share.

- **A printer share** A logical printer on a Windows server that allows multiple users to print to the same physical print device. This device can be attached directly to the network or to a communications port on the server.

With these basic definitions under your belt, you can begin to define printers as they are seen and used in a MetaFrame environment. Such terms include

- **Client printers** Physical print devices connected to an ICA client device using a cable (such as a parallel cable) or a port (e.g., a network port, UNC share, TCP/IP port, and so on).

- **Network printers** Printers that reside on a network print server or on a MetaFrame XP server outside the server farm. A printer shared from an ICA client device or from a network workstation is also considered a network printer by all other clients on the network.

- **Local printers** Printers that are directly connected, via cable or port, to a MetaFrame XP server in the server farm.

Creating Client Printers

ICA clients have the option of using printers connected to their client device when they log on to an ICA session. This is also known as an auto-created client printer. It allows the user to run an application executed on the MetaFrame server and still print to their local printer.

To ensure that auto-created client printing functions properly, several steps must be taken prior to the ICA client connecting to the MetaFrame server, as shown in the following. (The auto-creation process is heavily dependent on the print driver name, as seen on the client workstation and on the MetaFrame XP server.)

- A print driver must be installed on a MetaFrame server in the farm that matches the printer driver installed on the client workstation.

- The print driver should then be replicated to all servers in the server farm that this client will connect to.

- If the name of the print driver installed in the MetaFrame farm matches the client print driver name verbatim, a print driver mapping must be created. This is often seen in LaserJet type printers, where a Windows 9*x* print driver may have a name like "HP LaserJet 4000 PCL5e," but the Windows 2000 or

Windows NT driver name may be "HP LaserJet 4000 Series PCL5e." In this case, printer auto-creation would fail unless a printer mapping was created.

Once the auto-creation process has completed, the printer will then be available to the end user. The user will be able to recognize their printer by the unique printer name created in the following format: *#clientname/printername. Clientname* is generally the computer name for Windows 32-bit clients, while *printername* is the logical name of the printer as it appears on their workstation. (See Figure 12-1.) If no print jobs remain in the print spooler when the user logs off their Citrix session, the auto-created printer will be deleted. During the time the user is logged on, the client printer is available to only that user and no others. The exception to this, of course, is administrators.

exam
ⓦatch

The exam is sure to test you on auto-created printers. As seen in previous chapters, user and connection settings have an effect on how, or if, auto-created printers are used. Remember, you must also have the proper settings configured in the Citrix Connection Configuration, as well as in the User's configuration.

FIGURE 12-1

Typical printer properties for an auto-created client printer (Note printer name)

on the **Job**

Troubleshooting auto-created client printers can be a challenge to a new administrator. You may find yourself looking at what you think are correct settings, yet the printer still fails to auto-create. The following listing outlines several things to look for when troubleshooting an auto-creation problem.

1. Verify that the ICA client name is unique. MetaFrame uses the client name as part of the printer name. This name is also used to redirect print jobs back to the client device. You can check/change the ICA client name by editing the WFCNAME.INI file at the root of the C: drive.

2. After the user has logged on successfully, view the application log in Event Viewer to see if any new MetaFrame events have appeared. If you see EVENT ID 1106, view the event details (See Figure 12-2). It will contain the name of the client device connecting and, most important, the name of the print driver being used on the client. This print driver needs to be installed on the MetaFrame server for auto-created client printers to function.

3. If the print driver for that printer is installed, but the printer fails to auto-create, verify that the driver name shown on the MetaFrame server matches the name of the client print driver exactly. If they do not match a print driver, mapping must be created to associate the client print driver with the appropriate server driver.

FIGURE 12-2

Event details for a MetaFrame event

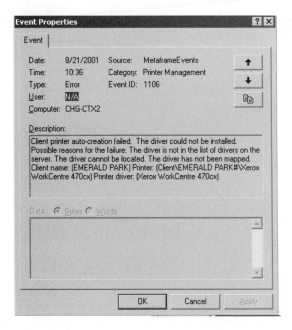

Client Printers for DOS and Windows CE Clients

Auto-created printers are generally used with 32-bit Windows clients but can be configured for other clients, such as Windows CE and DOS. These types of client printers do not auto-create natively, but an administrator can configure these clients to auto-create by using the Citrix Management Console.

By right-clicking the Printers icon in the Printer Management node (See Figure 12-3), a pull-down menu appears. From this menu, select Client Printers. The management window shows all DOS and Windows CE clients that have been configured to auto-create client printers.

To configure a new client for auto-creation, you must specify the following:

- **ICA Client Name**   This specifies the name of the client device you are configuring for printer auto-creation.

- **Printer Name**   Specifies a logical name (generally the type of printer) that you are auto-creating.

FIGURE 12-3	
Selecting Client Printers from the Printer Management node in the CMC	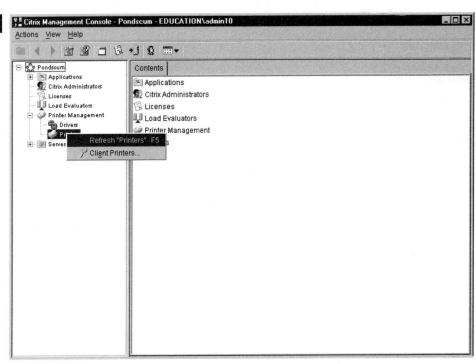

- **Driver**   This field associates a server side driver with the client printer. This driver name can be entered manually, or you can select from one of two menus. The first menu button is Browse Mappings, which allows you to select a client print driver name that has been mapped to a matching server side driver. The second menu button is Browse Drivers, which allows you to select a printer driver load on the MetaFrame servers in the farm. The driver you select from either of these lists should be installed or mapped on each MetaFrame server the client will connect to.

- **Port**   Specifies the physical LPT or COM on the client device that the printer is attached to. This is generally listed as LPT1:, but it can vary.

When a user connects to a MetaFrame server from a DOS or Windows CE client that has been configured this way, the user will be able to access the printer just as any other client would.

FROM THE CLASSROOM

Auto-Created Client Printers

Auto-created client printers are one of the most sought after functions in MetaFrame. This system allows users to connect from almost any device, use an application, and still print to their local printer even though the application is running on a server that could be thousands of miles away.

Auto-created client printers are generally a challenge to configure and maintain, however. This is generally due to the large number of inexpensive printers available to users and your need to have an appropriate driver for each printer the client wishes to use.

A good Citrix administrator will first determine which client printers they need to support. At this point, they will verify that these printers/drivers function properly in the MetaFrame environment. Once the solution is implemented, you can add driver/printer support as the farm or user base grows, and distribute a list of supported printers/drivers. Any addition to this list should be tested for functionality and stability prior to implementing it in a production environment.

—*Ron Oglesby, MCSE, CCEA, CCI, CSA*

Creating Network Printers

Citrix clients have the option of using network printers just like any Windows client on the network. They can add these printers through the Add Printer Wizard in the printers folder within the MetaFrame session, or they can use a NET USE command to map their LPT port to the network printer.

Though in a MetaFrame XP environment it is often easier for an administrator to configure the network printers to automatically create for the end user. This is extremely useful when the user only runs published applications and does not have the option or ability to run the Add Printer Wizard (such as when you are allowing the clients to run only Published Applications, or when you have restricted users from accessing the Control Panel functions including the Printers folder).

An administrator should follow these steps to configure ICA clients to auto-create network printers:

1. Import the print server into the MetaFrame farm using the Citrix Management Console.

2. Add the print drivers necessary to support those network printers to a MetaFrame server in the farm.

3. Replicate the print drivers to every server in the farm.

Then the printers will be configured (using the Citrix Management Console) with auto-creation settings that will assign it to a group or groups of users. To configure a Network Printer for auto-creation, right-click the printer in the Printers node and select Auto-Creation from the drop-down menu. (See Figure 12-4). The printers will then auto-create in the MetaFrame session for the user and be available for printing. Such auto-created printers will then be available from any client device. This is in contrast to auto-created client printers that are only available from that client device.

on the **Job**

DOS applications are not aware of Windows printers. These applications are written to send print jobs directly to an LPT port, mostly LPT1:. In such cases, mapping to a shared printer via UNC will allow a DOS application to print to the shared printer. Such a command would look like this:

```
NET USE LPT1: \\Servername\SharedPrinterName
```

Now that you have a better understanding of the three types of printers and how they function, here are some potential real-world scenarios and their solutions.

SCENARIO & SOLUTION

Is it possible for DOS ICA clients to auto-create client printers?	Yes. Though they do not auto-create in the same fashion as Win32 clients, they can auto-create with the proper configuration.
A client is attempting to connect to your MetaFrame XP server and their Client printer fails to auto-create. After investigating, you find there is no appropriate print driver to match the server operating system. Is it possible to auto-create this client's printer?	No. In order for the client printer to auto-create or be used in a MetaFrame environment there must be a suitable driver installed on the MetaFrame server.
When importing a network print server, do you need to install the print drivers on the MetaFrame server for those printers?	Yes. Importing the print server does not import the server drivers. You must manually install these drivers on at least one server in the farm, then replicate them to the remaining servers.

FIGURE 12-4

Using CMC to configure auto-created printers

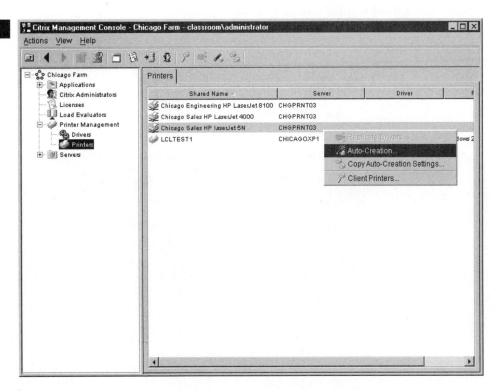

Using Local Printers

Local printers in a MetaFrame environment are added to the server just as you would add a printer to a Windows NT workstation or a Windows 2000 Professional Workstation. Adding a local printer to a MetaFrame server involves following the Add Printer Wizard in the Printers folder of the server.

1. Using the Add Printer Wizard, configure the printer as a local printer on the port where it is installed (LPT1:, COM1:, IP Port). Using this process, you can also install the appropriate driver for that print device.

2. Once the printer is installed there, it will automatically be available to users connecting to that server.

EXERCISE 12-1

CertCam 12-1

Adding a Local Printer to a MetaFrame XP Server

1. Log on to the XP server as a local administrator equivalent.

2. Access the Printers folder under Start-Settings or within the Control Panel.

3. Launch the Add Printers utility.

4. Deselect the Automatically Detect And Install My Plug-and-Play Printer check box.

5. Select LPT1: (or another port if you have a Local Printer).

6. Select the proper print driver for your printer.

7. Assign a name to your printer.

8. Follow the wizard and share your printer as LCLTEST.

9. Open the Citrix Management Console and verify that the printer shows up in the Printers node. (See Figure 12-5.)

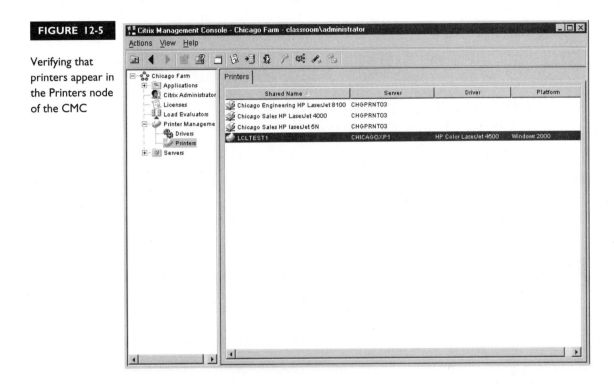

FIGURE 12-5

Verifying that printers appear in the Printers node of the CMC

CERTIFICATION OBJECTIVE 12.02

Replicating Print Drivers and Importing Print Servers

Several tools are available within the Printer Management node of the Citrix Management Console to make managing and working with Network printers easier than ever before. With MetaFrame XP, we can install a print driver to a single server in the farm and then replicate it to all other servers. We also have the ability to assign specific users or groups to specific network printers. In addition, we can create auto-replication lists for a standard set of print drivers so any new server in the farm will automatically have the supported printers installed.

Updating Printer Drivers in the XP Data Store

When viewing the driver list in the Citrix Management Console, you can determine easily which print drivers have been installed on any server in the farm. If a new driver is required in the farm, we need only add it to one server.

This driver can be installed two ways on Windows 2000, but only one way on NT 4.0 Terminal Server Edition.

In Windows 2000 and NT 4.0 Terminal Server Edition, we can add a driver by simply following the Add Printer Wizard, associating the printer with an unused port, adding our driver, and simply deleting the printer. The logical printer is removed but the driver remains installed on the server.

In Windows 2000, you can also add a driver by opening the Printers folder, selecting Print Server Properties, and from that window selecting the Drivers tab (see Figure 12-6). This window allows you to add or remove drivers without creating a logical printer. While both of these methods will install the driver in the same way, the second method reduces the amount of time involved by eliminating unnecessary steps, such as picking a port and naming a printer that will be deleted after it is created. One thing to remember is that since driver information is kept in

FIGURE 12-6

The Drivers tab from the Print Server Properties page in Windows 2000 Server

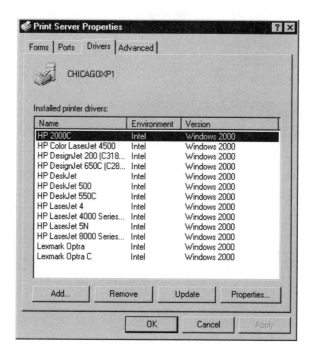

the data store, the number of drivers and servers you have can affect the data store performance and size.

So, how does the farm become aware of this new driver? By adding the driver to a server, you have basically installed a set of new files to the server along with driver specific registry entries. At regular intervals, IMA service for that server polls the print driver registry keys and compares that information against what is already listed in the data store. When the Independent Management Architecture subsystem discovers a new driver, that driver's information is then written to the data store.

EXERCISE 12-2

CertCam 12-2

Installing a Print Driver and Updating the Data Store

1. Open the Printers applet in the Control Panel.

2. Select the Add Printer Wizard.

3. Select Local Printer (if using Windows 2000, uncheck Automatically Detect Local Printer)

4. Select LPT1:.

5. Select HP as the driver manufacturer and HP LaserJet 4Plus as the driver.

6. Accept the default printer name.

7. Do not share the printer.

8. Do not print a test page.

9. Once the "logical" printer has been installed, select its icon in the Printers folder and delete it.

10. Using the Citrix Management Console, select the Drivers icon in the Printer Management node to verify that your driver is shown in the list of drivers for your server.

If the driver is not present in the list immediately, wait a minute or two and refresh the list by right-clicking drivers and selecting Refresh Drivers.

Importing a Network Print Server

Printers attached to a network print server outside the server farm are not readily available to ICA clients attaching to the farm. A Citrix administrator can ease this process by importing the network print servers he/she uses on the network. This can be done by right-clicking the Printer Management node and selecting Import Print Server. You will then be asked to supply the print server's name and a user account that has access to those printers (see Figure 12-7).

Currently imported network printer servers can be viewed by selecting the Printer Management node in the Citrix Management Console, then selecting the Network Printer Servers tab on the right side of the console (see Figure 12-8).

Once a Print Server is imported into the farm, its printers show up in the Printers icon under the Printer Management node. These printers can now be made available to the MetaFrame users that connect to the farm.

EXERCISE 12-3

Importing a Network Print Server

1. In the Citrix Management Console, right-click the Printer Management node.

2. In the pull-down menu, select Import Network Print Server.

3. When the Import Network Print Server dialog box appears, supply the name of a server that is sharing printers on your network, as well as the domain credentials necessary for access to those print shares.

4. Once the Printer Server is imported, it should be listed in the Printer Management node in the Network Print Servers tab. Verify this and also that its shared printers are listed under the Printers icon of the Printer Management node.

on the

Job

Once a print server is imported to the MetaFrame farm it cannot be reimported. The printer information that was imported to the data store is not updated dynamically from the current information on the print server. If a printer's properties have been changed or printers have been added or deleted from the print server, you must update or refresh the print server by right-clicking the server and selecting Update Print Server. Trying to import a network print server that is already imported will result in an error.

FIGURE 12-7

Importing a
network print
server

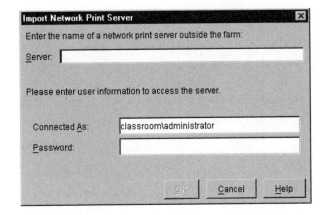

FIGURE 12-8

Viewing imported
print servers on
the Network
Print Servers tab

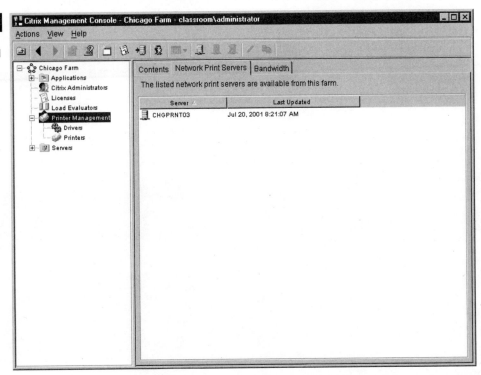

Assigning Users to Printers

By assigning network printers to the users' environment, we simplify the environment for both the end user and administrator. When the client connects and the user is authenticated, the IMA printer subsystem queries the data store to determine which printers the authenticated user has rights to. Only those printers that were assigned to the user are created for the session. The printers are then available to receive print jobs from applications running within the Citrix session.

To assign a user or group of users to a specific printer, right-click the printer in the Printer Management node and select Auto-Creation from the pull down menu that appears. From here, we can choose from a list of Available Accounts on the left (users or groups) and add them to the list of Configured Accounts on the right. (See Figure 12-9.)

When these users log in to the MetaFrame farm, the printer will be auto-created for them no matter what physical client they connect from. This is unlike the auto-created client printers. Remember, auto-created client printers are only available from a specific client device that the user is logging in from.

FIGURE 12-7

The
Auto-Creation
Settings page

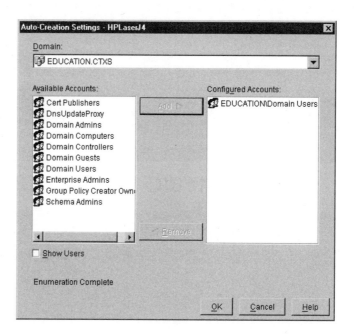

Now that you understand the basics of network printers and printer driver installation, here are a few possible scenarios and their solutions.

SCENARIO & SOLUTION

How would you allow your users to access printers that are shared on a server outside the farm?	Using the Citrix Management Console you can import the print server into the farm, then assign users or groups to the printers.
Is it possible to view which print drivers are installed on a MetaFrame server using the Citrix Management Console?	Yes. To do this you would select the Drivers icon in the Printer Management node, then select the server you wish to view.
Can a printer that has been imported from a network print server be assigned to an individual user?	Yes. When assigning users to printers, you can assign groups or individual users.

Replicating Printer Drivers Across a Server Farm

In order to ensure that all client and network printers function as they should, each server must have the drivers necessary to print to those printers. To keep an administrator from having to install the same print driver on several servers, the IMA architecture has a print driver replication function built into it.

This function will allow us to replicate a print driver to every server in the farm, or we can select specific target servers for the replication. It will also allow an administrator to create an Auto replication list that allows us to replicate drivers to any new server brought in to the farm automatically. This print driver information is stored in the IMA Data Store for future replication operations.

To replicate a driver to the entire server farm, select the Drivers icon under the Printer Management node. From this window, select the server from which the print driver should be replicated. This source server will be retained in the XP data store for replication to future servers. Selecting a source of "Any" is not recommended. Doing so will result in a warning from the system. (See Figure 12-10.) Citrix recommends having one server that all print drivers are replicated from.

Once the source is selected, the installed drivers on that source server are displayed. Right-click the driver you wish to replicate and select Replicate Drivers. The Replicate Driver dialog box will appear (see Figure 12-11). You can now replicate this driver to the entire farm and add it to the auto-replication list for new servers, or you can replicate it to specific servers of your choosing.

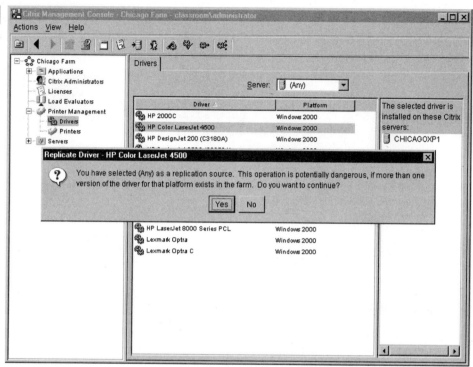

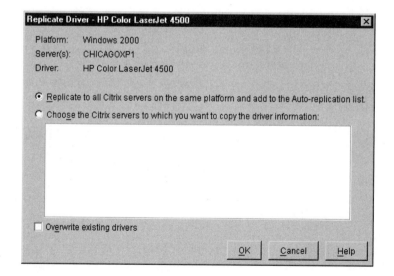

The Auto Replication list can also be viewed and edited by right-clicking the Drivers icon in the Printer Management node and selecting Auto-Replication from the pull-down menu. This list is platform-specific. You can choose the appropriate server operating systems from a platform pull-down menu at the top of the window. Drivers can only be replicated to similar platforms.

A check box is also available that will allow the administrator to select the option to overwrite existing drivers on the target servers. This is extremely useful if you are updating an existing print driver to a newer version.

EXERCISE 12-4

Replicating Print Drivers

Note: If you do not have multiple MetaFrame XP servers for this lab, you will need to stop at step 4 since you will not have any servers in your Replicate Drivers dialog box.

1. Using the Citrix Management Console, open the Printer Management node and select the Drivers icon.

2. Using the Server pull-down menu in the right pane of the Citrix Management Console, select the server you installed for the HP LaserJet 4Plus driver in Exercise 12-2.

3. Right-click the HP LaserJet 4Plus driver and select Replicate Driver.

4. In the Replicate Driver dialog box, select the option to Replicate To All Citrix Servers On The Platform And Add To The Auto-replication List; then click OK.

5. Return to the Drivers list in the Citrix Management Console and verify that the driver has been replicated to all servers in the MetaFrame farm. This can take several minutes. Refreshing the Drivers tab may speed the update of the Drivers list.

Managing Print Drivers

Deciding which printer drivers to support in a MetaFrame environment can be a tedious job. Some print drivers can cause server side problems when they are used to access client printers. These problems can include a stopped spooler service or even the infamous NT Blue Screen. It may be necessary to prohibit certain drivers from being used in your MetaFrame farm. Creating Driver Compatibility lists can allow you control over what drivers are used for client printers in your farm.

This list can be accessed and edited by right-clicking the Drivers icon and selecting compatibility. Again, this list is platform-specific, and you can choose your operating system with a pull-down menu at the top of the window (see Figure 12-12).

The default for this window is to allow all drivers except those listed. During a base install of MetaFrame, no drivers are added to this list. If you wish to restrict access to a certain driver in the farm, you can do so by clicking the Add button and selecting your driver.

Inversely, you can also make a list of supported drivers. Selecting the radio button Allow Only Driver In This List would create this type of list. You must then specify each driver that you will allow clients to use. Any printer using a driver not specifically

---

FIGURE 12-10

The Driver
Compatibility list

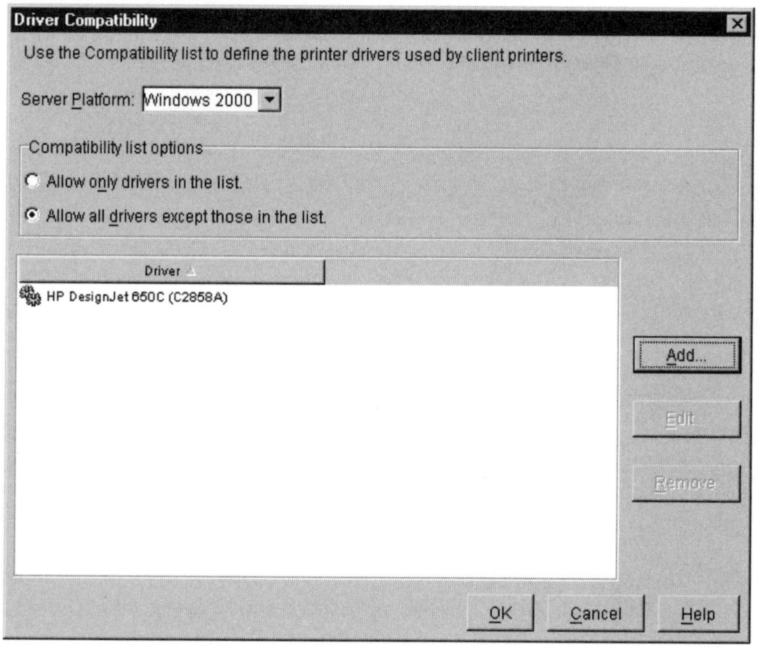

mentioned will not be allowed to auto-create, and the end user will receive a message at connection time stating they are attempting to use an unsupported print driver.

exam
Watch

Importing of network printers and the print driver management are new functions that were added with MetaFrame XP, and are not available with earlier versions of MetaFrame. The exam is sure to test your knowledge of these functions, along with your knowledge of how both systems work. Be sure to have a good understanding of network printers and print driver management before sitting down for the test.

Mapping Print Driver Names

As seen at the beginning of this chapter, an auto-created client printer can fail to auto-create if a matching print driver is not installed on the MetaFrame server. In some cases, print driver names vary between Windows 2000, Windows NT 4.0, and Windows 9x. This difference in driver names can also cause the printer auto-creation process to fail.

Example: Windows 98 client station has a local HP Laser 5Si using the HP LaserJet 5Si/Mx driver. You have installed the Windows NT 4.0 version of this driver on your Windows NT 4.0 Terminal Server. The driver name for NT 4.0 may look like this: HP LaserJet 5Si. In such cases, the driver on the server side may print fine to that print device, but it is the auto-creation sequence that is failing due to the differences in the driver names. Here we must create a mapping that will associate the client driver with an acceptable server driver.

To create this mapping you will right-click the Drivers icon again and select Mapping. This list again is platform-specific, so you need to verify that you have the proper operating system selected before editing the list. Select the Add button and you are presented with a Window that will allow you to enter the client printer driver name and use a pull-down menu to select the appropriate server print driver name (see Figure 12-13). This mapping will then be written to the WTSPRNT.INF file in the %SYSTEMROOT%\System32 directory on each MetaFrame server of your selected platform.

on the
Job

The auto-creation process is extremely sensitive. When entering the client driver, you must enter it verbatim. Respect upper- and lowercase characters, as well as spaces.

A quick way to get the client driver information is to view the auto-creation error message associated with this client in the Event Viewer's application log. In the details of this event, you see and copy to the clipboard the client's driver name as it is needed in the mapping window.

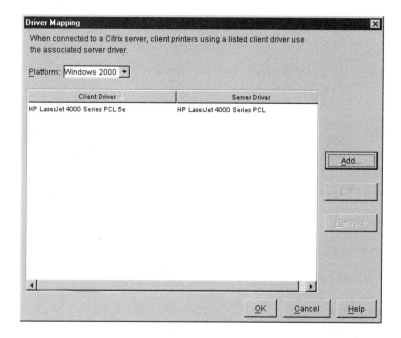

FIGURE 12-11

The Driver
Mapping list

With the knowledge you now have about driver replication and printer
auto-creation, here are a couple of real-world questions and there possible answers.

SCENARIO & SOLUTION	
True or False: Print driver information for the server farm is stored in each local server only.	False. The IMA service reads the print driver information from each server's local registry, but stores the information in the XP data store.
You have determined that every time your users print using a specific print driver, the spooler service on your server stops. You wish to restrict the use of this driver in your farm. How would you do this?	Using the Compatibility menu from the Drivers icon, you would select Allow All Drivers Except Those In The List, then add the unwanted driver to the compatibility list.

CERTIFICATION SUMMARY

Printing in a MetaFrame environment can be overwhelming to a new administrator, but with the proper planning and knowledge of how the system works, you will be well on your way to a smooth implementation and certification.

The test is sure to cover each type of printer in depth. Make sure you can define each type of printer in a MetaFrame environment and that you know how each is configured. Your knowledge of the Citrix Management Console will also be tested. Try to spend some time going through the various functions and workflows in the Console so you are familiar with every option as it relates to printing.

TWO-MINUTE DRILL

Creating Client, Network, and Local Printers

❑ A client printer is defined as a print device attached to an ICA client via a communications port or as a network printer for the local Windows operating system.

❑ Network printers are defined as printers that reside on a print server outside the server farm or as a printer shared with an ICA client device or network workstation.

❑ Local printers are defined as printers that are directly connected, via cable or port, to a MetaFrame XP server in the farm.

❑ To support a client printer, a matching driver must be installed on each MetaFrame server that the client will connect to.

❑ If an appropriate driver is installed on the MetaFrame server, Windows 32-bit clients will auto-create their printer by default.

❑ DOS and Windows CE clients must have auto-creation settings configured for the device using the Citrix Management Console.

❑ Auto-created printers are only available to the user's session they were auto-created in.

❑ Print drivers can be added to the server by adding a printer, selecting the proper driver, finishing the wizard, and deleting the printer.

Replicating Print Drivers and Importing Print Servers

❑ Print driver information is read from each server and stored in the data store.

❑ Print drivers can be replicated to all servers (and new servers) in the farm from a single MetaFrame XP server.

❑ Shared Printers outside the server farm are not readily available to ICA clients. The print server must be imported into the farm using the Citrix Management Console.

❑ You can replicate print drivers to a single server or all servers in the farm.

❏ Replicated print drivers can also be added to the auto-replication list so that new MetaFrame servers will automatically receive these drivers when added to the farm.

❏ Print driver replication is platform/operating system-specific.

❏ When a client driver name is different from its server driver name, use the Driver Mapping list to allow the client printer to auto-create.

❏ The Driver Compatibility list gives you the power to allow or restrict the use of client print drivers in your farm.

SELF TEST

The following questions will help you measure your understanding of the material presented in this chapter. Read all the choices carefully, as there may be more than one correct answer. Choose all correct answers for each question.

Creating Client, Network, and Local Printers

1. In a MetaFrame Environment, three types of printers can be used. Which of the following are defined in a MetaFrame farm? (Choose all that apply.)

   A. Local printers

   B. Global printers

   C. Client printers

   D. Farm printers

2. For a client printer to auto-create, you must have what installed on the Citrix MetaFrame server?

   A. The Citrix Management Console

   B. A print driver that matches the client's print driver

   C. The HP print system if the client printer is an HP

   D. A matching local printer

3. When a client printer auto-creates, it creates a name that looks like which of the following?

   A. *Servername#printername*

   B. *Servername#clientname\Printername*

   C. *Clientname#\printername*

   D. *Username#\printername*

4. You wish to configure several DOS clients to enable them to access their local printers. What is the best way to accomplish this?

   A. Import the DOS printers into the farm; then adjust the printers' auto-creation settings for the user of that workstation.

   B. Use the Auto-creation settings in the Printer Management node to configure the client with the following parameters: client name, printer name, print driver, and port.

    C. Upgrade the workstation to a Windows operating system to take advantage of auto-created printers.

    D. Log in from the DOS client and add the printer manually by specifying the client LPT 1: in the Add Printer Wizard.

5. Network printers can be accessed by users through which of the following methods? (Choose all that apply.)

    A. The user can add the printer through the Add Printer Wizard if the wizard is available when running a desktop.

    B. The administrator can add a network printer using the Add Printer Wizard, and it will be available for all users.

    C. The administrator can import the network print server and then assign users to the printers.

    D. The user can use the Client Printer Wizard to connect to the network printer.

6. Which of the following is true about local printers in a MetaFrame XP environment? (Choose all that apply.)

    A. If shared, these printers automatically show up in the printers list in the Citrix Management console.

    B. These printers are connected to the MetaFrame server via a communication cable or local port.

    C. These printers cannot be assigned to users.

    D. These printers can be assigned to users but only when the users are logged in to the server that hosts the local printer.

7. A user contacts you and states that whenever they log in to the Citrix server, they are not able to print to their client printer. After investigating the problem, you determine the print driver they are using has a name different from its server driver name. How can you rectify this situation?

    A. Check the printer manufacturer's Web site to see if a newer driver is available.

    B. Inform the user that his printer is not supported and will not work.

    C. Create a printer mapping, associating the client driver name with its matching server driver.

    D. Share the client's printer locally; then import the client as a network print server.

8. Which of the following clients can auto-create their client printers?

    A. Windows 32-bit clients

    B. DOS clients

    C. Unix clients

    D. Windows CE clients

9. Who has permissions to see auto-created client printers on a MetaFrame server?

    A. The user whose session auto-created the printer

    B. Administrators only

    C. All users logged in to the MetaFrame server

    D. The user whose session auto-created the printer and determined the members of the Administrators group.

10. Which of the following are true statements regarding print drivers?

    A. Print drivers are OS/platform-specific.

    B. Print drivers are required on the MetaFrame server to support network, client, and local printers.

    C. When a print driver is loaded, it installs files to the local operating system and adds keys to the local server's registry.

    D. Print drivers are installed using the Add Driver dialog box in the Citrix Management Console.

Replicating Print Drivers and Importing Print Servers

11. You have just imported a network print server into your MetaFrame XP farm. Which of the following items are required to allow your users access to these printers when they log on to MetaFrame? (Choose all that apply.)

    A. Installing the required print drivers on at least one server in the farm

    B. Assigning the printers to users through the Citrix Management Console

    C. Disabling all client printers so users will see the network printers

    D. Replicating the printer drivers to all MetaFrame XP servers in your farm

12. Where is the print driver and replication information kept for the server farm?

    A. In each MetaFrame server's registry

    B. In the IMA data store

    C. In the local zone's data collector

    D. In both the data collector and the IMA data store

13. When importing a network print server, you must provide what information?

    A. The name of the print server

    B. A username and password that has access to the shares on the print server

    C. The TCP/IP address of the print server

    D. The names of the print shares you wish to import

14. You have installed several new shared printers onto your network print server that is already imported into the MetaFrame farm. You wish to assign these printers to your users but cannot find them listed in the Citrix Management Console. What is needed to allow you to see these new printers?

    A. You should delete the Print Server from the Citrix Management Console and re-import it.

    B. The Independent Management Architecture service needs to be stopped and restarted.

    C. You need to select the print server in the Citrix Management Console and update it.

    D. Nothing. The MetaFrame Server will import the new printers as load allows.

15. Printers that have been imported into the farm from a network print server can be assigned to… ? (Choose all that apply.)

    A. Groups of users

    B. Individual user accounts

    C. Individual computer accounts

    D. Individual MetaFrame servers

16. The Citrix Management Console will show you which of the following in the Printer Management node?

    A. All network and local printers available to users in the farm

    B. All Win32 auto-created client printers

    C. A list of drivers installed on the Citrix farm

    D. A list of drivers installed on each of the MetaFrame servers

17. When replicating drivers, which of the following options are you given?

    A. Replicate the driver to every server in the farm

    B. Add the driver to the auto-replication list

    C. Remove the driver from the farm

    D. Overwrite existing drivers

18. There are two ways to view installed print drivers on a Windows 2000 MetaFrame XP server. (Choose the two ways from the list that follows.)

    A. Open the Printers folder in the Control Panel, right-click an open area in the window, and select drivers.

    B. Using the Citrix Management Console, select the Drivers tab; then select the server you wish to view information from.

    C. Open the Printers folder in the Control Panel, select Print Server Properties; then select the Drivers tab.

    D. Edit a file called WTSPRNT.INF in the WINNT\SYSTEM32 directory.

19. How can you remove a print server from the MetaFrame XP farm?

    A. By selecting the printers from that print server in the Printers node and deleting them

    B. By selecting the print server from the Printer Management node, right-clicking, and selecting Discard

    C. By removing the print server from the domain

20. A new MetaFrame server is being installed into the farm today. You want to ensure that all the printer mappings from your current server are used on the new server. What must you do to ensure that the printer mappings are exported to the new server?

    A. In the Printer Management node, open the Driver Mapping dialog box and select to replicate mappings to the new server.

    B. In the Printer Management node, open the Driver Mapping dialog box and select to replicate mappings to the all servers in the farm.

    C. Nothing. Print driver mappings are replicated to all servers in the farm automatically.

    D. On the new server, open the Citrix Management Console and duplicate the print driver mappings from the first server.

LAB QUESTION

You are faced with the following scenario:

Your company is about to implement a MetaFrame solution that will allow users at remote offices to run a new application based at the main corporate office. This application is Windows-based and will require that each user has a printer configured in their session.

All the clients connecting to your server will be Windows NT 4.0 Workstation using the Win32 ICA client. The majority printers they have configured at their workstations are network printers mapped to printer shares on servers at the remote offices. A handful of users have local printers connected to their workstations.

What is the best printing solution to implement in this environment that is easy to administer and allows every remote user to print?

SELF TEST ANSWERS

Creating Client, Network, and Local Printers

1. ☑ **A and C.** Local printers are connected directly to the MetaFrame server. Client printers are attached directly to the client device. Network Printers are the third type of printer available in a farm.
   ☒ **D and B** are not types of printers and are therefore incorrect.

2. ☑ **B.** You must have either a matching driver on the server side or a print driver mapping for the client driver.
   ☒ **A** is incorrect because the Citrix Management Console is installed on all Citrix servers. **C and D** are incorrect because only the driver files are needed.

3. ☑ **C.** This is the proper format for an auto-created client printer.
   ☒ **A, B, and D** are not in the proper format.

4. ☑ **B.** Using the Citrix Management Console, DOS and Windows CE clients can be configured to auto-create client printers.
   ☒ **A** is incorrect because the client device is not sharing its printer. **C** is incorrect as well, since there are much fewer steps and it's much faster using the auto-creation settings. **D** is also incorrect, since this can be done from the Citrix Management Console, no trip to the client device is required.

5. ☑ **A and B.** A user can add a network printer during their session if they have access to the Printers folder and the Add A Printer Wizard, or an administrator can import the print server and assign groups or users to specific printers.
   ☒ **C** is incorrect, since this will add the network printer only for the administrator, and **D** is incorrect because there is no such utility.

6. ☑ **A and B.** When shared, these local printers appear in the Citrix Management Console and the printers are connected to the server directly or via a local port.
   ☒ **C and D** are incorrect because local printers can be assigned to users, and since the printer is shared, the user does not have to be logged on to the server which hosts the printer.

7. ☑ **C.** Creating a printer mapping is the proper way to match client and server drivers that have different names.
   ☒ **A** is incorrect because we already have a driver installed on the server. **B** is incorrect

because you do have the ability to make it function. **D** is incorrect because while this may allow us to see the printer in the Citrix Management Console it still requires a matching driver name.

8. ☑ **A, B,** and **D.** Windows 32-bit clients will auto-create without administrator intervention, and DOS and Windows CE clients can be configured to auto-create their client printer.
   ☒ **C** is incorrect. Unix clients do not support auto-created printers.

9. ☑ **D.** Only the user who auto-created the client printer and the Administrators group has access to that printer.
   ☒ **A, B,** and **C** are incorrect because only the user who auto-created the client printer and the Administrators group has access to that printer.

10. ☑ **A, B,** and **C.** When installed, a print driver adds files and registry settings to the local operating system. Print drivers are also built specifically for different operating systems.
   ☒ **D** is incorrect. Print drivers are installed from the Printers folder on the server. No such utility exists in the Citrix Management Console.

Replicating Print Drivers and Importing Print Servers

11. ☑ **A, B,** and **D.** Each of these steps is required to assign a network printer to a user or groups of users.
   ☒ **C** is incorrect. Network printers assigned to users do not require that client printers be disabled.

12. ☑ **B.** Print driver and replication information for the farm is stored in the IMA data store.
   ☒ **A** is incorrect because the local server registry only holds print driver information for that server. **C** and **D** are incorrect because the zone data collector does not hold driver or replication information.

13. ☑ **A** and **B.** All that is required is the name of the print server and valid credentials to authenticate to the server.
   ☒ **C** and **D** are incorrect because the IP address is not required, and the printer shares will all be automatically imported.

14. ☑ **C.** The easiest way to see these new printers is to right-click the server in the Citrix Management Console and update it.
   ☒ **A** is incorrect. While this may work, it will also delete all the auto-creation settings configured for the existing printers. **B** and **D** are also incorrect because neither will have an effect on whether the new printers are available in the farm.

15. ☑ **A** and **B**. The Citrix Management Console allows you to assign printers to groups or users.
    ☒ **C** and **D** are incorrect. The Auto-Creation Settings window has no options for assigning printers to server or computer accounts.

16. ☑ **A**, **C**, and **D**. Each of these can be seen in the Print Management node of the Citrix Management Console.
    ☒ **B** is incorrect. There is no list for auto-created Win32 client printers available.

17. ☑ **A**, **B**, and **D**. Each of these options is available in the Replicate Driver dialog box window when configuring driver replication.
    ☒ **C** is incorrect. This option is not available in the Citrix Management Console. The process is done manually on the operating system side.

18. ☑ **B** and **C**. The Citrix Management console can show you installed drivers on a server, or you can view the drivers from the Server Properties in the Printers folder.
    ☒ **A** is incorrect. This does not give you the option to view printers. **D** is incorrect, because this will show you printer mappings on that server but not all the print drivers.

19. ☑ **B**. This is the proper workflow for removing a print server from the farm.
    ☒ **A** is incorrect. This will not remove the print server from the data store. **C** is also incorrect. This will not remove the print server from the farm, but will cause auto-created printer functions from this server to fail.

20. ☑ **C**. Any mappings entered in the Driver Mapping dialog box are automatically replicated to all servers in the farm.
    ☒ **A** and **B** are incorrect because there are no such settings in the Driver Mapping dialog box. **D** is incorrect because the mappings will be automatically replicated to this new server. These settings are configured for the entire farm.

LAB ANSWER

Import all network print servers into the farm. This will allow you to use the Citrix Management Console to assign printers to users at each remote location. Install print drivers to support these network printers and replicate the drivers to each server in the farm.

Next, determine which clients have printers attached locally to their PCs. Identify drivers for each printer and either install the appropriate driver or map it to another print driver.

At first glance, some may want to use auto-created client printers for the entire install, but this would require more setup time because of the need to determine each client's print driver. By using network printers, we have limited the number of possible drivers needed, except for those few clients who have local printers.

13

Monitoring and Troubleshooting MetaFrame XP Servers

O f all the skills involved in installing, configuring, deploying, and managing servers, the ability to fine-tune and troubleshoot is among the most highly prized. All the rest is similar to following a recipe. If you're careful and follow all the instructions, you can build a server or a server farm. Well, maybe that's oversimplifying it a little, but what happens when things go wrong? No book can possibly list every error message you might receive, or detail each performance problem that might crop up. Every server and server farm is unique (unless they are cloned), and each can have different hardware, installed applications, policies, and even users that will affect how the server performs.

Because perfection is hard to come by and things can, and will, go wrong, it is essential to become adept at monitoring and troubleshooting your servers. Monitoring your servers on a regular basis can help to prevent problems from occurring in the future. Monitoring can also help you to establish baselines for your servers; to see what is normal for them, and what is not.

Windows and Citrix both provide tools that can assist you in efficiently managing and troubleshooting your servers. Windows NT 4.0 Terminal Server edition and the Windows 2000 Server family both provide the Event Viewer, System Information, and Task Manager. Citrix MetaFrame XP*e* includes Resource Manager and Network Manager, each of which merits a sizable role in your administration tool kit.

CERTIFICATION OBJECTIVE 13.01

Using Event Viewer and System Information

The Event Viewer is the one of the first tools to use for troubleshooting and monitoring your system. It is a front-end feature, used to view the event logs in which information is recorded about the computer and applications. Windows NT 4.0 Terminal Server Edition, has three logs: the Application Log, the Security Log, and the System Log. Windows 2000, meanwhile, has an additional three logs that are available on domain controllers running the associated services; they are the Directory Service Log, the DNS Server Log, and the File Replication Service Log. The Event Viewer is installed by default and located under Administrative Tools on both operating systems, while the logs themselves are stored in the

%systemroot%\system32\config folder. Table 13-1 lists the logs and the type of information contained in each.

With the Event Viewer, you can monitor the events that take place on your systems and detect activities that may require your attention. Analyzing these events can help you resolve issues related to security, resource allocation, and system problems. When saved, log files also provide a historical view of these events. It is a good idea to archive the log files from each of your servers for future reference.

on the **Job** *Remote servers and workstations can also be monitored from your local Event Viewer, providing they have accounts in the domain or in a trusted domain and are connected to the network. To view the logs of remote computers, right-click Event Viewer (local), and from the context menu, select Connect to Another Computer.*

TABLE 13-1 Event Viewer Log Data

Log Type	Log Data	Windows NT 4 Terminal Server	Windows 2000 Server Family
System	Related to System components such as services, drivers, or hardware	✓	✓
Security	Events relating to logons, logon attempts, and resource usage	✓	✓
Application	Events logged by applications or programs	✓	✓
Directory Service	Problems related to Directory Services, Global Catalog, and Active Directory; Windows 2000 domain controllers only		✓
DNS Server	Directory Name Service information and errors; Windows 2000 domain controllers only		✓
File Replication Service	Events related to replication to other servers; Windows 2000 domain controllers only		✓

Event Log Categories

Three categories of events are generated in the System and Application logs and two additional event categories in the Security logs. It is important to understand what each of the categories pertain to and what they say about the server or application. The System and Application logs include the following event categories:

- **Information events**   Provide status information and details about "good" things such as the successful operation of a service, driver, or application. Typically, there are far more of these than any other type. Information events are represented by a blue "i".

- **Warning events**   Provide information on potential problems, such as low disk space, services that have not been configured, and lost or timed-out connections. These may not be significant but should be examined carefully and, if possible, corrected immediately. Warning events are represented by a yellow triangle with an exclamation point (!) inside.

- **Error events**   These are indicative of more serious conditions and logged when there is a failure such as a service failing to start, a duplicate IP address, a malfunctioning hardware device, or system crash. Error events are represented by red circles with white Xs through them, as shown in Figure 13-1.

FIGURE 13-1	
The Windows 2000 Event Viewer	

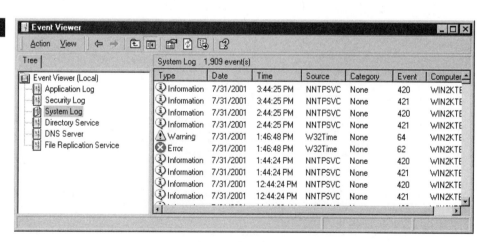

The Security Log contains events that are generated when auditing has been implemented. Auditing can be enabled on events such as logons, resources, or file access. The two types of Security Log events are

- **Success Audit events**   Provide information on successful logins or access.
- **Failed events**   Provide information on failed login attempts, failed access to resources, or other security threats.

Event Information

As you scroll through the log, each event listed provides several pieces of information:

- The type of event, whether information, warning, error, success or failure.
- The date and time the event was logged.
- The source of the event. The event source is the service, driver or application that reported the event to the log.
- The category of event, if applicable, is a number used internally by the component that reported the event.
- The event ID number that describes the event to Windows 2000.

To learn more about an event, double-click the entry to open its property sheet, as shown in Figure 13-2. The property sheet reiterates the preceding information and may also include a username, computer name, and a description of the event. The Source, Event ID, and description will often be referenced in the Microsoft and/or Citrix Knowledge Base and provide explanations and solutions to the problem.

Managing the Event Viewer

Because the event logs record information on a daily basis, they could become enormous if left unmanaged. Of course, Microsoft took care to set defaults to prevent this from happening, but you can adjust those defaults to meet your own needs. To change settings on a log, right-click the log and select Properties. As shown in Figure 13-3, there are two tabs: the General tab and the Filter tab. The General tab provides information about the log such as its location, size, creation date, last modified date, and last accessed date. It also allows you to specify the maximum size of the log, what to do once the log has reached its maximum size.

FIGURE 13-2

The Event
Properties
dialog box

FIGURE 13-3

The General tab
under System
Log Properties

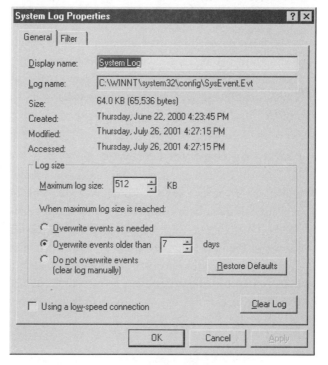

It even lets you clear the log manually so you can start fresh. If left at the default setting, the log maxes out at 512KB. If you choose to change the default size, however, you have the option to overwrite the events as needed, to overwrite those events older than a specified number of days, or to forego overwriting and clear the log manually. Unless you are absolutely certain you will never need those logs again, take a moment to save them before clearing. Citrix recommends you set the maximum log size to 1024KB and to overwrite events as needed. The reasoning behind this is to keep the event logs from filling up and generating errors of their own. The only problem with this configuration is that the older events will be wiped out and unavailable for reference in the future. The General tab also allows you to configure the event logs for a low-speed connection. This option can be used when monitoring a computer across a slow WAN link or dial-up connection.

e x a m
ⓦa t c h

Citrix recommends setting the Event Log's maximum size to 1024KB and to overwrite as needed.

o n t h e
ⓙo b

If you choose to set the logs to "Do not overwrite events," do not forget to archive and clear them on a regular basis. Be especially careful when security auditing is enabled. Select only the events you need to audit. Logs can fill up quickly and, if left unchecked, could crash the server.

Filtering and Searching for Events

The Filter tab (Figure 13-4) allows you to select the type of events displayed in the Event Viewer. By default, the Event Viewer displays all events in a log sorted by most recent date. The Filter tab allows you to select events based on the following criteria shown in Table 13-2.

Windows 2000 provides a Find utility for searching through event logs. Find can be used to locate related events to determine how frequently the event has occurred. To use Find, open the Event Viewer, click View, and select Find. Under Types, select the type of events you want to find. On both operating systems, events can be sorted by clicking the column heading you wish to sort by. For example, if you want to see all events related to a particular service, click on the Source column heading and scroll down until you find the service you are tracking. All other events relating to this service will be grouped together and easy to locate.

The Event Viewer is typically the tool used in troubleshooting Windows systems. Learning to use it is relatively easy, the hard part is figuring out what the

System Log Properties

| General | Filter |

Event types
- ☑ Information
- ☑ Warning
- ☑ Error
- ☑ Success audit
- ☑ Failure audit

Event source: [All]

Category: [All]

Event ID:

User:

Computer:

From: First Event 6/22/2000 4:23:45 PM

To: Last Event 7/27/2001 8:35:45 AM

Restore Defaults

OK   Cancel   Apply

TABLE 13-2 Event Viewer Filters

Property	Description
Event Type	Information, Warning, Error, Success Audit, Failure Audit.
Event Source	The source is the application or component that logged the event. A source could be a specific application, driver, or system component.
Category	Category is most useful for security events, because most system events do not belong to categories and application categories are numbered.
Event ID	Useful when you are looking for all the occurrences of a specific event.
User	This filters on all events associated with a particular user. Can be useful for troubleshooting user complaints.
Computer	Filtering on Computer will display all events for that computer.
From and To	Allows filtering on a range of dates.

information means and how to resolve the issues it reports. We'll get to that in the sections that follow, but for now, try Exercise 13-1 to familiarize yourself with the Event Viewer and its configuration options.

EXERCISE 13-1

CertCam 13-1

Changing Event Log Settings

1. Choose Start | Programs | Administrative Tools.

2. Double-click Event Viewer.

3. Right-click the System Log and select Properties. This opens up the System Log's Property sheet. At the top, you should see two tabs, the General tab and the Filter tab.

4. Select the General tab and move down to Log Size. Change Maximum Log Size to 1024 KB.

5. Below the maximum log size, select Overwrite Events As Needed.

6. Click once on the Filter tab.

7. By default, all event types are selected. Deselect all but the Warning and Error event types.

8. Click OK to finish.

9. Now, open the System Log. There should be no Information events displayed. If you're very lucky, you will not have any error or warning events, but if you do, double-click them to open their Information Properties sheet. Take note of the information provided, especially the Event ID, Source, and Description.

Now that you are more familiar with the Event Viewer, it's time for a pop quiz. Test your knowledge by trying to answer the questions that follow. Try not to look at the answers first!

SCENARIO & SOLUTION

What tool should you use in Windows 2000 to monitor System and Application events?	The Event Viewer is used to view the logs in which the System and Applications report information, warnings, and errors.
What type of information does the System Log provide?	The System Log provides information, warnings and errors pertaining to system events, such as drivers starting/stopping, and low disk space.
What type of information does the Application Log provide?	The Application Log provides information, warning, and errors pertaining to applications and programs.
How can you view the event logs on another networked computer?	By right-clicking Event Viewer and selecting Connect To Another Computer.
How can you keep the event logs from overwriting older events?	Right-click the log, select Properties, and on the General tab, change the setting to Manual.
What does Citrix recommend concerning the event logs?	Citrix recommends setting the maximum size of the event logs to 1024, and to Overwrite As Necessary.

System Information Tool

In Windows 2000, most of the system management tools have been centralized within the Microsoft Management Console or MMC. To open the console, you can either right-click My Computer and select Manage, or go to Start | Programs | Administrative Tools | Computer Management. From here, you can view and monitor your local system or a remote system in your domain. To monitor a remote system, right-click Computer Management (Local) and select Connect To Another Computer.

System Information Tool contains vital information relating to your server in a read-only format. It cannot be used to test or change server hardware or software, only to display the servers configuration and components. Information contained in the folders can be saved as a text or .inf file and kept as historical data or e-mailed to a vendor's technical support. To save folder information, right-click the folder and select Save As.

If you do need to test or change hardware devices or drivers, use the Device Manager. From within Device Manager, devices can be tested, disabled, uninstalled, or updated. For problem services, use Services, located under Applications and

Services. Both the Device Manager and Applications and Services are found under the Computer Management Console.

There are three main sections within Computer Management: System Tools, Storage and Services and Applications. The System Information Tool is appropriately located under System Tools. You can also get to System Information by typing **winmsd** from the command prompt. Within the System Information Tool there are five subfolders that provide a wealth of information about your system. The five subfolders are: System Summary, Hardware Resources, Components, Software Environment, and Internet Explorer 5.

The System Summary displays a list of the system's basic configuration. This is where you'll find, among other things, the version and build of your operating system, the BIOS version installed memory, available memory, virtual memory, available virtual memory and page file size. Don't be surprised if you are asked to look here if you ever call a vendor for support.

The Hardware Resources folder has several subfolders devoted to information about the system's hardware (Figure 13-5).

FIGURE 13-5	

Hardware Resources

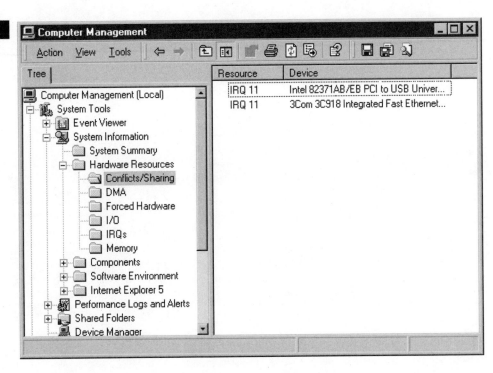

Don't overlook this one. It is one of the most important pieces of the System Information Tool because it provides information on hardware conflicts and IRQ sharing. If you've ever installed new hardware only to find that either it will not work, or another device has stopped working, you will appreciate the importance of this resource. Table 13-3 explains some of the information found in these subfolders.

The Components folder is another that you should become familiar with. It displays a list of components, all of which may not be installed on your system, and shows the resources they are using. If a component is actually installed, you can right-click it and view its property sheet. The property sheets provide all the details relevant to the device, including the driver versions, I/O, and IRQs it is using. The Component folder has eleven subfolders that represent the different classes of components that may be installed. One of the most interesting is the Problem

TABLE 13-3   System Information Hardware Resources

Resource	Description
Conflicts/Sharing	This folder lists all the components that are sharing an IRQ or are in conflict over one. If you have installed a new component and there are IRQ conflicts, you will see it listed here.
DMA	Direct Memory Access channels are rare these days, but you may see them used by audio devices. As you might recall, DMAs have the ability to move data from the device to RAM without involving the processor. If you have any DMA devices in your system, you will see them listed here.
Forced Hardware	Older hardware that is not supported by Plug-and-Play will be listed here.
I/O	The Input/Output folder lists the hardware devices and the areas of virtual memory being used by them.
IRQs	Interrupt request lines are the lines over which the device sends information to the processor. The IRQ folder will list the IRQs in use and also show those that are sharing an IRQ.
Memory	This folder shows information regarding the virtual memory areas used by devices. This is similar to what is shown in the I/O folder, but it is from the perspective of the device, not the memory.

Devices folder. Inside, devices that are not performing as expected or devices that have been removed incorrectly will be listed. The other ten folders are as follows:

- **Multimedia**   Audio and video codecs, CD-ROMs, sound devices
- **Display**   Adapter information, such as name, type, resolution, and pixels
- **Infrared**   Properties of any infrared devices installed
- **Input**   Keyboard and pointing device information
- **Modem**   Information on installed modems
- **Network**   Adapter, protocols, and WinSock information
- **Ports**   Serial and parallel port information
- **Storage**   Drivers associated with storage devices
- **Printing**   Any print drivers installed
- **USB**   Information on USB devices

The Software Environment folder contains ten subfolders that detail the software running on your system, as well as the files and services in use and who's using them. Table 13-4 lists the subfolders and describes the information contained in each.

The Internet Explorer 5 folder is fairly self-explanatory and contains those settings unique to Internet Explorer (IE). This is a great place to view paths, file versions, proxy settings, encryption, and other IE configuration information. The subfolders include

- **Summary**   Version, build, path, cipher strength, content advisor and Internet Explorer Administration Kit (IEAK)
- **File Versions**   Information on all IE files, version, date, vendor
- **Connectivity**   Dial-up, Local Area Network (LAN) or Proxy connection information
- **Cache**   Summary, list of objects in cache, page refresh, temp folder
- **Content**   Summary, personal and other peoples certificates, publisher
- **Security**   Local intranet, trusted sites, Internet security and restricted site

TABLE 13-4 The Software Environment Folder

Folder	Description
Drivers	Lists all installed drivers, their type (kernel or file system), state (stopped or running), and a brief description of what the driver does.
Environment Variables	Environmental variables listed include the path information for system files, location of temporary folders and files, the processor identification and operating system version.
Jobs	This folder contains a folder for each type of job that may be running.
Network Connections	All network connections and the associated drive letters will be displayed.
Running Tasks	This is a bit different than the Jobs folder. It contains a list of all executable files currently run by the services. Information such as file version, date, and file size are given. This is a good place to look if you need to know a file version or date.
Loaded Modules	This folder lists all the dynamic link libraries (dll) currently running on the system, their version, date, manufacturer, and path.
Services	This folder lists all the nonsystem services available on the system, whether they are running or not, and the start mode (manual, automatic, or disabled).
Program Groups	Terminal Server profile associations and all the groups available in the Start menu will be displayed here.
Startup Programs	This folder shows the programs that are configured to start at boot.
OLE Registration	Object Linking and Embedding associations can be found here.

Now that you've gotten more familiar with the type of information found in the System Information Tool, let's try a hands-on exercise.

EXERCISE 13-2

CertCam 13-2

Saving System Information to a File

In this exercise, we will assume that you are the administrator of XYZ Company, and you are having some difficulties with one of your servers after installing a new application. You've tried all the tricks you know, but are stumped, so you call the vendor for assistance. The technical support person you speak with asks you to e-mail her your system information summary. Here's what to do:

1. Log on to a Windows 2000 Server as Administrator.

2. Right-click My Computer and select Manage. This will open the Computer Management Console.

3. Expand System Information by clicking on the "+" on the left.

4. Right-click System Summary. This will bring up a menu that allows you to save the System Summary as a text file or an information (.inf) file, search the information using Find, Print the information, refresh or get Help.

5. Select Save As Text File. Save the file as testlog.txt.

6. Locate the file you just saved and double-click it to open it. The information saved in the file should look similar to that in Figure 13-6 that follows. It contains information about your server's hardware and environment that may help the vendor's technical support people resolve your problem.

FIGURE 13-6	
System Information Report	

```
testlog - Notepad
File  Edit  Format  Help

System Information report written at: 07/30/2001 01:58:49 PM
[System Summary]

Item     value
OS Name Microsoft Windows 2000 Server
Version 5.0.2195  Build 2195
OS Manufacturer Microsoft Corporation
System Name     WIN2KTESTDC
System Manufacturer      Dell Computer Corporation
System Model     OptiPlex GX1 550L+
System Type      X86-based PC
Processor        x86 Family 6 Model 7 Stepping 3 GenuineIntel ~550 Mhz
BIOS Version     Phoenix ROM BIOS PLUS Version 1.10 A08
Windows Directory        C:\WINNT
System Directory         C:\WINNT\System32
Boot Device      \Device\Harddisk0\Partition1
Locale  United States
User Name        W2KTEST\Administrator
Total Physical Memory   261,688 KB
Available Physical Memory        114,076 KB
Total Virtual Memory    895,056 KB
Available Virtual Memory         599,708 KB
Page File Space 633,368 KB
Page File        C:\pagefile.sys
```

Handling Events

So, you've been monitoring your Event Logs and have discovered warning and/or error events. What should you do now? What does all this stuff mean?! The dialog found in the logs is not always intuitive. Sometimes it's down right confusing. But in most cases, a cure can be found. Both Microsoft and Citrix have a Knowledge Base that contains articles relating to practically every problem you might encounter. To find the article that relates to the event, you will need to have the information found on the event's property sheet handy. Three key pieces of information are the Event ID, the Source and the Description, if there is one. Take these three pieces of information with you to Microsoft and/or Citrix's support Web site and begin your search. For Microsoft, go to http://search.support.microsoft.com/kb/c.asp, and for Citrix, go to http://www.citrix.com/support/.

on the
job

The Citrix support site also provides a link to their Solution Forums. The forums are active discussion areas where administrators can interact with other administrators and Citrix support technicians. The forum is extremely helpful when you cannot locate the right Knowledge Base article to resolve your issue. Typically, problems are not isolated to just one server, location, or administrator. If you are seeing it, chances are others are, too. Try searching the forums using keywords that describe the problem first. If you don't find any postings that address your issue, post a message asking if anyone else has seen the same problem and what they did to resolve it. Check back frequently to see if anyone has posted a response. Questions are frequently answered by other administrators, and often Citrix support technicians will point you in the right direction, or confirm another's solution. The forums can also be used to research products prior to purchasing or installing. It's a great source of real-world information—and it's FREE!

Deciding which Web site to visit first is usually determined by the Source and Description information. If the information is clearly related to MetaFrame, it might save time going to Citrix first. Generally, both Knowledge Bases will provide similar information or at least a pointer to the right article on the other's Web site. Other support resources offered by Microsoft and Citrix are

■ **Microsoft Online TechNet**   A site devoted to IT professionals that provides troubleshooting tools, information about known issues, hotfix, and service pack downloads. TechNet can be found at http://www.microsoft.com/technet/.

- **Microsoft TechNet Subscription**   Monthly TechNet subscriptions can be purchased for a mere $299 (single-user license) or $499 per year for TechNet Plus (single-user license). TechNet subscriptions provide monthly CD-ROM updates containing Knowledge Base articles, information, utilities, hotfixes, and service packs. The TechNet Plus subscription also includes software betas.

- **Citrix Solution Tools Plus**   Citrix provides quarterly subscriptions that include the Citrix Knowledge Base and Practices CD. In addition to the CDs, Citrix sends out a monthly Solution News online newsletter and Solution Flash, which notifies the subscriber of updates to Citrix products and Knowledge Base articles.

If you are unable to locate information about your particular warning or error, you may need to contact Microsoft or Citrix support. Both provide for-fee support services to fit various organizations or needs. Microsoft even provides per-incident support for those who rarely need assistance. The pricing depends on whether or not you or your company meet certain criteria, but it usually begins at $149 per year.

Preventing Disasters

When you've found the information you need to resolve your issue, there are a few steps you should take to ensure that the fix doesn't make matters worse. It is a well-known fact that fixes, such as service packs, hotfixes, and registry and configuration changes, frequently backfire and break what was not already broken. This can be an administrator's nightmare if the right precautions are not taken. Here are a few tips that may save you if your fix backfires:

- Keep your Emergency Repair Disks (ERDs) current. Windows NT 4.0 Terminal Service Edition included the RDISK utility for creating ERDs, but because the registry is so much larger on a Terminal Server, the registry can no longer fit on a single disk. Windows 2000 has improved upon the ERD process by eliminating the System hives. The new ERD is useful if your system will not boot. It can be used to repair a damaged boot sector, a damaged Mast Boot Record (MBR) and replace or repair a damaged NT Loader (NTLDR). It is important to keep your ERD disk up-to-date. The one created when you initially install the system is no longer valid once you've added accounts and customized your system. Create a new ERD after you have changed or updated your system configuration. An ERD can be created through the Windows 2000 backup utility, found in Start | Programs | Accessories | System Tools | Backup (Figure 13-7) or by typing **ntbackup** at the command prompt.

- If the problem is reproducible, run the fix on a test server first. If your test server is a duplicate of your production servers, you should see exactly the same results.

- When installing service packs, respond **YES** to creating a backup of the previous system files. If the service pack produces unexpected results, you can back out of the upgrade. The same should be done for application updates and hot fixes.

- Document everything! This is one of the most important things you can do. Make sure you save the documentation where it will be easy to access and backed up.

FIGURE 13-7

Windows 2000 Emergency Repair Disk

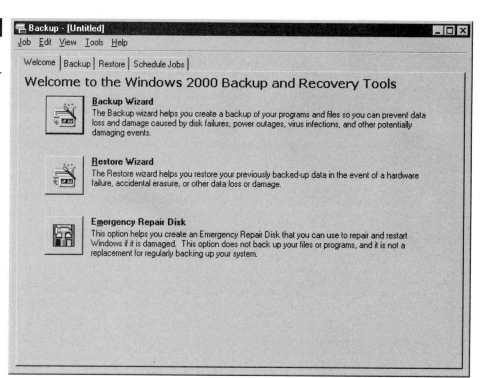

FROM THE CLASSROOM

What To Do When Things Go Wrong

No matter how careful you are, things can happen, it's just a matter of time. All you can do is take every precaution possible and have an arsenal of tools ready to combat whatever problem occurs. Backing up your servers and registry, testing, and backing out of upgrades are all very good practices, and I'd recommend employing them all just in case, but there are a few other tools out there that can make your life easier, or save you in a pinch. Windows 2000 comes with a few new or improved features that can really help you out of a jam.

First, Windows 2000 Backup is a big improvement over the old NT Backup. The new backup utility, located under System Tools in the Accessories folder, allows you to back up not only onto tape, but also on disks, CDs, and network-accessible volumes. A "System State" backup will back up the registry, Component Services Class Registration database, system startup files, and Certificate Services database on a nondomain controller.

Another improvement in Windows 2000 is the advanced startup options. To access these, press F8 during the Windows startup process. The new options provide enhanced troubleshooting and resolution features such as Safe Mode, Safe Mode with Networking, and Safe Mode with Command Prompt. These features were a part of Windows 9.*x* operating systems, but have been improved

upon in Windows 2000. If you have a driver that's gone astray and your machine blue screens at startup, try starting it in Safe Mode. It loads only the bare essentials and allows you to uninstall the problematic driver and reboot normally.

Consider this scenario: Suppose you've installed a device driver and after restarting the system, it freezes just after boot. What can you do? You've already logged in so it's too late for Last Known Good and your server locks up once you're in. Restart your server and press F8 during the Windows startup process. Select Safe Mode. Once the system starts up, right-click My Computer and select Manage. From Management Console, go into Device Manager, right-click the device in question and select Disable or Uninstall, then restart your system. An even slicker way to take care of the problem driver is to go to the command prompt and type: **Listsvc**. This will produce a list of drivers and services loaded, as well as their status. Once you have located the driver, type **disable** *<drivername>* and press ENTER. The problem driver will now be disabled and you should be able to function normally.

One of my favorite startup options is the Enable Boot Logging feature. When selected, Enable Boot Logging creates a log file that lists all the drivers and services the system loads or fails to load. The log, called Ntblog.txt, is located under the \Winnt folder. By starting up with this option, prior to and after an upgrade or new installation, you can document the new drivers or services that were installed. Just remember to rename the log after the first boot. If problems occur, you can use these logs to locate the problem driver or service.

Windows 2000 has also added the Recovery Console (RC) that can be run from the command line to perform troubleshooting and recovery tasks. The Recovery Console can be installed from the Windows 2000 \I386 directory by running the winnt32 command with the /cmdcons switch or booting from the Windows 2000 Setup disks or CD. Running the Recovery Console allows you to start/stop services, read and write data on local drives, even if they are formatted with NTFS and to format hard disks. You can even troubleshoot and repair an NT system with RC; just run RC from the CD-ROM or install onto the NT system.

Aside from the tools that come packaged with the operating system, there are a few other tools that can round out your toolkit. Absolutely no administrator's tool kit is complete without Winternal's RegMon and FileMon. Both tools are monitoring utilities that can be used to troubleshoot application problems. Common problems seen in server-based environments such as corrupt application files, invalid file paths, or user hive entries and locked down files that need less stringent permissions, can be tracked down and corrected using these two tools. Just start up RegMon or FileMon and run the application in question. Once the error has occurred, stop the monitor and check the log. Typically you'll see an entry that says "failed," "file not found," or "no access." These two utilities are must haves and well worth the money. Working demos can be downloaded from http://www.winternals.com.

—*Connie S. Wilson, MCSE, MCP+I, CCA, CNA*

Establishing a Baseline

What is a baseline and how can it help you? A baseline helps to determine how well your system is performing and to spot potential problems before they happen. Developing a baseline will help determine how many users the system can support concurrently, and the impact of running certain applications. It's a much better plan than waiting for your users to inform you of how slow the system is! It's also the first step in assuring that your system is running at optimum performance levels and that you have enough resources to support your environment.

How do you establish a baseline for your system? There are two techniques commonly used to develop a baseline. The first is to perform benchmarks or tests on your servers before and after placing them in production. In other words, once you have configured your server and installed all the applications, you perform tests to see how the server is performing. The same tests are run again after the server is in active use. This can be done in a nonproduction, test environment as well if you can round up enough users to act as guinea pigs.

The second method of developing a baseline is to gather server resource statistics over time while the server is in use. The tests can be run at intervals, over a period of weeks, for a trend analysis. The results are documented and compared. Both methods can help you determine system throughput and where potential bottlenecks may lie. Problems occur when demand for resources exceed supply. Typically, the server's processors, memory, physical and logical disks, network interface cards and software are monitored and the results compared.

Various tools can be used to monitor performance and develop a baseline. Both NT and Windows 2000 include Performance Monitor, while Citrix MetaFrame XP*e* includes Resource Management, which we'll discuss in the next section. Both can be extremely helpful in monitoring and developing a baseline for your server.

Performance Monitor

Performance Monitor or PerfMon is a graphical tool incorporated into Windows NT Terminal Server Edition and the Windows 2000 family of servers. It gathers and examines information about server activity by examining system objects or components. Objects are server components that possess a set of measurable properties such as the following:

- Server
- Processors
- Memory
- Physical and logical disks
- Users
- Connections

Objects are defined that represent individual processes, sections of shared memory, and physical devices. Each object has a series of counters associated with it, which represent the measurable characteristics of objects. An example is the Processor object which has several counters associated with it, such as % Processor Time, %User Time, and so on. Certain objects exist on all systems; others only exist if the system is running the associated software.

Each object can also have several instances. An instance shows how many of an object are available in the system. For example, if a server has multiple processors, the Processor object will have multiple instances. If the server has four disk drives, the Physical Disk object will have four instances and so on. Other objects such as Memory and Server do not have instances. Objects with multiple instances produce the same counter information for each instance.

To view the objects and counters that can be used to monitor your system, go to Start | Programs | Administrative Tools | Performance. Make sure System Monitor is selected on the left-hand side of the screen and click the "+" sign at the top of the monitor screen. (You can also right-click a blank area of the System Monitor and choose Add Counters from the context menu.) At this point, the monitor screen on the left is blank. Objects, instances, and counters must be selected and added. To select objects and their related counters, use the Performance Object drop-down menu and select the counters to monitor from the list. (See Figure 13-8.)

FIGURE 13-8

The Performance Monitor Add Counters window

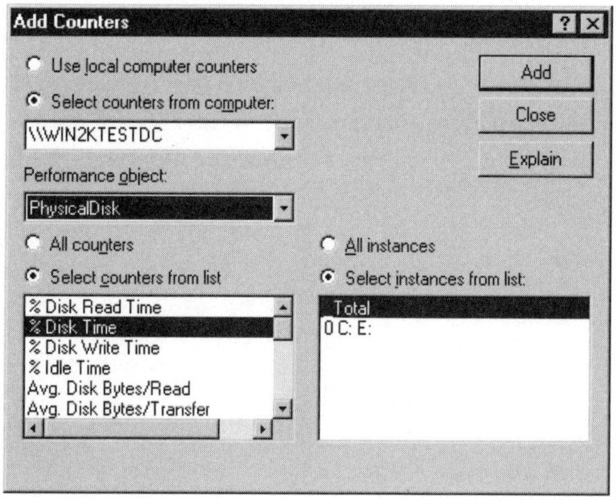

In the following sections, we will look at some of the objects Performance Monitor tracks, as well as their associated objects.

Processor   Process threads require processor cycles to run, and if the demand exceeds the supply, long processor queues develop and system response time will degrade. Two counters that can help you monitor the overall processor load are % Processor Time and Interrupts/sec.

If processor utilization is over 75 percent on average, the processor is working pretty hard. You might consider increasing the number or the speed of the existing processors in the server. To determine processor utilization, monitor the %Processor Time counter under the Processor object. The %Processor Time shows the percentage of elapsed time that a processor is busy executing non-idle threads. If the %Processor Time counter consistently registers at or near 75 percent, the processors might be slowing the system response time.

Common causes of excessive interrupts are defective device adapters or badly designed device drivers. Interrupts degrade system performance because most of the processor time is spent handling them. A moderately busy server (32-bit hard disk adapter, network card, and about 12 users) will experience an average of 100 interrupts per second. If the interrupts per second increases noticeably without a corresponding increase in system activity, it could indicate a hardware problem or faulty drivers.

Memory   Server memory takes the biggest hit on a Windows 2000 system. As we all know, every new version of the operating system and each new version of an application requires more and more memory. If you don't have sufficient memory on your system, you will definitely feel the pain and so will your users. Table 13-5 lists a few important memory counters you may want to keep an eye on.

Physical and Logical Disks   Disk problems on MetaFrame XP servers are usually related to paging because of the memory load the applications place on the server. When the physical memory is maxed out by the load of applications and users, the server begins using the hard disks to support virtual memory. Two counters that should be monitored on both physical and logical disks to measure performance are

- **% Disk Time**   Displays the percentage of the physical disk that is busy. If the disk is busy more than 90 percent of the time, you should probably add another disk.

- **Current Disk Queue Length**   Displays the current number of data transfers waiting in the queue. If you are averaging more than two, you will notice the degradation. Keep this number as small as possible.

on the

job

To enable disk counters, use the DiskPerf –Y switch but don't leave them running permanently as they incur overhead. Use DiskPerf –N to disable the counters.

Regularly monitoring your servers with Performance Monitor is one way you can establish a baseline. Try monitoring at intervals throughout the day, for short periods of time to keep the overhead low. Check and compare your results to find heavy use times and any possible bottlenecks.

Now that you have a good idea what monitoring server performance and developing a baseline are all about, here are a few questions you may want to remember for the exam:

TABLE 13-5   Performance Monitor Memory Counters

Counter	Description	Explanation
Available Bytes	Displays the size of the virtual memory available for applications.	There should always be at least 4MB available. If not, you may not have enough memory or you could have an application experiencing a memory leak.
Pages/sec	Displays the current rate at which pages are read from disk back into physical memory because of page faults or written to the disk to free RAM.	More than 20 pages per second indicates excessive paging and may suggest that your system needs more memory.
Commit Limit	Displays the amount of memory that can be committed without making the page file larger.	The page file should be at least 2 1/2 times the size of your system's RAM, but can be increased if the required space is available.
Committed Bytes	Displays the amount of memory committed to processes currently running on the system.	This is the amount of memory in use that isn't available to other processes.

SCENARIO & SOLUTION

Where can information be found about server hardware and potential IRQ conflicts?	In the Computer Management Console under System Information | Hardware Resources | Conflicts/Sharing.
What type of information does the System Summary display?	The System Summary displays the server's basic configuration, including OS and version, system name, manufacturer, model, processors, BIOS version, installed RAM, available RAM and Page File space.
What steps can be taken to protect your system prior to installing or upgrading applications?	Create a current ERD, back up your system, test installations on a test server, and document everything.
What is a baseline and what does it do?	A baseline monitors and documents system performance before and after it is placed into production. It helps determine whether your server has enough resources for your environment and what the normal status is.
What tool native to Windows NT and the 2000 Server family can be used to monitor and log system performance?	Performance Monitor is native to Windows NT and the 2000 Server family.
Where can I look to find all the drivers installed on my system?	In the Computer Management Console choose System Information | Software Environment | Drivers.
What should you do if processor utilization is 75 percent or above on a regular basis?	Add more or faster processors to your system.

CERTIFICATION OBJECTIVE 13.02

Managing Resource and Citrix Network Manager and Troubleshooting Network Monitor

Resource Manager is a monitoring tool made specifically for the MetaFrame XP server-based environment. Older, less "server-based aware" utilities often do not give accurate readings because they are not in tune to the server-based environment.

They don't take into account that the server is doing 100 percent of the processing and that multiple users are running sessions from it at one time.

Resource Manager allows you to view and monitor information about your server or farm and capture real-time data or produce reports. It can show you the applications you are running, how many instances are running and who is running them. You can track the resources consumed by each user and application and associate a charge with the usage so you can charge back for the use of applications and resources.

Resource Manager can be used on a server or server farm to

- Manage resources
- Monitor and analyze system performance, application usage, and user behavior
- Identify and diagnose potential problems
- Gather statistical data
- Create billing reports
- Produce reports
- Gauge and justify future resource needs
- Plan and scale servers and server farms

System Requirements

As you may have already read in earlier chapters, Citrix Resource Manager is not included with the base MetaFrame XP license and is not available in MetaFrame XP or MetaFrame XP*a*. Resource Manager is part of Citrix's Advanced Management Features. There are currently three MetaFrame XP solutions:

- **MetaFrame XP**   Designed as the base solution for departments or workgroups with up to five non-load-balanced servers
- **MetaFrame XP*a***   Designed for organizations with 2–100 load-balanced servers
- **MetaFrame XP*e***   Designed as the complete Enterprise solution for organizations with 20–1000+ load-balanced, managed servers

Remember, Resource Manager is not included with the base MetaFrame XP license or with MetaFrame XPa. It is only included in MetaFrame XPe.

Citrix Resource Manager can be installed on Microsoft Windows NT 4.0 Terminal Server Edition with Service Pack 5 or later, Windows 2000 Server, and Advanced Server. If installed on Terminal Server Edition, the Microsoft Data Access Component (MDAC) version 2.51, Service Pack 1 must be installed prior to installing MetaFrame XP and Resource Manager. In addition, you must be sure all servers that will run Resource Manager can connect to the MetaFrame XP data store and that the data store is currently running. Resource Manager uses the data store to hold configuration information about the servers, applications, and users.

MDAC 2.51, SP1 must be installed on NT Terminal Server Edition prior to installing MetaFrame XP and Resource Manager.

Installing Resource Manager

Installing Resource Manager is a snap. Once you have installed the operating system and MetaFrame XP, you are ready to install Resource Manager. Don't forget to activate your MetaFrame XP*e* license because it is required before you can use some of Resource Manager's features. Rinse and repeat on each server you plan on monitoring.

1. Make sure your system has the required resources to run Resource Manager. This should not be a concern if your system met the required resources for the operating system, Terminal Services, and MetaFrame XP.

2. Make certain all users have logged off and that all applications are closed.

3. Place the Citrix System Monitoring and Analysis CD-ROM in the CD-ROM drive. If your CD-ROM drive supports auto-play, the splash screen will appear shortly. If not, type **d:\autorun.exe** to start the program.

4. Click Citrix Resource Manager Setup once.

5. If prompted, restart the server after the installation.

A valid, activated MetaFrame XPe license is required before you can use some of the features of Resource Manager.

The Citrix Management Console The Citrix Management Console (CMC) is a centralized management facility that can be used to manage your server or farm. During installation, Resource Manager is integrated into the Citrix Management Console. To open the Citrix Management Console, choose Start, Programs | Citrix | Citrix Management Console. Double-click to open the CMC and log in. (MetaFrame XP allows you to specify MetaFrame administrators, as opposed to Windows administrators.) The CMC screen is divided into two panes. The left pane displays a list of components in the server farm. The right pane displays the information about the item selected in the left pane (Figure 13-9.)

Using Resource Manager

To access real-time information about the servers in a farm, click Servers in the left pane and select the server you want to monitor. In the right pane, click the Resource Manager tab to display the current status of all the servers currently monitored (Figure 13-10). You can also display a real-time list of all the components currently in an alarm state by clicking Watcher Window. The Watcher Window can remain visible on the desktop while the CMC is open to notify you of any problems. Components running normally will not be shown in the Watcher Window. To view the Resource Manager Server Log, right-click a server and select Resource Manager Server Log or press CTRL-ALT-B.

FIGURE 13-9	
The Citrix Management Console	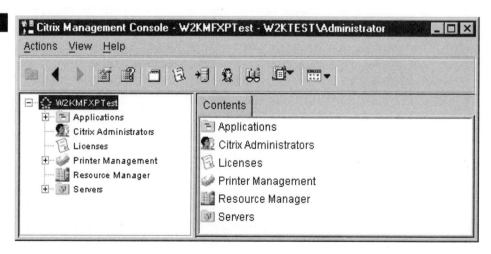

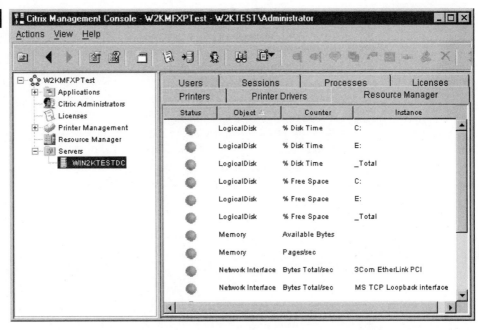

FIGURE 13-10

Real-time status

If you have applications with limited licenses, you may want to configure Resource Manager to monitor them. You can add limits to the count metric that will warn if a defined number of instances is approaching or generate an alarm if the limit number has been exceeded. To add applications for Resource Manager to monitor:

1. Right-click the Applications folder in the CMC.

2. From the menu, select New Resource Manager Application (Figure 13-11). The Resource Manager Application Wizard will guide you through adding the application.

3. Your application will now be listed under the Application folder in the left pane.

4. Highlight the Application folder in the left pane, then double-click the application in the right pane. You should see only the application in question under the Resource Manager tab.

5. Right-click the application and select Add/Remove Metrics.

6. The next screen allows you to select Count as your metric and gives you the option to remove all metrics or apply to other applications. If you have added other applications, you can add the metric to them at this time as well. Click OK to finish. Now that you have added your metric, it should be listed under the Counter column.

7. To set the number of applications allowed to run, right-click the application again and select Properties. From this screen, you can set limits for the number of instances of the application running at the same time. Settings can be configured for Yellow, Red, and what to do once the limit has been reached, such as e-mailing the administrator. This screen also allows you how to apply these settings to other applications being monitored. Click OK to finish.

Once you have configured the applications, click the Applications folder in the left pane and select Resource Manager in the right pane. Your applications should now be listed with a colored indicator next to them. If an application's instances exceed the limits you placed on them, the indicators will change colors (Figure 13-12).

Resource Manager uses metrics or conditions that relate to each component and application running on your server or within your farm. The metrics have threshold variables and when the threshold for a given component has been reached, Resource Manager will produce an alert and can even notify the administrator. Colored

FIGURE 13-11

Adding applications to Resource Manager

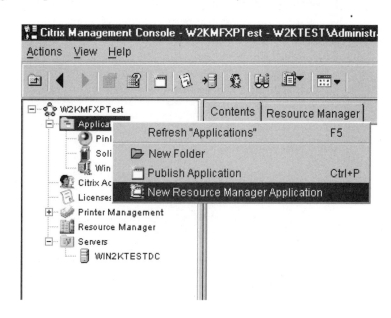

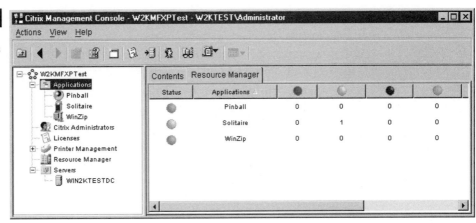

FIGURE 13-12

Application status

indicators are used to display the status of each monitored component. The status
indicator colors are shown in Table 13-6.

Metrics   Resource Manager defines a default set of metrics that are specific to
your server and operating system. Alarm thresholds are also defined for the metrics
that will alert you to potential problems. There are default metrics for Microsoft
Windows NT Terminal Server Edition and for the Windows 2000 Server family.
This is all very similar to the terminology used for Windows Performance Monitor!
The metrics can be fine-tuned, changed, added, or removed to better fit your

TABLE 13-6   Status Indicator Colors

Indicator Color	Meaning
Green	Indicates Normal Operation.
Yellow	Indicates a potential problem that may need further analysis. Indicates an alarm state.
Red	Indicates a problem that requires attention. Indicates an alarm state.
Blue	The metric is inactive and needs to be configured.
Black	The metric is set to "sleep" (an indefinite pause) and is not currently being monitored.
Gray	The metric is set to "snooze" (a timed pause) and is not currently being monitored.

environment. Once you get accustomed to what is normal for your server farm, you can adjust the metrics as needed.

Within a server farm, one server acts as the Farm Metric Server and interprets the metrics for the entire farm. The Farm Metric Server is the first server Resource Manager was installed on but can be changed to any other server in the Farm that has Resource Manager installed. If for some reason the Farm Metric Server is not available, a backup server will take its place until it is operational again.

A metric consists of objects, instances, and counters. As we learned in the preceding section, objects are server components that possess a set of measurable properties; they are physical or logical server resources. The default set of metrics for a Windows 2000 server and their associated counters are

- Network Interface
- Processors
- Memory
- Logical Disks
- System
- Page File
- Terminal Services

It's a good idea to keep an eye on these metrics and know what the norm is for your server or farm. For management and users to buy into server-based computing, they must feel as if they are running their applications from their own desktop machine. Be sure you know what the default metrics are, what they monitor and what it is they could be telling you about your server.

- The default metric for Network Interface is Bytes Total/sec. This metric monitors the network traffic coming into and from the server. A high metric counter can mean that there are too many user sessions connected for the network interface card to handle.

- There are two metrics for Processor, %Interrupt Time and %Processor Time. A high count for %Interrupt Time means your system is spending an inordinate amount of time processing interrupts rather than processing requests. This can be indicative of hardware problems or a very busy server. If the %Processor Time count is high, it could also mean that your server is too busy or it could be a runaway or hung program. To find out if it is a program or process causing the problem, use the Current Process report.

- Memory has one default metric: Available Bytes. A low reading here can mean that your system is short on memory and accessing the page file too often. This condition is called "thrashing." If this is the case, disk usage and paging counters will also be high. It could also mean that the system is overloaded, there are too many applications running that consume large amounts of memory, or an application or process is as fault.

- The metrics for Logical disk are %Disk Time and %Free Space. %Disk Time monitors disk usage and indicates how busy a disk is. This could be the result of too little physical memory, an application or process that makes frequent and extensive use of the disk. A value of 100% may indicate that the disk is too slow to support the number of requests it receives. If the server is running out of disk space, the %Free Space counter will be low. This usually indicates that larger or additional disks are required.

- The System metric monitors Context Switches/sec. A high reading means that too many processes are competing for processor time. To resolve this issue, you might consider adding additional or faster processors.

- The Page File metric is %Usage and a high reading will usually indicate that the page file is too small.

- The Terminal Services metric monitors Active and Inactive sessions and can indicate that there are too many users either logged in using resources, or disconnected and using resources. Even though a session is disconnected, it is still consuming server resources. It's a good idea to limit the time a session can be in the disconnected state.

exam
ⓦatch

Disk thrashing is an indication that there is not enough physical memory and the page file is being accessed frequently. The metric to watch is: Memory/ Available Bytes.

Resource Manager Reports

Resource Manager provides a variety of reports that can be used to examine the data reported by your server or farm. As shown in Figure 13-13, reports can be based on real-time system information or snapshots, current processes, and current users. The

FIGURE 13-13

Resource
Manager reports

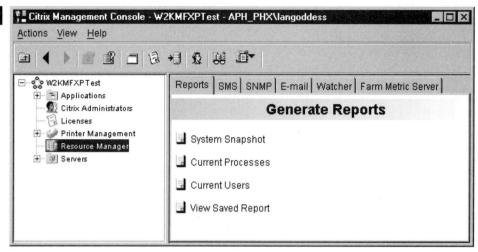

information can be used for historical reference, baselines, usage billing, to justify
future resource purchases or any number of other instances.

The System Snapshot allows you to pinpoint a moment in time and examine
the status of the server at that very moment. This can prove extremely useful for
troubleshooting problems that occurred at a time when you were not available.
Say for instance you are in a meeting when a problem occurs on the server. The
Jr. Administrator manages to handle the situation but has no idea what caused the
problem. You can use the System Snapshot to run a report for the time the problem
occurred, and use it to diagnose the problem. Data is gathered and stored every 15
seconds by default and kept for 48 hours. The arrow buttons under Time of Current
View, allow you to scroll backward and forward in time in 15 second intervals
(Figure 13-14).

Current Process can produce reports based on the applications and processes
running on servers within the farm. You might use this report if a process currently
running has entered into an alarm state.

Current Users produces reports on user and application activity. A user activity
report can be helpful in determining how many sessions a user has open and which
applications are being run by the user. The report also provides information on
when their session began, how long it's been established, the number of processes
running and the number of instances of each.

The last option on the Reports screen is View Saved Report. This option allows
you to retrieve and view saved reports.

FIGURE 13-14

A System
Snapshot report

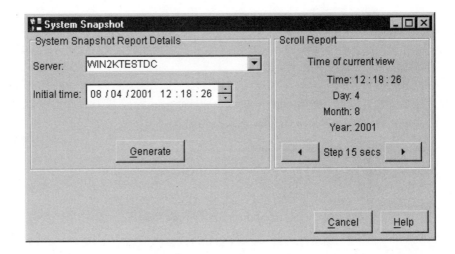

Now that you've been introduced to Resource Manager, try your hand at
Exercise 13-3 that follows. Remember, hands-on experience is extremely important
in the real world. (I'm assuming you have a MetaFrame XP*e* test server to practice
on. If you don't, it would behoove you to locate or build one to practice on.)

EXERCISE 13-3

CertCam 13-3

Creating Reports with Resource Manager

1. Log in as an administrator.

2. If the Citrix Administration bar is on the desktop, use the last icon at the
   bottom to open Citrix Management Console. If not, choose Start | Programs
   | Citrix | Citrix Management Console.

3. Log in as a MetaFrame XP administrator.

4. From the Citrix Management Console, click Resource Manager in the left
   pane. In the right pane, make sure the Reports tab is selected. You should
   see the report options available, as shown previously in Figure 13-13.

5. Select Current Users. The Report Details screen (Figure 13-14) allows you
   to choose the server to gather the data from and the individual user or all
   users to report on.

6. Select the server you are currently monitoring.

7. Select All Users.

8. Click Generate.

The report will be generated using an HTML (Hypertext Markup Language) form and will display

- The server name
- The date and time the report was run
- The number of open sessions
- The number of active processes
- The names of the users currently logged in
- The session name
- The protocol being used
- The session's start date and time
- The duration of the session
- The process count for each user
- The active process and instances of each for each user

From within the report itself, you are also given the option to save the report, either as an HTML file or as a comma-separated values (CSV) file that can be imported into a spreadsheet.

Sending Alerts   Resource Manager can be configured to sent alert messages to designated administrators when the status of a monitored component changes, either to an alarm state or back to normal operating status. Each monitored component can be individually configured to trigger an alert and notify the appropriate person. The alerts can be sent in the following ways:

- Short Message Service (SMS) text messages to cell phones or pagers
- Simple Network Management Protocol (SNMP) messaging
- E-mail messages

To configure the alerts, highlight Resource Manager from within the Citrix Management Console and select the type of alert you want to configure from the right pane.

And now, it's time for another pop quiz. Again, try not to read the answers before you've attempted to answer each question on your own.

SCENARIO & SOLUTION

Where is Resource Manager located?	Resource Manager is located within the Citrix Management Console.
What types of things can Resource Manager monitor?	Resource Manager can monitor hard disks, logical disks, processors, memory, network interfaces, Terminal Services, user sessions, application usage, page files usage, and the system.
What are metrics as used in Resource Manager?	Metrics are the measurable units that Resource Manager monitors. Each component or object has a set of metrics. Each metric has a definable set of thresholds or limits that describe normal operation.
How can servers be monitored in real time?	Either by clicking Servers in the left pane of the CMC or by selecting the Watcher Window tab from Resource Manager.
Why would you want to add and monitor specific applications?	Applications can be added to Resource Manager and a metric for Count enabled. You would do this if you wanted to keep track of how many instances of the application were running at one time. A reason for doing so could be that there are limited licenses available.
What type of reports does Resource Manager provide?	System Snapshots, Current Processes, and Current Users.

Citrix Network Manager

Citrix Network Manager works with third-party SNMP consoles to provide systems management capabilities to MetaFrame XP servers. The Network Manager consists of an SNMP agent and plug-ins that support HP OpenView and Tivoli NetView. With the SNMP console, it is possible to remotely manage your MetaFrame XP*e* servers using the same network management package that may be in use elsewhere on your network. With Network Manager and your third-party SNMP console of choice, you can shut down and restart MetaFrame XP*e* servers, disconnect, log off, and send messages to active session on a MetaFrame XP*e* server, as well as terminal processes running on MetaFrame XP*e* servers. If these all sound like things you can accomplish with MetaFrame XP*e*, you're right! MetaFrame XP*e* can perform many of the same functions third-party Network Management products do, but only for MetaFrame servers. If your environment requires a solution that will work for all the various servers in the network, Citrix Network Manager can help.

exam
ⓦatch

Citrix Network Manager is available only with Citrix MetaFrame XPe. It is not packaged with the base MetaFrame XP or XPa products.

System Requirements

Like Citrix Resource Manager, Citrix Network Manager comes only with Citrix MetaFrame XP*e*. It does not come with the base MetaFrame XP or XP*a* license and it cannot be purchased separately. The requirements for Network Manager are the same as those for MetaFrame XP*e* with the addition of

- Microsoft SNMP services
- Tivoli NetView 5.1.2 or later
- HP OpenView Network Node Manager 6.1 or later

exam
ⓦatch

Citrix Network Manager can be used with Tivoli NetView 5.1.2 or later or with HP OpenView Network Node Manager 6.1 or later.

Installing Network Manager

As mentioned earlier, Microsoft SNMP services must be installed prior to installing Network Manager. The SNMP services are not installed by default on either Windows NT 4.0 or Windows 2000. To install SNMP:

1. Exit all open applications.
2. Open the Control Panel and select Add/Remove Programs.
3. Select Add/Remove Windows Components.
4. Click Management and Monitoring Tools and then click Details.

5. Select Simple Network Management Protocol and then click OK.

6. Reapply any installed service packs.

After SNMP has been installed, you are ready to install the Citrix Network Manager plug-ins. To install the plug-ins:

1. Exit all applications.

2. Load the Network Manager CD-ROM. If your CD-ROM drive supports 3.autorun, the Network Manager splash screen will appear. If not, go to Start, choose Run and type **d:\autorun.exe** to start the installation.

3. Once the splash screen has appeared, select the plug-in you wish to install, either HP OpenView or Tivoli NetView.

4. Follow the on-screen prompts to complete the installation.

on the **job**

If you are running the SNMP management console on a computer other than the MetaFrame XPe server, it is a good idea to install the Citrix Management Console on that computer as well because it provides other management capabilities not found in Network Manager.

Troubleshooting Network Monitor

Network Monitor or NetMon is a network diagnostic tool provided by Windows NT and Windows 2000. The version that comes with NT and Windows 2000 is the lite version, the full version is part of Microsoft Systems Manager Server (SMS). Network Monitor is used to monitor network traffic and troubleshoot network-related events, such as a server that is sending or receiving an inordinate amount of traffic, misconfigured workstations, printers, and servers.

Network Monitor provides a graphical display of local area network statistics such as

- The source address of the computer sending the packet
- The destination address of the computer receiving the packet
- The protocols used to send the packets
- A portion of the data being sent

Network Monitor is able to do all this by collecting or capturing data on the frames going across the network. The data is then stored in a capture buffer, which is a reserved area of memory. Once the data has been captured, it can be saved to a text or capture file for later examination.

It's a good idea to check your capture buffer before capturing data. The default maximum size for Windows 2000 is 1GB. NT's default maximum is 8MB less than the total amount of RAM installed on the system. To check or set the buffer size, go to the Capture menu and select Buffer Settings.

If you know what type of frame you are looking for, Network Monitor can filter the frames and collect information only on the type you have specified. If you were interested in seeing only data about a particular protocol, you could enable filtering and capture only those specified. A real life situation might be to locate workstations that have unnecessary protocols installed or to look at the amount of ICA traffic on the network. Network Monitor can help you locate network bottlenecks, servers that are receiving too many requests and even Internet browsing traffic. It is another must-have tool for your administrator toolkit.

Network Monitor can be used to locate servers on the network that are sending or receiving an inordinate amount of data. It can also be used to track down heavy Internet browsing and unnecessary protocols.

System Requirements

Network Monitor requires a network interface card that supports promiscuous mode. If you are running Network Monitor on a remote computer, the local machine's network card does not need to support promiscuous mode.

Installing Network Monitor

To install Network Monitor:

1. Exit all open applications

2. Open the Control Panel and select Add/Remove Programs.

3. Select Add/Remove Windows Components.

4. Click Management and Monitoring Tools and click Details.

5. Select Network Monitor and click OK.

Capturing Traffic

To start Network Monitor, go to Start, select Programs | Administrative Tools | Network Monitor. If you have more than one network card installed on your machine, you will need to select a network to enable the Capture menu. If you have only one network card installed, the Capture menu will already be enabled. To begin capturing network data, select Start from the Capture drop-down menu. Network Monitor will immediately begin capturing frames and will continue until you stop the capture or the capture buffer fills up. To stop the capture, select Stop from the Capture menu. Figure 13-15 shows the Network Monitor interface. To save the captured data, click File | Save As.

FIGURE 13-15

Network
Monitor

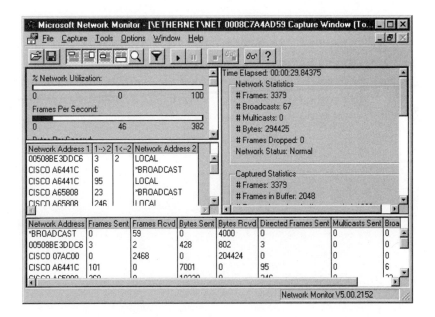

CERTIFICATION SUMMARY

Whew! So many tools, so little time! But seriously, this chapter has covered several tools that every administrator needs to know about and have in their toolkits. Each topic was covered only briefly, but there is so much more information on them to be had. If you're looking for more, try going to the vendor's Web site (Microsoft and Citrix both have a wealth of information on their sites. Another source of information is the applications Help menu. They're doing so much more with them these days. Remember, troubleshooting is a tough job, but one of the most prized in the IT industry. It doesn't hurt to have a variety of tools handy to make the job easier. Good Luck with your exam!

✓ TWO-MINUTE DRILL

Event Viewer and System Information

- ❑ The Event Viewer can be used to monitor, detect, and troubleshoot events that take place on a server.

- ❑ The Event Log can be managed through the associated property sheets. Properties include maximum log size, overwrite/clear log manually, and filtering.

- ❑ The System Information Tools are located in the Microsoft Management Console and contains information about the server hardware and software that can be monitored and viewed but not modified.

- ❑ The System Summary provides information about the system's basic configuration, including OS version, BIOS version, installed/available memory, and page file size.

- ❑ The information contained in the System Information Tool can be saved to a text or .inf file by right-clicking the desired folder and selecting Save As.

- ❑ The Event ID, Source, and Description are important because they can point you to the component that reported the event and they can be used to locate information in the Microsoft and Citrix Knowledge Bases.

- ❑ In Windows 2000, ERD disks can be created from the Backup utility located under Accessories | System Tools. Windows 2000 ERDs no longer include the registry hives, but can be useful when you cannot boot your system.

- ❑ A baseline can help to determine how well a system is performing and help spot potential problems or bottlenecks before they happen.

- ❑ Performance Monitor and Resource Manager are tools that can be used to monitor and develop a baseline for your system.

Managing Resource and Citrix Network Manager and Troubleshooting Network Monitor

- ❑ Citrix Resource Manager is not included with the base Citrix MetaFrame XP license. Resource Manager cannot be purchased separately; you must purchase MetaFrame XP*e*.

- ❑ Resource Manager is a monitoring tool specifically designed for MetaFrame XP servers.

- ❑ If installing Resource Manager on a Windows 4.0 Terminal Server Edition server, MDAC 2.51, SP1 must be installed prior to installing MetaFrame XP and Resource Manager.

- ❑ Resource Manager is located within the Citrix Management Console.

- ❑ Network Manager is not included with the base MetaFrame XP license. It can only be obtained when purchasing MetaFrame XP*e*.

- ❑ Network Manager works with third-party SNMP consoles. It consists of an SNMP agent and plug-ins for the third-party management application.

- ❑ Network Manager works with HP OpenView Network Node Manager, version 6.1 or later, as well as Tivoli NetView 5.1.2 or later

- ❑ SNMP services must be installed prior to installing Network Manager.

- ❑ Network Monitor is included with Windows NT and Windows 2000 and can be used to monitor and troubleshoot network problems such as unnecessary protocols, misconfigured workstations, excessive traffic to/from servers, or heavy Internet browsing.

SELF TEST

The following questions will help you measure your understanding of the material presented in this chapter. Read all the choices carefully as there may be more than one correct answer. Choose all correct answers for each question.

Using Event Viewer and System Information

1. In the Event Viewer, what three pieces of information about an event are key in locating the cause and resolution of a problem?

   A. Date, Time, and Type

   B. Username, Computer Name, and Source

   C. Source, Event ID, and Description

   D. Time, Computer Name, and Type

2. What five types of events are recorded to the event logs?

   A. Information, Warning, Error, Successful Audits, and Failed Audits

   B. Application, Security, System, Directory Service, and File Replication

   C. Source, ID, Description, Username, and Computer Name

   D. Daily, Weekly, Monthly, and Yearly

3. What does Citrix recommend the Event Log's maximum size be set to?

   A. 512KB

   B. 256KB

   C. 1024KB

   D. 2GB

4. How can you use the Event Viewer to view the Event Logs on a remote system?

   A. Connect using RAS and open the Event Viewer on the remote system.

   B. Right-click Event Viewer (local) and select Connect To Another Computer.

   C. Open the Event Viewer and from the Action drop-down menu, select Connect to a remote computer.

   D. Add the remote computers you wish to monitor to the Event Viewer (local) tree.

5. Jack has called his software vendor support line for help in troubleshooting an error he's receiving. The support technician wants to know what type of system Jack is using, the BIOS version, OS build, installed RAM, and other basic system configuration information. What is the best way Jack can quickly get this information to the support tech?

   A. Locate the documentation that came with his system and fax it to the technician.

   B. Right-click System Summary in Information Tools. Save the information to a text file and e-mail it to the tech.

   C. Quickly make a list of all the information the tech wants; then check system documentation and configuration files for the answers. Type this into an e-mail and send it to the tech.

   D. Promise the tech the information will be forthcoming and assign the task to your Jr. Administrator.

6. The System Information Tool can be used to

   A. Modify or add a new component to your system

   B. Display system configuration settings

   C. Remove or disable device drivers

   D. Connect to another computer

7. Diane has installed a new USB port on her computer but it doesn't appear to be functioning. Where can she look to see if there's a problem with the new port? (Select all that apply.)

   A. The Event Viewer

   B. System Information | Hardware Resources | Conflicts | Sharing

   C. Device Manager

   D. Performance Monitor

8. Scott, the new Jr. Administrator, has been monitoring the Event Logs on the Sales server farm. For several days now an event warning has been logged that doesn't make any sense to him. It doesn't seem to point to a particular system component. He's worried that it could escalate and become a real problem if he doesn't discover what is causing it. What can Scott do to find out what the event means?

   A. Call the Sr. Administrator who is away on vacation and ask for assistance.

   B. Keep monitoring the event and hope that nothing further happens before the Sr. Administrator gets back.

C. Check the Microsoft and Citrix Knowledge Bases for any reference to the Event ID and description.

D. Wait until someone calls to complain of a problem that is occurring around the same time.

9. How can you display all the pertinent details about a device including driver version, IRQs, and I/O?

A. Open Device Manager and double-click the device.

B. Open System Information and go to the Component Folder. Right-click the device to view its property sheet.

C. Locate the device's documentation.

D. Use Explorer to navigate to the device's software installation folder. Look for .txt or .inf files and read through them.

10. In Windows 2000, where can the environmental variables be found?

A. In the Control Panel under System.

B. Under Administrative Tools/System.

C. In System Information Tools under the Software Environment Folder.

D. In Start | Programs | Accessories | System Tools.

Managing Resource and Citrix Network Manager and Troubleshooting Network Monitor

11. What are two tools included with Windows 2000 Server and MetaFrame XP*e* that can facilitate developing a system baseline?

A. Event Viewer and System Information Tool

B. System Information Tool and Connection Manager

C. Citrix Resource Manager and Performance Monitor

D. Citrix Load Manager and Citrix Resource Manager

12. A server in the server farm Maurice manages has been experiencing some performance problems lately and he has decided to use Resource Manager to help him find out why. He suspects that there may be a hardware problem or a faulty device driver. What object and associated metric can he monitor to confirm this?

A. Maurice should monitor the Network Interface Bytes Total/sec.

B. The Terminal Services, Active/Inactive Sessions will provide the information needed.

    C. The problem is most likely a processor problem, so Maurice should check the %Processor Time metric.

    D. Because he suspects it is a hardware or device driver problem, Maurice should monitor the Processor %Interrupt Time metric.

13. Citrix Resource Manager is included in which base MetaFrame license?

    A. MetaFrame XP

    B. MetaFrame 1.8 for Windows 2000

    C. MetaFrame XP*a*

    D. MetaFrame XP*e*

14. Randy has decided to install Citrix Network Manager on his MetaFrame XP*e* server. He has made sure that the hardware exceeds the necessary minimums for Windows 2000 and MetaFrame XP*e* and he has applied all the necessary service packs and hotfixes. In preparation for the install, Randy logs in as Administrator and makes sure there are no applications running or users connected to the server. He places the Network Manager disc in the CD-ROM drive, uses Add/Remove Programs for the install, and selects the Tivoli NetView plug-in. The installation begins, but ends abruptly with an error message. What could be wrong?

    A. Randy has forgotten to log in as Administrator.

    B. He does not have Tivoli NetView installed on the server.

    C. He has not installed SNMP services.

    D. You cannot install Network Manager on a MetaFrame XP*e* server.

15. What needs to be installed on Windows NT 4.0 Terminal Server Edition prior to installing Resource Manager?

    A. The SNMP services

    B. The Microsoft Access runtime version

    C. MDAC 2.51, SP1

    D. MetaFrame 1.8.

16. Susan has been monitoring her server farm with Resource Manager for several weeks now. Everything has been good so far; all the indicators are green for her servers. Next week, due to corporate reorganizing, her location will house another small division and its employees. The new employees will be connecting to her server farm and she's not sure whether she has enough resources on her servers to accommodate the new users. What objects and metrics can she monitor in Resource Manager to help her decide? (Select all that apply.)

A. Network Interface, Bytes Total/sec

B. Processor, %Interrupt Time

C. Processor, %Processor Time

D. System, Context Switches/sec

17. Diane wants to find out what applications her users are running most often and how many instances of each they are running. How can this be accomplished?

A. Diane should create an online survey and distribute it to all her users.

B. Diane should use Resource Manager to produce Current User Reports. The reports will display the users, the applications they are running, and the number of instances of each that are running and who is running them.

C. Diane should use Network Monitor to trace network packets to see who is running the applications.

D. Diane should use System Information Tool to monitor Applications.

18. Citrix Network Manager can use the SNMP consoles of which two third-party management solutions? (Select all that apply.)

A. Tivoli NetView 5.1.2 or later

B. Resource Management Services 1.0b

C. HP OpenView Network Node Manager 6.1 or later

D. Bline Extra Management Services

19. John has been noticing that his network slows to a crawl during the afternoon. He's used Resource Manager to monitor the Network Interface metric and found there is usually one server that appears to be generating and receiving a lot of network activity, but it is seldom the same server from day to day. What could be the problem and how can John track it to its source? (Select the best answer.)

A. John's servers are load-balanced, that would explain why it is never the same server producing the alerts in Resource Manager. A high count for Network Interface, Bytes Total/sec could indicate the server is engaging in a high amount of activity. A likely reason could be that a user is either up/downloading files from the Internet or playing Internet online games. John can run Network Monitor and enable filtering on the Internet proxy server if this is true. He can then trace the packets back to the originating workstation and user.

B. John suspects that a user is playing online Internet games every afternoon. The reason it is seldom on the same server is because the user is attempting to escape detection by logging in to a different server each day. John will use Resource Manager to run Current User reports to discover who it is.

C. John has assembled a task force that will covertly visit each user's desk during the afternoon hours. The user in question will not know who the spies are and will not take precautions to prevent detection.

D. The user has been logging in to a different server each day in an attempt to prevent detection. John suspects that the reason has something to do with the Internet and will enable filtering in Network Monitor to trace packets to and from the Internet proxy server.

20. What type of network interface card does Network Monitor require to function?

A. One that can run in Liberal mode

B. One that can run in Promiscuous mode

C. One that runs extremely fast

D. One that can work with another NIC in tandem

LAB QUESTION

This exercise is designed to test your knowledge of monitoring and troubleshooting MetaFrame XP.

You are a consultant with XYZ Consulting Services. You've been sent out on a job to assist a company in troubleshooting their Windows 2000 Advanced Server/MetaFrame XP*e* server farm. The administrators on site tell you they have followed a step-by-step process when planning, testing, and implementing the server farm. They cannot understand why there are so many performance problems.

The administrators inform you there has only been one change in their environment since they originally implemented the server farm: the addition of several new users. They go on to say that the new users were the source of many complaints about applications loading slowly, and they only ran one specific application, which had just recently been installed. As for when the complaints started, some users had been complaining about slow logons since before the new users arrived.

The administrators on site have been monitoring the servers using System Information Tool, Event Viewer but have not discovered what the problem is. There are no errors in the Event Log and no installed devices appear to be faulty. They have kept a log of the complaints they have been receiving over the last week. It is your job to track down what their problem(s) may be.

As you read through the log, you see the following items:

- Monday, users complaining of slow logons and applications loading slowly.

- Tuesday, user logons still slow but applications loading a little faster.

- Wednesday, a third of the users are out of the office for a seminar and those left behind haven't complained too much about applications loading slowly, but logging on is still slow. A few times during the day the network just crept along.

- Thursday, logons still slow, applications loading slowly again, but network seems to be faster today.

- Friday, logons still slow, applications loading a bit faster, especially as the day progressed. The network appeared to be okay.

SELF TEST ANSWERS

Using Event Viewer and System Information

1. ☑ C is the correct answer. The Source can lead you to the component that reported the event, while the Event ID and Description will help you track down the appropriate Knowledge Base article for a resolution or explanation.

   ☒ Answers **A, B,** and **D** are all types of information found on the Event Properties sheet, but are not as important in the troubleshooting process as the items in answer **C**.

2. ☑ **A.** The five types of events recorded in the event logs are Information, Warning, Error, Successful, and Failed Audits.

   ☒ **B** lists the types of logs that Event Viewer can monitor, while answer **C** provides only one of the correct answers. **D** is totally fictitious.

3. ☑ **C.** Citrix recommends setting the Event Log's maximum size to 1024KB and to overwrite as needed.

   ☒ **A** is the default log size on Windows 2000, **B** is smaller than the default size and would fill up quickly in most environments, and **D** is overkill, no Event Log should ever get that big.

4. ☑ **B.** As long as the remote workstation or server has an account in the domain, or is in a trusted domain and is currently on the network, you can right-click Event Viewer (local) and select Connect To Another Computer.

   ☒ **A** is possible, but not the best choice. **C** is incorrect because there is no option to Connect To Another Computer within the Action drop-down menu. **D** is incorrect because you cannot add items to the Event Viewer (local) tree.

5. ☑ **B** is the correct answer. The System Summary provides the basic system configuration information the tech is looking for, and it's the quickest, most accurate way to provide it.

   ☒ **A** is incorrect because the original system documentation may not provide all the details the tech needs and it most likely will not be up-to-date. **C** is possible but definitely not the quickest and easiest way to get things done. **D** is also possible if Jack doesn't need a resolution to his problem any time soon.

6. ☑ **B** is correct. The System Information Tool can only be used to display the configuration settings because it is read-only.

   ☒ **A** is incorrect because you cannot add or modify settings in the System Information Tool. These tasks can be performed in Device Manager. **C** is also incorrect for the same reason; use the Device Manager to uninstall or disable device drivers. **D** is also false. You cannot connect to another computer through the System Information Tools, but you can through System Tools.

7. ☑   **A, B,** and **C** are all correct. Diane can check the Event Viewer to see if an error report has been logged. She can also check for IRQ conflicts under System Information | Hardware Resources | Conflicts | Sharing, and **C** is correct because a device that isn't functioning properly will also show up in the Device Manager displayed with a warning or error symbol.

☒   **D** is incorrect because Diane can look at the Event Viewer, the System Information | Hardware Resources | Conflicts | Sharing, and the Device Manger, but not the Performance Monitor, to determine if there's a problem with the new port.

8. ☑   **C** is the best answer. Even if there is no source that points to a particular device or component, the Event ID and/or the description of the event can usually locate a Knowledge Base article that will explain the event.

☒   While **A** is a possibility, it wouldn't look good for Scott, and the Sr. Administrator probably wouldn't like being called off the beach. **B** is also a possibility. Some warnings are innocuous and never really turn into a problem, but there's always the chance that it might. It's better to be safe than sorry. **D** is also a possibility but again, it wouldn't be in Scott's favor to wait until someone complains. Finding the answer before a problem occurs could make him the hero.

9. ☑   **B.** The Components folder lists all the components that may or may not be installed on your system. If you right-click an installed component, it will open its Property Sheet which provides all the pertinent details.

☒   **A** is incorrect because the key word here was "display." From within the Device Manager, you can install, uninstall, and modify settings for a device. **C** is incorrect because the original documentation may not be the current driver version. **D** is also incorrect as the driver installation may not have created a folder.

10. ☑   **C** is correct. The Software Environment folder lists the environmental variables, network connections, running task, and other useful information.

☒   **A** is correct for Windows NT, but incorrect for Windows 2000. **B** is also incorrect. Environmental variables are not located in the Administrative Tools folder. Although there are some useful utilities under Accessories | System Tools, environmental variables is not one of them.

Managing Resource and Citrix Network Manager and Troubleshooting Network Monitor

11. ☑   **C.** Both Citrix Resource Manager and Microsoft's Performance Monitor can facilitate developing a system baseline. Resource Manager was created specifically for MetaFrame XP and is more server-base aware.

☒ **A** is incorrect because although both the Event Viewer and System Information Tool are good tools for monitoring and troubleshooting, they have no real-time or historical monitoring capabilities. **B** is also incorrect because the Citrix Connection Manager has nothing to do with performance monitoring and System Information Tool does not provide real-time or historical information. **D** is partially correct. Resource Manager could help, but the Citrix Load Manager does not monitor system performance or provide real-time or historical information.

12. ☑ **D.** The Processor %Interrupt Time metric, if consistently high, can mean that there is a hardware problem or a faulty device.
☒ **A** is incorrect because the Network Interface Bytes Total/sec monitors the network activity the server is generating and receiving. **B** is incorrect because the Terminal Services Active/ Inactive Sessions pertains to users who are currently logged in and either active or disconnected. **C** is close—it is most likely a processor problem, but %Processor Time implies there are too many users on the server or that a rogue program is running.

13. ☑ **D** is correct. Citrix Resource Manager is available only with MetaFrame XP*e* and it cannot be purchased separately.
☒ **A** is incorrect because MetaFrame XP is the basic solution and does not include Resource Manager. **B** is also incorrect because MetaFrame 1.8 did not include Resource Manager. However, Resource Management Services (RMS) could be purchased separately. **C** is also incorrect. Resource Manager is only available with MetaFrame XP*e*.

14. ☑ **C.** He has forgotten to install SNMP services on the server.
☒ **A** is incorrect because Randy did log in as Administrator. **B** is also incorrect because Tivoli NetView does not need to be installed on the server, only the plug-in needs to be installed. **D** is incorrect as well because you can install Network Manager on a MetaFrame XP*e* server.

15. ☑ **C** is the correct answer. MDAC 2.51, SP1 must be installed prior to installing MetaFrame XP*e* or Resource Manager.
☒ **A** is incorrect. SNMP services do not need to be installed to run Resource Manager. **B** is incorrect because Resource Manager installs the runtime version of Access automatically. **D** is also incorrect because MetaFrame 1.8 does not need to be installed.

16. ☑ **A, B, C,** and **D.** Network Interface, Bytes Total/sec can tell her if her servers are generating or receiving high levels of activity. This could mean there are too many users connecting at one time. If Processors, %Processor Time is consistently high, it could indicate there are too many users on the system, while System, Context Switches/sec can indicate that there are too many users on the system competing for processing time. **B** is also correct because the Processor, Interrupt Time can indicate the server is too busy.

17. ☑ **B** is the correct answer. Diane should use Resource Manager Current User reports to monitor the users, applications, and instances.

☒ **A** is not the correct answer, but if Diane had no other tools at her disposal, she could do this. **C** is incorrect because Network Monitor can trace packets based on protocol, sending/receiving computer, and various other variables but cannot tell her what applications are running or how many instances there are of each. **D** is also incorrect because System Information Tool can display installed applications but cannot provide information regarding who is using the applications or how many instances of each are running.

18. ☑ **A** and **C** are correct. Tivoli NetView 5.1.2 and HP OpenView Network Node Manager are both supported by Citrix Network Manager.

☒ **B** is incorrect as this is the earlier version of Resource Manager used with MetaFrame 1.8 and is not a third-party solution. **D** is incorrect, as it does not exist.

19. ☑ The best answer is **A**. John's servers could be load-balanced, which would explain why the activity is seldom on the same server. If Resource Manager is reporting high metrics on Network Interface, Total Bytes/sec, this is a good indication that the server or servers are generating and receiving high traffic. By using Network Monitor and enabling filtering on the Internet Proxy server, John can discover which workstation the packets are being sent to and from.

☒ **B** is incorrect because Resource Manager Current User reports will only show that the Internet browser is being used, not the games which are running on a server somewhere on the Internet. **C** is the Gestapo method and may work, but there really must be an easier way. **D** is partially correct, but a more plausible reason for the movement from server to server is load-balancing.

20. ☑ **B** is the correct answer. The network interface card used to run Network Monitor must support Promiscuous mode.

☒ **A** is incorrect as there is no Liberal mode. **C** is also incorrect, although it would be wise to use the interface cards that support 100MB transfer rates or more, and **D** is incorrect because it is not required that there be two network cards for Network Monitor to work. If there are two cards, you must select the network to be monitored before the console will open.

LAB ANSWER

If the onsite administrators were careful in their planning, testing, and implementation, it's likely that they sized their servers correctly; at least in the beginning. Here's a list of the clues you should have picked up on:

- The addition of several new users.

- The addition of a new application installed on the servers.

- The fact that the new users were among the users complaining about how slow their applications loaded, even though they only used the server farm for the one application.

- Slow logons had been happening since before the new users arrived, so it is most likely a separate problem

- The problem with the network also appears unrelated to the new users, but it could be significant that it occurred when many of the users were out of the office.

- Monday and Tuesday appear to be the days when users complain most about the programs loading slowly.

- Wednesday, when many users were out of the office, there were few complaints about applications.

- Friday, the application behavior was somewhat better.

- Slow logons appear to be the only consistent problem.

Plausible answers and resolutions:

Since the server farm is running MetaFrame XP*e*, you could ask to install Resource Manager on the servers to be monitored. With Resource Monitor, you can track application usage and system health. After running the Resource Manager for a few days, you should be able to see some trends. It is quite likely that the new users' application is a resource hog. It could also be possible that the additional users themselves are overloading the servers.

In Resource Monitor, check the Network Interface; Bytes Total/sec can tell you if the servers are receiving more traffic than the NIC can handle. If this is the case, it might be wise to add an additional server, but in this scenario, it doesn't sound necessary. Memory Available Bytes should also be monitored. This metric can tell you if your servers are low on memory. An application that is a resource hog could be causing the problem. If the Memory Available Bytes counter is high, the Disk Use and Page File %Usage will also be high because the system must use the Page File when supplementing its physical memory with virtual memory. If the counters are indeed high, adding additional RAM to the servers may solve the problem of applications loading slowly.

The slow logons were a gimme. This is typically the case when user profiles are out of control. Make sure that temp files, temporary Internet files, Favorites, user documents, Outlook .pst files, and any other data that can be saved elsewhere is. Logons are guaranteed to speed up dramatically once this is done.

As for the slow network response and faster application loading on Wednesday, a good guess would be that the users who were out of the office for the day included at least some of the new users running the memory-hungry application, while the other half were probably managers. Users left with no supervisor looking over their shoulder might take the opportunity to browse the Internet, play online games or download MP3s. This theory could be tested by employing Network Monitor the next time a similar situation occurred.

CITRIX® CERTIFIED ADMINISTRATOR

A

About the CD

his CD-ROM contains the CertTrainer software. CertTrainer comes complete with ExamSim, Skill Assessment tests, CertCam movie clips, the e-book (electronic version of the book), and Drive Time. CertTrainer is easy to install on any Windows 98/NT computer and must be installed to access these features. You may, however, browse the e-book directly from the CD without installation.

Installing CertTrainer

If your computer CD-ROM drive is configured to autorun, the CD-ROM will automatically start up upon inserting the disk. From the opening screen you may either browse the e-book or install CertTrainer by pressing the *Install Now* button. This will begin the installation process and create a program group named "CertTrainer." To run CertTrainer use START | PROGRAMS | CERTTRAINER.

System Requirements

CertTrainer requires Windows 98 or higher and Internet Explorer 4.0 or above and 600 MB of hard disk space for full installation.

CertTrainer

CertTrainer provides a complete review of each exam objective, organized by chapter. You should read each objective summary and make certain that you understand it before proceeding to the SkillAssessor. If you still need more practice on the concepts of any objective, use the "In Depth" button to link to the corresponding section from the Study Guide or use the CertCam button to view a short .AVI clip illustrating various exercises from within the chapter.

Once you have completed the review(s) and feel comfortable with the material, launch the SkillAssessor quiz to test your grasp of each objective. Once you complete the quiz, you will be presented with your score for that chapter.

ExamSim

As its name implies, ExamSim provides you with a simulation of the actual exam. The number of questions, the type of questions, and the time allowed are intended to be an accurate representation of the exam environment. You will see the screen shown in Figure A-1 when you are ready to begin ExamSim.

When you launch ExamSim, a digital clock display will appear in the upper left-hand corner of your screen. The clock will continue to count down to zero unless you choose to end the exam before the time expires.

There are three types of questions on the exam:

- **Multiple Choice**   These questions have a single correct answer that you indicate by selecting the appropriate check box.

- **Multiple-Multiple Choice**   These questions require more than one correct answer. Indicate each correct answer by selecting the appropriate check boxes.

FIGURE A-1

The ExamSim opening page

■ **Simulations** These questions simulate actual Windows 2000 menus and dialog boxes. After reading the question, you are required to select the appropriate settings to most accurately meet the objectives for that question.

Saving Scores as Cookies

Your ExamSim score is stored as a browser cookie. If you've configured your browser to accept cookies, your score will be stored in a file named *History*. If your browser is not configured to accept cookies, you cannot permanently save your scores. If you delete this History cookie, the scores will be deleted permanently.

E-Book

The entire contents of the Study Guide are provided in HTML form, as shown in Figure A-2. Although the files are optimized for Internet Explorer, they can also be viewed with other browsers, including Netscape.

FIGURE A-2

Study Guide contents in HTML format

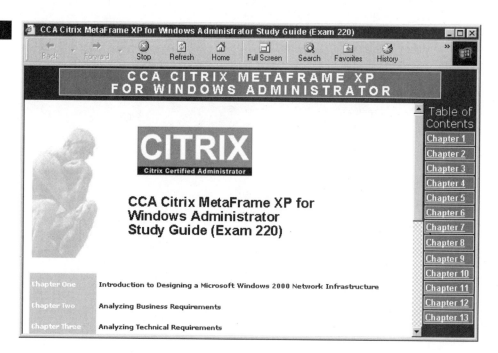

CertCam

CertCam .AVI clips provide detailed examples of key certification objectives. These clips walk you step-by-step through various system configurations and are narrated by Kevin Wing, CCEA, CCNA, MCSE. You can access the clips directly from the CertCam table of contents (shown in Figure A-3) or through the CertTrainer objectives.

The CertCam .AVI clips are recorded and produced using TechSmith's Camtasia Producer. Since .AVI clips can be very large, ExamSim uses TechSmith's special AVI Codec to compress the clips. The file named tsccvid.dll is copied to your Windows\System folder when you install CertTrainer. If the .AVI clip runs with audio but no video, you may need to reinstall the file from the CD-ROM. Browse to the "bin" folder and run TSCC.EXE.

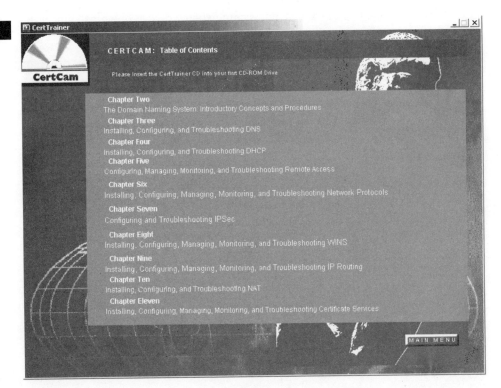

FIGURE A-3

The CertCam Table of Contents

DriveTime

DriveTime audio tracks will automatically play when you insert the CD-ROM into a standard CD-ROM player, such as the one in your car or stereo. There is one track for each chapter. These tracks provide you with certification summaries for each chapter and are the perfect way to study while commuting.

Help

A help file is provided through a help button on the main CertTrainer screen in the lower right hand corner.

Upgrading

A button is provided on the main ExamSim screen for upgrades. This button will take you to www.syngress.com, where you can download any available upgrades.

CITRIX® CERTIFIED ADMINISTRATOR

B

About the Web Site

A t Access.Globalknowledge, the premier online information source for IT professionals (http://access.globalknowledge.com), you'll enter a Global Knowledge information portal designed to inform, educate, and update visitors on issues regarding IT and IT education.

Get *What* You Want *When* You Want It

At the Access.Globalknowledge site, you can

- Choose personalized technology articles related to your interests. Access a news article, a review, or a tutorial, customized to what you want to see, regularly throughout the week.

- Continue your education, in between Global courses, by taking advantage of chat sessions with other users or instructors. Get the tips, tricks, and advice that you need today!

- Make your point in the Access.Globalknowledge community by participating in threaded discussion groups related to technologies and certification.

- Get instant course information at your fingertips. Customized course calendars show you the courses you want, and when and where you want them.

- Obtain the resources you need with online tools, trivia, skills assessment, and more!

All this and more is available now on the Web at

http://access.globalknowledge.com.

Visit today!

Glossary

Add ICA Connection   This launches a wizard to create your custom connection. An ICA Dial-in connection allows you to connect directly to a modem or modem pool connected to the Citrix server and can be used instead of a Dial-Up Networking (PPP/RAS) connection. An ICA Dial-in differs from a RAS connection in that you're authenticated within the session instead of making a network connection outside of the session beforehand.

AppEnumerator   This provides an interface for accessing a user's application set information.

Application load   An accurate measure of work load cannot be taken without considering the type of applications that will be deployed on the server. Certain applications will consume more memory than others, as well as processing time and disk space. Microsoft Office 2000 applications will eat up at least 10MB of RAM each, while Office XP consumes 12MB, and Outlook another 2MB!

Application Location   When you choose the Publish Application radio button, the Command Line box within this tab refers to the location of the local executable files for the published application. The Working Directory is the directory where the application's executable file resides.

Application Name   Use this tab to view or update the reference names and description of the application. This must be a name that uniquely identifies the application in the farm. On this tab you have the option to disable the application. When the application is disabled, no users will be able to access the application.

Application Properties   The Application Properties dialog box allows an administrator to adjust a number of application specific settings. The tabs displayed within the Application Properties dialog box allow an administrator to "tweak" an application's properties. Any changes made to the properties of an application will affect the properties of that application, when it is accessed through an ICA session, on every server for which it is configured.

Appsrv.src   This program allows you to edit parameters relating to custom ICA connections, specifically application servers and the client settings Seen in the

Custom ICA Connections View. You can use this file to restrict users to a particular view and remove icons you do not want them to use.

Asynchronous (Async) connections　Async connections have many of the same security features as network connections, but each Async listener is limited to one connection. Asynchronous connections also have additional configuration options not available with network connections. If the transport option is set for asynchronous connections, administrators will see a list of devices that are available for asynchronous connectivity. A list of COM ports and/or modems will be displayed, along with a set of options for the device being used. If asynchronous connections are configured for dial-up access, the properties of the selected modem are accessible through the Citrix Connection Configuration tool.

Authentication Tickets　These are used to keep the user's credentials secure in the ICA file downloaded to the user. The ICA file, by default, contains the user's username and domain name in clear text. The password is "scrambled" in the ICA file. If the ICA file was captured, these credentials could be cut and pasted into a new ICA file and reused over and over. An Authentication ticket is issued to the user and used in place of the user's credentials. This ticket is encrypted and good for only one use or 200 seconds. Once it has been used or the timeout has expired the ticket will no longer be accepted by the MetaFrame servers.

Auto-created client printers　These are one of the most sought after functions in MetaFrame. This system allows users to connect from almost any device, use an application, and still print to their local printer though the application is running on a server that could be thousands of miles away. Auto-created client printers are generally a challenge to configure and maintain, however. This is generally due to the large number of inexpensive printers available to users and your need to have an appropriate driver for each printer the client wishes to use.

Auto-created printers　A type of client printer that is generally used with 32-bit Windows clients but can be configured for other clients, such as Windows CE and DOS. These types of client printers do not auto-create natively, but an administrator can configure these clients to auto-create by using the Citrix Management Console.

AutoLogon The AutoLogon option can be configured so all connections to a selected listener automatically log on with a specified user account. However, administrators should carefully consider the security implications of using this option. If this option is used carelessly, administrators may not be able to control who accesses the Citrix server.

Baseline This helps to determine how well your system is performing and to spot potential problems before they happen. Developing a baseline will help determine how many users the system can support concurrently and the impact of running certain applications. It's a much better plan than waiting for your users to inform you of how slow the system is! It's also the first step in assuring that your system is running at optimum performance levels and that you have enough resources to support your environment. The second method of developing a baseline is to gather server resource statistics over time while the server is in use. The tests can be run at intervals over a period of weeks for a trend analysis. The results are documented and compared. Both methods can help you determine system throughput and where potential bottlenecks may be.

Basic Input/Output System (BIOS) A set of programs encoded in ROM on IBM PC-compatible computers programs handle startup operations such as Power On Self Test (POST) and low-level control for hardware such as disk drives, keyboards, etc.

BIOS: See *Basic Input/Output System*

Browsers: See *Web browsers*

Central Processor Unit (CPU) utilization This monitors overall processor utilization. This rule by default will report full load when processor utilization is greater than 90 percent and will report no load when processor utilization is less than 10 percent.

Ciphersuites tab This contains the settings that configure which ciphersuites the SSL relay will accept from the web server. A ciphersuite is an encryption/decryption algorithm. This tab contains a list of all Citrix supported ciphersuites.

From the list of available ciphersuites you may select which ciphersuites you wish to use.

Citrix Connection Configuration   The Citrix Connection Configuration utility is a granular tool used to configure and manage server connections. When MetaFrame is installed on a Terminal Server, one ICA connection is created for each network protocol. The Citrix Connection Configuration tool can be used to add more listeners or edit the existing ICA and RDP connections.

Citrix Installation Manager (CIM)   The Citrix Installation Manager (CIM) is used to install applications on multiple XP servers. The three key components of the CIM are the CIM plug-in, which resides in the CMC console, the Installer service which resides on target servers that do not run the CMC, and the Packager, which runs on a Windows NT 4.0 TSE service pack 5 or later or Windows 2000 Server running terminal services in application server mode. When the Citrix Installation Manager is loaded on your server, The Citrix Installation Manager, or CIM, plug-in is displayed in your CMC. Used to manage MSI and ADF packages and install applications on the target servers, the CIM packages are created using the packager component of the CIM on a separate dedicated MetaFrame XP application server. The CIM plug-in in the CMC is used to manage and schedule package installations across a server farm.

Citrix Management Console (CMC)   A comprehensive interface that combines all MetaFrame administrative functions into a single application, ensuring that administrators no longer need switch between several task specific applications to manage a server farm. The CMC provides a single point of contact for the administration of all facets of a MetaFrame XP server farm. CMC is a Java-based console capable of running on any Windows NT or Windows 2000 computer, thus freeing the administrator from having to perform administrative functions on a Citrix server.

Citrix Server Administration   This utility allows Citrix administrators to manage users and sessions across the entire enterprise. There are several ways to manage users with the Citrix Server Administration tool. The way administrators manage users in a Citrix environment depends on the size and architecture of the Citrix environment. Some administrators may have only one or two Citrix servers, in which case finding a particular Citrix user or session may be relatively easy. In large Citrix environments, administrators may have to navigate through the Citrix Server Administration and utilize the sorting features to locate users and sessions.

CitrixTextCredentials This encapsulates user credentials for transference to the server farm.

Citrix Win32 Program Neighborhood client This client allows graphical access to applications published on a Citrix server. Users can browse the Program Neighborhood to access application sets that have been configured on the Citrix server. They can then launch the application from the Program Neighborhood window. This client can also be used with NFuse to run applications configured to launch a separate window. Application icons can be pushed to the client desktop or the Start menu, allowing the user to run the application without opening the client program.

CitrixWireGateway This creates a communication link between the Web page requesting a user's application information and the server farm containing the applications.

Client auto-update This allows users to connect to the Citrix server and download the latest Citrix client. This frees the administrator from having to touch every machine when a new client becomes available. Clients are stored in the central Client Update Database. New clients can be added to the database using the Client Distribution Wizard on the MetaFrame Toolbar.

Client drive mapping This allows remote drives to be mapped to local drives on a user's computer. For example, a home directory on a server can be mapped to the user's C: drive. The drive can then be accessed by all standard file tools. The Win32 client supports client device mapping during a Citrix session. This allows local drives, printers, and COM ports to be accessed while running remote applications.

Client printers Physical print devices connected to an ICA client device using a cable (such as a parallel cable) or a port (e.g., a network port, UNC share, TCP/IP port, and so on).

Client settings   The Client Settings button, which can be located by editing the properties of an ICA listener, provides access to several settings that are used to restrict access to certain client mappings. By default, a Citrix server will map resources from the Citrix server to an ICA client device to provide a seamless user experience.

CMC: See *Citrix Management Console*

Component Object Model (COM)   This is a method for different software components to communicate with one another, regardless of hardware, operating system, or language being used.

Component Object Model (COM) port mappings   These permit almost any peripheral that connects through the COM port to be accessed in a Citrix application session. COM ports must be manually mapped to the server.

Context switches   Monitors the number of context switches on the server. By default this will report full load when the number of context switches is greater than 16,000 per second and will report no load when the number of context switches is less than 900 per second.

Control commands   Control commands are a category of ICA command packets that manage the connection to the application server and the relationship to the local client user interface.

Current Process   This produces reports based on the applications and processes running on servers within the farm. You might use this report if a process currently running has entered into an alarm state.

Current Users   This produces reports on user and application activity. A user activity report can be helpful in determining how many sessions a user has open and which applications are being run by the user. The report also provides information on when their session began, how long it's been established, the number of processes running and the number of instances of each.

Custom ICA Connections view This view allows the user to create direct connections to specific MetaFrame servers or connect directly to a published application. If applications are published to a NT Domain instead of a Farm, custom connections will need to be created for each published application to which the users need to connect.

Data collectors Data collectors in MetaFrame XP are analogous to an ICA master browser. Each zone contains one MetaFrame XP server that is configured as the data collector. The data collector receives information from each of the other XP servers in the zone. Like the master browser in previous versions, the data collector maintains a list of all servers and the applications they serve, along with the TCP/IP addresses of each server. Data collectors are chosen via elections much like NT domain controllers and MetaFrame 1.x ICA master browsers.

Data store The data store is another critical component that must be properly planned. Available in several different flavors, the data store allows administrators to customize their environment to meet the business needs. Based upon ODBC compliant database engines, MetaFrame XP currently supports three database formats and two connection methodologies.

Diffie-Hellman key algorithm The Diffie-Hellman key agreement algorithm was designed to allow to computers to exchange information that would allow both computers to arrive at the same exact symmetric key with out ever transmitting data in the communication that would compromise the symmetric key used in that session.

Diffie-Hellman parameters These are used during key negotiation. When a secure ICA client establishes an encrypted session, the MetaFrame server and client use a public key algorithm to pass public keys and these parameters over the communication path. Using these parameters, the client and server's Private Keys and Public keys both the client and the server arrive at the same unique Symmetric Key.

Digital Independence This is the marketing term Citrix uses to describe the concept of being able to run any application, on any device, over any network connection, wireless to Web. Attaining Digital Independence means being freed from the traditional restrictions and intricacies of technology so everything can compute.

Digital Subscriber Line (DSL)   There are many variants of digital subscriber line (xDSL). All versions utilize the existing copper loop between a home and the local telco's Central Office (CO). Doing so allows them to be deployed rapidly and inexpensively. However, all DSL variants suffer from attenuation, and speeds drop as the loop length increases. Asymmetrical DSL (ADSL) and Symmetrical DSL (SDSL) may be deployed only within 17,500 feet of a CO, and Integrated Services Digital Network emulation over DSL (IDSL) will work only up to 30,500 feet. All DSL variants use Asynchronous Transfer Mode (ATM) as the data-link layer.

Direct Memory Access (DMA)   These channels are rare these days, but you may see them used by audio devices. As you might recall, DMAs have the ability to move data from the device to RAM without involving the processor.

Direct mode   Direct mode allows servers to communicate directly with the data store database to maximize performance, however this requires more sophisticated database engines such as MS SQL or Oracle.

Disconnect   Allows the administrator to disconnect a user from their current session. The session remains open on the server, and the user is able to reconnect to the disconnected session the next time they log on, provided that the server has not been rebooted.

Disk caching/compression   This allows the Win32 client to work well over low speed links, whether they are asynchronous or WAN links. The amount of drive space given over to caching can be modified (the default is one percent), the cache directory can be chosen, and the minimum size bitmap to be cached can be configured.

Disk data I/O   Monitors disk I/O per second in kilobytes. This rule by default will report full load when the total disk I/O in kilobytes per second is greater than 32,767 and will report no load when the disk I/O in kilobytes per second is equal to zero.

DNS: See *Domain Name System*

Domain Name System (DNS)   Because the actual unique Internet Protocol (IP) address of a web server is in the form of a number difficult for humans to work with, text labels separated by dots (domain names) are used instead. DNS is responsible for mapping these domain names to the actual IP numbers in a process called resolution. Sometimes called a Domain Name Server.

Driver   This field associates a server side driver with the client printer. This driver name can be entered manually, or you can select from one of two menus.

DSL: See *Digital Subscriber Line*

ECC RAM: See *Error-correcting code memory (ECC RAM)*

Error-correcting code memory (ECC RAM)   ECC memory includes special circuitry that tests for the accuracy of data as it passes through memory and corrects any errors it finds.

Error events   These indicate more serious conditions and logged when there is a failure such as a service failing to start, a duplicate IP address, a malfunctioning hardware device or system crash. Error events are represented by red circles with white Xs through them.

Event Viewer   This is the one of the first tools to use for troubleshooting and monitoring your system. It is at the front end and used to view the event logs where information is recorded about the computer and applications. The Event viewer is installed by default and located under Administrative Tools on both operating systems, and the logs themselves are stored in the %systemroot%\system32\config folder. With the Event Viewer, you can monitor the events that take place on your systems and detect activities that may require your attention. Analyzing these events can help you resolve issues related to security, resource allocation and system problems.

Explicit users   These are by definition normal user accounts and can be domain accounts or local user accounts if no domain is present. You should always use explicit users when security is important. Explicit users will use their normal logon credentials when connecting to an application set or custom connection, and unlike anonymous accounts, their user profile information will be saved when the explicit user logs off.

Farms: See *Multiple farms; Single farms*

Frame Head   Optional framing protocol header. Prefix for framing stream-oriented transport data.

Frame Relay   A packet switching communication service that neither detects nor corrects routing relays. It typically provides for a bandwidth within the range of 56 Kilobits per second (56 Kbps) to 1.544 Megabits per second (Mbps) rates emerging.

GPO: See *Group Policy Object*

GroupCredentials   This contains a list of group names with an associated domain for use in retrieving applications for user groups.

Group Policy Object (GPO)   After you create a group policy, it is stored in a Group Policy Object (GPO) and applied to the site, domain, or Organizational Unit (OU). GPOs are used to keep the group policy information; essentially, it is a collection of policies. You can apply single or multiple GPOs to each site, domain or OU. Group policies are not inherited across domains, and users must have Read permission for the GPO that you want to have applied to them. This way, you can filter the scope of GPOs by adjusting who has read access to each GPO.

Hardware Compatibility List (HCL)   The Hardware Compatibility List is published by Microsoft for each of its operating systems and is updated on a monthly basis. There is a copy of the HCL on the Windows 2000 Professional CD, located in the Support folder and named Hcl.txt.

HCL: See *Hardware Compatibility List*

Hotkeys   This option allows you to change the mapped out hotkeys within a session. This is useful when applications have hard coded hotkeys that cannot be changed. These hotkeys are set by default to not interfere with local client Windows hotkeys.

Hot-swappable components   Hot-swappable server components are available that can be changed out while the server is online, without interrupting service. Others can detect a failure and automatically swap over to a redundant component (automatic-swap). Components that are typically hot-swappable include hard disks, power supplies, and NICs.

HTML: See *HyperText Markup Language*

HTTP: See *HyperText Transport Protocol*

HyperText Markup Language (HTML)   The format used to create documents viewed on the World Wide Web (WWW) by the use of tags (codes) embedded within the text.

HyperText Transfer Protocol (HTTP)   HTTP is an Internet standard supporting World Wide Web (WWW) exchanges. By creating the definitions of Universal Resource Locators (URLs) and their retrieval usage throughout the Internet.

ICA: See *Independent Computing Architecture*

Ignored processes   Processes that Resource Manager, if installed, is configured not to monitor. To stop monitoring a process, choose add process and type the exact name of the process.

iDen   Motorola's new service that allows 64Kb connections from your laptop via your mobile phone.

IIS: See *Internet Information Server*

IMA: See *Independent Management Architecture*

Independent Computing Architecture (ICA)   A Distributed Presentation Services protocol that allows clients to establish sessions with the MetaFrame XP server and to run server-based applications as if they were installed locally. Though the client device does not require a hard drive, it can still run the most up-to-date programs. Being platform independent, ICA can run on practically any client platform.

Independent Computing Architecture (ICA) browsing Citrix servers communicate with each other through a process known as ICA browsing. ICA browsing is protocol-specific, and the browser settings of a particular Citrix server can be managed for each protocol. By default, a Citrix server will be able to communicate with all other Citrix servers on its subnet through ICA browsing. When two or more Citrix servers are on the same subnet, they will perform an ICA browser election, and one of the servers will declare itself the ICA Master browser. This process happens automatically, and a set of rules allows the servers to determine which server will be the ICA Master browser. However, by configuring the ICA browser settings in the Citrix Server Administration utility, administrators can control which servers will participate in the browser elections and which server or servers will become ICA browsers.

Independent Computing Architecture (ICA) Client device This component is defined within an NFuse system as any computing device capable of launching an ICA session and a Web browser. Several examples include PCs, Net appliances such as PDAs or thin client terminals, and UNIX workstations. The ICA Client device works together with the Web browser and the ICA Client as a two-part system. The Web browser is capable of viewing the application set and downloading the ICA files while the ICA Client acts as the engine to launch the ICA sessions.

Independent Computing Architecture (ICA) display This tab controls the manner in which data is transmitted to the client. The default setting in this section of the server farm properties are optimized for client performance. In most cases, there will be no need to change these settings. However, if you have users who access the farm across low-bandwidth links, you may want to adjust these settings for optimal performance.

Independent Computing Architecture (ICA) gateways ICA gateways provide virtual links between servers and farms to tunnel all traffic to allow MetaFrame to scale outside a single network. Although MetaFrame XP does not require ICA gateways to perform this function, they are still used for backward compatibility with MetaFrame 1.8. Because ICA browser information is protocol-specific, ICA gateways are bound to one protocol. ICA gateways can be set up for

TCP/IP, IPX, or both. When a gateway is set up for one protocol, the server will be able to obtain updates from remote servers for that protocol exclusively.

Independent Computing Architecture (ICA) PassThrough   This is essentially publishing Program Neighborhood to ICA clients that do not support connecting to server farms. ICA PassThrough is installed on a MetaFrame XP server by default and resides on the server in the subfolder %systemroot%\system32\ICA PassThrough. To enable ICA PassThrough, publish PN.EXE in an NT Domain scope and create a custom connection to the published application. Essentially, this type of connection is an ICA session within an ICA session, but special modifications to ICA PassThrough increase the overall performance.

Independent Management Architecture (IMA)   IMA is an architectural model and a communications protocol. IMA provides not only an architectural foundation, but also a server-to-server communications bridge on UDP 2512 for license pooling, published applications, and load balancing information. IMA enables you to group servers into farms regardless of their location or subnet. IMA provides a scalable architecture that allows server farms to be installed quickly, span several subnets, and yet still be managed from a centralized perspective. It also introduces a level of fault tolerance that permits any one server to fail without affecting the entire farm.

Indirect mode   This was designed to work around the limitations of access as a database application. By utilizing indirect mode, each server must communicate directly with the IMA services on the host server. The single host server is then the only service directly communicating with access preventing database corruption.

Installation diskettes   These are created from the ICA Client Creator in the Citrix toolbar. This is also the most tedious and time-consuming method of distributing the ICA client. The client installation disk method of deployment is mostly for smaller companies that do not want to set up a network share point or remote locations that need to be sent disks when installing over a wide area network (WAN) line is too costly or too slow to be practical.

Integrated Services Digital Network (ISDN)   Integrated Services indicates the provider offers voice and data services over the same medium. Digital Network is a reminder that ISDN was born out of the digital nature of the intercarrier and intracarrier networks. ISDN runs across the same copper wiring that carries regular telephone service. Before attenuation and noise cause the signal to be unintelligible, an ISDN circuit can run a maximum of 18,000 feet. A repeater doubles this distance to 36,000 feet.

Internet Information Service (IIS)   Windows NT Web browser software that supports Secure Sockets Layer (SSL) security protocol from Netscape. IIS provides support for Web site creation, configuration, and management, along with Network News Transfer Protocol (NNTP), File Transfer Protocol (FTP), and Simple Mail Transfer Protocol (SMTP).

Internet Protocol (IP) range   This rule monitors the Client's Transmission Control Protocol/Internet Protocol (TCP/IP) address. Within this rule you are able to allow or disallow a range or several ranges of IP addresses.

Interoperability mode   Within interoperability mode, MetaFrame XP provides the ability to operate in cooperation with MetaFrame 1.8 to continue providing application services to users. Due to the nature of the operation of interoperability mode, several factors must be taken into consideration when using it.

Interrupt ReQuest (IRQ)   An electronic signal that is sent to the computer's processor requiring the processor's attention. Also, a computer instruction designed to interrupt a program for an Input/Output (I/O).

IRQ: See *Interrupt ReQuest*

ISDN: See *Integrated Services Digital Network*

Java   An Internet and intranet application programming language.

Java Server Pages (JSP)

Java Virtual Machine (JVM)   An interpreter able to convert byte code language into machine code. After the conversion, the JVM executes the code.

JSP: See *Java Server Pages*

JVM: See *Java Virtual Machine*

LAN: See *Local Area Network*

License pooling   One of the most important features of using mixed mode operation is the capability to share licenses between MetaFrame 1.8 and MetaFrame XP servers. MetaFrame 1.8 servers with connection licenses installed can share these with all servers located within the mixed mode server farm. In addition, MetaFrame XP servers can pool connection licenses it maintains to any MetaFrame 1.8 server within the farm located on the same subnet.

License threshold   This monitors both assigned and pooled MetaFrame XP connection licenses in use on the server. This rule by default will report full load when either the number of assigned licenses in use is greater than ten or the number of pooled licenses in use is greater than 50. By default it will also report no load when either of these counts are equal to zero.

Load balancing   Load balancing works by distributing the clients that connect across the servers in the server farm. Applications or entire desktops can be published and load balanced, providing that all servers have the application or desktop in common. Unfortunately, this capability is not available in a mixed mode server farm. When load balancing applications across a mixture of MetaFrame versions, only the basic load balancing parameters available in MetaFrame 1.8 are available.

Load Evaluators   A Load Evaluator is a set of rules used to calculate load on a MetaFrame server in your farm. These Load Evaluators can be assigned to specific servers or to published applications in the MetaFrame farm. Each rule within a Load Evaluator consists of an identifier, a description of the rule and threshold settings that can be adjusted on a rule-by-rule basis. A Load Evaluator can consist of only one rule or use many in concert. When several rules are used the Load Management system uses the rules together to determine the overall load of the server. The MetaFrame servers use Load Evaluators to determine their current load. When the load for a server changes, whether it increases or decreases, this new information is sent to the Zone Data Collector. This means all new client connections are routed through the Data Collector.

Load Manager   Load Manager is an option that installs with MetaFrame XP but requires a separate license to activate. Its function is to balance the workload across servers in a MetaFrame XP server farm. When a user launches a published application or desktop, Load Manager determines which server in the farm has the lightest load and places the user on that server. Load Manager is not a fault-tolerant solution like clustering, but a high-availability feature.

Local Area Network (LAN)   A system using high-speed connections over high-performance cables to communicator among computers within a few miles of each other, allowing users to share peripherals and a massive secondary storage unit, the file server. By default, the listener will be bound to all the LAN (local area network) adapters that are configured with the selected protocol, and there will be unlimited connections available on the listener. *See also* Wireless LANs.

Local host cache   The local host cache is an Access database that is stored locally on each server in the farm to cache farm information. This database increases performance because it is not necessary to contact the data store every time a client queries the server. The local host cache also maintains enough information to allow the server to operate for up to 48 hours in the absence of the data store. During this period, the server will continue to attempt to contact the data store on a regular basis. If the data store is not contacted within 48 hours, the server will invalidate its licensing information and discontinue taking new connections.

Local printers   Printers that are directly connected, via cable or port, to a MetaFrame XP server in the server farm. Local printers in a MetaFrame environment are added to the server just as you would add a printer to a Windows NT workstation or a Windows 2000 Professional Workstation. Adding a local printer to a MetaFrame server involves following the Add Printer Wizard in the Printers folder of the server.

Memory   The amount of RAM needed increases linearly with the number of users connected to the server. Users are typically Power Users or Typical Users. Citrix recommends an additional 8MB for each Power User and 4MB of RAM for each Typical User. To do the math for a Windows 2000 Server with MetaFrame XP having eight Power Users and seven Typical Users, the equation would look something like this: 256MB + 128MB + (8 × 8) + (7 × 4) = 476MB. That's 256MB required for Windows 2000, 128MB required for MetaFrame XP and Citrix Management Console, 64MB recommended for the eight Power Users and 28MB recommended for the seven Typical Users.

MetaFrame XP   The next platform release for Citrix and is optimized for use with advanced Windows platforms, and tuned specifically for Internet use. This new architecture should allow Citrix to deploy any application, to any device, over any connection, with a highly competitive power and flexibility. XP*a* and XP*e* versions are available.

Metrics   Metrics are the measurable units that Resource Manager monitors. Each component or object has a set of metrics. Each metric has a definable set of thresholds or limits that describe normal operation. For management and users to buy into server-based computing, they must feel as if they are running their applications from their own desktop machine. Be sure you know what the default metrics are, what they monitor and what it they could be telling you about your server.

Microsoft Management Console (MMC)   The MMC provides a standardized interface for using administrative tools and utilities. The management applications contained in an MMC are called Snap-ins, and custom MMCs hold the Snap-ins required to perform specific tasks. Custom consoles can be saved as files with the .msc file extension. The MMC was first introduced with NT Option Pack. Using the MMC leverages the familiarity you have with the other snap-ins available within MMC, such as SQL Server 7 and Internet Information Server 4. With the MMC, all your administrative tasks can be done in one place. In Windows 2000, most of the system management tools have been centralized within the MMC.

Mixed mode   To support backward compatibility in a MetaFrame 1.8 server farm environment, mixed mode operation can be enabled. Although recommended only as a migration or temporary option, it does offer additional services and capabilities to administrators. Once MetaFrame XP is operating in mixed mode, the ICA browser service is enabled on all servers in the farm.

MMC: See *Microsoft Management Console*

Module.src   This program contains information about network protocols and transports, including COM ports.

Multiple farms   Based upon the business requirements of organizations, some implementations require the use of multiple farms. Although this adds an additional level of complexity to an environment, it also comes with its own set of benefits as well. Benefits for using multiple MetaFrame XP farms include decentralized administration; minimized network traffic; minimized security risks associated with network traffic and traversal of firewalls for intrafarm communication; data store replication is not required; and segmented licensing—the ability to license farms separately versus one large pool.

Native mode   Native mode provides compatibility within a server farm consisting of Citrix MetaFrame XP 1.0 servers only. Advantages for using native mode include that ICA Browser service is disabled on all servers within the farm limiting the broadcast traffic required on your network. IMA traffic used in its place is not based on broadcast traffic; Program Neighborhood services are disabled on all servers within the farm; data collectors are used instead of the ICA browser service; and data are not shared with Citrix MetaFrame 1.8 servers located within the same farm.

Net appliances   Net appliances typically come with a keyboard, mouse, and small screen, but no hard drive. The OS is usually embedded in ROM or FLASH, and no files are stored locally. The low power of the CPU prevents the appliance from running mainstream applications natively, but with the use of an ICA client, the appliance can run any application the server can provide. Most net appliances provide a parallel or USB port for a printer, so documents created in an ICA session can be printed locally.

NetBEUI: See *NetBIOS Extended User Interface*

NetBIOS: See *Network Basic Input/Output System*

NetBIOS Extended User Interface (NetBEUI) The transport layer for the DOS networking protocol called Network Basic Input/Output System (NetBIOS).

Network Address Translation (NAT) Most firewalls have the ability of using a technology called network address translation (NAT). Using NAT with Citrix, each MetaFrame server receives an alternate IP address. Only ICA Clients that know the alternate address will pass through the firewall.

Network bandwidth Network bandwidth plays an important role in system performance and user experience. Since all the processing occurs on the server and clients are in constant communication, server-based computing requires more, not less, available network bandwidth.

Network Basic Input/Output System (NetBIOS) A program in Microsoft's operating systems that links personal computers to Local Area Network (LAN).

Network Interface Card (NIC) A board with encoding and decoding circuitry and a receptacle for a network cable connection that, bypassing the serial ports and operating through the internal bus, allows computers to be connected at higher speeds to media for communications between stations.

Network Manager This works with third-party SNMP consoles to provide systems management capabilities to MetaFrame XP servers. The Network Manager consists of an SNMP agent and plug-ins that support HP OpenView and Tivoli NetView. With the SNMP console it is possible to remotely manage your MetaFrame XP*e* servers using the same network management package that may be in use elsewhere on your network. With Network Manager and your third-party SNMP console of choice, you can shut down and restart MetaFrame XP*e* servers, disconnect, log off and send messages to active session on a MetaFrame XP*e* server and Terminal processes running on MetaFrame XP*e* servers.

Network Monitor (NetMon) This is a network diagnostic tool that is provided with Windows NT and Windows 2000. The version that comes with NT and Windows 2000 is the light version, the full version is part of Microsoft Systems Manager Server (SMS). Network Monitor is used to monitor network traffic and troubleshoot network-related events and such as a server that is sending or receiving an inordinate amount of traffic, misconfigured workstations, printers and servers.

Network printers   Printers that reside on a network print server or on a MetaFrame XP server outside the server farm. A printer shared from an ICA client device or from a network workstation is also considered a network printer by all other clients on the network. Citrix clients have the option of using network printers just like any Windows client on the network.

Nfuse   NFuse provides some industry standard techniques for securing information across communication channels in addition to providing some added security of its own, allowing secure communication between all three tiers. NFuse also provides a large number of client devices and server platforms to participate within this Web-enabled technology. In addition, server-side scripting and configuration can create a single point of access for all users connecting to NFuse. When using NFuse and forcing encryption at the connection level, you may experience problems where users have a secure client, launch an application via NFuse but still receive the message that they do not meet the required encryption level. The easiest way to fix this, if you do not mind running encryption for every session (which you must not, since you set it at the connection level), is to set each application to use the encryption level you forced at the connection level.

NIC: See *Network Interface Card*

Node item   Node items are containers (and management tools) which contain objects that represent resources or items that can be managed in the server farm such as Applications and Citrix Administrators. Each *node item* with a (+) next to it will reveal nested specific items and features of the server farm beneath them.

Non-Windows ICA clients   Other operating systems can also act as clients and connect to the MetaFrame XP server. This allows MetaFrame XP to coexist in various computing environments, thus earning the name "Independent Computing Architecture."

NT File System (NTFS) The NT File System (with filenames up to 255 characters) is a system created to aid the computer and its components recover from hard disk crashes.

ODBC: See *Open DataBase Connectivity*

Open DataBase Connectivity (ODBC) A database programming interface that allows applications a way to access network databases.

Page fault This monitors the number of page faults per second. This rule by default will report full load when the number of page faults a second are greater than 100 and will report no load when the number of page faults a second are equal to zero.

Page swap This monitors number of Page Swap operations per second. This rule by default will report full load when the number of page swaps are greater than 100 and will report no load when the number of page swaps a second are equal to zero.

Pass-through authentication This allows local usernames and passwords to be automatically forwarded to servers to allow users to log in to their applications. This reduces the number of logon windows a user will face. The main drawback of this feature is that pass-through authentication is enabled, meaning automatic client update will not work.

PassThrough: See *Independent Computing Architecture PassThrough*

Performance Monitor (PerfMon) This is a graphical tool incorporated into Windows NT Terminal Server Edition and Windows 2000 family of servers. It gathers and examines information about server activity by examining system objects or components. Objects are server components that possess a set of measurable properties.

PN: See *Program Neighborhood*

Pn.src This program configures settings in relation to application sets and contains two sections: Program Neighborhood and Application Set. The Program

Neighborhood section defines the application sets. The Application Set section defines all configuration information for those defined sets.

Point-to-Point Protocol (PPP) . A serial communication protocol most commonly used to connect a personal computer to an Internet Service Provider (ISP). PPP is the successor to Serial Line Internet Protocol (SLIP) and may be used over both synchronous and asynchronous circuits. Also, PPP is a full-duplex, connectionless protocol that supports many different types of links. The advantages of PPP made it de facto standard for dial-up connections.

Port   Specifies the physical LPT or COM on the client device that the printer is attached to. This is generally listed as LPT1, but it can vary.

Power users   Power Users will utilize more resources than Typical Users. Power Users are depicted as being more computer savvy, running more applications at one time, cutting and pasting between remote and local applications and generally stressing the system more. One Power User is equivalent to two Typical Users in terms of processor utilization and RAM consumption. The exact processor, RAM and network bandwidth requirements cannot be accurately determined until a baseline using at least five users, has been established. Citrix recommends an additional 8MB for each Power User and 4MB of RAM for each Typical User.

PPP: See *Point-to-Point Protocol*

Print device   The physical printer that produces the print jobs. A print job is the binary translation of the file you are printing into a language the printer understands.

Print driver   The software used by the operating system to interpret an application's print commands and convert these into a language that the printer will use to produce a print job. A print driver must be installed on a MetaFrame server in the farm that matches the printer driver installed on the client workstation. The print driver should then be replicated to all servers in the server farm that this client will connect to. If the name of the print driver installed in the MetaFrame farm matches the client print driver name verbatim, a print driver mapping must be created. Deciding which printer drivers to support in a MetaFrame environment can be a tedious job. Some print drivers can cause server-side problems when they are used to access client printers.

Print queue   The holding area for print jobs waiting to be printed on a print device. These queues are generally located on a print server and accessed in Windows environments by a printer share.

Printer   The Windows icon you *See* in the Printers applet in the Control Panel. This icon is a logical reference to a print device attached to the local system bus via a communications port.

Printer mapping   Printer mapping allows clients to use their local printers in remote applications, just like they would with local applications. Printer mappings can also be forced to the default printer on the client by checking the box labeled Default To Main Client Printer.

Printer name   Specifies a logical name (generally the type of printer) that you are auto-creating.

Printer share   A logical printer on a Windows server that allows multiple users to print to the same physical print device. This device can be attached directly to the network or to a communications port on the server.

Program Neighborhood (PN) client: See *Citrix Win32 Program Neighborhood client*

Program Neighborhood (PN) folders   These allow you to publish applications in a logical folder structure, similar to the logical layout of a hard drive partition. You can group common applications in their own folders, so when a user connects to an application set, he or she can more easily navigate the list of published applications.

Public Key-Private Key encryption   This uses one key to encrypt the data and one key to decrypt the data. The public key is used during the encryption process. Once the information is encrypted, it is sent to the recipient who then uses the Private Key to decrypt the data. The public key in this scenario can be transmitted freely across public lines. No data are contained in the public key that can compromise the Private key. If an unauthorized user was to obtain the public key, he or she could only encrypt data and not decrypt it. This means that since the Private Key is used to decrypt your data, it must be kept secure at all times. The draw back to Public Key-Private key is its speed. Though it is considered more secure than symmetric key encryption, it is also slower.

Query server (qserver)   You can use the **qserver** or **query server** command to determine which server is acting as the master browser. Before telling the selected server to become the Master Browser, you should check the current status of the ICA browser by using the qserver command from a command line. Running the qserver command displays the IPX address of the Citrix servers on a subnet.

RAID: See *Redundant Arrays of Inexpensive Disks*

RC5   This is an encryption algorithm that Citrix employs to encrypt session information from ICA Client devices to Citrix MetaFrame for Windows servers. RC5 encryption uses the RC5 encryption algorithm developed by RSA Data Security, Inc. and the Diffie-Hellman key agreement with a 1024-bit key to generate RC5 public and private keys. RC5 encryption supports 40-, 56-, and 128-bit encryption that can be enforced by Citrix administrators on a per-connection basis. In addition, minimum encryption levels can be used to enforce encryption if a connection is to be made.

Reboot Schedule   Periodic server reboots can be scheduled using the reboot schedule tab for each server. It is a good practice to reboot servers on a regular basis. The reason for this is that applications housed on the server can cause memory leaks, which tie up valuable resources on your servers.

Redundant Arrays of Inexpensive Disks (RAID)   RAID is a disk subsystem made up of several drives of the same size that appear as a single drive thereby improving reliability, response time, and/or storage capacity. Selecting the correct RAID level is a complex process, and each has its own strengths and drawbacks. Typically, a RAID setup is recommended in a multiprocessor environment. Hardware RAID is highly advised, as it consumes fewer resources than software

RAID on both Windows 2000 and Windows NT 4.0 Terminal Services Edition. If RAID is not an option, stick to fast SCSI drives.

Remote Access Service (RAS)   Remote Access Service is a built in feature of the Microsoft NT operating system. It allows users to dial establish a connection to an NT network over a standard phone line. Remote Access allows users to access files on a network or transfer files from a remote PC, over a Dial-Up Networking connection. The performance of transferring files over a dial-up connection is very similar to the performance you would get if you were downloading a file from the Internet.

Remote Display Protocol (RDP)   This is Microsoft's version of a thin-client protocol. RDP operates on many of the same principles as the ICA protocol. RDP allows users to access and control Windows Terminal Servers remotely, using a minimal amount of resources on the client device. However, the RDP protocol is not as robust as the ICA protocol. The RDP protocol only supports TCP/IP and lacks many of the ICA features that create a seamless user experience for Citrix clients.

Resource Manager   This is a monitoring tool that was made specifically for the MetaFrame XP, server-based environment. Older, less "server-based aware" utilities often do not give accurate readings because they are not in tune to the server-based environment. They don't take into account that the server is doing 100 percent of the processing and that multiple users are running sessions from it at one time. Resource Manager allows you view and monitor information about your server or farm and capture real-time data or produce reports. It can show you the applications you are running, how many instances are running and who is running them. You can track the resources consumed by each user and application and associate a charge with the usage so that you can that you can charge back for the use of applications and resources.

Ricochet   Ricochet enables laptop and Windows CE users to utilize PC Card-based modems to access the Internet at up to 128 Kbps in most major cities.

Secure Hypertext Transfer Protocol (HTTPS)   This is a secure version of HTTP used on the internet. It uses SSL to secure provide security for data that is passed over it. The NFuse Web pages should be configured to use HTTPS in order to guarantee that the user credentials are encrypted when they are passed from the client browser to the Web server.

Secure Sockets Layer (SSL)   SSL is an open, non-proprietary, industry standard Web protocol designed to provide secure server authentication, data encryption, message integrity, and optional client authentication. By combining the SSL technology with HTML, HTTPS was created. SSL and therefore HTTPS use the TCP port 443 by default for its communications.

Secure Sockets Layer (SSL) Relay   This works much the same as the SSL technology enabled between a Web server and a Web browser, except that now the secure tunnel is being passed between the Web server and a Citrix server farm. SSL Relay is a default component of Citrix MetaFrame XP for Windows 1.0 and Citrix MetaFrame 1.8 with SP2 with FR1 licensed and activated. By default, the SSL Relay used TCP port 443 for its SSL communication.

Security Log   This contains events that are generated when auditing has been implemented. Auditing can be enabled on events such as logons, resources or file access. The two types of Security Log events are Success Audit events (providing information on successful logins or access) and Failed events (providing information on failed login attempts, failed access to resources, or other security threats).

Server-to-server communication   Within MetaFrame XP, server-to-server communication is accomplished by utilizing TCP port 2512. Each server uses a direct channel to other servers as required via this single port. As compared to MetaFrame 1.8 using UDP port 1604, this new architecture provides a much more reliable and scalable solution.

Shadow   Allows the administrator to view and remote control a user's session from their desktop. Be aware that shadowing has limitations. If your server is configured to ask permission from the user in the ICA session before shadowing can commence. Additionally, the client device you are shadowing from must be capable of supporting the video resolution of the ICA session or shadowing will terminate.

Shadowing   Shadowing is the ability to remotely control a user session. This capability allows administrators to manage and troubleshoot user sessions thereby providing further functionality to this multiuser environment. This service allows administrators to interact directly with users sessions including providing keyboard and mouse input into the MetaFrame XP session simultaneously with the user. Used commonly for training exercises, user monitoring, and troubleshooting; this adds to the administrators arsenal of tools when using Citrix MetaFrame XP.

Simple Network Management Protocol (SNMP)   A standard for managing hardware devices connected to a network, approved for UNIX use, which lets administrators know, for example, when a printer has a paper jam or is low on toner.

Simultaneous installations   An issue facing administrators when completing multiple installations of Citrix MetaFrame XP is the ability to perform simultaneous installations. Although this can be done successfully, there are a few guidelines that must be followed to minimize issues they may arise. As servers are installed, the must all communicate with the data store to properly complete the implementation process. When multiple servers access the same data locations within the data store, timeouts can occur. Proper planning for these types of issues can immediately resolve most problems before they occur.

Single farm   The most common implementation of Citrix MetaFrame XP is using a single server farm. Single farms can be used in small business to large enterprises due to the increased scalability and reliability. Factors such as database performance, hardware platforms, and network connectivity all play a role in deciding upon using a single farm.

SNMP: See *Simple Network Management Protocol*

Sound support: Win32 client sound support allows users with a compatible sound card to play sound files on the server and hear them through their local computer sound system. The sound files can be compressed to meet bandwidth requirements for the network. Sound support can be managed on the client side from the settings of the application set.

Speed Screen 3 This enhances the feel of responsiveness of an application and further reduces bandwidth usage. SpeedScreen 3 shows significant measurable improvement over previous versions. SpeedScreen 3 provides the user with an immediate change in the cursor to inform the user the action is pending. SpeedScreen 3 enables users to receive almost instantaneous responses to mouse movements and keystrokes. SpeedScreen can also be customized by using the Latency Reduction Manager from the Citrix | MetaFrame XP program group.

Speed Screen Latency Reduction Manager Use the SpeedScreen Latency Reduction Manager to customize SpeedScreen settings for a MetaFrame XP server, individual published applications, and input controls within applications. You can save a SpeedScreen configuration file and then deploy the file across your server farm. With SpeedScreen Latency Reduction Manager, you can configure local text echo settings for individual input fields within an application. SpeedScreen Latency Reduction settings can be applied to servers, applications, and input fields of a specified application.

Subscription advantage Citrix provides a service known as Subscription Advantage, of which clients meeting defined criteria defined receive free upgrade licenses to MetaFrame XP. Additional information related to these licenses can be found at the Citrix web site.

Symmetric Key encryption This is a little different. It uses the same key to both encrypt and decrypt the message we are sending. While this encryption method is generally faster than Public key-Private Key, it also depends on the symmetric key remaining totally secure and never being compromised. This means that the Symmetric Key must be sent over a secure channel or hand delivered to the parties involved in the communication.

System Information Tool This contains vital information relating to your server in a read-only format. It cannot be used to test or change server hardware or software only to display the server's configuration and components. Information contained in the folders can be saved as a text or .inf file and kept as historical data or e-mailed to a vendor's technical support.

System Summary　This displays a list of the system's basic configuration. This is where you'll find, among other things, the version and build of your operating system, the BIOS version installed memory, available memory, virtual memory, available virtual memory and page file size.

Tab view　The tab view allows administrators to configure a number of parameters for each item simply by clicking on its associated tab within the tab view pane.

TCP/IP: See *Transmission Control Protocol/Internet Protocol*

Telephony Application Program Interface (TAPI)　A Microsoft and Intel programming interface. TAPI allows the user to connect with and use voice services on a server.

TemplateParser　This performs the substitution tag processing on text files. This allows for the customizing of ICA files before being presented to users.

Terminal Server　Terminal Server is a special edition of Windows NT that adds UNIX-like multiuser capabilities and support to Windows NT Server 4.0. The current version is Windows NT Server 4.0 Terminal Server Edition (code named Hydra).

Terminal Services　This is not installed by default under the Windows 2000 Server family operating systems and must be installed prior to installing MetaFrame XP.

Thinwire　Thinwire is a logical data stream that flows encapsulated in an ICA packet. ICA must guarantee the delivery of the thinwire data stream with no errors and no missing or out-of-sequence data. The output of the thinwire protocol driver is a logical data stream that is sent through a virtual channel API, which takes the data stream and encapsulates it into an ICA packet.

Thrashing　A high reading indicates the system is short on memory and accessing the page file too often. This condition is called thrashing. If this is the case, disk usage and paging counters will also be high. It could also mean that the system is overloaded, there are too many applications running that consume large amounts of memory, or an application or process is as fault.

Timeout settings   These can be configured to terminate connected, disconnected, or idle sessions after a given amount of time elapses. Administrators may wish to use a combination of these settings to keep users from inadvertently wasting server resources. Citrix users may not know the difference between disconnecting from a remote session and logging off from a session, in which case administrators may want to configure timeout settings so that disconnected sessions will be reset.

Transmission Control Protocol/Internet Protocol (TCP/IP)   A set of communications standards created by the U.S. Department of Defense (DoD) in the 1970s that has now become an accepted way to connect different types of computers in networks because the standards now support so many programs.

Tree view   A view which displays, for example, at the top of the left pane with all management tools or node items displayed beneath it.

Typical users   Typical Users are depicted as having one or two applications open at a time, and tend to be less sophisticated in their approach. One Power User is equivalent to two Typical Users in terms of processor utilization and RAM consumption. The exact processor, RAM and network bandwidth requirements cannot be accurately determined until a baseline using at least five users has been established. Citrix recommends an additional 8MB for each Power User and 4MB of RAM for each Typical User.

UDP: See *User Datagram Protocol*

Universal Serial Bus (USB)   A low-speed hardware interface (supports MPEG video) with a maximum bandwidth up to 1.5 MBytes per second.

USB: See *Universal Serial Bus*

User Datagram Protocol (UDP)   A Transmission Control Protocol/Internet Protocol (TCP/IP) normally bundled with an Internet Protocol (IP) layer software that describes how messages received reached application programs within the destination computer.

User load   The user load on a system can drastically affect its hardware requirements. The more users, the more resources are needed. It is not only the number of users that can affect system performance, but the way they use the system. Generally speaking, users can be divided into two groups: Power Users and Typical Users.

User profile overrides   This option simply allows administrators to disable wallpaper that is associated with a user's profile. Some users may have graphically intensive wallpaper associated with their mandatory or roaming profile. Disabling wallpaper could provide these users with better performance over slow network connections.

Users: See *Power users; Typical users*

Virtual channel   A virtual channel is used by application layer objects on a session-based connection to provide additional functions to the client in parallel to the ICA protocol.

Virtual Private Network (VPN)   VPNs reduce service costs and long distance/usage fees, lighten infrastructure investments and simplify Wide Area Network (WAN) operations over time. To determine just how cost-effective a VPN solution could be in connecting remote offices, use the VPN Calculator located on Cisco's Web site at www.cisco.com.

VPN: See *Virtual Private Network*

WAN: See *Wide Area Network*

Web browsers: This allows users to access Citrix NFuse sites where they receive the same applications that would be provided by a full Program Neighborhood client. The users can then launch their applications using either an ActiveX-, Netscape Plug-In-, or Java-based ICA client.

Web ICA client   Web ICA clients are necessary to run published applications via the Internet. The ICA Web client is an add-in to Microsoft Internet Explorer and Netscape Navigator or Communicator. The Internet Explorer version uses Active X Control and the Navigator version uses the Netscape Plug-in.

Wfclient.src   This program defines general PN client configuration, including keyboard settings and video defaults.

Wide Area Network (WAN)   A network using high-speed long-distance common-carrier circuits or satellites to cover a large geographic area.

Win16 ICA client   The Win16 ICA client is for use on older operating systems and does not support Program Neighborhood. Win16 clients use Remote Application Manager and must configure specific access to published applications.

Win32 ICA client   The Win32 ICA Web client allows connections to applications through an NFuse server using a Web browser. The Win32 ICA client is used for newer operating systems and provides the Citrix Program Neighborhood, which allows users to browse published applications within the server farm. Windows CE ICA clients are available through Citrix OEM partners.

Win32 ICA Web client   This includes encryption levels of 40-, 56-, or 128-bit. Published applications and Citrix sessions can require a specific encryption level from the client. If encryption is not set, the client will not be able to connect. The encryption requirement can be set on either the application, or applied to an entire connection. The choices of Basic, 40-, 56-, 128-bit (Logon Only), or 128-bit are available.

WinCE ICA client   The Windows CE client is required for many handheld and Windows Terminal devices. Before installing the client, make sure you have the correct client for the device you will run it on.

Wireless LANs   These are becoming more prevalent now with the 802.11b standard equipment being available to home users as well as corporations. Many companies are installing wireless access points throughout their offices to provide easy access to corporate data as employees move about the building conferring with other staff on various projects. Conference rooms are a common place to find wireless connectivity because it provides LAN access to everyone in the room without the hassle of wires.

XP: See *MetaFrame XP*

Zones   Zones are responsible for collecting data from other server within the farm and distributing it effectively. Each zone elects a data collector whose role replaces the need for the ICA master browser in earlier versions of MetaFrame. Placement and configuration of zones within a MetaFrame XP farm can greatly affect performance and efficiency of the Citrix farm.

INDEX

C

INTERNATIONAL CONTACT INFORMATION

AUSTRALIA
McGraw-Hill Book Company Australia Pty. Ltd.
TEL +61-2-9417-9899
FAX +61-2-9417-5687
http://www.mcgraw-hill.com.au
books-it_sydney@mcgraw-hill.com

CANADA
McGraw-Hill Ryerson Ltd.
TEL +905-430-5000
FAX +905-430-5020
http://www.mcgrawhill.ca

GREECE, MIDDLE EAST,
NORTHERN AFRICA
McGraw-Hill Hellas
TEL +30-1-656-0990-3-4
FAX +30-1-654-5525

MEXICO (Also serving Latin America)
McGraw-Hill Interamericana Editores S.A. de C.V.
TEL +525-117-1583
FAX +525-117-1589
http://www.mcgraw-hill.com.mx
fernando_castellanos@mcgraw-hill.com

SINGAPORE (Serving Asia)
McGraw-Hill Book Company
TEL +65-863-1580
FAX +65-862-3354
http://www.mcgraw-hill.com.sg
mghasia@mcgraw-hill.com

SOUTH AFRICA
McGraw-Hill South Africa
TEL +27-11-622-7512
FAX +27-11-622-9045
robyn_swanepoel@mcgraw-hill.com

UNITED KINGDOM & EUROPE
(Excluding Southern Europe)
McGraw-Hill Education Europe
TEL +44-1-628-502500
FAX +44-1-628-770224
http://www.mcgraw-hill.co.uk
computing_neurope@mcgraw-hill.com

ALL OTHER INQUIRIES Contact:
Osborne/McGraw-Hill
TEL +1-510-549-6600
FAX +1-510-883-7600
http://www.osborne.com
omg_international@mcgraw-hill.com

Well-practiced